Continued from front flap

the impact of two revolutions. Before the first — the shopping-center revolution — had run its course, the second — the discount store revolution — began to make itself felt.

To cover these and other changes of the past decade and to interpret their impact on the chains required this revised and enlarged edition.

This comprehensive history of the chains divides itself into three parts: (1) the birth and growth of the system; (2) its struggle for self-preservation in the face of violent and sustained opposition; and (3) its maturity and adjustment to changed conditions.

A major section of the book reviews the events of the years when the chains had to fight for their existence against discrimnatory taxation and other measure signed to check their growth or elim them. The public-relations aspect chain-store operation are fully exami

How the chains offer an improved tribution system for the farmer and ot mass producers, unique vocational opportunities in retailing, leadership in community activities and a higher standard of living for the consumer is discussed at length and documented.

With no less than eight chains now in the billion-dollar a year sales category, and several others rapidly approaching that status, the "big business" aspect of this segment of retailing has not escaped the scrutiny of monopoly-hunters. Recent developments in this area are covered in this new edition.

Invaluable as a reference work but, as one reviewer said, "as delightful in style as it is in content," this up-dated edition of CHAIN STORES IN AMERICA is indispensable for a clear understanding of the background of chain-store development, the current status of the system and the factors which will shape its future.

CHAIN STORES
IN AMERICA
1859-1962

CHAIN STORES
IN AMERICA

1859-1962

By Godfrey M. Lebhar

Editor-in-Chief, CHAIN STORE AGE

THIRD EDITION

CHAIN STORE PUBLISHING CORPORATION

NEW YORK

CHAIN STORES IN AMERICA: 1859-1962.

PRINTED IN THE UNITED STATES OF AMERICA
BY THE COLONIAL PRESS INC., CLINTON, MASS.

CONTENTS

(Continued on next Page)

v

Contents (Continued)

CHARTS AND TABLES

PREFACE TO THIRD EDITION

ALTHOUGH ONLY four years have elapsed since the Second Edition of this work went to press, enough changes in our retailing picture have occurred in the interim to require substantial revisions of certain of the statistical data as well as additions to the text. The new material includes not only obvious additions to the annual records of individual chains, the inclusion and interpretation of the latest Census figures and a review of recent governmental action and court decisions affecting the chains, but, more significantly, the impact on the chains of the continued growth of shopping centers and the almost revolutionary emphasis on low-margin retailing stemming from the success of discount stores.

GODFREY M. LEBHAR

New York, January 31, 1963

PREFACE TO SECOND EDITION

THE SEVEN years which have elapsed since the publication of the first edition of this book have served to complete a century of continuous operation for this country's oldest and biggest chain, The Great Atlantic & Pacific Tea Company. And since the history of the chain store system in this country starts, for all practical purposes, with the birth of A&P, 1959 may well be regarded as the 100th anniversary not only of that company but of the chain store system itself.

That fact in itself might not provide a sufficient reason for issuing a revised edition of a book which carried chain store history up to 1950, but changes occur so rapidly in such a dynamic field as retailing that the 1950 picture hardly suffices for 1959. More to the point, however, is the fact that the exhaustion of the first edition provides an opportunity to bring out this Centennial Edition covering the full span of the chains' first century, 1859 to 1959.

GODFREY M. LEBHAR

January 2, 1959

PREFACE TO FIRST EDITION

Since 1932, when the present author offered *The Chain Store—Boon or Bane?* as his contribution on what was then generally referred to as the "chain-store question," the chain store has ceased to be a question.

The "question" about chain stores then was: "If chain stores keep expanding at their present rate, how long will it be before the independent merchant is wiped out entirely?" And, of course, that question implied another: "Is it in the public interest for the independent merchant to be replaced by chain stores?"

The main question has been answered by events. The chains did *not* "keep expanding at their present rate." On the contrary, subsequent events showed that the *indications* of 25 years ago rested on a false premise. The possibilities for chain-store expansion were not unlimited. The rapid and spectacular progress the chains made between 1920 and 1930 carried them to a certain point, but that apparently was as far as they were destined to go. The competitive position the chains had attained by 1930 was a substantial one, but since then their main task has been to hold it.

Today the chain-store system is recognized as an established feature of our distribution set-up and an extremely valuable one. Its main economic function is to provide a type of low-cost distribution designed to lower retail prices and make more things available to more people. Its social function is to raise the general standard of living by stretching the purchasing-power of the consumer's dollar. That it can achieve both these functions to a marked degree without eliminating the independent merchant the events of the last 20 years clearly show. Indeed, the independent merchant is not only just as strong numerically today as he was back in 1929, when the "chain-store question" was beginning to gain nationwide attention, and enjoying the same share of the total retail business as he accounted for them, but he is actually doing a much better job. The spur of competition provided by the chains has proved his salvation rather than his ruin.

The purpose of this book, then, is not to attempt again to answer the "chain-store question," which has answered itself, but to record the history of a movement which has meant and means so much to our domestic economy.

The book naturally divides itself into three parts: (1) the birth and growth of the system; (2) its struggle for self preservation in the face of violent and sustained opposition; and (3) its maturity.

Both the history of the chains and the so-called chain-store problem have been well covered in several recognized works. Particularly valuable were *Chain Stores,* by Hayward & White, 1928; *The Chain Store Problem,* by Beckman & Nolen, 1938; *Chain Stores and Legislation,* by Daniel Bloomfield, 1939; and *The Chain Store Tells Its Story,* by John P. Nichols, 1940. The only trouble with these books is that they are all out of print, besides being to some extent out of date. More recent works covering retailing or marketing in general devote some space to the chain-store system, but obviously the treatment is necessarily limited.

In undertaking the task involved in preparing this book the author has been moved by a sense of responsibility based on his own connection with the chain-store field since 1925 as editor and one of the publishers of *Chain Store Age.* In that capacity it was his privilege to know and to work with many of the chain store leaders whose names appear in these pages and to play a part in some of the events recorded. Much of the data used herein is based on material gathered through the years and published in the pages of *Chain Store Age* or preserved in its files.

For their cooperation in reading the manuscript, in whole or in part, the author acknowledges his gratitude to John A. Logan, president of the National Association of Food Chains; John F. Deegan, National Marketing Director, Atlantic Commission Co., Dr. Paul C. Olsen, assistant to the president of the Limited Price Variety Stores Association; Mrs. Gladys M. Kiernan, executive secretary of the Institute of Distribution; Rowland Jones, Jr., president of the American Retail Federation; Dr. Charles F. Phillips, president of Bates College; Don Francisco, vice president of J. Walter Thompson Co.; E. W. Simms, of White & Simms, formerly general counsel for the Institute of Distribution; Arnold D. Friedman, president of Lebhar-Friedman Publications, Inc., publisher of *Chain Store Age;* and the following members of the editorial staff of that publication: the late Frank E. Landau, editorial director; Lawrence Drake, Ben Gordon and John G. Poulos. A special acknowledgment goes to Samuel O. Kaylin, editor of the Administration Edition of *Chain Store Age,* and to the author's brother, Lionel M. Lebhar, for their assistance in preparing the manuscript for the press and their wise suggestions in regard to it.

If, in this effort to record the history of chain stores in America, the author reveals a endency to stress the virtues of the chains and to minimize their shortcomings, no apology is offered. Convinced as he is of the merits of the chain-store system, social as well as economic, the author sees no reason to conceal his convictions on that score.

GODFREY M. LEBHAR

New York, December 1, 1951

CHAIN STORES
IN AMERICA
1859-1962

PART I

BIRTH

CHAPTER I

WHAT THE CHAIN STORE
SYSTEM IS

THIS COUNTRY has approximately 1,800,000 retail stores
of all kinds, types, and sizes in operation.

That figure is based on the latest official count, the 1958
U.S. Census of Business, which puts the figure at 1,788,325,[1]
plus the fact that the number of stores does not change materially from year to year. Indeed it has changed hardly at
all over the past 20 years, the 1939 Census accounting for
1,770,355 stores, the 1948 Census for 1,769,540, and the 1954
Census for 1,721,650.

This constancy might seem remarkable in view of the substantial growth of our population during the period in question—from approximately 131 million in 1939 to 174 million
in 1958. Such a substantial increase in population, amounting
to 33%, would develop a need, one might expect, for at least
some increase in the number of stores.

That they were not provided is explained by the fact that
the period in question saw a definite and continued trend toward *larger* stores. Sparked by the introduction of the supermarket in the early '30s and its rapid development thereafter,
the new stores in all fields followed the trend and became ever
larger than their predecessors. Thus the need for greater retail

[1] Why this number is somewhat less than the actual number of stores in operation is explained on page 67.

3

facilities which did indeed develop was met by providing larger rather than more stores.

On the other hand, how has this relatively constant number of stores been maintained in view of the deplorably large number of retailers who drop out of the picture every year?

Without discussing here the reasons for the high rate of mortality which has always marked retail enterprise, the record indicates that for every merchant who goes out of business another is always ready to take his place. Vacant stores in a good location do not remain that way very long. Every year brings a new crop of hopefuls eager to set up shop in any spot which seems suitable for the purpose. Few are deterred by the fate of the previous tenant, if, indeed, they become aware of it.

But how about the new stores which are constantly being built to meet the needs of new or expanding communities? How is it that they fail to swell the total? A logical explanation would seem to be that these additions are offset by the elimination of store property which has been converted to other uses.

Even the development of shopping centers in recent years cannot have swelled the total appreciably in the interim between the 1954 and the 1958 Censuses, even though such projects obviously bring many new stores into the picture where none existed before. For assuming that as many as 2,200 centers came into the picture during the period in question, and assuming that they averaged 10 stores each, they would still have added only 22,000 stores to the nation's total. That is certainly no small number, and the importance of this revolutionary trend must not be minimized, but still it is not enough to change the overall statistical picture substantially. Actually, as is revealed by Table 15, page 74, the number of stores increased by 66,675 between 1954 and 1958. Among them, shopping center stores were undoubtedly well represented.

Accepting 1,800,000 then as a reasonably accurate basis for the brief analysis of the current retail set-up which follows, the first thing to note is that these stores are of all kinds, types, sizes and grades.

So far as size goes, at one end of the scale, we have, on the one hand, the huge department stores found in our big cities, each occupying a large multi-storied building with thousands of square feet of selling space on each floor, employing a veritable army of workers, drawing customers from a wide area, and doing many millions of dollars' worth of business a year. On the other hand, we have many thousands of modern supermarkets, discount stores, and other kinds of stores, which are typically single-storied but make up in area what they lack in height, and which likewise develop huge volume per unit. In 1958, 25,178 stores had annual sales in excess of $1,000,000, as shown in Table 1, and of these, the Census breakdown reveals, only 2,128 were department stores.

At the other end of the scale, we have hundreds of thousands of small neighborhood stores, usually specializing in particular lines of merchandise, occupying relatively little space, having limited capital, employing few, if any, workers, and doing such a small volume of business that their ability to stay in the picture for more than a few years is highly questionable.

In between these two extremes, we have hundreds of thousands of well-established, efficiently operated stores of all kinds and types, occupying the better retail locations, adequately capitalized, stocked, and manned, and operating profitably enough in most cases not only to insure their survival but to provide for possible expansion.

Quantitatively, these three groups, considering only the stores which were in operation for the full year, shaped up in the 1958 Census as shown in Table 1.

As might be expected and as is revealed in Table 3 (page

TABLE 1

RETAIL STORES IN OPERATION THROUGHOUT 1958,
BY SALES SIZE

(Source: U.S. Census of Business: 1958)

GROUP	NUMBER	%	SALES (MILLIONS)	%
Doing $1,000,000 or more	25,178	1.5	$ 58,591	31.1
Doing $50,000 to $999,000	685,208	41.6	109,843	58.3
Doing less than $50,000	936,523	56.9	20,045	10.6
All stores	1,646,909	100.0	$188,479	100.0

12), 912,642, or 97% of the stores doing less than $50,000 a year, were single stores.

Looking at our stores from another angle which is more to our present purpose, namely, that of ownership, they can be divided into two groups—one very large and the other correspondingly small.

The larger group, accounting for 1,605,590, or 89.8%, of the total enumerated in the 1958 Census, consisted of what the Census Bureau classified as "single units," which are more generally referred to as "independent stores." Their common characteristic is that each is separately owned and self-operated. In other words, the storekeeper is both the owner and the boss. He is referred to as an independent because he is responsible only to himself for his policies, his methods, and his results.

The smaller group, consisting of the remaining 182,735, or 10.2%, of the total, were classified in the Census as "multiunits." A multiunit was defined as "one of two or more establishments in the same general kind of business operated by the same firm." According to many authorities, all the stores in this group are chain stores,[2] but, for its own reasons, the Census Bureau abandoned the use of that designation completely in connection with its 1948 Census and followed the

[2] See p. 68, *post.*

same policy with its 1954 and 1958 enumerations. In all previous Censuses, however, commencing with the original one in 1929, the Census Bureau had regarded and designated all stores operated by firms with *four* or more as "chain stores," designating as "multiunits" only those operated by firms with two or three.

But no matter how you designate the stores in this group, their common characteristic is that each belongs to a group of two or more similar stores, and is typically operated by a hired *manager* rather than by an individual *owner*. Unlike the independent merchant, the manager of a chain store does not own it, nor does he set its policies, and he is definitely responsible to someone else—the individual or company owning the chain—for his operating results.

A breakdown of the 182,735 multiunits, or chain stores, as they will usually be referred to in this volume, is shown in Table 2.

TABLE 2

MULTIUNIT STORES, 1958, BY SIZE OF FIRM
(Source: U.S. Census of Business: 1958)

SIZE OF FIRM	STORES IN CATEGORY	SALES (MILLIONS)
2 stores	52,258	$ 9,626
3 stores	16,307	4,140
4 or 5 stores	13,310	4,176
6 to 10 stores	12,366	4,816
11 to 25 stores	14,670	5,115
26 to 50 stores	11,888	6,263
51 to 100 stores	11,708	4,597
101 or more stores	50,228	28,476
	182,735	$67,209

From the fact that the chains (including within that category all firms operating two or more stores) account for only 10% of all retail stores, their importance to our domestic economy might appear to be correspondingly small.

But that would be a mistake for two reasons.

In the first place, the chains account for a much larger percentage of the total dollar volume done by all retail stores than their meager percentage of the total number of stores might suggest. In 1958, with aggregate sales of $67 billion, as appears from the foregoing table, they accounted for approximately 34% of total sales.

Furthermore, even that figure of 34% does not tell the whole story of chain-store importance. For in some fields the chains are naturally a more important factor than they are in others. In those fields which lend themselves best to the chain-store type of operation, the chains play a far more important role than they do in retailing as a whole.

The 1958 Census reveals this quite clearly. It shows, for instance, that in the variety-store field, in which the chains were the pioneers, they operated 45% of the stores and accounted for 84% of the total sales in this field; in the shoe field, the chains operated 42% of the stores and accounted for 58% of the sales; in the grocery field, the chains operated only 9.6% of the stores but they accounted for 55% of the sales; while in the drug field, the chains with 13% of the stores accounted for 29% of total sales. All the figures in this paragraph include chains with *two* or *three* stores. For this reason, they do not agree with those shown in Table 15, *post*, which include only chains with *four* or more stores.

In the second place, certain basic characteristics of the chain-store type of operation have had a greater impact on the retail business as a whole, and on our general economy, than the number of their stores or even the volume of their sales might lead one to expect.

One of the outstanding characteristics of chain-store merchandising, for instance, has been its emphasis on lower prices. It has provided a competitive factor which other retailers could not ignore. Thus, such price advantages as the chains have been able to offer their own customers have benefitted their competitors' customers as well. For the lower prices or better values offered by one retailer or one type of retailing are bound to be reflected in the market more or less generally. Prices may not be reduced to a uniform level as a result of competition but the spread between the lowest and highest prices is bound to be narrowed. To the extent that chain-store pricing policies have tended to bring all prices down, their impact on retailing has been far-reaching and significant.

But behind the chains' lower prices, of course, are the various operating and merchandising factors which make them possible. Some of them are inherent in the chain-store type of operation and are unavailable to single-store merchants. But many of them can be adopted or adapted by *any* retailer. Take, for instance, as an outstanding example of the latter, the cash-and-carry method of operation—the elimination of credit sales, on the one hand, and delivery of merchandise from store to home, on the other. Although the chains did not invent that idea, they did see in it an effective means to lower prices, and they adopted it almost universally. Chain stores and cash-and-carry became almost synonymous terms. But the chains had no patent or monopoly on the plan and all retailers were free to use it. To the extent, however, that the chains' competitors failed to follow characteristic chain-store methods and policies, such as the cash-and-carry idea, the impact the chains have made on distribution in general has been out of proportion to the number of their stores or their share of total retail volume.

Having divided all retail stores into two groups, independents and chains, and having referred to certain operating and merchandising features *inherent* in the chain-store system, the question arises: What is the basic difference between the two systems?

Broadly speaking, the chain-store system is nothing more nor less than a method of distribution involving the use of *more than one* retail outlet. That is a very rough and incomplete description of the chain-store system, but it really covers the outstanding difference between the chain store, on the one hand, and the single, or independent, store, on the other.

The biggest chain in the country today, and incidentally the oldest, the Great Atlantic & Pacific Tea Company, with some 4,400 stores (at one time it had 15,700) and an annual volume in the fiscal year ending February 24, 1962, of $5,240,-315,000, differs only in degree from the newest infant in the chain-store family, which may operate but two or three units, for they both differ from the independent store primarily because they transact their business not through a single store but through more than one.

In emphasizing the fact that the difference between the chain store and the independent store is based fundamentally on *the number of units* operated under one ownership and control, there is no intention to minimize the importance of the distinction. On the contrary, whatever advantages the chain-store system may possess must be attributed directly to the economies accruing from the operation of more than one unit and the increase in the scope of operation thereby achieved, while, on the other hand, whatever weaknesses are inherent in the system are due almost exclusively to the special problems involved in the operation of more than one unit.

Most of the advantages the chains enjoy may be traced directly to the fact that the business is conducted through more than one unit because most of those advantages come from *volume,* and the volume the chains are able to attain depends mainly upon the number of stores they operate.

The fact that *large* volume may likewise be attained by a retailer with a single store, and frequently is, does not weaken the foregoing statement. For although, under a single roof, a merchant may attain a very large volume, his possibilities in that direction are nevertheless limited just so long as he confines his operations to a single establishment.

Offhand, it might seem unnecessary to elaborate the point that more volume is possible with two stores than with one, but the truth of that statement may be so easily befogged by reference to the stupendous business done in *some* instances by single stores that it may be useful to look into the matter a little further.

The truth of the matter is that while large volume is attainable in a single store, as has been demonstrated not only in the case of our big department stores but, more recently, in the grocery field with the advent of the supermarket and in the general merchandise field with the development of mammoth discount stores, the *maximum* possibilities for volume can be secured only through the operation of more than one store. But more fundamental is the fact that, while some single-store merchants do develop large volume, a large percentage remain relatively small.

The situation is clearly revealed in Tables 3 and 4.

Table 3, covering 1,470,454 *single* stores which were in operation for the full year of 1958 shows that 912,642, or 62.1%, of them did *less* than $50,000. How much less than $50,000 a year most of them did is indicated by the fact that, with a combined volume of $19,667,000,000, this group averaged only $21,500 per store. Indeed, the Census breakdown reveals that the number of stores doing less than $30,000 in 1958 was 642,463, averaging less than $15,000 each.

Table 4 tells the same story in another way. It discloses that 591,150 stores, or 36% of all stores, including multiunits, which were in operation throughout 1958, had *no* paid employees, while an additional 596,403, had 3 employees or fewer. Together these groups comprised some 72% of all stores, but they accounted for only 24% of all retail sales. That the advantages which accrue from large-scale retail operations are beyond the reach of stores of this caliber so long as they remain single-store operations would seem to be obvious, even though by affiliation with voluntary chains and cooperative groups, even small-scale independent merchants may improve their competitive position.[3]

Turning now to the other end of the scale, Table 3 shows that single stores doing *more* than $300,000 a year in 1958

TABLE 3

SINGLE STORES IN OPERATION THROUGHOUT 1958, BY SALES SIZE

(Source: U.S. Census of Business: 1958)

SIZE GROUP (ANNUAL SALES)	STORES IN GROUP	%	SALES OF GROUP (MILLIONS)	%
$300,000 or more	66,488	4.5	$ 50,085	40.6
$50,000 to $299,000	491,324	33.4	53,580	43.5
Less than $50,000	912,642	62.1	19,667	15.9
All stores	1,470,454	100.0	$123,332	100.0

numbered 66,488, or 4.5% of the total. They accounted, however, for 40.6 of the total sales of all single stores, and because of the huge volume which some of them developed they averaged approximately $750,000 a year.

Included in this group, of course, are most of our big department stores, many of which do many millions of dollars' worth of business a year. But even the biggest of them is limited in the amount of business it can do so long as it confines itself to a single store.

This is well illustrated in the case of R. H. Macy & Co.'s huge store on 34th Street and Sixth Avenue, New York.

In 1921, Macy's sales amounted to $46,000,000, a tremendous volume to be attained under a single roof. Nevertheless, year by year the volume increased until, in 1929, it reached a record figure of $98,600,000. In that year, however, the company acquired Bamberger & Co., a Newark, N.J. department store, and the following year the *combined* sales amounted to

[3] See "Those Hardy Independents," *Chain Store Age*, Grocery Edition, July, 1960, page 35.

$135,000,000. Of that total, Macy's contributed $99,000,000 and Bamberger's the balance.

The illustration is particularly in point because Newark is sufficiently close to New York to warrant the conclusion that Macy's enjoyed a certain amount of Newark patronage be-

TABLE 4

RETAIL TRADE, 1958, BY EMPLOYMENT SIZE

(Source: U.S. Census of Business: 1958)

EMPLOYEES PER STORE	NUMBER OF STORES	%	SALES OF GROUP (MILLIONS)	%
None	591,150	35.9	$ 12,583	6.6
One to three	596,403	36.2	32,527	17.3
Four or more	459,356	27.9	143,369	76.1
All stores in operation throughout 1958	1,646,909	100.0	$188,479	100.0

fore it took over Bamberger's, and yet $35,000,000 more was apparently to be had at that time only by the acquisition of that store or another store of like capacity.

Incidentally, it should be pointed out that because of the delivery system maintained by stores like Macy's and the mail order facilities they have at their command, their possibilities for volume are not necessarily limited to their immediate neighborhoods. Indeed, they seek and obtain a certain amount of patronage from communities far removed from their natural trading area. But despite their effort and their success in that direction, their real possibilities for volume seem nevertheless to be limited to the business they can draw from their immediate vicinities.

Realization of this limitation in recent years led most of our leading department stores to open suburban branch stores. Macy's, today, operates not only a number of large stores which it acquired, as it did Bamberger's, but also a number of branch stores which it established in its own backyard, so to speak—in Parkchester, in the Bronx; Jamaica, L.I.; Flatbush, Brooklyn; White Plains, N.Y.; and Roosevelt Field, L.I. —because that was the only way to capture millions of dollars of additional volume which the "miracle" store on 34th Street could not hope to draw.[4]

Other New York department stores and specialty shops and similar stores in other cities have followed the same general pattern. The trend has usually been referred to as "decentralization." Traffic congestion and limited parking facilities in the downtown areas, plus the tremendous growth in suburban population, have undoubtedly been largely responsible for it. Taking the store to the customer who can no longer shop conveniently at the main store may be as much a matter of holding existing volume as a means of achieving additional volume. In either event, however, the trend illustrates that even our most successful stores recognize the limitations inherent in any given location and attempt to overcome them by opening branch stores.

If big stores like these, with their extensive delivery systems, find themselves at a disadvantage with a single store, how much more limited must be the chances of a merchant who must rely exclusively on his immediate neighborhood for all of his business!

Not only are the possibilities for volume at any single location definitely limited, but the converse is also true: Once the limitations incident to single-store operation are eliminated, the volume attainable is dependent only on the number of stores which can be successfully operated. The history of the chains is replete with instances of merchants who, once they realized the limitations of single-store operation, found that the road to unlimited volume presented practically no obstacles.

[4] Macy's sales for the fiscal year ending July 28, 1962, were $541.5 million. At that time, the company's various department store divisions were operating 41 stores in all, with 11 more under construction or planned.

The experience of the J. C. Penney Company is typical of the manner in which most of the chain-store companies, which loom large in today's distribution set-up came into being. As a matter of fact, practically all chains, small as well as large, started in precisely the same way, achieving various degrees of success.

The first Penney store, which operated under the name of the "Golden Rule," was established by James Cash Penney and a couple of partners in Kemmerer, Wyo., in April, 1902. It was a most insignificant 25x45-foot dry-goods store located in a community hardly more promising. Certainly, from the pictures of it which have been preserved, it gave no indications that it was to be the progenitor of the 1,700 outstanding apparel and general-merchandise stores which dot the country today. For his one-third interest in the store, Mr. Penney put up $500 of his own money plus $1,500 which he was able to borrow from a bank.

The sales the first year were approximately $29,000—indicating that this first Penney unit was somewhat more successful than the majority of single stores are today, particularly as $29,000 in those days meant considerably more than it does now.

In 1903, Mr. Penney and his partners opened a second establishment in another frontier community, and in that year the combined volume of the incipient chain was $63,000. Store No. 3 was opened in 1904. In 1907, Mr. Penney bought out his partners' interest in the three stores for $30,000, and he was in business on his own.[5]

That same year, Mr. Penney took into his organization a man who was later on to become the president of the company and to direct its operations through many of its most successful years—the late Earl C. Sams. How Mr. Sams came to get in touch with Mr. Penney is best told in his own language.

[5] Norman Beasley, *Main Street Merchant* (New York: McGraw-Hill Book Co., 1948).

"In 1907, I was operating, with the backing of some friends, a store in my small native town of Simpson, Kan.," he said, in the course of his testimony before a Congressional committee[6] 33 years later. "I was an independent merchant. . . . We operated a good store to the best of our knowledge and I was pretty much my own boss. However, I couldn't see any real opportunity ahead. A livelihood—yes, perhaps—but not much more. In looking around for a much bigger opportunity, an employment agency told me about a man named J. C. Penney who had a store in the little coal camp of Kemmerer, Wyo., and who had a vision of something beyond a single small store. After some correspondence, I left Kansas and joined Mr. Penney."

One of the things which attracted Mr. Sams to Mr. Penney, he went on to say, "was the vision he had of more than one store—maybe a dozen, maybe even 50, which might be opened through the years and which would work together."

That vision of "even 50" stores may have seemed far off in 1907 but, as a matter of fact, it was realized sooner than either Mr. Sams or Mr. Penney himself could ever have dreamed. Within four years after Mr. Sams' decision to throw in his lot with Mr. Penney, the company had 22 stores in operation and the sales passed the $1,000,000 mark! By 1914, the vision of "even 50" stores was actually achieved. That year the 71st store was opened and the company's sales totaled $3,600,000.

A particularly interesting milestone in the company's progress, however, is the fact that its sales in 1921, when it had 312 stores, amounted to $46,000,000. Both the year and the amount are significant because it happens that Macy's sales that very same year hit the very same level. The significance lies in the fact that, whereas the department store, operating under a single roof, had required 63 years to reach that point (Macy's was established in 1858) the chain-store company,

---

[6] Hearing on Patman Bill, 76th Congress, 3rd Session, Vol. 1, p. 559.

operating under a number of separate roofs scattered over a wide area in communities far smaller than New York, had reached the same point in only nineteen years.

TABLE 5

GROWTH OF J. C. PENNEY COMPANY, 1902-1962

YEAR*	STORES	SALES	YEAR*	STORES	SALES
1902	1	$ 28,898	1932	1,473	$ 155,271,981
1903	1	63,523	1933	1,466	178,773,965
1904	2	94,165	1934	1,474	212,053,361
1905	2	97,654	1935	1,481	225,936,101
1906	2	127,128	1936	1,496	258,322,479
1907	2	166,314	1937	1,523	275,375,137
1908	4	218,432	1938	1,539	257,963,946
1909	6	310,062	1939	1,554	282,133,934
1910	14	662,331	1940	1,586	304,539,325
1911	22	1,183,280	1941	1,605	377,571,711
1912	34	2,050,642	1942	1,611	490,295,173
1913	48	2,637,294	1943	1,610	489,888,091
1914	71	3,560,294	1944	1,608	535,362,894
1915	86	4,825,072	1945	1,602	549,149,148
1916	127	8,428,144	1946	1,601	767,584,135
1917	177	14,881,203	1947	1,601	775,889,615
1918	197	31,338,104	1948	1,601	885,203,023
1919	197	28,783,956	1949	1,609	880,192,488
1920	312	42,846,009	1950	1,612	949,729,400
1921	313	46,641,928	1951	1,621	1,035,201,519
1922	371	49,035,729	1952	1,632	1,079,256,505
1923	475	62,188,979	1953	1,634	1,109,507,675
1924	569	74,261,343	1954	1,644	1,107,156,633
1925	674	91,062,616	1955	1,666	1,220,085,325
1926	747	115,683,023	1956	1,687	1,291,867,267
1927	892	151,957,865	1957	1,694	1,312,278,407
1928	1,023	176,698,989	1958**	1,687	1,409,972,649
1929	1,395	209,690,418	1959	1,683	1,437,489,357
1930	1,452	192,943,765	1960	1,695	1,468,917,982
1931	1,459	173,705,095	1961	1,686	1,553,505,660

* Calendar years until 1957. Thereafter fiscal years ending January 31 following year given.
** 13 months.

The progress of the chain from that time on is revealed in Table 5, which gives the number of stores and the annual sales in each year from 1902 to 1961.

The growth of the J. C. Penney Company from a single

store in 1902, with sales of $29,000, to a chain of 1,686 stores in 1962, with sales of $1.5 billion, amazing as it is, was the outcome of no magic formula, no secret process, no patent or monopoly, no unusual opportunity which was not available to any other single-store merchant in 1902, or at any other time before or since. Of course, the idea of operating more than one store did not originate with Mr. Penney. On the contrary, the Great Atlantic & Pacific Tea Co. had been in operation for more than 40 years, Jones Brothers Tea Co. (later to become Grand Union Co.) for 30 years, and the F. W. Woolworth Co. for more than twenty years, when Mr. Penney opened his first store, while at least a score of other chains had preceded him.

But, what is more to the point, thousands of single-store merchants have followed the identical path which Mr. Penney and his predecessors trod and have likewise developed highly successful chains in a number of different fields of retail activity.

Full-length books have been written about the chains built by Frank Woolworth, J. C. Penney, Louis K. Liggett and Sears, Roebuck.[7] Hundreds of other chains have been the subjects of success stories in leading magazines and business papers. But the fact is that a human-interest story lies behind practically every one of the chains now in existence. Only the limitations of space and the fact that all the stories follow the same basic pattern, differing only in details, prevent their inclusion in these pages. Inspiring and useful as these success stories are, too many of them in this volume would make monotonous reading.

However, two of them which were told by the author years ago in the course of an address on "Opportunity in the Chain

---

[7] John K. Winkler, *Five and Ten* (New York: McBride, 1940); Norman Beasley, *op. cit.*; Samuel Merwin, *Rise and Fight Againe* (New York, Boni & Co., 1935); Emmett & Jeuck, *Catalogs and Counters* (Chicago: University of Chicago Press, 1950); see also case histories of many chains in *Chain Store Age* (all editions), June, 1950.

Store Field"[8] may be told again if only for the purpose of bringing them up to date.

The first involved the history of the Badger Paint & Hardware Stores, of Milwaukee, which was then only ten years old.

In 1918, Robert Jacobi opened a paint store. He had no idea of starting a chain at the time. All he saw was the possibility for a paint store that would be different from the general run.

In the first place, he decided to paint his store attractively so that the store itself would be a standing advertisement of the virtue of paint. In the second place he decided to go aggressively after business instead of waiting for it to come to him.

Although his entire capital was only $1,400, he spent $900 of it the very first month for advertising. The attractive appearance of the store, the energy its proprietor put into the management of it, the advertising effort, all combined to make the store successful. The first year's sales were $23,000. The greatest single item of expense was advertising.

Then the big idea came to this single-store merchant. The advertising he was doing would work just as well for two stores as it would for one, so that, in effect, this heavy item of cost would be cut in two.

He opened a second store. Sales for the two stores were $50,000. His operating expenses were substantially reduced proportionately because some of them, like advertising, were shared by the two stores instead of being carried entirely by one.

The following year, out of profits, he opened a third store. Then he began to realize some of the additional benefits the operation of more than one store makes possible. He found that his buying power had increased and, by buying in larger quantities, he paid less for his merchandise.

[8] Delivered before Retail Clothiers and Furnishers Associations of New York, New Jersey and Pennsylvania, Hotel Ambassador, Atlantic City, February 22, 1928.

From that time on his progress was rapid. By 1928, he had his own paint factory, was operating nearly 50 stores, and his sales were in excess of $1,000,000.

What was the sequel of that story? According to the company's report for 1949, the Badger Paint & Hardware chain was operating 117 stores and sales totaled $4,500,000. Included in the assets of the company, which had started in 1918 with a capital of $1,400, were land and buildings valued at more than $1,000,000. As of January 1, 1962, the company was operating 128 stores in Wisconsin, Illinois, and Missouri. Its assets had grown substantially since its report of 1949, and its sales were $7,497,869.

The other story related to an independent merchant in another field—a druggist in Chicago. Back in 1909, when he was 36 years old, this druggist was operating a small store which he had bought from his employer in 1901, and he was just about making both ends meet. That year he got a chance to buy a second store from another former employer. To raise the money for the down payment, he would have to sell a half-interest in the store he had. His friends advised him against it.

"Chicago has too many drug stores already," they warned. "Why buck the tide?"

"Chicago may have too many drug stores," he replied, "but it hasn't enough *Walgreen* drug stores!"

For the independent druggist in question was the late Charles Walgreen, and his purchase of a second store in 1909 against his friends' advice marked the beginning of the Walgreen chain of drug stores which, in 1928, at the time of the address in question, had 170 stores in operation and was doing more than $20,000,000 a year. The independent druggist of nineteen years earlier had become the president of the second largest drug chain in the country.

What happened was told in detail in a special issue of the

Walgreen *Pepper Pod,* June, 1951, the company's house organ—the 50th anniversary issue.

In 1911, a third store was opened, in 1913 a fourth, and by 1916, seven Walgreen stores, each separately incorporated, were in operation. That year the separate corporations were merged to form the present Walgreen Company. Its growth from 1920 to 1961 is shown in Table 6.

TABLE 6

WALGREEN CO. GROWTH, 1920-1962

YEAR	STORES	SALES (MILLIONS)	YEAR	STORES	SALES (MILLIONS)
1920	23	$ 2.2	1942	480	95.3
1921	29	2.6	1943	460	112.2
1922	33	2.5	1944	442	120.0
1923	41	3.6	1945	427	118.8
1924	56	5.6	1946	412	140.7
1925	87	9.3	1947	410	154.5
1926	107	13.5	1948	413	163.3
1927	170	20.9	1949	414	163.4
1928	230	31.4	1950	410	163.4
1929	397	46.6	1951	406	171.5
1930	440	39.1*	1952	400	177.9
1931	468	54.0	1953	390	181.5
1932	471	47.6	1954	388	184.3
1933	474	46.0	1955	388	192.7
1934	487	53.7	1956	386	212.3
1935	501	58.1	1957	407	235.1
1936	496	61.8	1958	406	260.0
1937	504	67.9	1959	422	285.1
1938	508	67.7	1960	451	312.4
1939	494	70.8	1961	467	331.7
1940	489	74.3	1962	476	353.3
1941	487	82.5			

* For 9 months only. Fiscal years thereafter ending September 30 of year given.

In 1939, Charles Walgreen died and his son Charles Walgreen, Jr., took over as president. The chain has gained consistently under his direction not only in volume of sales but in leadership in its field and in the pharmaceutical profession. Although it now has somewhat fewer stores than it had at one time, as is revealed in the following table, this merely reflects the trend towards bigger stores to which reference has already been made. As a result, the combined selling area of the 467 stores in operation at the end of the 1961 fiscal year greatly exceeded that of the 508 stores operating in 1938. The annual sales reported include sales to several hundred agency stores —independent drug stores which serve as Walgreen agencies for the company's own products and which also use the facilities Walgreen has for supplying them with many other items.

The founder of Walgreen Company was a typical single-store druggist when the opportunity came to him to acquire a second store. After that he made his own opportunities. He enjoyed no advantage over his fellow independent druggists except, perhaps, a livelier imagination and a greater ambition. These were apparently enough to lay the foundation for what was to become the biggest drug chain in the country.

That most chains started with modest capital and financed their early expansion entirely out of earnings is not only a fact but was more or less inevitable. Until they had demonstrated their ability to operate a chain of stores profitably over a number of years, their chance of attracting outside capital would obviously have been slim.[9] The first public financing for the Woolworth Company did not come until 1912.[10] J. C. Penney Company financed itself until it had 197 stores and sales of $21,000,000; the S. S. Kresge Co. until it had 66 stores and sales of $7,900,000; and McCrory Stores Corporation until it had 113 stores and sales of $4,900,000.

In the shoe field, the present Melville Shoe Corporation, which was founded by Frank Melville, Jr., in 1892, was financed out of earnings for the first 24 years of its existence. Not until 1916, when the present corporation came into existence, was outside capital sought. The G. R. Kinney Company, founded in 1894, followed a similar course. It was incorporated in 1917, but the stock was closely held. Not until 1923,

[9] Luigi Criscuolo, "Financing the Chain," *Chain Store Age*, June, 1925, p. 13.
[10] *Five and Ten*, note 7 *supra*.

by which time the company had 152 stores in operation and shoe factories of its own and sales of $14,000,000, was any common stock offered publicly.

That has been the almost universal formula responsible for the chain-store system today. Not all the chains it has produced have grown to the point where public financing was either feasible or desired. The fact is that the great majority of the chains which comprise the system are extremely small compared with A&P, the Woolworth Co., J. C. Penney Co., Walgreen's, Melville Shoe Corporation and other leaders in their respective fields.

On the other hand, in between the top-flight companies and the smallest ones are thousands of regional and local companies each operating relatively few stores but doing an annual business running well into the millions.

But, large or small, national, regional or local, these companies collectively make the chain-store system. Almost without exception they have three basic points in common:

1. They started as single-store merchants.

2. None of them was content to remain a single-store merchant.

3. By escaping the limitations of single-store operation, they were able to develop a volume of sales which, judging from the experience of most single-store merchants, they would have secured *in no other way.*

CHAPTER II

THE BIRTH OF THE SYSTEM

CHAIN-STORE history conveniently divides itself into three periods:

1. 1859-1900, the period in which the pioneers in several important chain-store fields got their start and had their early development.

2. 1900-1930, the period in which the chain-store idea captured the imagination of many alert retailers, brought hundreds of new chains into existence, and witnessed the expansion of the system at such a rapid rate and on such a conspicuous scale as to threaten its destruction.

3. Since 1930, the period in which the system had to fight for its very existence but emerged the stronger for its experience and better equipped to fill its particular niche in the distribution set-up on a sound and abiding basis.

That the chain-store idea had its beginnings, of a sort, long before 1859, the year A&P was founded, is beyond question. John P. Nichols, in his outstanding book on chain stores,[1] refers to a chain of stores operating in China 200 years before Christ, a chain of drug stores founded in Japan in 1643, mercantile operations of a chain-store character carried on by the Fugger family in Germany and the Merchant Adventurers in England, the chain of outposts developed in Canada by the Hudson's Bay Company, chartered in 1670, and the fact that

[1] John P. Nichols, *The Chain Store Tells Its Story* (Institute of Distribution, 1940), p. 13. For more complete data on early history of chains, "of a kind," see *"Economics of Retailing,"* Paul H. Nystrom, 1930, Ronald Press.

24

our own Andrew Jackson at one time owned a small chain of retail stores in Tennessee. And, no doubt, many another early American merchant might have qualified as a pioneer chainstore operator by reason of the fact that he had a second, a third or even a fourth store.

Nevertheless, the date of the founding of the A&P is chosen as the take-off point for this record of chain stores in America because *all* the chains which have helped in any way to make the system what it is today came into being within A&P's lifetime.

1. *The Pioneer Grocery Chains*

A&P had its beginnings in a small store on Vesey Street, New York, opened in 1859 by George F. Gilman and George Huntington Hartford. It was not a grocery store and it did not have the name Great Atlantic & Pacific Tea Co. Whether the founders at that time had any idea that they would ever have more than one store may be doubted, for the success of their first store was by no means assured. The only idea they had then was to make tea available to the public at much below the prevailing price by simply importing tea direct from China and Japan and cutting out some of the middlemen's costs and profits.

However, the Gilman & Hartford venture on Vesey Street did prove so successful that before very long they opened a second store. By 1865, they had no less than 25 stores in operation and had assumed the name of the Great American Tea Company. By that time they were so well established and so sure of their ground that they decided to add a line of groceries, figuring that if they could sell tea at reduced prices, they could sell other items at reduced prices also.

It was not until 1869 that the name Great Atlantic & Pacific Tea Company was adopted. By that time the company had begun to spread westward and undoubtedly felt that a more comprehensive title would reflect the scope of its operations more clearly.

In 1878, Mr. Gilman retired and Mr. Hartford was left to carry on alone until two of his sons, George L. and John A., were old enough to join him, the former in 1880 and the latter in 1888.[2]

A&P's 100th store was opened in 1880. Considering that the company was then 21 years old, its rate of expansion, although rapid enough, no doubt, for those days, had been at a snail's pace compared with what was to happen later on. One hundred stores in 21 years! A time was to come when A&P was to open as many as that in two weeks—to open an *average* of 50 stores a week for a whole year!

Even twenty years later, at the turn of the century, A&P was still operating less than 200 stores, although by 1900 the company was 41 years old.

Turning for a moment from A&P, a number of other grocery chains came into existence during that period, to say nothing of the appearance of the first Woolworth store, in 1879, and the early development of the Woolworth chain and other chains in the 5-and-10-cent-store field, of which more will be said later.

In the grocery field, the year 1872 saw the organization of its second oldest chain—Jones Brothers Tea Co., of Brooklyn, which was later to become the successful Grand Union Company of today.

Ten years later, in 1882, was sown the seed of the present Kroger Company, the third largest grocery chain today in number of stores and volume of sales. That year, Bernard H. Kroger, of Cincinnati, 22 years old, with a couple of years of experience as a grocery clerk, opened a store under the name of Great Western Tea Company. It made a profit the very first year and, before very long, a second store was opened

[2] *Time*, November 13, 1950, p. 93.

and the combined profits made a third store possible. But, although the rate of expansion was necessarily slow, by 1891 the Great Western Tea Co. had seven stores and by 1902, it had 36. That year it became the Kroger Grocery & Baking Company. Its growth thereafter was more rapid. Indeed, the day was to come when it would have more than 5,500 stores.[3] Today, as a result of the trend toward larger but fewer stores, the Kroger Company, as it is now called, operates only 1,354 stores but its sales in 1961 totalled $1,842,342,667—making it the third biggest chain in the food field.

Another food chain established the same year as Kroger, James Butler Grocery Co., of New York, followed a different course. Although it developed successfully for many years—to the point where it was operating more than 500 stores in the metropolitan area—its owners decided in 1936 to retire from the field. Some of the stores were sold to their managers. The remainder were liquidated.

Five other food chains established well before the turn of the century were:

	Founded
Childs Grocery Co.	1883
Acme Tea Co.	1887
Geo. M. Dunlap Co.	1888
The Bell Company	1890
Robinson & Crawford	1891

In 1917, these companies, all operating in the Philadelphia area, merged and became the American Stores Co. With some 1,100 stores in the combined operation at the start, and annual sales aggregating $68,300,000, the company followed the expansion trend and by 1932 reached its peak of 2,977 stores with sales in that depression year of $115,500,000. In its fiscal

---

[3] In 1929, the company reached its peak in number of stores, 5,575, and its sales that year were $286 million.

year ending March 31, 1962, with only 785 stores, the company's sales totalled $1,034,878,658, the fourth biggest chain in the food field. It is now known as Acme Markets, Inc.

Two pioneer New York chains which were to retain their identities all through the years and which are operating today at peak efficiency are H. C. Bohack Company, of Brooklyn, and Gristede Bros., of New York.

The former goes back to 1887, when H. C. Bohack opened his first store. Following the traditional pattern, he opened store after store until eventually his chain spread all over Long Island. At the end of its 1962 fiscal year, the company operated 197 stores and its sales for the year totalled $176,797,000. More significantly, as it approached its 75th year, it was planning substantial expansion in Staten Island and in Manhattan and the Bronx.

The Gristede story goes back to 1891, when two brothers, Charles and Diedrich Gristede, who had both worked as grocery clerks, decided to open a store of their own. Their obvious determination to please their customers and make a success of their business, the long hours they put into their self-bossed jobs and their friendly personalities did not go unrewarded. They were the kind of men who would have been reasonably successful in the grocery business even with a single store.

As it was, however, they were not content to continue on that basis, and they opened a second store. Although their subsequent expansion proceeded always at a slow pace, the company today is operating 123 stores in New York and Connecticut, and their sales are estimated to be in the neighborhood of $125,000,000. Incidentally, this chain specialized in a more complete range of groceries and delicacies than the typical grocery chain was accustomed to stock, and it also has the distinction of being one of the very few food chains in the whole country which gave credit and made deliveries while its competitors in the chain-store field stuck rigidly to the cash-and-carry principle.

One of the most successful regional chains whose roots go back to the period under consideration is First National Stores, of Somerville, Mass., although it did not actually come into being until it was organized under that name in 1926. In that year, The Ginter Company, which had been established in 1895, and the John T. Connor Co. and the O'Keeffe Company, all of Boston, merged to form First National.

The combined operation involved 1,681 typically small stores and the 1927 annual sales amounted to $59,038,304, or an average of $35,000 a year per store. At the end of its 1962 fiscal year, the chain reported only 632 stores in operation but sales of $711,303,869, or an average of $1,125,000 per store. The comparison provides further concrete evidence of the trend toward bigger stores which has been previously noted.

Two other extremely successful chains in today's picture came into existence in 1899—National Tea Co. and Jewel Tea Company. Both originated in Chicago.

Starting with a single store, National Tea's early growth was relatively slow. By 1921, however, it had 261 stores and an aggregate volume of $16,300,000, and accelerating its expansion in line with the trend of that decade, by 1929 its stores reached a peak in number of 1,627, with sales of $90,200,000. Today the chain and its subsidiaries operate stores in 18 States extending from Canada to the Gulf of Mexico. Although at the end of 1961 its stores numbered only 897, their sales totalled $888,853,000, making National the sixth largest food chain in the country.

The Jewel Tea Co. of today does indeed stem from a seed sown in 1899, but this successful chain did not operate even a single store until 1932! Starting a very small business as tea and coffee merchants, the founders of what was to become Jewel Tea rapidly developed a horse-and-wagon home service business that was eventually to require a fleet of more than 2,500 salesmen-driven motor trucks to handle its ever-growing trade. Sales in 1929 reached a total of $16,800,000. Then, in 1932, came an opportunity to acquire an established Chicago chain of some 75 stores, and Jewel entered the food-chain field as a supplement to its home-service set-up.

Today, Jewel Tea still maintains 1881 home service routes, but its food stores numbered 286 as it completed its 63rd year of operation on December 31, 1961, it was operating a successful drug chain of 31 stores which it acquired that year, a group of 4 self-service department stores and it had a substantial interest in a Belgian supermarket chain which had 10 units in operation at the end of the year and was planning a number of additional units. Jewel's sales in 1961, including those of its home-service routes as well as those of its supermarket, drug and department stores in this country totalled $552,200,000.

Many local food chains in operation today in various parts of the country likewise had their beginnings back in the period under consideration, but no attempt has been made to list them all. Typical of the group are Henke & Pillot, Houston, Tex., founded in 1872, which is now owned by the Kroger Co.; Ralph's Grocery Co., Los Angeles, founded in 1873; Daniel Grocer Co., Murphysboro, Ill., founded in 1882; Fred W. Albrecht Co., Akron, Ohio, founded in 1891; and Standard Grocery Co. (now owned by National Tea Co.), Indianapolis, founded in 1897 by Lafayette Jackson, who was to figure as plaintiff some 30 years later in a case which made chain-store history.[4]

Returning now to A&P for a resumption of the account of that company's progress through its first 100 years, its real expansion program did not get under way until 1912. Then, as a result of a successful experiment with a new type of store

[4] See page 138, *post.*

suggested by John A. Hartford,[5] a decision was made to open as many of them as possible as rapidly as they could be established.

These new stores, called "economy stores," were designed to sell groceries as cheap as possible by the simple device of selling on a cash-and-carry basis instead of making deliveries and extending credit, as A&P had done up to that time in common with other grocers.

Furthermore, the new stores were to be small, low-rent, one-man affairs, with modest fixtures, all making for low operating costs, and were to be satisfied with a minimum of profit. Increased volume was to be depended upon to make up for the low profit rate.

The first economy stores proved so successful that A&P decided to open them wherever they could be established with a reasonable prospect of success—which, because of their low prices, meant practically anywhere and everywhere. The 500th A&P store was opened in 1913 and the company had 585 in operation by the end of that year. In the next two years it opened some 1,600 more and, by the end of 1919, it had no less than 4,200!

But that was only the beginning of an expansion program which was to *add* nearly 10,000 stores in the next six years, the company having 14,000 stores in operation by the end of 1925. From that point, further expansion at a slower rate carried the chain to its peak of 15,700 in 1930, as is shown in Chart I on page 32, and Table 7 on page 33.

What happened after that to reduce the number of A&P stores to its present level of 4,400 was the revolutionary change in the grocery field brought about by the introduction of the supermarket in the early '30s.

This newcomer was much bigger than the largest combination stores which immediately preceded it—stores which han-

[5] He died September 20, 1951. George Hartford died September 23, 1957.

CHART I
GROWTH OF GREAT ATLANTIC & PACIFIC TEA COMPANY
1920-1962*

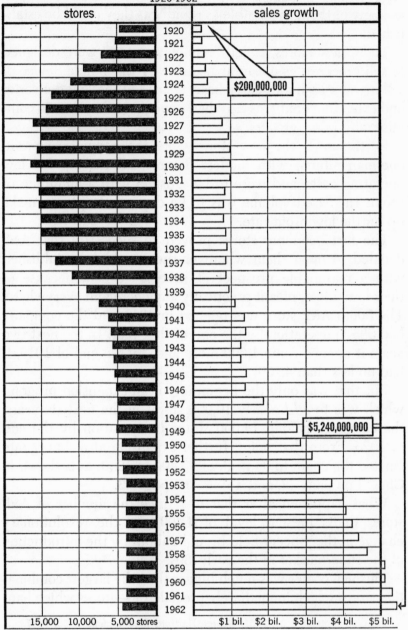

stores	sales growth

$200,000,000

$5,240,000,000

| 15,000 | 10,000 | 5,000 stores | | $1 bil. | $2 bil. | $3 bil. | $4 bil. | $5 bil. |

*Fiscal years ending last Saturday in February of year given

32

dled fresh meats and a wide range of fresh fruits and vegetables as well as groceries all under one roof. It was four or
five times bigger than the traditional straight grocery stores

TABLE 7

GROWTH OF A&P, 1859-1961

YEAR*	STORES	SALES (MILLIONS)	YEAR*	STORES	SALES (MILLIONS)
1859	1	—	1934	15,035	842
1865	25	—	1935	14,926	872
1880	100	—	1936	14,746	907
1900	200	—	1937	13,314	882
1906	291	—	1938	10,900	879
1910	372	—	1939	9,200	990
1911	400	—	1940	7,230	1,116
1912	480	—	1941	6,170	1,379
1913	585	—	1942	6,000	1,471
1914	991	—	1943	5,900	1,311
1915	1,817	—	1944	5,800	1,402
1916	2,866	—	1945	5,600	1,435
1917	3,782	—	1946	5,200	1,909
1918	3,799	—	1947	5,075	2,546
1919	4,224	$ 195	1948	4,900	2,837
1920	4,621	235	1949	4,700	2,905
1921	5,217	202	1950	4,500	3,180
1922	7,350	247	1951	4,400	3,392
1923	9,303	303	1952	4,300	3,756
1924	11,421	352	1953	4,250	3,989
1925	14,034	440	1954	4,200	4,140
1926	14,811	574	1955	4,150	4,305
1927	15,671	761	1956	4,200	4,482
1928	15,177	973	1957	4,200	4,769
1929	15,418	1,054	1958	4,252	5,095
1930	15,737	1,066	1959	4,276	5,049
1931	15,670	1,008	1960	4,351	5,247
1932	15,427	864	1961	4,409	5,240
1933	15,131	820			

* Fiscal years ending February 28 following year given until 1955; thereafter on
last Saturday in February following year given.

which had previously constituted the grocery field. But besides being bigger, the supermarket presented many new
operating and merchandising features.

In the first place, it was operated on a self-service basis, so far, at least, as the grocery department was concerned.[6] Secondly, it featured huge displays of groceries of all kinds as well as fresh meats and fruits and vegetables. Some of the early versions of the supermarket carried many other lines as well, having no relation to the grocery business—clothing, shoes, furniture, for example—which were sold in departments operated by concessionaires. But the development of the supermarket followed a more conservative pattern although interest in non-food items was to be reborn later on. Finally, and probably most significant, everything was featured at aggressively low prices made possible by the economies flowing from the self-service set-up and the advantages inherent in large volume.

Although the first supermarkets were established by independents for the most part, the chains eventually recognized their basic advantages and possibilities and decided that the only thing to do was to build supermarkets themselves. Some chains acted faster than others but, by 1937, most of the leading food chains, including A&P, were building supermarkets as fast as they could find suitable locations—and closing up three or four of their existing smaller units to make

[6] The supermarkets did not originate self-service. This revolutionary idea in food retailing was the brain-child of the inventive mind of Clarence Saunders, of Memphis. He made it the basis of an entirely new type of grocery store which he introduced, in 1916, under the intriguing name of Piggly Wiggly. The special lay-out of the Piggly Wiggly store required customers to pass through a turnstile and then follow a more or less prescribed path exposing them to the appeal of all the merchandise displayed on the shelving. The idea was so successful that the company was able to sell franchises to thousands of others who wanted to adopt it and operate under the Piggly Wiggly name. Many of the leading chains, including Safeway, Kroger, National Tea and Colonial, operated Piggly Wiggly stores in certain areas for many years before they converted their own stores to self-service. The two basic features of the Piggly Wiggly idea—specially designed self-service stores and the franchise arrangement—were likewise employed by other companies. Two of the most successful were Jitney Jungle, of Jackson, Miss. and Handy Andy, Inc. of San Antonio, Tex. The original Piggly Wiggly stores were no bigger than the typical grocery store of the period but, with the trend toward bigger stores, Piggly Wiggly stores of super-market dimensions naturally evolved. That these original self-service stores laid the foundation for the modern supermarket would seem to be beyond question. The Piggly Wiggly Corporation, Jacksonville, Fla., is servicing today some 2,000 Piggly Wiggly stores of all sizes, many of them being operated by extremely successful regional chains.

way for each of the supermarkets they established.

The net result of the trend toward bigger stores in the case of A&P was, as has been pointed out before, to reduce the number of its stores from 14,700 at the beginning of 1937 to some 4,000 since 1952. This apparent elimination of 10,700 stores actually reflected the elimination of an even greater number of small stores, approximately 13,700, and their replacement by some 3,000 supermarkets. The conversion, drastic as it was, resulted in no loss of sales. On the contrary, whereas the 14,700 stores in operation at the end of 1936 had produced sales that year of $889 million, A&P's sales in the fiscal year ending February 24, 1962, with only 4,400 stores in operation, totalled $5,240,300,000, a figure never before attained by any retail enterprise, except by A&P itself in the preceding year, when its sales were fractionally higher.

True enough, this increase, amounting to 477%, in a period of 25 years, was accounted for partly by the change in the dollar's value. The main reason for it, however, was an actual increase in unit sales which reflected the greatly increased capacity of the modern supermarket compared with that of the typical grocery store which it replaced. The fact is that the type of supermarket A&P and other food chains are operating today averages more than twenty times as much business as their average store produced 20 years ago.

A&P's modern supermarkets are indeed a far cry from the "economy stores" with which the company embarked on its cash-and-carry, minimum-profit, low-price policy back in 1912, but the goal is still the same. Furthermore, the operating economies made possible by the introduction of self-service and the tremendous increase in volume per store are substantially greater than those achieved when the cash-and-carry idea was first adopted.

Since it celebrated its 100th anniversary in 1959, the big company has been distributing more than $5 billion of groceries annually at just about the lowest prices an inflated economy permits. Its success reflects the soundness of the low-price policy the company adopted early in its history and which it has followed persistently ever since. A natural result of A&P's low-price leadership was to keep *all* food-store prices at relatively low levels and thus to raise the buying-power of the consumer's food dollar and the nation's standard of living. To conclude, however, that the policy was adopted with any such altruistic purpose rather than as a practical formula for achieving success in a highly competitive business would be erroneous.

2. *Pioneer Variety Store Chains*

Another single-store venture which was destined not only to develop into a huge chain but was to provide the inspiration and the pattern for an entirely new field in retail merchandising was the 5-and-10-cent store started by Frank W. Woolworth in Lancaster, Pa., in 1879.[7]

While a clerk in a Watertown, N.Y., dry-goods store, young Woolworth had had an experience which impressed him deeply. A table of miscellaneous smallwares over which he had placed a sign: "Anything on this table, 5¢" was almost cleared the first day. It convinced young Woolworth that a whole store devoted exclusively to 5-cent items would prove equally successful. He determined to try it out.

With $300 worth of merchandise, which he obtained on credit from his former boss, and his own meager savings, he opened a store in Utica, N.Y.

The store did fairly well for a few months but then the novelty wore off. The young pioneer, still convinced that the idea was basically sound, decided to close up shop, clear up his debts and try his luck elsewhere.

Having heard from a friend that Lancaster, Pa., was an up-and-coming town, he made a trip there to look the place over. He found what he thought he wanted in a vacant 14x35-foot store on North Queen Street, and rented it. With the re-

[7] See *Five and Ten, supra;* and the company's own booklets.

mainder of his stock from the Utica store and additional merchandise which he obtained on credit from his former employer, the new store opened for business June 21, 1879.

Writing to his father the following day, young Woolworth reported enthusiastically that his first day's sales had amounted to $127.65—"the most I ever sold in one day!" As he had had an opening stock costing only $410, his enthusiasm would seem to have been justified.

At any rate, he was apparently so confident of success that in that very letter he added: "I think some of starting a branch store in Harrisburg, Pa., and putting Sum [his brother Charles Sumner Woolworth] in it."

The Harrisburg store, a 12x16-foot affair, was indeed opened the following month, but although it survived longer than the first Utica venture, the following March it, too, folded up.

A fourth store was tried out in York, Pa., opening April 3, 1880, but it, too, failed to turn the corner. It was closed June 30.

That fall, however, the fifth store, opened in Scranton, Pa., proved to be the second successful venture. The combined sales of the Lancaster and Scranton stores in 1881 amounted to $18,000. The following year they increased to $24,125.

By that time, Woolworth was convinced that the 5-and-10-cent-store idea was basically sound, provided you found the right locations. He was also convinced, however, that the possibilities of a single store of that kind were definitely limited—that real success would require a number of such stores. Only in that way would purchases be big enough to command the most favorable prices, and thus extend the range of items which could be sold profitably at 5 cents or 10 cents.

Nevertheless, expansion in those early years proceeded slowly. To find promising locations was only one of the problems. To train or to find trustworthy men to manage them, either as employees or partners, took even more time. Partners with capital to invest were particularly desirable at that stage of Mr. Woolworth's progress and he was lucky enough to find several of them.

By 1886, he had seven stores in operation. His sales totalled $100,000. But it was not until 1895, by which time he had 25 stores, that his year's sales passed the $1,000,000 mark. His first venture in New York City was a store on 6th Avenue and 17th Street, opened in October, 1897.

By the turn of the century only 59 Woolworth stores were in operation, but they were all flourishing. Their total sales exceeded $5,000,000. A few years later, expansion was accelerated by the purchase in 1904 of 21 stores in the middle-west, twelve in Pennsylvania and four in Massachusetts from various operators.

For, almost from the start, Woolworth's success with this new type of store had attracted the attention of others and tempted them to try it themselves. As early as 1881, John G. McCrory had opened his first store in Scottsdale, Pa.—the forerunner of a chain which was to grow with the years and which today, as McCrory Stores Corporation, operates a complex of 600 variety stores plus 687 stores in other fields.[8]

Back in 1900, McCrory had twenty stores, S. H. Kress & Co., whose first store had been opened in Memphis in 1896, had eleven, while S. S. Kresge Company, which was destined to become the second largest variety chain, was still operating its first store, which it had acquired in 1899. A couple of years earlier, Mr. Kresge had gone into partnership with Mr. McCrory with respect to two stores, one in Memphis and the other in Detroit. Then they had decided to travel their separate ways and Mr. McCrory took over the Memphis store while Mr. Kresge became the sole owner of the Detroit store.

In 1961, the Kresge Company operated 777 stores and its sales reached $433 million.

S. H. Kress & Co., successful right from the start, expanded

[8] See comprehensive study of this Company in June, 1962, Variety Store Editions, Chain Store Age.

gradually through the years. At the close of 1952, it was operating 261 stores, with sales of $176 million for the year. Then its sales started to decline until in 1960, they totalled only $144 million. In 1961, however, under new management, the picture improved and a slight gain in sales was achieved.

Returning to the pioneer company, up to 1905, Mr. Woolworth was the sole owner of all the stores which operated under his name alone. In addition, he had an interest in a number of other stores which he had started in partnership with others and which invariably bore the joint names of the partners. In 1905, he decided, for reasons of prudence, to incorporate the stores which he owned outright, and F. W. Woolworth & Co. was the result. All the stock, both preferred and common, was held by Mr. Woolworth and his friends.

By 1911, F. W. Woolworth & Co. had 318 stores, but some of his former associates had come along too. S. H. Knox & Co., Buffalo, N.Y., for instance, had 112 stores; F. M. Kirby & Co., Wilkes-Barre, Pa., 96; and E. P. Charlton & Co., Fall River, Mass., 53.

Why not a merger? That possibility was seriously discussed by the respective owners of the companies in question, all of whom knew and respected each other, and by the end of that year the union was effected.

The new company was the present F. W. Woolworth Company. It was made up as follows:

Company	Stores
F. W. Woolworth & Co.	318
S. H. Knox & Co.	112
F. M. Kirby & Co.	96
E. P. Charlton & Co.	53
C. S. Woolworth	15
W. H. Moore	2
	596

C. S. Woolworth was Frank's brother. Who was W. H. Moore? And why did his two stores figure in the big merger?

William H. Moore was the man who had given young Woolworth his first job as a clerk in the dry-goods store he ran in Watertown, N.Y. There it was that Woolworth had learned all he knew about the dry-goods business and where, indeed, he had picked up the idea of running a store devoted exclusively to 5-and-10-cent items. What is more to the point, it was Mr. Moore who had given his ambitious young clerk the goods with which to stock his first unsuccessful venture in Utica and his second store, which took root. Six years later, by which time Woolworth had five successful stores in operation, he learned that his old boss was in difficulties and about to go into bankruptcy. He promptly went to his benefactor's rescue by establishing him in a new business—a 5-and-10-cent store! And where did he locate it? In the very store where the idea of a 5-and-10-cent store had first occurred to him. At the time of the merger, Mr. Moore had two 5-and-10's in operation.

The inclusion of those two stores in the $65,000,000 merger could not have been much of an inducement to the investing public which was given an opportunity to invest in the stock of the new company,[9] but to Mr. Woolworth it meant a whole lot. It meant that he had not forgotten his indebtedness to the man who had made the whole thing possible.

The amazing progress of the Woolworth company from 1912 to date, as revealed in Table 8, is actually only part of the story. It covers only the Woolworth operations in the United States, Canada, Cuba and Mexico. But Mr. Woolworth established a chain in England, also, and it, too, has been very successful.

The British Woolworth Co.—F. W. Woolworth & Co. Ltd. —dates back to 1909, when Mr. Woolworth and some of his younger executives went over to England for the express pur-

---

[9] The company was capitalized at $65,000,000, consisting of $15,000,000 preferred stock, representing the value of the physical assets, and $50,000,000 of common stock, representing the value of the good will and future possibilities. See *Five and Ten, supra,* pp. 162 *et seq.*

pose of starting a similar chain there. For their first store they selected a site in Liverpool, organized the British company, and within a very few months had the company well on its way towards duplicating the performance of the American

TABLE 8

GROWTH OF F. W. WOOLWORTH CO. BY STORES AND SALES, 1911-1961

YEAR	STORES	SALES	YEAR	STORES	SALES
1911	596	$ 52,616,000	1937	2,010	304,775,000
1912	631	60,558,000	1938	2,015	304,305,000
1913	684	66,228,000	1939	2,021	318,840,000
1914	737	69,620,000	1940	2,027	335,475,000
1915	805	75,996,000	1941	2,023	377,148,000
1916	920	87,089,000	1942	2,015	423,221,000
1917	1,000	98,103,000	1943	2,008	439,009,000
1918	1,039	107,179,000	1944	2,004	459,847,000
1919	1,081	119,496,000	1945	1,971	477,136,000
1920	1,111	140,919,000	1946	1,958	552,369,000
1921	1,137	147,655,000	1947	1,945	593,359,000
1922	1,176	167,319,000	1948	1,944	623,942,000
1923	1,260	193,447,000	1949	1,938	615,650,000
1924	1,356	215,501,000	1950	1,936	632,136,000
1925	1,423	239,033,000	1951	1,943	684,180,000
1926	1,480	253,645,000	1952	1,960	712,655,000
1927	1,581	272,754,000	1953	1,981	713,870,000
1928	1,725	287,319,000	1954	2,021	721,313,000
1929	1,825	303,047,000	1955	2,064	767,779,000
1930	1,881	289,289,000	1956	2,101	806,198,000
1931	1,903	282,670,000	1957	2,121	823,895,000
1932	1,932	249,893,000	1958	2,152	864,570,642
1933	1,941	250,517,000	1959*	2,319	986,213,902
1934	1,957	270,685,000	1960	2,430	1,035,292,793
1935	1,980	268,750,000	1961	2,502	1,061,401,832
1936	1,998	290,387,000			

* Includes stores and sales of German and Mexican subsidiaries, for this and subsequent years.

company. Within a year, six stores were in operation. By the date of the American merger, the British company had 28 stores. They were known as "3d-and-6d" shops—three pence and six pence being the nearest equivalent to our nickels and dimes.

Progress from that time on was rapid and spectacular. In fact, the British proved themselves to be even more receptive to the lure of the 5-and-10-cent-store idea than Mr. Woolworth's own countrymen had been. Although the company has less than half as many stores as its American parent, opening its 1000th store in 1958, its net profits are substantially greater than those of the company here.

But even if Table 8 were expanded to reflect the operations of all the Woolworth stores abroad, it still would not tell the full story of what Woolworth's success has meant to this country.

For the contribution the company has made has by no means been confined to Woolworth's own operations, extensive and important as they have been. On the contrary, it properly includes the development in this country of an entirely new type and kind of retailing—the variety store—which owes its existence to the example and inspiration provided by the pioneer.

What that means in terms of stores and sales is easily shown. For whereas the Woolworth stores in this country in 1958 numbered some 2,100, the entire variety store field, including independent as well as chain stores, comprised some 21,000. And whereas Woolworth's sales for that year totalled $864 million, the sales of the entire field totalled $3.6 billion.[10]

In economic terms, the variety-store field makes a tremendous contribution to the national welfare in many ways. It provides an outlet for many millions of dollars' worth of items which would not be produced at all but for the facilities the variety stores provide for their distribution on a mass basis. It provides millions of jobs not only in distribution but in production. It gives 12,000 individuals an opportunity to engage in a profitable business of their own, as proprietors of independent variety stores. It provides responsible and well-paid positions for thousands of chain-store executives and the man-

[10] U.S. Retail Census, 1958.

agers of the individual stores. Finally, although incidentally, because of the income it produces in the shape of profits, salaries, wages and dividends, the variety-store field makes a substantial contribution to its silent partner, Uncle Sam, in the shape of Federal taxes.

But, in broader terms, perhaps the greatest virtue of the variety-store field lies in what it has added to the American standard of living. By making available a wide range of merchandise at popular prices it has stretched the consumer's dollar to the point where it has meant more things to more people—more *good* things for better living, culturally as well as materially.[11] The "5-and-10-cent store" has become such an accepted feature of American life that the special contribution it makes, social as well as economic, is apt to be overlooked.

Besides the variety-store chains and the grocery chains which were founded between 1859 and 1900 and which are still in operation, a score or more of chains in other fields can make the same boast.

3. *Pioneer Chains in Other Fields*

In the drug field, for instance, at least 13 chains now operating in various parts of the country can trace their lineage back to a parent store established in the second half of the 19th century. Among the oldest are Schlegel Drug Stores, Davenport, Iowa, established in 1850, and Meyer Brothers Company, Fort Wayne, Ind., in 1852. T. P. Taylor & Co., Louisville, Ky., and Jacobs Pharmacy Co., Atlanta (now owned by Haag Drug Co., Indianapolis) were both founded in 1879—the year young Frank Woolworth got his first suc-

[11] In 1929, John Cotton Dana, director of the Newark Museum, staged an exhibit of five cases of items bought in Newark and New York variety stores at prices ranging from 10 cents to 50 cents to demonstrate that "beauty has no relation to price, rarity or age." Beauty of form, design or color in merchandise is no longer reserved for those who can afford to pay high prices, thanks to mass producers and mass distributors who long ago found out that beauty costs no more than ugliness. See *Chain Store Age*, General Merchandise Section, August, 1929, p. 55; Variety Stores Edition, April, 1949, p. 67.

cessful store under way. These embryo drug chains were joined by Read Drug & Chemical Co., Baltimore, in 1883; Marshall Drug Co., Cleveland (now owned by Cunningham) in 1884; Skillern's Drug Stores, Dallas, in 1885; Kinsel Drug Co., Detroit (now owned by Cunningham) in 1888; Cunningham Drug Stores, Detroit, in 1889; Bartell Drug Co., Seattle, in 1890; Owl Drug Co., San Francisco, in 1892; Eckerd Drug Stores, Erie, Pa., in 1898; and Standard Drug Stores, Cleveland (now owned by Regal Drug Stores) in 1899.

Several other small chains which were later to become a part of the Louis K. Liggett Co., organized in 1907, were likewise founded prior to 1900. They included the Jaynes Co., Boston; Hegeman Co., New York, which had four stores in 1900; and Wm. B. Riker Co., New York, which had two stores. They were later merged to become the Riker-Hegemen-Jaynes Co., which was acquired by the Liggett company in 1916.

But none of the drug chains of that era had made any conspicuous progress when it ended. Whether all the drug chains in existence in 1900 had as many as 75 stores in the aggregate is doubtful.

In the shoe field, the story is the same. Although two of the chains founded in this period were to become and remain the two biggest companies in their field, their progress during their early years was negligible. The Melville Shoe Corporation dates back to 1892, but although it operated 1,212 stores (including 42 leased departments in discount stores) as of December 31, 1961, most of them—873, to be exact—are accounted for by its chain of Thom McAn stores which was not established until 1922, at which time the company had only nineteen other stores in operation.

The G. R. Kinney Company, founded in 1894 by George Romanta Kinney in Waverly, N.Y., is now one of the largest shoe chains, in number of stores, with 560, but by 1920, when the company was 26 years old, it was operating only 75 stores.

The development of chains in the shoe field was eventually to carry them to the point where they accounted for some 50 per cent of all shoe-store sales (not 50 per cent of all shoe sales, as department stores and other stores sell shoes as well as shoe stores) but the situation in 1900 gave no such indication.

One of the oldest chains in the general-merchandise field which traces its origin back to the period under consideration is Belk Brothers, of Charlotte, N.C. It grew out of a 22x70 foot "racket store" [12] opened in 1888 by William Henry Belk in Monroe, N.C. It was operated by him and his brother, Dr. John Belk, for five years before a second unit was ventured, and expansion thereafter proceeded at a slow rate for many years. Thus, by the turn of the century, the brothers had only five stores in operation. Their progress thereafter was more rapid as appears from the fact that, with 22 stores in operation in 1920, they added 41 in the next decade, 115 more between 1930 and 1940, and another 107 between 1940 and 1950. As of August, 1961, they had 410 stores in operation.

A unique feature of the development of this chain was the fact that most of the stores were separately incorporated, with the ownership of the stock divided between the manager selected to operate it and the Belk family. That is why many of the stores have always been operated under hyphenated names, such as Belk-Hudson Company, organized in 1893, Gallant-Belk Company, organized in 1919, and Parks-Belk Company, organized in 1929. Many of these companies now have a number of units operating under their respective cor-

[12] The "racket store" of the period in question was the forerunner of the variety store and general-merchandise store of today. The original Belk store was called the "New York Racket" in the hope that "everybody would think that sounded big." LeGette Blythe, *William Henry Belk, Merchant of the South* (University of North Carolina Press, Chapel Hill, 1951).

porate names. The connecting link between them, besides the stock interest which the Belk family owns in each of them, is a centralized buying agency and operating service bureau which the company maintains for the benefit of all Belk stores although none is required to avail itself of the services offered.

In the restaurant field, of the chains in existence today, John R. Thompson Co., of Chicago, dates back to 1891, and the Childs Co. of 1899. But neither of them became much of a factor in the areas in which they operated until many years later.

In the tobacco field, a retail cigar store in Syracuse, N.Y., opened in 1892 by George Whelan, a wholesale tobacconist, was to provide the background and the inspiration for what became one of the biggest and most important chains in the country—the United Cigar Stores Co. But Mr. Whelan had been running his retail store for eight years before the idea of developing a chain occurred to him. What happened then is related in a later chapter.[13]

Originating in this period and therefore deserving mention at this point because of the important part they were destined to play in the chain-store field although neither of them operated even a single retail store until after the post-war depression of 1921, are two Chicago companies. That seeming paradox is explained by the fact that the companies in question, Montgomery Ward & Co., hereafter referred to as Ward's, and Sears, Roebuck & Co., hereafter referred to as Sears, both started in life as mail-order houses and confined their retail activities to that type of distribution for more than 50 years in the one case and for nearly 40 years in the other before they decided that the time was ripe to operate retail stores as well.

Ward's was founded in 1872, Sears in 1886. The latter was destined to become the second largest retail organization in the world. Its sales for the year ending January 31, 1961, were $4.3 billion. Only A&P, with sales that year of $5.2 billion,

[13] P. 107 *post*.

sold more. Ward's had sales of $1.2 billion. Although both Ward's and Sears still do a substantial volume by mail through their catalogs, most of their sales today are made over the counters of their retail stores, of which Ward's as of January 31, 1962 had 517 and Sears 740. The record of Ward's growth from 1926 to date is detailed in the appendix, page 409, *post*.

The astounding history of Sears, Roebuck & Co. is told in great detail in *Catalogues and Counters,* by Boris Emmet and John E. Jeuck, to which reference has already been made.[14] Suffice it to say here that it all started when Richard W. Sears, a railway station agent at North Redwood, Minn. got a shipper's permission to dispose of a box of watches which the consignee refused to accept. Sears undertook to sell the watches to his friends *by mail.* And when he found out how easy it was —largely because the small mark-up he required enabled him to offer the watches far below the regular retail price—he set himself up in the mail-order business, first in Minneapolis and later in Chicago. He was soon joined by Alvah C. Roebuck, who had had some experience in watch repairing which Sears figured might be useful.

Working together under various trade names until 1893, when the name Sears, Roebuck & Co. was adopted, the young firm had apparently made substantial progress, for its sales that year totalled $388,000. In 1895, when sales approached $800,000, Julius Rosenwald, a clothing merchant, joined the firm because "he recognized in the mail order methodology a pioneer effort towards mass distribution." [15] His influence on the company's subsequent success may be judged by the principles which he formulated and which became known as the "Rosenwald Creed." Its cardinal conclusions were:

(1) "Sell for less by buying for less. Buy for less through the instrumentality of mass buying and cash buying. *But maintain the quality.*

---

[14] See p. 18, *supra.*
[15] Sears, Roebuck & Co., Annual Report for 1940.

(2) "Sell for less by cutting the cost of sales. Reduce to the absolute practical minimum the expense of moving goods from producer to consumer. *But maintain the quality.*

(3) "Make less profit on each individual item and increase your aggregate profit by selling more items. *But maintain the quality."*

By the turn of the century, Sears' volume had reached $11,-000,000. In 1906, the company opened its first branch mail-order plant, in Dallas, and that year the company was reincorporated with a capital of $40,000,000. Four years later, in 1910, the second branch plant was opened, in Seattle, and sales that year totalled $61,000,000. In 1920, they reached their peak, for that period, at $245,000,000. Incidentally, that year Woolworth was operating 1,111 stores, with aggregate sales of $141,000,000.

Then, in 1921, came the post-war crash and Sears' volume nose-dived to $160,000,000. In the years which followed that debacle, both Ward's and Sears apparently considered the possibility of opening retail stores to augment their mail-order sales. Particularly enthusiastic regarding such a move was Gen. Robert E. Wood, vice president in charge of merchandising for Ward's, and when, in 1924, he left Ward's to become a vice president of Sears, he carried his enthusiasm for retail stores with him. Sears decided to take the step, although they proceeded gingerly at first.

The first Sears store was opened February 2, 1925. Actually it was just a part of the Chicago mail-order plant converted into a department store. Three months later, the same course was taken in Seattle, and the other branch plants rapidly followed suit. The first retail outlet outside of a mail-order plant was opened in Evansville, Ind., on October 5, 1925. The year ended with eight stores in operation.

The growth of the retail operation by number of stores, store sales and ratio to total sales for each year from 1925 to 1941 inclusive is revealed in Table 9 compiled from data in

"Catalogues and Counters," to which reference has already been made.

Reference to the table in question discloses the remarkable fact that the chain of 378 stores which Sears developed in the short space of six years was able, in 1931, to outsell the

TABLE 9

SEARS, ROEBUCK STORES, 1925-1941

YEAR	STORES	STORE SALES (000 OMITTED)	RATIO TO TOTAL SALES
1925	8	$ 11,819	4.5
1926	9	23,046	8.5
1927	27	40,001	13.6
1928	192	107,179	30.9
1929	319	174,623	39.6
1930	338	180,830	46.3
1931	378	185,339	53.4
1932	374	159,026	57.7
1933	400	167,860	58.2
1934	416	204,075	60.5
1935	428	243,291	58.6
1936	440	324,604	61.8
1937	473	366,285	64.4
1938	482	344,800	64.8
1939	520	435,406	66.6
1940	595	515,322	69.2
1941	617	662,394	68.4

far-flung mail-order set-up which had been in successful operation for more than 50 years! And from that time on, as more and more stores were added, the store operation accounted for an ever greater proportion of gross sales, even though the mail-order sales climbed too as retail volume generally improved after the depression years.

For several years after 1941, Sears was unable to build additional stores because of the ban on civilian construction during World War II. As a matter of fact the number of stores in operation in 1946 was only 610 compared with 618 in 1941.

As soon after the war as conditions permitted, however, Sears embarked on a policy of steady expansion which carried the number of its stores to 740 by the end of 1961—without including 51 foreign stores. During this period, too, it expanded the number of its domestic catalog sales offices—from 338 in 1947 to 957 in 1961.[16]

The substantial growth of the company since World War II, which is reflected in the following table, is a tribute to

[16] Annual Report.

TABLE 10

GROWTH OF SEARS, ROEBUCK & CO.,
1941-1961

YEAR	STORES	CATALOG SALES OFFICES	TOTAL SALES (IN MILLIONS)
1941	618		$ 915
1942	599		868
1943	596		853
1944	606		989
1945	604		1,045
1946	610		1,613
1947	623	338	1,982
1948	628	341	2,296
1949	647	358	2,169
1950	654	404	2,556
1951	674	479	2,657
1952	684	546	2,932
1953	694	570	2,982
1954	699	609	2,965
1955	707	694	3,307
1956	717	772	3,556
1957	724	815	3,601
1958	728	849	3,721
1959	734	913	4,036
1960	740	947	4,134
1961	740	957	4,267

the vision and courage of Gen. Wood and his colleagues.

As a chain, Sears dates back only to 1925, but because its entry into the chain-store field was made possible by the success it had already achieved as a mail-order house, a line of business in which it had been engaged continuously since 1886, this brief historical sketch of the company's career may not be deemed out of place in a discussion of the 1859-1900 period.

So much for some of the pioneer companies which came into the picture prior to 1900 and which are still in operation —many of them being the leaders in their respective fields.

The significant fact about the 1859-1900 period is that it saw the foundation laid for what was to become one of the most important features of our distribution set-up—the chain-store system—but that was all. The real development of the system did not begin until after the turn of the century.

CHAPTER III

THE MOVEMENT GAINS
MOMENTUM

How MANY chain stores in all were in operation at the turn of the century is not known. From the data available with respect to the larger companies then in existence, the total would probably not have exceeded 500. In any event, although the two biggest companies, A&P and Woolworth, may have begun to attract some attention individually as enterprising and progressive concerns, the chains as a group were certainly too insignificant a factor to have rated notice as a new type of operation which might bear watching.

But if a census had been taken ten years later, it would have reflected a more significant situation. For the first decade of the century saw the birth of a number of new companies which were destined to become outstanding chains in their respective fields. More directly to our present point, some of them, by reason of original and aggressive merchandising policies, attracted more attention right from the start than those which had been established many years earlier.

That was particularly true of United Cigar Stores Co., whose new type of cigar store spelled the doom of the old model which had prevailed up to that time.[1] It was also true of the new chains in the drug field who found it necessary not only to join the ranks of the cut-rate stores then in exist-

[1] See p. 107, *post*.

ence but to take the lead in merchandising standard products aggressively. For only in that way could they drive home to the consumer that they could and would pass on to their customers the benefit of large-scale retailing.[2] To the extent that such aggressive merchandising policies achieved their purpose, the chains made their presence felt quickly not only by the public but by their competitors.

A list of some of the chains which came into the picture between 1900 and 1910 and which went on to become important factors in their respective fields is presented in Table 11.

In the next decade, 1910 to 1920, so many new chains came into the picture that to list them all would serve no useful purpose. In addition, the chains already in existence were expanding at a far more rapid rate than in their earlier years.

It was in this period, it will be recalled, that the A&P started its "economy store" program and, within six months after Mr. Hartford was convinced that he was on the right track, the company started adding stores just as fast as it was physically possible to open them. The 500th store was opened in 1913. By April 3, 1915, the company had 1,670. In the next two years, no less than 1,600 stores were added. Sales jumped from $31,000,000 in 1914 to $76,000,000 in 1916. By the beginning of 1920, A&P was operating 4,200 stores.

A&P's example could not escape the notice of the many other grocery chains which were then in operation in all areas of the country. How far some of the others had progressed is indicated by the fact that when five of them, all in the Philadelphia area, merged in 1917 to become the American Stores Co. they were operating in the aggregate 1,223 stores, and became the second largest grocery chain at that time. The Acme Tea Co., the largest of the group, had 433 stores; Childs Grocery Co. 268; The Bell Co. 214; Robinson & Crawford 186; and George N. Dunlap Co. 122.

[2] See p. 111, *post*.

In the variety-store field, Woolworth opened no less than 480 stores between 1912 and 1920, jumping from 631 to 1,111; Kresge added 99 stores in the same period; Grant, which had started in 1906, had four stores in 1910 and 33 by 1920;

TABLE 11

SOME CHAINS FOUNDED BETWEEN 1900 AND 1910

1900

D. Pender Grocery Co., Norfolk (now Colonial Stores, Inc.).
Hook Drugs, Indianapolis.
Daniel Reeves (grocery), New York, later acquired by Safeway.
Dockum Drug Stores, Wichita, Kans. (now owned by Adams Drug Co., Inc.).

1901

United Cigar Stores Co., New York.
F. & W. Grand-Silver (variety), New York, now H. L. Green Co.
Lane Bryant (apparel), New York.
A. L. Duckwall Stores Co. (variety), Abilene, Kans.
Walgreen Co. (drug), Chicago.
J. Weingarten, Inc. (grocery), Houston, Tex.

1902

J. C. Penney Co. (apparel), New York.
Schultz Bros. (variety), Chicago.

1903

Morris Stores (variety), Bluffton, Ind. Now owned by the G. C. Murphy Co.

1905

Peoples Drug Stores, Washington, D.C.

1906

W. T. Grant Co. (variety), New York.
G. C. Murphy Co. (variety), McKeesport, Pa.

1907

Louis K. Liggett Co. (drug), New York.
Mading's Drug Stores, Houston, Tex.
Fisher Brothers Co. (grocery), Cleveland.

1908

A. S. Beck Shoe Corporation, New York.
Katz & Besthoff (drug), New Orleans.

1909

Western Auto Supply Co., Kansas City, Mo.
Gallaher Drug Co., Dayton, Ohio.
Hested Stores (variety), Fairbury, Nebr. (now owned by J. J. Newberry).

Murphy jumped from ten in 1910 to 51 in 1920; Kress, which had started the century with eleven stores, had 84 by 1910 and 145 by 1920; and McCrory, which had twenty stores in 1901, had 60 by 1910, and 156 by 1920.

A quick run-down of the status of some of the other chains in 1920 will be sufficient to indicate that, by that time, the shape of what was to come was becoming definitely discernible.

In the grocery field, Kroger had 799 stores; the predecessors of First National, 803; Daniel Reeves, 202; Southern Grocery, 119; National Tea, 163; and Bohack, 152.

In the shoe field, Melville had only twenty stores, but Kinney had 75.

In the drug field, Louis K. Liggett Co., which in 1916 had acquired the 106 stores operated by the Riker-Hegeman-Jaynes chain, was nearing the 200 mark; Walgreen's, which had not actually become a chain until 1909 when the second store was opened, now had 23; and People's Drug, organized in 1905, had eight stores in operation.

In the restaurant field, J. R. Thompson had 104 units; Childs, 88; Waldorf System, 79; and F. G. Shattuck, later to be known as Schrafft's, an even dozen.

Perhaps the most spectacular development of all had been that of the United Cigar Stores Co., which by 1920 had 1,096 stores. Schulte, another cigar-store chain, was second with 196.

How many stores in the aggregate all the chains had in operation in 1920 is not definitely known. It has been estimated by John P. Nichols[3] that, whereas in 1914 the total number of stores was 8,000, the number in 1920 was 27,000. The Federal Trade Commission put the figure at 50,000!

[3] *The Chain Store Tells Its Story, op. cit.*

TABLE 12

GROWTH OF 20 LEADING CHAINS
BY NUMBER OF STORES
1920-1949

	1920	1925	1930	1949
GROCERY CHAINS				
A&P	4,544	14,034	15,737	4,820
American	1,223	1,792	2,728	1,671
First Nat'l*	803	1,642	2,548	1,083
Kroger	799	2,559	5,165	2,190
Safeway	191	1,050	2,675	2,202
National Tea	163	761	1,600	655
	7,723	21,838	30,453	12,621
VARIETY STORE CHAINS				
Woolworth	1,111	1,420	1,881	1,938
Kresge	184	306	678	702
Kress	145	166	212	256
McCrory	156	181	242	201
Murphy	53	88	166	218
McLellan	43	94	277	230
Grant	38	77	350	480
Newberry	17	86	335	482
Neisner	4	13	75	121
	1,751	2,431	4,216	4,628
APPAREL CHAIN				
J. C. Penney	312	676	1,452	1,607
SHOE CHAINS				
Kinney	75	250	366	305
Melville	20	148	480	561
	95	398	846	866
DRUG CHAINS				
Walgreen	23	87	440	414
Peoples	8	18	117	141
	31	105	557	555
TOTAL (20 CHAINS)	9,912	25,448	37,524	20,277

* Predecessor companies for 1920 and 1925.

The probability is that the actual figure was somewhere between these two estimates, but the exact number is not of great significance. For what happened between 1920 and 1925 has a more direct bearing on subsequent chain-store history than anything that preceded those active chain-store years.

In the absence of an official census to record the full expansion of the chains during the five-year period in question, what happened in the case of twenty leading chains, whose

CHART II

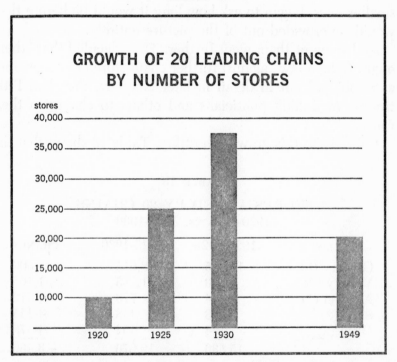

statistics are available, will have to suffice. Table 12 and Chart II tell their own story, showing that the twenty chains which had 9,912 stores in operation in 1920 had 25,448 only five years later! And that scale of expansion, of course, was on top of what had been becoming more and more apparent in the years immediately preceding 1920.

Keeping in mind that Table 12 presents a partial list of the chains then in existence, even though it does include most of the bigger ones, and that hundreds of other chains all over the country were also expanding during that period, some idea is provided of the impact of this phenomenon on other types of retailing. To aggravate the situation was the fact that the majority of the new chain stores were opened in areas in which the chains were already established.

Little wonder that the chains' competitors, particularly the smaller ones, began to ask how long it would be before they would be crowded out of the picture entirely.

And some of them went further. They decided that "there ought to be a law" against further chain-store expansion and, as is pointed out in detail in later chapters, they had little trouble in finding politicians and others to champion their cause.

But despite this growing hostility, Table 13 shows that the

TABLE 13

STORES ADDED BY 20 CHAINS,
1920-1925 vs. 1925-1930

FIELD	1920-1925	1925-1930	CHANGE
Grocery (6)	14,115	8,615	−5,500
Variety (9)	680	1,785	+1,105
Apparel (1)	364	776	+412
Shoe (2)	303	448	+145
Drug (2)	74	452	+378
	15,536	12,076	−3,460

chains which expanded so spectacularly between 1920 and 1925 did not stop then. On the contrary, in the next five-year period, they added another 12,000 stores. Although that was less than the 15,536 stores added in the preceding five-year period, an analysis of the Table will show that the only let-up was in the grocery field, in which only 8,615 stores were added compared with 14,115 in the preceding period.

The expansion of the chains in the other fields made up in part for the slow-up in the grocery field. That is revealed in Table 13, which gives the number of stores added in each of the two periods by each of five fields covered.

Undoubtedly the fact that the grocery chains were not expanding as rapidly between 1925 and 1930 as they had been in the preceding five-year period would have been less perceptible than the substantial strides the chains in the other fields continued to make, particularly as the grocery chains continued to grow even though not at such a rapid rate.

But the significant fact about the chain-store movement is that despite all the indications that it would continue indefinitely, actually it did nothing of the kind. Although, in the decade from 1920 to 1930, the chains listed in Table 13 added no less than 27,612 stores to the 9,912 they had had in operation at the start of it, a gain of nearly 280%, the era of all-out expansion came to an end in 1930. How precipitate the drop was is revealed in Chart II (page 57).

Having reached a peak of 37,524 stores in 1930, the number of stores operated by the twenty leading chains in question started steadily to decline until, in 1949, the total was only 20,047, or 17,477 fewer. True enough, this 41% decline is accounted for entirely by what happened in the grocery field alone, where, as has been pointed out already,[4] the introduction of the supermarket brought about the elimination of most of the smaller stores formerly operated. But even when that controlling factor is eliminated, the significant fact remains that the fourteen other chains listed added only 728 stores between 1930 and 1949, a span of nineteen years, compared with the 4,794 in the ten years preceding 1930. The rate of expansion dropped from an average of 479 stores a year to 38!

[4] See pp. 31-35, *supra*.

What brought about the decline in the number of grocery stores has been explained, but why did the chains in the other fields stop expanding, except to a negligible extent, after 1930?

Several factors were involved.

In the first place, after the rapid pace they had set for themselves in those hectic years preceding 1930, most of the companies needed a breathing spell—a chance to consolidate their gains. The larger scale of operations called for major organization changes in some cases. To open additional stores was easier than to develop men to direct and manage them.

In the second place, more stores meant not only more trained men to operate them but more capital to finance them. The collapse of the stock market in 1929 plus the onset of the depression naturally dried up many of the sources of investment capital and put a damper on further investment for the time being.

Thirdly, by the time the depression had worked itself out and the chains might have been ready and tempted to resume expansion on a moderate scale, along came Pearl Harbor and World War II. The resulting shortages of manpower and merchandise created operating problems for the chains which additional stores would only have magnified. In any event, wartime bans on civilian construction would have prevented the chains from expanding during this period even if they could have manned and stocked additional stores.

Finally, the trend toward bigger stores which brought the supermarket into the grocery field had also made itself felt in other fields of retailing. Bigger drug stores, bigger variety stores, bigger apparel stores, and bigger stores in various other fields made the chains less dependent on additional stores for the additional volume from which, in retailing, "all blessings flow." Table 14, showing the average sales per store for leading chains in 1950 and 1961 compared with what they were in 1930, reflects the effect of the trend in question. Although the increase in dollar sales per store resulted in part from the rise in prices, the main reason for it was that the chain stores of 1950 were typically two to five times as big as those of 1930 and those of today are even bigger.[5]

To keep in step with the trend, the chains directed their attention principally to their existing stores. To bring them up to the new standards as rapidly as possible became the main objective. Where existing locations permitted enlargement and modernization, the chains followed that course. As soon as the restrictions on civilian construction were lifted after World War II, the chains proceeded to modernize their stores as fast as they could. But where existing locations were too small to permit the kind of enlargement called for, re-location became necessary. While this policy gave the chains many *new* stores, it did not add to the number in operation.

One incidental result of this trend to bigger stores was that the number of stores a chain was operating lost much of its significance as an index of its growth. With one new unit doing as much business as ten smaller ones, most of the chains have been showing substantial sales increases from year to year even though the number of their stores may have been consistently declining. Reference to the data presented in the Appendix (p. 391 *et seq.*) shows this quite clearly.

Because of this a number of chains seem to feel that a better index of their growth is provided today by the total number of square feet their stores occupy, and in recent years their annual reports have been giving such information as well as the

[5] Walgreen's first "super-drug" store was opened in Tampa, Fla., in October, 1934. The company described it as "a revolutionary new kind of drug store which not only provided the space for additional lines but took merchandise out of the traditional show-cases and presented it instead on open display counters where customers could see it, touch it and buy it. The success of this new type of drug store sounded the knell of the old-fashioned kind of 'small corner drug store.'" The company opened a gigantic store in Miami in 1937 and another in New Orleans in 1938. In October, 1949, the company opened Chicago's biggest drug store, at State and Madison Streets, with 30,000 square feet on two floors. At the end of 1961, Walgreen's was operating 254 self-service stores averaging $834,000 a year, and 213 service stores averaging $546,000. (See Chain Store Age, Druggist Editions, January, 1962.)

number of stores operated. The soundness of this course is indicated by the fact that whereas Jewel Tea Co. reported 160 stores with a total of 1,057,469 square feet of floor space in

TABLE 14

AVERAGE ANNUAL SALES PER STORE
27 Chains, 1930, 1950 and 1961
($ Thousands)

	1930	1950	1961		1930	1950	1961
GROCERY CHAINS				VARIETY STORE			
A&P	$ 68	$680	$1,119	CHAINS			
Safeway	82	568	1,235	Woolworth	$154	$327	$402
Kroger	50	419	1,360	Kresge	222	424	570
American[1]	52	312	1,225	Kress	327	624	535
First National	42	380	1,109	Grant	236	522	603
National Tea	53	497	990	McLellan[4]	87	245	
Colonial[2]	35	487	987	McCrory[4]	179	481	
Bohack	49	370	900	Murphy[5]	105	687	534
				Neisner	220	474	441
APPAREL CHAIN				Green[4]	159	459	
J. C. Penney	133	589	921	Newberry	90	302	516
SHOE CHAINS				MISCELLANEOUS			
Melville	60	125	132	CHAINS			
Kinney	44	118	162	Western Auto[6]	136	311	261
				J. R. Thompson	120	215	593
DRUG CHAINS				Schraffts	630	835	1,150
Walgreen[3]	93	399	700	Waldorf System	106	196	218
Peoples	143	332	481				

[1] Now Acme Markets, Inc.

[2] 1930 refers to predecessor companies.

[3] 1950 and 1961 estimated, as chain's reported sales includes those to agency stores; but this chain's 254 self-service stores averaged $834,000 per store in 1961.

[4] McLellan, Green and McCrory now combined as McCrory Stores Corporation; separate sales for 1961 not available.

[5] Reflects acquisition of chains operating smaller stores since 1952.

[6] Company-owned stores only.

1952, in 1956, with 184 stores, the floor space had increased to 1,635,046 square feet. The net increase in stores was 24, or 15%, but the increase in floor space was 54%! It was significantly reflected in a corresponding 50% increase in sales during the period in question.

To what extent was chain-store expansion checked by the wave of anti-chain agitation which developed in the 1920s and brought with it special chain-store taxes graduated in severity according to the number of stores operated?

That is a natural question. Certainly the purpose of such taxes was to produce the result which actually occurred. Chain-store expansion did slow up almost to a stop. But that chain-store taxes had much to do with it may well be doubted, for several reasons:

1. The factors already listed were sufficient in themselves to account for the result in question.

2. Although the purpose of such taxes was to impose an additional burden on chains heavy enough to discourage the addition of new stores, actually the top tax imposed, $750 per store in Texas, was hardly serious enough to have had that effect—except in the case of extremely small-volume units, such as filling stations.[6] Certainly the trend toward bigger stores tended to make a tax of that kind increasingly negligible.

3. The states which imposed such taxes showed no greater decline in the number of chain stores than those in which such taxes have never been imposed.[7]

4. The trend toward fewer but bigger stores in the chain grocery field has been attributed by some to the effect of chain-store taxes. Actually it reflected a change in grocery merchandising in which the question of chain-store taxes played no part.[8] The supermarket idea was introduced not by the chains but by the independents. The chains adopted it because it was a good idea, and experience has demonstrated the wisdom of their move.

That the agitation against chain stores might have had a greater deterrent effect on chain-store expansion policies than

[6] See p. 146, *post*.

[7] Willard L. Thorp, "Economic Planning via Chain-Store Taxes," *Dun's Review*, August, 1937.

[8] See pp. 31-35, *supra*.

the weight of the taxes actually imposed is, of course, true. Such a conclusion, however, would rest only on surmise. It is negatived in too many cases to have much weight. From a public-relations standpoint, the hostility to "big business" in certain quarters might give any really big company something to think about before embarking on any major expansion program, but relatively few chains are big enough to have to take that factor into consideration.

The most reasonable conclusion seems to be, therefore, that the tremendous momentum the chain-store movement developed between 1920 and 1930 carried it to a point at which a levelling-off process was natural if not inevitable. The chains went no further because, whether they knew it or not, they had actually arrived at their destination. Although their sales were to expand more than twofold between 1930 and 1950, the share of the market they had gained for themselves by 1929 was not materially changed thereafter. That, at least, is the clear indication of the U.S. Census figures for 1929, 1939, 1948, 1954 and 1958.

Because these official figures provide the only objective measurement of what chain stores have come to mean to America, a separate chapter is devoted to them.

CHAPTER IV

WHAT THE RETAIL
CENSUS SHOWS

THE FIRST counting of retail noses on an all-out basis was undertaken in 1930 by the U.S. Department of Commerce, Bureau of the Census. It covered the year 1929. It was known as the Census of Distribution.

Similar enumerations were made later by the Bureau for the years 1933, 1935, 1939, 1948, 1954 and 1958.

Before summarizing any of the findings, one important point must be made. As each successive Census was taken, certain changes in classification were deemed desirable. To make the current results comparable with previous ones, adjustments and revisions of previous enumerations were necessary. The result was inevitable discrepancies between the figures originally obtained and given out at the time the Census was made and the figures for that year as they appeared in a subsequent Census for purposes of comparison.

By way of illustration, when the results of the 1929 Census were first released they showed total retail sales of $50,033,-850,792 rung up on the cash registers of 1,549,168 retail stores. But, lo and behold, when the 1939 Census came out, for comparability's sake, the figures for 1929 were revised as follows: Total sales $48,329,652,000; total number of stores: 1,476,365.[1]

A footnote explains the discrepancy as follows:

[1] U.S. Census of Business, 1939, Vol. 1, Retail Trade, Part 1, p. x.

"Previously published totals for 1929 and 1935 revised to exclude data for service garages and other automotive business whose receipts from service sales exceed their sales of merchandise. These are included in the Census of Service Establishments for 1939."

Although such revisions are obviously inescapable unless the original classifications are to be frozen forever, the use of Census figures is unsafe unless these periodic changes are kept in mind and due allowance is made for them.

Particularly important is it to note in this connection that the 1954 Census is not comparable with the 1948 Census not only because it was compiled in a different way but because it used a different base. For our present purpose, the different base is the more significant difference. The scope of the 1954 Census was narrower. Whereas the 1948 Census included all retailers with annual sales of $500 or more, the 1954 Census was confined to those with annual sales of at least $2,500.

The obvious result was to throw out of the 1954 count many thousands of small retailers who would have been included if the 1948 base had been retained. One unfortunate effect was to show a decline in the number of retailers between 1948 and 1954, whereas if the same base had been used, 1954 would have shown an increase!

Because of the erroneous conclusions which would arise from a direct comparison of the 1954 Census with the 1948 Census without making allowances for the change in base, the Census Bureau provided a *revised version* of the 1948 data to make it as comparable as possible. This revision reduces the 1948 total from 1,771,317 stores to 1,668,479. Comparing that figure with 1954's 1,721,650, we have an increase of 53,171 stores in 1954 instead of a decrease of 49,667. This does not mean, of course, that the original 1948 figure was erroneous but merely that it took in more territory than the 1954 compilation.

Unfortunately, the effort of the Census Bureau to avert misinterpretation of the 1954 Census was ineffective. Direct comparison between it and the preceding Census led many to the conclusion that the number of retailers had decreased substantially during the six-year period which separated them.[2] Lest others make the same mistake in referring to the data shown in Table 15, the appropriate warning can hardly be repeated too often: *The 1954 Census is not comparable with those which preceded it!*

The 1958 Census followed the 1954 pattern in that it excluded all stores with no paid employes which had sales of less than $2,500 in the census year. To that extent, therefore, it, too, is not comparable with the censuses which preceded that of 1954 so far as the number of stores is concerned.

A major change adopted for the 1958 Census is thus explained in the Census:

"Whereas in the 1954 Census, leased departments (businesses operated as a department of a retail business, under different ownership) were counted as separate establishments and separately classified by kind of business, in the 1958 Census they have been combined with the retail business in which located. As a result, it is anticipated that the count of establishments will be approximately 25,000 less in the 1958 Census than would have been the case if the 1954 Census procedure had been followed. In addition, there will be some redistribution in the data among the various kinds of business categories, e.g., the figures for a leased shoe department located in a department store which were tabulated in the 'shoe store' kind of business in 1954, are included with 'department store' figures in the 1958 Census. Leased departments in the 1954 Census reported sales of approximately one billion dollars."

Another important observation to make, before proceeding with a summary of the Census figures relating to the chain-

<hr>

[2] *Chain Store Age,* Administration Edition, March, 1957, p. 58; Grocery Edition, December, 1956, p. 35.

store picture, concerns the Bureau's definition of a chain store. It naturally had to define the term before it could tell how many chain stores were in operation.

Whether or not the definition should be broad enough to include every merchant who operates more than one store was the first hurdle to be taken. On the one hand, the claim could be made that because the man who operates two stores has overstepped the boundaries of single-store operation he is at least an embryo chain. That is the viewpoint the author has always taken and which is reflected in the foregoing pages. That was the position the courts took, too, when the question came up in connection with a tax on "chain stores" which applied to chains "with two stores or more." As is related later on,[3] the law was declared constitutional because of the "real and substantial difference" between merchants with "two or more stores" and those with only one.

On the other hand, the Census Bureau felt that because many two-store and three-store operations lack certain characteristics typical of chain stores, they should *all* be excluded from the chain-store category.

To meet the situation, the Bureau decided to break down all retail stores into three main classes: (1) independents; (2) two-and-three-store multiunits; and (3) chain stores.

Thus originated the conception that a minimum of four stores was needed to make a chain—a conception which has undoubtedly had the effect of understating the scope of the chain-store field from the standpoint of both the number of stores they operate and their relative share of the total retail business.

This effect has not gone unnoticed by students of distribution. Thus, Theodore N. Beckman and Herman C. Nolen, in their book "The Chain Store Problem," published in 1938, took emphatic exception to what they term the "artificially

[3] See p. 136, *post*.

concocted definition of chains," [4] used by the Census Bureau. They complained that as a result of that definition "the importance of chain stores is grossly understated."

To illustrate their point, they note that whereas, according to the 1929 Census (as subsequently revised) chain stores then numbered only 148,037, the number would have been 212,620 if the two-and-three-store multiunits had been included. Furthermore, whereas chain-store sales in 1929 were given as $9.8 billion, or 20% of all retail sales, they were actually $14.1 billion, or 29.7% of total sales, if the sales of the two-and-three-store units are included.

Nevertheless, the Census Bureau stuck to its original definition in all subsequent compilations until the 1948 Census was undertaken.

Then it decided to abandon the use of the terms "chain" and "chain store" altogether. Instead, the term "multiunit" was adopted to cover not only the stores of firms with two or three, which had previously been grouped separately, or included with independents, but also those of firms with four or more, which the Bureau had previously designated as chain stores.

To make the 1948 statistics comparable with previous Census data, multiunits with four or more stores were separated from those with only two or three and could, therefore, be compared with what were formerly designated as chain stores. The same plan was followed in compiling the 1954 and 1958 Censuses. But by reason of this long-deferred revision in nomenclature, each of us must now define a chain according to his own lights. The Bureau of the Census can no longer be cited as an authority for the present size or importance of the chain-store field, *as such*, or for anything else relating to chain stores, *as such*, for it no longer designates any type of operation by that name.

[4] *The Chain Store Problem* (New York: McGraw-Hill Book Co., 1938), p. 23.

With the foregoing observations in mind, the Census figures for the years 1929, 1939, 1948, 1954 and 1958 as revised for purposes of comparison and as presented in Table 15, may now be considered.

The 1929 Census is particularly interesting not only because it was the first complete count of chain stores ever undertaken but because, having covered the year 1929, it reflects the status of the chains at the peak of the expansion program which marked the 1920-1930 period, as was brought out in the preceding chapter.

What did this Census show? It showed that we then had 1,476,365 retail stores of all kinds in operation and that 159,-638 or 10.8% of them, were chain stores—using that term to denote stores owned and operated by organizations of all types with four or more retail outlets.

Total retail sales that year were $48,329 million, of which the chain stores accounted for $10,740 million, or 22.2%.

The fact that the chains accounted for less than 11 per cent of all retail stores, despite their expansion, and for only 22 per cent of the total retail volume, may be somewhat surprising, but that is because the over-all figures fail to tell the real story.

For as was pointed out earlier,[5] the chains have always been a more important factor in some fields than in others. In such fields as variety stores, for instance, in which, of course, the chains were the pioneers, they accounted for 90% of the total sales in 1929; in the shoe field for 45.7% of shoe store sales, in the grocery field for 39%; and in several other fields they likewise exceeded the over-all ratio of 22%.

By contrast, as Table 15 reveals, the chains accounted for considerably less than 22% of the total retail volume in a number of other fields, and indeed, in many retail fields, the chains did not figure at all. Thus, the fact that their share of

[5] See p. 8, *supra*.

all retail sales was only 22% obscures their more important status in the fields in which they were particularly active.

Certainly the overall picture gave no comfort to the independent grocer. What concerned him, of course, was what had happened and what seemed to be happening in his own field. What the 1929 Census revealed to him was that the chains, with only 17% of the stores, already accounted for 39% of the sales. At the rate they had been expanding, how long would it be before the independent would be crowded out altogether? He could not know then what the subsequent Census figures were to make quite clear—that by 1930 the chains had gone about as far as they were destined to go— for the next 25 years at any rate.

What actually happened between 1929 and 1948 is revealed in Table 15. The data for 1954 and 1958 is likewise included in the Table, but, for reasons which have already been given, it is not strictly comparable with that of the earlier Censuses.

So far as the whole retail field is concerned, Table 15 shows that the competitive position of the chains remained practically unchanged from 1929 to 1948. In 1929, the chains accounted for 22.2% of total sales and, in 1948, for 22.8%. The 1954 figure of 23.7% is obviously higher than it would have been if the 1954 Census had been compiled on the same basis as those which preceded it. That is likewise true of the 1958 figure.

In the grocery field, a substantial decline in the number of stores operated by the chains between 1929 and 1954 reflects, of course, the trend toward bigger but fewer stores to which reference has already been made. The chains' share of total food store sales showed a slight decline between 1929 and 1948, but it was more than made up by 1954, even though the 43.3% figure is somewhat higher than the actual percentage which would have been shown but for the changes made in compiling the 1954 Census. That, again, is also true of the gain shown in the 1958 Census.

That the variety store chains accounted for a somewhat smaller share of the total market in 1954 than they did in 1929 is apparent from the Table. Although they increased the number of their stores 40% and their sales 200% during the period, the number of independent stores grew at an even greater rate, from 6,663 to 12,294, a gain of 84%. This increase in number of stores gave the independents 20.4% of the market in 1954 compared with only 10.4% in 1929. By 1958, the Census figures show, the chains were operating a somewhat greater percentage of the stores than in 1954 and were enjoying a somewhat larger share of the sales, but in both instances the gain was slight.

In the shoe field, Table 15 discloses a substantial gain in the relative number of stores operated by the chains between 1929 and 1958, but their share of the sales did not increase to the same extent.

The drug chains accounted for 18.5% of the total retail drug trade in 1929, according to the Census data and showed but a slight gain in 1954—to 19.9%. The accuracy of the 1954 figure was seriously questioned, however,[6] and if the challenge was well-founded, the drug chains with four or more stores actually operated 4,497 stores in 1954 and had sales of $1,321 million, or 25.2% of the total. On the same basis, their share in 1958 was considerably greater than the Census data indicates.

In the department store field, Table 15 reveals a major change in the status of the chains, accounting as they did for 78% of the sales in 1958 compared with only 15.3% in 1929. The change is accounted for partly by changes in this classification since 1929 but mainly by the shopping-center trend which meant the opening of branch stores by department stores. The effect of this trend was naturally to switch many a department store from the single-unit or two or three store

[6] *Chain Store Age,* Drug Edition, November, 1956.

multiunit column to the chain store column. Since 1948, it will be noted, the number of chain department stores increased by 750, whereas department stores with fewer than 4 units declined by 173 in number of stores operated. Obviously when a department store, doing perhaps $50 million a year, attains chain store status by opening its third branch suburban store, whether in a shopping center or elsewhere, its *total* volume goes into the chain store column at the expense of the single unit column. The transfer naturally results not merely in a gain for the chains but a corresponding deduction from independent department store sales. With the current growth of so-called *discount* department stores, which is dealt with in a later chapter, the chains will figure even more heavily in the department store classification in future Censuses unless the Bureau decides to set discount stores up as a separate classification.

That the status of the chains in the grocery, variety store, shoe and drug fields in 1948 as compared with 1929 is typical of what happened in a number of other fields as well is revealed in Chart III from a study made by Clement Winston and Reba L. Osborne, of the U.S. Department of Commerce.[7] It covers thirteen selected fields, including several in which the chains had made relatively little progress by 1929 as well as those in which their progress had been most pronounced.

The combined sales of the chains in these thirteen fields stood at 28% of total sales in those fields in 1929, the chart shows, and at approximately the same level in 1948. Covered in the study were grocery stores; department store and general merchandise; drug; eating and drinking establishments; men's clothing and furnishings; women's apparel and accessories; shoes; auto accessories; hardware; building materials' furniture and house furnishings; family wear; and variety stores.

The outstanding fact disclosed by the Census figures is that

[7] *Survey of Current Business,* January, 1949. The chart appears on p. 78, *post.*

TABLE 15

RETAIL CENSUS, 1929, 1939, 1948, 1954 AND 1958

(Source: U.S. Department of Commerce, Bureau of the Census)

KIND OF BUSINESS	YEAR	NUMBER OF STORES			SALES (MILLIONS)		
		TOTAL	CHAIN*	%	TOTAL	CHAIN	%
ALL KINDS	1929	1,476,365	159,638	10.8	$ 48,329	$10,740	22.2
	1939	1,770,355	132,763	7.5	42,041	10,105	24.0
	1948	1,769,540	105,109	5.9	130,520	29,736	22.8
	1954	1,721,650	105,139	6.1	169,968	40,297	23.7
	1958	1,788,325	114,170	6.3	199,646	53,443	26.7
FOOD GROUP	1929	481,891	61,416	12.7	10,837	3,514	32.4
	1939	560,549	51,110	9.1	10,165	3,409	33.5
	1948	504,439	32,574	6.5	30,966	10,493	33.9
	1954	384,616	25,212	6.5	39,762	15,478	38.8
	1958	355,508	25,005	7.0	49,022	21,592	44.0
Grocery Stores	1929	307,425	53,466	17.4	7,353	2,873	39.1
(With and without	1939	387,337	40,159	10.4	7,722	2,841	36.8
meat)	1948	377,939	25,047	6.6	24,770	9,319	37.6
	1954	279,440	19,076	6.8	34,421	14,918	43.3
	1958**	259,796	19,935	7.6	43,696	21,056	48.2
Meat Markets and	1929	49,865	2,804	5.6	1,337	141	10.5
Fish Markets	1939	42,360	1,605	3.8	750	78	10.4
	1948	29,465	724	2.5	1,776	128	7.2
	1954	27,354	708	2.5	2,128	144	6.7
	1958	28,183	489	1.8	2,520	124	4.9
Dairy Products and	1929	8,478	1,201	14.2	727	336	46.2
Milk Dealers	1939	16,834	3,308	19.7	740	323	43.6
	1948	11,727	1,799	15.3	1,887	622	33.0
	1954	(Not separately enumerated)					
	1958	7,628	1,326	17.3	412	124	30.0
Candy, Nut and	1929	63,265	1,461	2.3	572	54	9.4
Confectionery Stores	1939	48,015	2,225	4.6	295	51	17.3
	1948	32,876	3,051	9.3	649	187	28.8
	1954	20,507	1,954	9.5	568	127	22.3
	1958	17,593	1,498	8.5	528	122	23.1
Fruit Stores and	1929	22,904	383	1.7	308	15	4.9
Vegetable Markets	1939	27,666	453	1.6	222	17	7.7
	1948	15,763	177	1.1	399	17	4.3
	1954	13,136	134	1.0	485	15	3.1
	1958	12,689	83	0.6	505	18	3.2
All Other	1929	29,954	2,101	7.0	540	95	17.6
	1939	38,337	3,030	7.9	435	99	22.8
	1948	36,669	1,776	4.8	1,485	220	14.9
	1954	40,943	1,898	4.6	2,094	143	6.8
	1958***	29,619	1,674	5.6	1,361	148	10.9

* Only stores operated by companies with four or more are included in the chain store category in this table. See page 66 for comment on 1954 and 1958 data.

** Includes delicatessen stores, whereas previous data for this category did not.

*** Derived by deducting total of specified categories from Food Group total.

TABLE 15 (Continued)

RETAIL CENSUS

| KIND OF BUSINESS | YEAR | NUMBER OF STORES | | | SALES (MILLIONS) | | |
		TOTAL	CHAIN*	%	TOTAL	CHAIN	%
DRUG STORES	1929	58,258	3,513	6.0	$ 1,690	$ 312	18.5
	1939	57,903	3,928	6.8	1,563	379	24.2
	1948	55,796	3,715	6.7	4,013	869	21.6
	1954	56,009	3,470[1]	6.2	5,252	1,044	19.9
	1958	56,232	3,888	6.9	6,779	1,456	21.5
GENERAL MERCHANDISE GROUP	1929	54,636	12,029	22.0	6,444	2,163	33.6
	1939	50,267	11,785	23.4	5,665	2,643	46.7
	1948	52,544	12,727	24.2	15,975	8,751	54.8
	1954	76,198	13,199	17.3	17,872	10,637	59.4
	1958	86,644	14,144	16.3	21,879	14,629	68.2
Department Stores	1929	4,221	2,560	60.6	4,350	665	15.3
	1939	4,074	2,672	65.5	3,975	1,195	30.0
	1948	2,580	1,565	60.7	10,645	5,523	51.9
	1954	2,761	1,856	67.2	10,558	6,956	65.6
	1958	3,157	2,315	73.2	13,359	10,156	78.0
Variety Stores	1929	12,110	5,447	45.0	904	810	89.6
	1939	16,946	6,390	37.7	977	850	87.0
	1948	20,210	7,418	36.7	2,507	2,077	82.9
	1954	20,917	7,623	36.4	3,067	2,444	79.6
	1958	21,017	8,007	38.1	3,621	2,932	81.4
Dry Goods and General Merchandise Stores	1929	38,305	3,932	10.3	1,190	688	57.8
	1939	29,247	1,578	5.4	713	99	13.9
	1948	29,754	3,744	12.6	2,824	1,151	40.8
	1954	51,814	3,720	7.2	4,233	1,237	29.4
	1958	62,470	3,822	6.3	4,899	1,541	31.5
EATING AND DRINKING PLACE GROUP	1929	134,293	3,392	2.5	2,125	299	14.1
	1939	305,386	5,222	1.7	3,520	298	8.5
	1948	346,556	6,133	1.8	10,683	742	7.0
	1954	319,657	7,521	2.3	13,101	992	7.6
	1958	344,740	10,333	3.0	15,201	1,287	8.6
Eating Places	1929	134,293	3,392	2.5	2,125	299	14.1
	1939	169,792	5,058	3.0	2,135	292	13.7
	1948	194,123	5,824	3.0	6,468	718	11.1
	1954	169,867	7,251	4.2	8,096	969	11.9
	1958	229,815	10,067	5.6	11,038	1,263	11.5
Drinking Places	1929	—	—	—	—	—	—
	1939	135,594	164	0.1	1,385	6	0.4
	1948	152,433	309	0.2	4,215	24	0.6
	1954	123,887	270	0.2	4,360	23	0.5
	1958	114,925	266	0.2	4,164	24	0.5
APPAREL GROUP	1929	114,296	17,218	15.1	4,241	1,197	28.2
	1939	106,959	17,591	16.4	3,259	1,001	30.7
	1948	115,246	14,515	12.6	9,803	2,729	27.8
	1954	119,743	19,881	16.5	11,078	3,197	28.8
	1958	118,759	19,414	16.3	12,525	4,004	32.0

* See footnote on first page of this table.
[1] See page 72, *supra*.

TABLE 15 (Continued)
RETAIL CENSUS

KIND OF BUSINESS	YEAR	NUMBER OF STORES			SALES (MILLIONS)		
		TOTAL	CHAIN*	%	TOTAL	CHAIN	%
Men's and Boys'	1929	28,197	3,054	10.8	$ 1,193	$ 271	22.7
Clothing, Hat, etc.,	1939	21,501	1,798	8.4	773	171	22.1
Stores	1948	23,730	1,663	7.0	2,166	360	16.6
	1954	19,247			2,299		
	1958	24,199	1,982	8.2	2,597	488	18.8
Women's	1929	18,253	2,132	11.7	1,088	292	26.8
Ready-to-Wear	1939	25,820	3,242	12.6	1,009	291	28.8
Stores	1948	30,677	3,747	12.2	3,305	966	29.2
	1954	45,213	8,220	18.2	4,333	1,327	30.8
	1958	44,628	6,732	15.0	4,909	1,598	32.5
Shoe Stores	1929	24,259	6,099	25.1	807	369	45.7
(All Kinds)	1939	20,487	5,721	27.8	617	306	49.7
	1948	19,551	5,417	27.7	1,467	697	47.5
	1954	23,847	7,625	31.7	1,895	878	45.9
	1958	24,437	7,786	32.4	2,129	1,026	49.0
Family Clothing,	1929	43,587	5,933	13.6	1,154	265	23.0
Accessories and	1939	39,151	5,717	14.6	859	195	22.7
All Other Stores	1948	41,288	3,697	9.0	2,865	704	24.6
	1954	25,012			2,416		
	1958	25,495	2,914	11.4	2,890	892	30.7
FURNITURE, HOUSE	1929	58,941	6,796	11.5	2,755	560	20.3
FURNISHINGS, AND	1939	52,827	6,918	13.1	1,733	393	22.7
APPLIANCES GROUP	1948	85,585	6,031	7.1	6,914	1,027	14.9
	1954	91,797	5,576	6.1	8,619	1,131	13.1
	1958	103,417	6,055	5.8	10,074	1,361	13.5
Furniture Stores	1929	25,153	922	3.9	1,510	208	13.8
	1939	19,902	779	3.9	973	141	14.5
	1948	29,031	1,051	3.6	3,427	399	11.6
	1954	50,729	1,399	2.7	5,374	572	10.6
	1958	36,096	1,317	3.6	4,783	606	14.7
Other Home	1929	8,820	468	5.3	303	47	15.5
Furnishings	1939	12,012	444	3.7	227	47	20.7
Stores	1948	19,623	575	2.9	944	164	17.4
	1954						
	1958	26,336	585	2.3	1,792	131	7.3
Home Appliances	1929	24,968	5,366	21.5	941	304	32.3
and Radio Stores	1939	20,913	5,695	27.2	533	206	38.6
	1948	36,913	4,405	11.9	2,543	464	18.2
	1954	40,542	4,177	10.3	3,227	559	17.5
	1958	40,985	4,153	10.1	3,499	624	17.8
AUTOMOTIVE GROUP	1929	69,379	3,516	5.1	7,043	750	10.6
	1939	60,132	4,464	7.4	5,549	373	6.7
	1948	86,162	3,682	4.3	20,104	741	3.7
	1954	85,953	3,561	4.1	29,915	955	3.2
	1958	93,656	4,273	4.5	31,808	1,318	4.1

* See footnote on first page of this table.

TABLE 15 (Continued)
RETAIL CENSUS

KIND OF BUSINESS	YEAR	NUMBER OF STORES			SALES (MILLIONS)		
		TOTAL	CHAIN*	%	TOTAL	CHAIN	%
Motor Vehicle	1929	42,204	1,290	3.1	$ 6,267	$ 617	9.8
Dealers	1939	33,609	438	1.3	4,810	136	2.8
	1948	43,999	170	0.4	15,953	253	1.6
	1954	61,547	221	0.3	27,531	272	0.9
	1958	63,886	245	0.3	28,309	323	1.1
Tire and Accessory	1929	22,313	2,049	9.2	599	122	20.4
Dealers	1939	18,525	4,014	21.7	524	235	44.8
	1948	20,628	3,342	16.2	1,360	455	38.5
	1954	18,845	3,212	17.0	1,814	652	36.2
	1958	20,912	3,738	17.9	2,425	914	38.0
All Other	1929	4,862	177	3.6	177	11	6.2
	1939	7,998	12	0.2	215	2	0.9
	1948	21,535	171	0.8	2,792	33	1.2
	1954	5,307	128	2.4	565	31	5.5
	1958	8,858	290	3.3	1,074	81	7.5
GASOLINE	1929	121,513	30,038	24.7	1,787	629	35.2
STATIONS	1939	241,858	10,397	4.3	2,822	294	10.4
	1948	188,253	5,445	2.9	6,483	470	7.3
	1954	181,747	6,344	3.5	10,744	875	8.1
	1958	206,302	9,692	4.7	14,178	1,368	9.6
LIQUOR STORES	1929	—			—	—	—
	1939	19,136	2,854	14.9	586	257	43.9
	1948	33,422	2,998	9.0	2,580	803	31.1
	1954	31,240	2,830	9.1	3,181	901	28.3
	1958	37,068	3,291	8.9	4,202	1,104	26.3
LUMBER, HARDWARE,	1929	90,386	9,001	10.0	3,846	526	13.7
FARM IMPLEMENT	1939	79,313	7,958	10.0	2,735	395	14.4
STORE GROUP	1948	98,938	7,951	8.0	11,151	1,558	14.0
	1954	100,519	7,696	7.7	13,124	1,550	11.9
	1958	108,248	7,276	6.7	14,309	1,483	10.3
ALL OTHER STORES	1929	292,772	12,701	4.3	7,561	790	10.4
	1939	236,025	10,536	4.5	4,444	662	14.9
	1948	202,599	9,336	4.6	11,847	1,552	13.1
	1954	226,903	10,874	4.8	15,987	2,552	15.9
	1958	277,751	10,799	3.8	19,669	3,841	19.5

* See footnote on first page of this table.

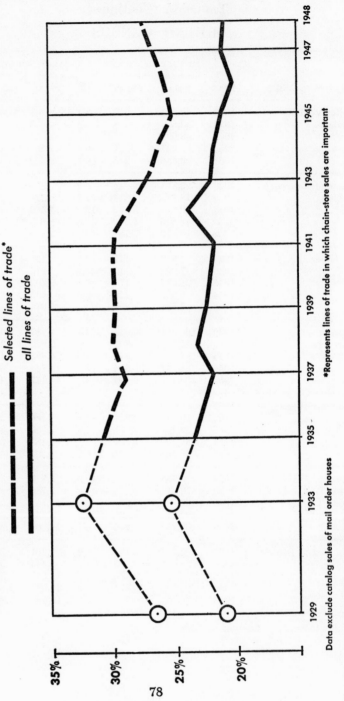

CHART III

Ratios of chain to total retail sales, 1929-1948

Selected lines of trade*

all lines of trade

*Represents lines of trade in which chain-store sales are important

Data exclude catalog sales of mail order houses

Source: U. S. Department of Commerce, Office of Business Economics

78

while the total number of retail stores increased by 311,960 between 1929 and 1958, or 21.1%, the gain came entirely from the increase in the number of independent stores. Actually, as the following tabulation discloses, independent merchants were operating 357,418 more stores in 1958 than in 1929, a gain of 27.1%, while the chains (four or more stores) were operating 45,468, or 28.5%, fewer.

RETAIL STORES, 1929 AND 1958

(Derived from Table 15)

	1929	1958	CHANGE	%
All stores	1,476,375	1,788,325	+311,960	+21.1
Independents[1]	1,316,737	1,674,155	+357,418	+27.1
Chains[2]	159,638	114,170	− 45,468	−28.5

[1] Includes 2 and 3 store multiunits.
[2] Includes only multiunit stores of firms with 4 or more.

True enough, the substantial decline in the number of chain stores is more than accounted for by what happened in two categories—grocery stores and gasoline stations. In the former, the chains had 33,351 fewer stores in 1958 than in 1929, and, in the latter 20,346 units. But if these two categories are left out of consideration, while the chains will be found to have increased the number of their stores during the period, the independents show considerably greater relative gains. Chains in fields other than grocery or gasoline stations, increased their stores from 76,134 in 1929 to 84,453 in 1958, a gain of 8,409 stores, or 11.1%. But on the same basis, independent stores increased from 971,293 to 1,237,684, a gain of 266,391 stores, or 27.4%.

The significance of the story these Census statistics tell lies in the fact that instead of being wiped out of the picture completely as he had expected to be in the '20s, the independent merchant remained very much alive. Not only was he able to withstand the challenge of the chains, but he found ways of adjusting himself to other new competitive factors which developed during the period.

The two main conclusions to be drawn from the Census figures are:

1. The chains had attained an important place in our distribution set-up by 1929, particularly in those fields in which their development had been most pronounced.

2. The important status attained by the chains as of 1929 has not materially changed since that time. In other words, the fear that the chains would go on expanding indefinitely proved to have been ill-founded. As the late Hugh M. Foster pointed out in 1937 in an outstanding study of chain store development from 1920 to that date,[8] the chains "had come of age" in the early 1930's. Certainly they seem to have attained most of their growth by that time.

But although these facts are clear enough now, they could hardly have been foreseen 30 years ago. Then it seemed, as has already been pointed out, that the chain-store juggernaut would crush everything in its path unless something were done to stop it.

What followed gave the chains plenty to worry about and to combat for many years. The story is told in detail in later chapters. But before entering into that hectic phase of chain-store history, a consideration of the basis of chain-store strength is necessary to provide the proper background.

[8] "The Chain Store Comes of Age," *Printers' Ink Monthly*, April, 1937.

CHAPTER V

THE BASIS OF CHAIN-STORE
STRENGTH [1]

BEFORE THE chains came into existence, the need for retail stores was supplied almost exclusively by independent merchants who secured their merchandise from either wholesalers or manufacturers direct. The system which then prevailed and which, of course, still exists, is commonly referred to as the wholesaler-retailer system because most products had to find their way from manufacturer or producer to the consumer through both wholesalers and retailers.

In the early days of chain-store development, the wholesaler-retailer system was so well intrenched that manufacturers and producers refused to deal directly with the chains, compelling them to buy through wholesalers, just as the independent merchants did, or at least to pay the same prices as independents paid. [2] Such policies were inspired mainly by a desire to protect the old-line distributors from the "cut-price" competition which the chains would be in a better position to wage if they could obtain their merchandise on a wholesale basis.

Eventually, however, the chains in almost every line succeeded in gaining recognition as wholesale as well as retail

[1] This chapter is taken almost word for word from *The Chain Store—Boon or Bane?* by the author (Harper & Brothers, New York, 1932), by permission of the publisher. It has been revised, however, to bring it up to date.
[2] See pp. 119 *et seq.*

distributors and, from that time, two distinct channels of distribution came into general use—the wholesaler-retailer system and the new chain-store system.

Although from the technical standpoint of marketing, the independent store and the chain store represent two distinct types of operation—the former to be considered solely as a retailing operation and the latter as a type of combined wholesaling and retailing—that distinction has little significance to the consumer. To him, a store is ordinarily just a store, whether it be an independent store or part of a chain, a store to be patronized or passed by, according to the appeal it registers or fails to register.

Whatever success the chain stores have won for themselves reflects, therefore, the public's reaction to what they have to offer. Of course, chain-store critics used to assert that one of the principal advantages chain stores seem to offer, namely, lower prices, was illusionary. Such criticisms have been completely refuted in recent years, however, by comparative price studies made under impartial auspices.[3] In any event, the sustained success of the chains over the years would, in itself, refute such a contention, unless it is to be assumed, contrary to Lincoln's famous aphorism, that a very large proportion of the public can be hoodwinked continuously.

What, then, is the basis for chain-store growth, as revealed by the foregoing statistics, in the face not only of widespread and well-established competition but the early opposition of those upon whom the chains had to depend for merchandise?

Let us try to answer the question first from the standpoint of the consumer for, obviously, the impression the chain stores have registered with the public, whether conscious or subconscious, accounts for their success. Later we will consider the various factors which have enabled the chains to do what apparently their competitors left undone.

Listing them in the order of their probable importance to

[3] See pp. 102 et seq.

the customer, the following factors may be said to have been responsible in the early days of chain-store growth for whatever preference the chains enjoyed over the existing competition:

1. Better values, mainly in the form of lower prices.
2. Better physical appearance of the stores themselves.
3. Superior locations.
4. Fresher merchandise and wider assortments.
5. Advertising.

As against these positive influences, the popularity of chain stores developed in the face of the following counteracting obstacles:

1. No deliveries and no credit.
2. Loyalty to old established order.
3. Store-management by *employes* as against the management of independent stores by their owners.
4. The superior ability and aggressiveness of a certain percentage of the independent merchants.

Taking up first the influences that have worked in favor of the chains, the factor of lower prices has undoubtedly been largely responsible for the following they have developed. Although these lower prices were made possible to some extent by the elimination of delivery and credit, services for which consumers should be willing to pay, the fact remains that so many consumers are more interested in lower prices than in such service that the cash-and-carry system fills a definite need in our distribution system, and the chains were the first to cash in on it on a big scale.

Of course, nothing prevents an independent merchant from following the same policy, and many do. Nor is there anything inherent in the chain-store system which precludes the extension of credit or the making of deliveries. Indeed, in the clothing field, credit chains proved singularly successful and furniture, jewelry and other kinds of chains likewise operated on a credit basis even while cash-and-carry prevailed almost universally among the grocery, drug and variety store chains. In recent years, moreover, the intense struggle for added volume has led practically all chains to extend credit. This includes the two big mail order houses, J. C. Penney, nearly all the variety store chains, the department store chains, and, remarkable as it may seem, even the discount department stores, like E. J. Korvette! At the same time, most of these chains have provided for deliveries of items which customers would find it inconvenient to carry away.

Nevertheless, the fact remains that the chains, as a class, adopted the cash-and-carry idea right from the start, and the independents, as a class, stuck generally to the credit-and-delivery basis and, because a definite demand exists for both types of retailing, the chains opened a rich vein for patronage which the independents had almost entirely neglected.

But the lower prices the chains have always emphasized were made possible not only by the economies of cash-and-carry operation but, to an even greater degree, by the benefits that come from large-scale operation, of which we shall have considerably more to say later on.

Obviously, an attractive-looking store, well-lighted and well-equipped, will attract more trade than one which is run-down-at-the heels, inadequately lighted and lacking in modern equipment. The chains, as a class, have always recognized the importance of the physical appearance of their stores and, what is more to the point, they have had the resources to a greater extent than their independent competitors to maintain high standards in that respect. This factor has undoubtedly contributed greatly to the appeal chain stores have made and the customer traffic they have been able to draw.[4]

With more experience in the choice of locations, with more capital at their command and with greater prospects of being able to cover high rents, the chains have generally located

[4] For data on the heavy expenditures the chains make to keep their stores up-to-date see *Chain Store Age* annual store-construction surveys.

their stores to better advantage than the average independent.

One of the guiding principles which inspired pioneers in the food-chain field was the merchandising advantage to be gained by speeding up the *turnover*. To achieve that end the chains had to concentrate on items for which a constant demand existed and which therefore moved most rapidly, and to be satisfied with smaller profit per unit.[5] That policy, which is perhaps the most characteristic feature of food-chain-store merchandising, not only made for lower prices but, in the case of perishables, it minimized stale merchandise. Thus, consciously or subconsciously, the consumer showed a preference for chain stores because their merchandise was more apt to be fresh.

Finally, consumers were undoubtedly influenced by the advertising the chains were in a better position to use than their smaller competitors. This was true especially in the larger cities, where newspaper space is relatively expensive. The chains could use it liberally because, by dividing its cost among all their stores which benefited by it, the cost per store was relatively small. The single-store merchant, as a rule, found this sales-stimulant beyond his reach.

No doubt the list of factors which helped to make friends for the chain stores might be materially lengthened but those which have been mentioned include the more important ones.

In considering the obstacles the chains had to overcome and which, in the course of the years, they have largely surmounted, the loyalty of the consumer to old-established merchants in preference to newcomers was a natural one. Such attachments undoubtedly worked against the chains in their early days and were strengthened by the anti-chain campaigns which were to develop later on, but, in the long run, they offered little real resistance to chain-store development.

More serious, perhaps, was the inherent disadvantage in

[5] Incidentally, this policy left a field open for grocers carrying broader lines and accounts for the ability of so many single-store grocers to withstand chain-store competition.

the chain-store system which makes it necessary to entrust the management of the various units to employes. To the extent that employes cannot be expected to exert themselves as much for others as the owner of a store would for himself, the chains undoubtedly suffered some disadvantage. On the other hand, the incentives they offered to capable employes in the way of promotion and other methods they used to get satisfactory performance from their employes probably reduced this handicap to a minimum. Furthermore, the assumption that all independent stores are owner-operated and that all store-owners have and use what it takes to impress their customers favorably is, of course, wrong on both counts.

Although a large percentage of independent stores are one-man operations,[6] the percentage of total retail business they do, compared with that done by their larger and more successful fellow independent merchants, is small.

Whatever disadvantage may be involved in relying upon paid employes in retailing is felt by the bigger and better independent stores as well as by the chains and, of course, those are the stores whose competition means most to the chains.

So far as the personality and salesmanship of the average owner of a one-man store is concerned, common experience confirms that they are apt to be a negative factor as frequently as a positive one.

If the net balance of advantages and disadvantages may have favored the chains, certainly the difference was never great enough to give the chains a clear path. A large number of efficient, wide-awake, energetic independent merchants have disputed the advance of the chains every inch of the way. The statistics heretofore presented show clearly enough that the independents, as a group, have held their own since 1930 despite all the progress the chains had made in the years of their greatest development.

[6] See p. 11, *supra.*

But, with all due deference to the more progressive and successful independents, the great majority of independents were not of that caliber when the chains first came into the picture. Had it been otherwise, perhaps the chains would never have made the headway which carried them so far. As it was, however, the new methods the chains introduced were in such striking contrast to the less satisfactory practices of the great majority of independent merchants that the public must have recognized the difference instinctively. The rapid growth of the chains was the inevitable consequence.

The truth of the matter is that the chains grew because they introduced a method of retail distribution for which there was a definite need and which the old wholesaler-retailer system failed to supply. To what extent the old system was inherently deficient and to what extent its shortcomings could be and have been corrected must be discussed now, not for the sake of stressing the imperfections of a competive system but in order to contrast certain features of the chain-store system.

The ideal distribution system would bridge the gap between production and consumption with maximum efficiency at minimum cost.

Without any question, the outstanding inherent defect of the old wholesaler-retailer system lay in the fact that, under it, the wholesale function and the retail function are performed by separate, independent factors, whereas, under the chain-store system, the two functions are, to a major extent, combined.

In no sense does the chain-store system eliminate the wholesale function: it still has to be performed, but, whereas under the old system the wholesaler exercised no control over his retail outlets nor did the retailer have any control over his sources of supply, under the chain-store system both functions are performed by the same organization and the control is unified. That this basic difference between the two systems has been partly nullified by the development of voluntary chains of various kinds is true. But the fact remains that such organizations did not come prominently into the picture until the chains had established themselves on a firm basis. When the chains were making their greatest strides, the old wholesaler-retailer set-up provided their principal competition.

Reduced to its simplest terms, the main result of the essential difference between the two systems lies in the fact that under the old plan it is necessary for the wholesaler to *sell* to the retailer before the merchandise can find its way into consumption. Under the chain-store system, this intervening selling process, with all its disadvantages, is obviated.

A. C. Hoffman, of the U.S. Bureau of Agricultural Economics, stressed the advantages of integrating wholesaling and retailing, as in the chain-store system, in a monograph published by the Temporary National Economic Committee appointed by the 76th Congress, 3rd Session, and published in 1940.[7]

"Another important aspect of mass distribution from the standpoint of marketing efficiency," he declared, "is the fact that mass distributors have tended to integrate successive marketing functions within a single organization. The number of bargaining transaction and ownership transfers necessary to move goods from producer to consumer is thus greatly reduced as compared with the regular channels.

"The importance of this is commonly overlooked. No inconsiderable part of the total cost of distributing food products is incurred for the purpose of bringing about ownership transfer at various stages in the marketing process. Brokers' fees, wholesalers' commissions, salesmen's salaries, advertising expenditures—all are partially chargeable to the efforts of sellers and manufacturers to find retail outlets for their goods. . . . In the regular channels, comprised as they are of many small, specialized handlers, the product moves forward

[7] A. C. Hoffman, *Large-Scale Organization in the Food Industries*, Monograph 35, Temporary National Economic Committee, Senate Committee Print, 76th Congress, 3rd Session.

chiefly by means of numerous buying and selling transactions. In contrast, the mass distributor moves it forward on an inter-company basis, with the orders and requirements of its various parts largely supplanting the bargaining transactions of the regular system.

"This is the key to much, if not most, of the advantage which the grocery chains have over the independent retailer-wholesaler system. When the function of wholesaling is integrated with that of retailing, it is no longer necessary to 'sell' the retail store. The average independent retailer is visited daily by at least half-a-dozen salesmen, each trying to sell him a small bill of merchandise which he may or may not need. Those who seek the retailer's business cannot permit him simply to order his merchandise as he needs it; the competition between them is such that they constantly must persuade, cajole and coax him.

"The cost of this sort of thing in time and money is nothing short of stupendous. Yet it is seldom mentioned when methods for reducing the costs of food distribution are being considered because most people, including a fair share of the economists, are more concerned with the preservation of competition under old institutional forms than with economic efficiency as we have defined the term."

Putting it in another way, under the old system, the wholesaler, in making his purchases from producers, must *guess*, so to speak, what he will be able to resell to his retail customers. After he has made his guess, he can sell only what his retail customers *guess*, in turn, they will be able to sell to their customers, the consumers. Under the chain-store system, the chain has to guess only what its stores will be able to sell the consumer. Thus, the new system eliminates one of the *guesses*.

What this means in helping to bridge the gap between production and consumption is considerable from the standpoint of both efficiency and cost.

From the standpoint of efficiency, the old system tends to

suffer because, to the extent that the wholesaler's guess as to what the retailer will buy is *wrong*, the process of distribution, so far as those particular items are concerned, is definitely blocked. As a device for moving goods into consumption, the wholesaler-retailer system, to this extent, falls down completely. Via this channel, goods can never get into consumption until they have bridged the gulf between wholesaler and retailer. The chain-store system eliminates that gulf. Everything the chain buys, the consumer will have a chance to buy, but that is not true of everything the wholesaler buys.

Then, too, because the wholesaler exercises no effective control over the purchases of the retailer, he must compete with other wholesalers for the retailer's patronage. This limits the efficacy of the old system in several ways.

In the first place, it slows up the rate of turnover because it compels the wholesaler to carry more varieties of merchandise than would be necessary if he were the final arbiter as to the items that were to be offered at retail.

In the second place, with many wholesalers serving the same territory and naturally seeking the patronage of the same retail outlets, a certain part of the selling effort expended must inevitably prove fruitless. To the extent that this selling effort fails, it represents economic waste.

Finally, although theoretically the competition between wholesalers need not lead them to employ uneconomic methods, such as opening unprofitable accounts, granting unsafe credits, and overloading their customers, we know that, practically, that is just what happens.

Still another inherent weakness which affects the efficiency of the wholesaler-retailer system lies in the fact that the wholesaler is out of direct touch with the consumer. Because he has no direct way of gauging consumer preferences or buying habits, his job of "guessing" just what he can sell the retailer, outside of staples, is made so much harder and is attended with greater risk. This disadvantage is obviated to a large extent in the chain-store system because the chains maintain direct consumer contacts through the medium of their own retail outlets.

When we come to consider the relative costs of the two systems, the first fact to be noted is that, although the chain is relieved of the heavy expense involved in *selling* what it buys to its retail outlets, it cannot escape the cost of corresponding operations. The goods the chain takes into its warehouse do not automatically take their places on the shelves of the retail units without a system, without supervision or without expense. Thus, although the chains do not have to sell merchandise to their retail units, they do have to maintain adequate machinery and manpower to see that the stores are suitably stocked and the merchandise effectively displayed.

Before considering the relative cost of the two systems, let us look at the defects of the old system as they have developed in the retail end, where we will find additional reasons to explain the rise of the chains.

Perhaps the outstanding characteristic of independent retailing as it existed in the days when the chains were coming up, and which is almost as pronounced today, is that the great majority of retailers are essentially small-scale operators, accounting for but a small proportion of the total volume done by independents. The major part of that volume is done by a small proportion of independents who operate relatively large stores.

Data compiled by the Census Bureau in connection with the 1929 Census clearly reveals the situation which then prevailed. Of the 1,543,158 retailers reported for that year, 986,551, or 64%, had an annual volume of less than $20,000. As a group they accounted for only 15% of total store sales. These figures include all retail stores, chain as well as independent. However, since the total number of chain stores in 1929 was only 159,000, the number of small stores in operation must have been preponderantly independent stores. The 1929 Census also showed that at the other end of the scale, retail stores doing upwards of $100,000 a year numbered only 77,513, or 5% of the total, but they accounted collectively for 45% of total retail sales.[8] The heavy preponderance of small stores in 1929 is shown graphically in Chart IV.

CHART IV

Retail stores in 1929 by volume of sales

(% of total number of stores in operation)

5.03% did more than $100,000 a year each

did $20,000 to $100,000 a year each

31.04%

63.93%

did less than $20,000 a year each

Source: U. S. Department of Commerce, Bureau of the Census

Why is it that so large a proportion of those engaged in retailing attain such a comparatively small volume, and what is the significance of that fact so far as the efficiency of our present system of distribution is concerned?

The reason we have so many *small* retailers is that we have so many retailers. The 1958 Retail Census data on the 1,470,-454 single stores which were in operation the entire year tells the story. Their sales totalled $123.3 billion. Obviously they could not *all* have done a *large* volume because if the total sales had been divided among them *equally*, none would have done more than $83,000 for the year.

The amount of money spent at retail does not vary with the

[8] See Tables 3 and 4, pp. 12 and 13, for the situation regarding single stores in 1958.

number of stores we have. It is governed largely by the amount of disposable income—income less taxes—consumers, as a whole, have to spend. Furthermore, consumers spend their money in stores they like best. The great bulk of it, the statistics demonstrate, goes into the larger-volume stores. The inevitable result is indicated by the 1958 Census. Instead of every independent store doing as much as $83,000, which would have been their volume if all had shared equally, no less than 642,463 of the 1,470,454 which were in operation throughout 1958—43.7% of them—actually did less than $30,000, averaging less than $15,000 each.[9] Despite the number of them they accounted for only 7.8% of total sales of the group. On the other hand, 40.6% of the sales were rung up by stores doing $300,000 and up, of which there were 66,488, or 4.5% of the group.

As has been pointed out, the amount of money spent at retail is not unlimited and it would therefore be impossible for all merchants to do a large business, so long as we have so many of them, even if all possessed the genius of a John Wanamaker or a Marshall Field. It might therefore seem to be a gratuitous observation to refer to the appallingly large number of independent retailers who would never be successful even if there were enough volume available for all who might merit it.

In other words, if the public buying-power were to be doubled tomorrow, the great bulk of the additional funds would be spent, in all probability, in the stores which enjoy the lion's share of the present volume. The position of the rank and file of the small independent merchants would not be measurably improved.

And yet the make-up of our merchant class is important because the fact that so many of them are doomed to mediocrity or failure serves to explain a lot of things we want to know more about.

[9] U.S. Census of Business: 1958.

It serves to explain (1) why we have so many small stores; (2) why, despite the fact that we already have too many stores, we could still use more *good* ones; and (3) why the field was wide open for the chains when they came into the picture and is still wide open for all the latent A. T. Stewarts, Marshall Fields, John Wanamakers, Frank Woolworths and J. C. Penneys the present generation may provide.

Common experience confirms the opinions which have been expressed on this point by all authorities on retailing.

"The ease with which entry may be made into the retail business," declared Dr. Paul H. Nystrom, "throngs its channels with people who have no aptitude, no education, no experience, nor other necessary qualifications for this business. The wonder to many students of the retail business is that more do not fail." [10]

When James L. Palmer[11] was professor of marketing at the University of Chicago, in discussing the "Economic and Social Aspects of Chain Stores," he said:[12]

"The business methods of most retailers and wholesalers prior to the development of chains were appallingly wasteful. Even after ten years of intensive chain competition, we find many wholesale and retail distributors employing methods which should have been obsolete decades ago. The fact that some chains have been successful despite their own inefficiency rather than because of the perfection of their methods certainly demonstrates conclusively the wastefulness of the methods employed by some of our established institutions. It is difficult for an impartial observer to become enthusiastic about the preservation of individual enterprise in the field of distribution if, in preserving it, we perpetuate the existence of the host of incompetents that have been engaged in retailing and wholesaling in the past."

Discussing particularly the independent merchant in the

[10] Paul H. Nystrom, *Economics of Retailing* (New York: Ronald Press, 1930), 3rd Edition, Vol. 1, p. 119.

[11] Now president of Marshall Field & Co., Chicago.

[12] *Journal of Business*, University of Chicago, Vol. II, No. 3, July, 1929.

grocery field, although what he says of the grocer undoubtedly applies with equal force to small-scale retailers in general, Carl N. Schmalz, then assistant director of the Harvard Bureau of Business Research, now president of R. H. Stearns Co., Boston department store, probably hit the nail squarely on the head in the following summary of the small retailer's shortcomings:[13]

"It seems, therefore, that independent grocery stores on the whole have been poorly managed, and there is strong reason for believing that this poor management has been almost unavoidable.

"As a rule, independent grocery stores necessarily are small,[14] so that the net earnings of each are strictly limited. Nevertheless, their managers are confronted with practically all the problems of any independent business.

"These men should have the knowledge, the judgment, and courage necessary in formulating and executing sound financial policies, not only in interpreting local demand but also, in changing fundamental conditions, in keeping sales and stocks in balance, in controlling expense and in granting credit.

"These qualities are seldom found in a man able and willing also to work long hours as salesperson, bookkeeper, janitor, stock boy and general detail man.

"Because of these management problems and the small sales volume, it is extremely difficult to make a single grocery store yield an income in salary and profit sufficient to compensate adequately the ability required to manage that store successfully.

"It seems reasonable to assume that many independent stores have been, and will continue to be, managed by men incompetent to operate them at a profit, and that one may expect a continuation of the high failure rates found by such

[13] *Harvard Business Review*, July, 1931.
[14] This was written before the advent of the supermarket, which has changed the picture somewhat for the progressive independent in the food field. But the observations still apply to small-scale retailers in all fields, including the food field.

investigators as Nystrom and McGarry. The old system placed an impossible burden upon the independent retailer."

If the foregoing appraisals of independent merchants, as a class, were reasonably accurate at the time they were made, of which there can be little doubt, they go a long way to explain why the chains grew so rapidly and account for the relative strength the system has consistently displayed. By contrast with the weaknesses so prevalent among the independents, the advantages offered by the chains must have seemed even bigger than they were to a large percentage of the consuming public.

But, it may be asked, assuming that an individual lacks the ability, the skill or the resources needed to enable him to develop a *large* retail business, what is to prevent him from performing a useful public service as a *small* retailer? Why cannot he sell five or ten thousand dollars worth of merchandise a year just as efficiently and as economically as a larger operator might sell seventy-five or one hundred thousand dollars a year?

The first answer is that, unless a retailer realizes at least a fair volume of business, he cannot make both ends meet and must inevitably go on the rocks. Although many small stores do manage to hang on year after year, they are the exception and, even if they survive, their stores are not the kind the public prefers to trade in. All stores, the smallest as well as the largest, incur certain inescapable operating expenses— rent, light, and heat. Such expenses, not to say anything of a reasonable return to the proprietor on his invested capital, can be covered only if the merchant does enough business to pay for them after he has paid for the merchandise itself.

Back in 1928, the U.S. Department of Commerce and the U.S. Chamber of Commerce published the results of a census of distribution it had made in eleven cities[15] as a pilot survey in preparation for the nationwide census it was to make for

---

[15] *Retail and Wholesale Trade of Eleven Cities,* Chamber of Commerce of the United States, May, 1928, in conjunction with the U.S. Department of Commerce.

the year 1929. Commenting on the number of small-scale retailers in the grocery field, the Department said:

"The average store with an annual volume of $5,000 has little chance of surviving and, while the possibility of profitable operation increases with the annual volume, it is not until we reach a volume of more than fifty thousand dollars that more than mere existence seems possible." [16]

The significance of that comment is confirmed by various studies on retail mortality. In Buffalo, for instance, Dr. Edmund D. McGarry, of the University of Buffalo,[17] found that between 1921 and 1928, 27% of the independent druggists that opened up in Buffalo passed out of business during their first year; in the hardware field, 34%; in the shoe field, 44%; and in the grocery field no less than 60%.

Similar studies made in Louisville, revealing the same lamentable situation, led to the important Louisville Grocery Survey, an investigation of distribution conditions made under the auspices of the U.S. Department of Commerce and other cooperating bodies.[18]

Of course, the main weakness of the small-scale retailer, from the standpoint of the consumer, is that his prices are inevitably higher than those charged by his larger competitors and, generally speaking, his store will be a less attractive place to shop in than the larger and more up-to-date establishments operated by his competitors.

Turning now from the weaknesses of the small-scale retailer to the specific elements of strength in large-scale retailing, the advantages offered are not dependent upon the type of operation involved. They are enjoyed by the independent merchant who achieves large volume, whether through a department store, a supermarket or in any other way, just as they are by the mail-order houses and the chains.

Increased volume brings not only lower merchandise costs

[16] See p. 11 *supra* which discloses that in 1958 no less than 642,463 single stores averaged annual sales of only $15,000.

[17] *Mortality in Retail Trade*, University of Buffalo, 1930.

[18] Louisville Grocery Survey, U.S. Department of Commerce, 1930.

by reason of quantity purchases but results in many other operating and merchandising economies, although, of course, there is a limit beyond which such economies are no longer realized. The law of diminishing returns, which sets a limit beyond which the benefits of mass production may cease to exist, undoubtedly applies to mass distribution as well. But at just what point a company, whether in production or distribution, becomes *too* big for its own good is not easy to establish.

Up to the time this law of diminishing returns begins to exert itself, however, the advantages of large scale retailing are not to be doubted. Some of the more important ones may be thus enumerated:

1. The large scale distributor buys both his merchandise and his working equipment cheaper.
2. He can hire greater skill.
3. He can install more scientific methods and equipment.
4. He can resort to a more effective "division of labor."
5. He can command credit more readily.
6. He can better withstand business losses.
7. He can operate on less profit per unit.

The character and importance of these advantages must in most cases be more or less obvious.

Buying in large volume, for instance, results in a lower price because the seller can afford to share with the large buyer what he saves in selling cost. Although the really big buyers were once in a position to secure even greater price concessions than the volume of their purchases warranted, the passage of the Robinson-Patman Act in 1936 has made all discriminatory prices illegal unless they can be justified by actual savings to the seller.[19] However, the very fact that this

[19] The Robinson-Patman Act, which became effective June 19, 1936, amended the Clayton Act of 1914. It contains the following proviso: "Provided, that nothing herein contained shall prevent differentials which make *only due allowance* for differences in the cost of manufacture, sale or delivery resulting from the differing methods or *quantities* in which such commodities are to such purchasers sold or delivered."

law, which was designed to protect small buyers from un-economic advantages enjoyed by big buyers, recognized that quantity purchases do justify lower prices emphasizes the natural advantage enjoyed by large-scale operators in this important phase of their business.

The large operator can afford to employ the best brains available because high salaries distributed over a large number of units usually involve a lower burden per unit than lower salaries distributed among fewer units. That applies, too, to the methods and systems he installs and the equipment he uses. He commands greater credit and can better withstand business losses because large-scale operation involves the use of larger resources and the very size of the operation signifies, even if it does not guarantee, greater stability.

But without question the greatest advantage accruing to the large-scale distributor is that he can usually operate on less profit per unit and still secure a satisfactory return on his invested capital, because the scale of his operations is usually larger proportionally than the additional capital required to finance them. A low rate of profit per unit, added to lower merchandise costs resulting from quantity buying, and lower operating costs per unit resulting from quantity selling, spells lower prices to the consumer—a competitive advantage which accounts in large measure for the success the chains have achieved and works similarly to the advantage of other large-scale operators.[20]

When we consider the advantages accruing from a more

[20] The amount of net profit per dollar of sales needed to produce a satisfactory return on the invested capital depends upon various factors. One of the most important is the turnover rate—the rapidity with which the capital invested in merchandise can be recovered and reinvested. That, in turn, depends upon the kind of merchandise involved. Naturally, the necessities of life move into consumption faster than items which are less essential or are within the reach of fewer people. For the actual operating results of the chains in the grocery and variety store fields see the reports of the Harvard Bureau of Business Research issued annually. See also *Chain Store Age*, Grocery Edition, May, 1958, page 67, for comment on the small net profit per dollar of sales realized by the food chains.

effective "division of labor," some elaboration is necessary, for that feature of mass distribution has probably been given less credit for the results achieved than it deserves. If, for instance, we turn to the chain-store system as an example of mass distribution, the first thought in the minds of most people is that the chains' advantage lies mainly if not wholly in their buying advantages as compared with their smaller competitors.

Without minimizing the value of quantity purchases, the greater all-round efficiency a large-scale distributor achieves by utilizing the principle of a division of labor probably means far more to him in the long run than all his buying advantages.

Perhaps the best way to illustrate the advantages of a division of labor in distribution is to see what happens when it is not employed. The small-scale retailer provides a typical example. He has to do practically everything himself, just as a shoemaker had to produce a pair of shoes from start to finish before the introduction of shoe-making machinery. He has to select the location of his store, in the first place, although he may have had no experience whatever in that direction. Then he has to lay it out and equip it. He has to buy his initial stock of merchandise, relying mainly, perhaps, on the advice of those from whom he buys.

With his stock of merchandise on hand, he has to trim his windows, prepare his advertising, if he does any, open a set of books, if he keeps any, grant credit, take care of collections, superintend deliveries and wait on customers.

Once established in business, he must listen to visiting salesmen and decide what lines to carry and how much of each; he should be able to analyze his sales so as to determine what items to push and which ones to discontinue; he has to watch his competitors and he must handle his finances so that he may meet his obligations and maintain his credit.

Obviously, no merchant, no matter how smart he is or how hard he has tried to equip himself for all the manifold tasks involved in the successful conduct of a store, can reasonably expect to qualify as an expert in all its branches. He can hardly be an expert buyer, an expert accountant, an expert window-trimmer, an expert debt-collector, an expert advertising manager and an expert merchandiser, and even if he were actually an expert in every one of these departments, he would not have the time to capitalize his versatility.

Compare the situation of the typical small-scale retailer with the division of labor which prevails where the volume is great enough to require and to permit the employment of specialists in each department.

In a typical chain-store organization, for instance, you have a real-estate expert selecting the locations for the individual units and securing the most advantageous terms in the lease. You have merchandising specialists handling both the buying and the selling activities, a personnel director hiring the help and supervising them, a display expert taking care of the store windows and the interior arrangement of the merchandise. Accounting, control, warehousing, transportation, sales promotion, public relations, financial, construction and maintenance experts deal with their special fields. Trained executives establish the chain's policies and see that they are carried out. The store manager, who is the counterpart of the individual merchant so far as the public is concerned, can concentrate almost exclusively on selling.

Without any question, this division of labor, which is found in the department store or in the large independent store of any kind, as well as in the chains, and which is the direct result of large-scale operation, is one of the principal advantages of large-scale operation, although it is not generally recognized as such.

But, it may be asked, while the best skill available may be utilized by the large-scale operator, and while large-scale operation might, indeed, be impossible without it, is it *necessary* for a small store? It is not necessary, but without it the

small store must inevitably remain small. The only way out
for the individual retailer who is unable or unwilling to expand his operation is to affiliate himself with some organization, such as a voluntary chain, or a cooperative enterprise of
a similar type, which will give him the benefit of the expert
guidance and help he must lack as long as he plays a lone
hand.

Although a small-scale retailer can improve his position by
joining a voluntary chain, the full benefits of mass distribution
are available only to retailers large enough to utilize all of
them.[21]

The basis of chain-store strength lies primarily in the fact
that operating more than one store opens the way to greater
volume, with all the benefits which, as we have seen, flow
from it. But, in addition to operating more stores, the chains
have increased their volume per store in the various ways
which have been enumerated.

Whether the cost of bridging the gap between the producer
and the consumer via the old wholesaler-retailer channel is
greater than via the chain stores has been made the subject
of several studies. Although none of these comparisons of
operating costs is too satisfactory, even to their respective
authors, because of the absence of comparable data, the general conclusion is that the consumer pays less for distribution
via the chain stores than via independent stores.[22]

Of course, what is more important to the consumer are the
relative prices in the two types of stores—whether the lower
price is the result of buying advantages, operating economies,
or lower net profits, or a combination of any of those elements.
On that score, numerous studies have been made by impartial authorities, including the Federal Trade Commission,[23]

---

[21] Cf. A. C. Hoffman, *Large Scale Organization in the Food Industries*, Monograph No. 35, T.N.E.C. Study, 1940, pp. 9, 10.

[22] *Expenses and Profits in the Chain Grocery Business*, 1929, Bulletin No. 84,
Bureau of Business Research, Harvard University, June, 1931.

[23] Federal Trade Commission: "Chain Store Inquiry—Prices and Margins of
Chain and Independent Distributors," Vol. IV, 1933, 1934; *The Chain Store Tells
Its Story, op. cit.*, pp. 106, 116, 122, 124.

and the results show a consistent differential in favor of the chains, although its extent varies in different kinds of stores, lines of merchandise and geographical areas. Furthermore, these differentials have undoubtedly narrowed in recent years as a result of greater efficiency on the part of independent stores achieved through affiliation with voluntary chains and in other ways.

After reviewing no less than seventeen different comparative price studies made by others as well as a special study they undertook themselves, Profs. Beckman and Nolen, in their book *The Chain Store Problem*,[24] reached the following significant conclusion:

"From the data presented and analyzed in the present and preceding chapters there can be little doubt that chain stores substantially undersell their independent competitors. In every line of trade that has been studied the chains enjoy a price differential that increases, though not in exact proportion, with the number of units operated. . . . Another significant factor is that the independent merchants are apparently finding ways and means to cut down the chain price differential. The earlier studies revealed consistently wider price differences than the more recent ones."

A realistic, but striking, recognition of the fact that these differentials still obtained, in the grocery field, at any rate, as late as 1945 was the Office of Price Administration's classification of grocery stores, by type of operation and sales per store, as a basis for a differential in price ceilings.[25]

The retail markups established for Group 3, comprising chain stores doing less than $250,000, and Group 4 comprising all retailers doing more than $250,000, were substantially lower than those established for Group 1, comprising independent stores doing under $50,000, or Group 2, comprising independent stores doing between $50,000 and $250,000.

The differential varied from one group of commodities to

[24] *The Chain Store Problem, op. cit.*, p. 136.
[25] O.P.A. Maximum Price Regulations 422 and 423, February 3, 1945.

another, but in some cases the markup set for Groups 1 and 2 was 100% or more higher than that set for Groups 3 and 4. On sugar, for instance, the markups (the addition to the wholesale price to make the retail price) for Groups 1, 2, 3 and 4 were 17%, 12%, 7%, and 6% respectively; on canned milk, 20%, 20%, 10% and 9%; breakfast cereals, 22%, 20%, 13% and 11%; lard, 20%, 18%, 13% and 10%; and coffee, 17%, 17%, 12% and 11%.

Thus, for the first time, with the Government in complete control of the nation's food supply and price structure, the economies made possible by large-scale distribution—the economic facts of life—were officially applied in a practical way. And in 1951, when price control was again invoked, the Office of Price Stabilization—OPA's counterpart—again classified grocery stores by type of operation and sales volume as had been done in 1945.

But the fact that the chain-store system rested upon a sound foundation was not enough to justify its existence in the eyes of those who were bound to feel the effect of chain-store competition. Slowly at first but more rapidly as the tempo of chain-store growth quickened, a wave of anti-chain agitation spread through the country. The chains are still feeling some of the consequences of that crusade, as will be shown in succeeding chapters but, fortunately for them, the hue and cry died down appreciably 15 years ago and is hardly likely to be revived.

PART II

STRUGGLE

CHAPTER VI

THE CHAINS ENCOUNTER
OPPOSITION

AT THE TURN of the century the number of chain stores in operation in all fields was negligible. Certainly at that time nobody could have foreseen how quickly the chain-store idea was to spread and grow, and only the most imaginative and timorous could have regarded it as posing a threat to the existing order.

Shortly after the turn of the century, however, as has been pointed out, the situation began to take on a new aspect. Not only did the chains then in existence begin to expand at a somewhat faster rate, but the possibilities of the chain-store idea began to attract newcomers in increasing numbers. What is more to the point, some of the newcomers made a more spectacular entrance than their predecessors had done. This trend brought into the picture not only new chains but new kinds of stores, new standards of retailing and more aggressive forms of merchandising.

Outstanding in this category was the United Cigar Stores Company, which opened its first store in New York in 1901. The story of its conception, its plans, its principles and its remarkable growth in the 25 years which followed was told on the occasion of its 25th anniversary by Herbert S. Collins, its vice-president and one of its founders.[1]

[1] *Chain Store Age*, May, 1926, p. 13.

According to Mr. Collins, the idea of the chain originated with George J. Whelan in 1900. At that time he was in the wholesale cigar business in Syracuse, N.Y., and, in addition, had been running a retail cigar store there since 1892. The remarkable success of that store, which was years ahead of cigar stores of that period, suggested to Mr. Whelan that the retail tobacco trade was ripe for reform.

"The average cigar store of that time," Mr. Collins recalled, "hardly deserved to be called a *store* at all. Certainly it followed none of the fundamental principles of retail merchandising which even the poorest merchant recognizes today. It was inadequately stocked, the fixtures were of the most primitive kind, and little or no attempt was made at window or inside display. The principal attraction consisted of a row of chairs and cuspidors, newspapers and magazines for the convenience of idlers who elected to congregate there. An empty carton or two and several theatrical posters comprised the usual contents of the windows, and, but for the wooden Indian outside the store, the passerby would hardly have been able to tell whether it was a cigar store or a real estate office."

But Mr. Whelan's store was different. It had no wooden Indian and no chairs for loafers. Indeed, signs around the store announced: "No loafing, all room needed for business." The windows were tastefully stocked with cigars, cigarettes, pipes and tobacco, and, instead of theatrical posters, attractive signs announcing special sales or the contests which Mr. Whelan was constantly staging were conspicuously displayed.

Sales averaged about $250 a day—a tremendous volume for those days.

In 1900, came the big idea. If a cigar store run along these original lines worked out so profitably in Syracuse, why not duplicate it elsewhere? Why not establish a *chain* of them throughout the country?

A second store was accordingly opened in Elmira and, in

quick succession, others in Utica, Troy and Auburn. They were all money-makers right from the start.

The following year, Mr. Whelan and his associates opened an office in New York and laid their plans for organizing the United Cigar Stores Company. Within a very few months the corporation was launched with a capital stock of $2,000,000.

The first store to bear the name that was to make chain-store history opened on Nassau Street, New York, that year. It was only ten feet wide, with a 7-foot window, but it was set up after the style which had proved so successful in the Whelan stores upstate.

The underlying principles of the new venture were (1) to sell the best cigar to be had for the price asked and to sell smoking and chewing tobacco for less than it could be obtained elsewhere; (2) to operate on a cash basis; and (3) to extend genuine courtesy and service to customers.

Within a few days after the first store was opened, seven more were bought from an operator who had been running them along the old lines. The kind of stores they were is indicated, Mr. Collins pointed out, by the fact that the value of the stock and fixtures in all seven totalled less than $6,000.

From that time on, the chain spread as rapidly as suitable locations could be secured. How rapid that was is revealed in Table 16 showing the company's growth in sales year by year from 1901 to 1925.

"We had plenty of opposition," Mr. Collins noted. "The independents fought us tooth and nail—not because we were a chain but because we were supposed to be the outlet for the 'tobacco trust.' In those trust-busting days, it was the easiest thing in the world to raise a hue and cry against anything connected with 'the interests' and the 'tobacco trust' was regarded as one of the wickedest of them all."

But, as the sales record indicates, the louder the independents protested against the new cigar stores, the more eagerly the public flocked to them.

However, even though the complaints of the independent tobacconists failed to move the public, they could hardly have gone unnoticed by independent retailers in other fields. How soon would it be, they must have asked themselves, before some equally revolutionary type of store or method of merchandising appeared in their own fields?

TABLE 16

SALES OF UNITED CIGAR STORES
COMPANY, 1901-1925

1901	$ 93,374	1914	$29,902,712
1902	1,754,593	1915	31,038,849
1903	6,025,489	1916	35,822,984
1904	7,243,729	1917	42,913,234
1905	9,839,231	1918	52,035,735
1906	12,727,906	1919	61,874,070
1907	16,532,307	1920	78,918,582
1908	16,881,596	1921	76,521,198
1909	18,871,531	1922	72,484,254
1910	21,774,538	1923	74,199,273
1911	24,383,827	1924	79,738,566
1912	26,718,281	1925	85,060,104
1913	29,574,950		

So far as organized efforts to check the encroachment of chain stores were concerned, the most determined, at that time, appeared in the drug and grocery fields.

In the drug field, however, the effort was directed not against the chains, as such, but against "price-cutters" in general. Certainly the development of the drug chains prior to 1910 was negligible enough to have given the established order little cause for alarm so far as normal competition was concerned. But when it became apparent that the newcomers were to be aggressive merchandisers, lining up with the cut-rate independents and department stores, who had long been a thorn in the side of the trade as a whole, the character of their competition rather than its volume was naturally a most disturbing factor.

That the so-called "price-cutting evil" had plagued the drug trade long before the drug chains came into the picture, is revealed by the drastic measures the National Wholesale Druggists Association took to cope with it as far back as 1882 and even earlier. By influencing manufacturers of patent medicines and proprietaries—the principal items exploited by the price-cutters—to confine their sales to members of their association, who by their membership agreed to maintain standard prices, the NWDA was able to keep the evil within reasonable bounds. Their hand was strengthened when their methods were upheld by the N.Y. Court of Appeals[2] when a price-cutter claimed he had been "boycotted" by the association because he was not on the association's approved list. On the contrary, decided the Court, whatever "boycott" existed was of his own making, for all he had to do to get all the merchandise he needed was to give up his price-cutting practices and join the association.

In the fight against price-cutting, the manufacturers of many patent medicines and proprietaries cooperated fully with the regular distributors. They developed all sorts of "agency" and other plans designed to confine the sales of their products to wholesalers who agreed (1) to maintain established wholesale prices; and (2) to sell only to retailers who had likewise agreed to maintain established retail prices.

Despite these determined and persistent efforts of both manufacturers and wholesalers, the cut-rate stores somehow managed to get at least enough of the protected items to enable them to feature their cut-price offerings constantly and conspicuously.

When the drug chains came into the picture, they had no other practical course but to join the price-cutters. How could they pass on to the public the economies made possible by

[2] Park v. NWDA, 175 N.Y. 1.

chain-store operation unless they sold for less? And how could they drive home more effectively the fact that their prices really were lower than by featuring *standard* items below the prices which the independents generally were required by their sources of supply to maintain?

It is not surprising, therefore, that one of the many cases instituted by manufacturers against price-cutters in the days when price-maintenance agreements were held to be lawful (so far, at least, as proprietaries and patent medicines were concerned) was directed against one of the pioneer drug chains—the Jaynes Drug Co., which not only conducted a wholesale drug business but had launched a chain of drug stores in Boston. The manufacturer complained that Jaynes was getting its supplies of plaintiff's products from wholesalers who had agreed not to sell them to price-cutters, and was instrumental, therefore, in getting such wholesalers to violate their contracts. The injunction was granted on December 12, 1906,[3] the court overruling the chain's contention that such contracts were invalid because they restrained competition in violation of the Sherman Anti-Trust Act.

But this victory, and similar decisions won by the manufacturer of "Peruna,"[4] were short-lived, for, in 1911,[5] the U.S. Supreme Court decided unequivocally that all kinds of price-maintenance agreements were invalid except those involving items covered by patents or copyrights—and "patent" medicines and proprietaries did not come within that category.

In the face of that decision, the fight against price-cutters had to take a new tack. The only way price maintenance could be achieved legally now was through legislation specifically authorizing it. From that time on, various bills were introduced in Congress to achieve the desired objective, but although some of them got to the stage of public hearings, none

[3] Dr. Miles Medical Co. *v*. Jaynes, 149 Fed. R. 838 (1906).
[4] Park *v*. Hartman, 145 Fed. R. 358 (1906); reversed 153 Fed. R. 24 (1907).
[5] Dr. Miles Medical Co. *v*. John D. Park & Sons Co., 220 U.S. 373 (1911).

was ever enacted. Not until 42 States had legalized price maintenance through what were known as Fair Trade Acts did Congress add its blessing by recognizing such contracts in the Miller-Tydings Act of 1937.

The story of the long effort to legalize price maintenance is pertinent here only because the aggressive competition of the chains, and particularly the drug chains, was constantly held up as the horrible example of what made legalized price maintenance necessary.

Strangely enough, however, not many years were to pass before the drug chains, to whom price-cutting was supposed to be so vital, joined the independents in a nationwide demand for legislation designed to eliminate or curtail it. Most of them have been among the strongest supporters of Fair Trade, as price maintenance came to be known, ever since.

Undoubtedly the coming of the depression and its effect on retail sales in general had much to do with the drug chains' change of attitude. What happened is clearly shown by an analysis of the operating results in chain drug stores made by the Harvard Bureau of Business Research for the years 1929, 1931 and 1932. It showed that whereas average sales per store of $116,400 in 1929 had yielded a typical net profit of 3%, average sales dropped to $105,000 in 1931 and showed a fractional net loss; and to $90,398 in 1932, with a typical net loss of nearly 3%!

Under such conditions, cut-price merchandising lost much of its attraction. When price appeal failed to produce the volume needed to sustain it, it had little to commend it. The situation was further aggravated by the impact of a new and formidable type of price-cutter in the shape of what were called "pine-boards." These crudely set up outlets featured nationally advertised proprietaries, toiletries and other drug-store products at deep-cut prices which the chains were no longer interested in meeting.

At any rate, in 1932, the late Charles R. Walgreen came

out publicly for legalized price maintenance. His stand was quickly endorsed by George M. Gales, president of Louis K. Liggett Co., Malcolm G. Gibbs, president of Peoples Drug Stores, and other leading drug-chain operators.

The ensuing campaign for Fair Trade laws in state legislatures, with the chains lined up with the independent druggists, was singularly successful. Before many years were to pass, no less than 45 States had enacted such laws. When the first law of the kind, passed in California in 1931, proved abortive, because all it did was to legalize price contracts between those who would sign them, leaving untouched the price-cutters who naturally refused to sign such a contract, the weakness was eliminated by an amendment in 1933. The new California law made a price-maintenance contract with even a single retailer binding on *all* retailers in the state whether they were parties to it or not. Then the big question was whether such a unique provision was constitutional. In December, 1936, the U.S. Supreme Court held that it was.[6]

Following that decision, one State after another enacted a Fair Trade law. Within a couple of years, every State in the Union had one with the exception of Missouri, Vermont and Texas, in which three States no such law was ever passed.

But even when price maintenance agreements were enforceable in 45 States, not all manufacturers who would have liked to have availed themselves of the privilege felt free to do so. For such agreements were still condemned by Federal laws which manufacturers engaged in interstate commerce could not ignore. To remove that remaining obstacle, the Miller-Tydings Act was pushed through Congress in 1937. It exempted such agreements from the ban imposed by Federal laws provided they were authorized by the laws of the States in which they were made.

Thereafter, the Fair Trade set-up was widely adopted by

[6] The Pep Boys *v.* Pyroil Sales Co., Inc., and Kunsman *v.* Factor & Co., 229 U.S. 198 (1936).

manufacturers of branded lines, although it was favored in some fields more than in others. In the drug field, for instance, it became almost universal. That was because of the wide demand for it by distributors of all types—wholesalers, chains and independents. On the other hand, it made little headway in the grocery field, largely because the chains in that field were opposed to it on principle. They wanted no restriction whatever on their freedom to set their own resale prices. As they had become a substantial factor in the distribution set-up, their suppliers generally eschewed Fair Trade. In other fields in which trade-marked articles figured extensively, the adoption of Fair Trade was more or less spotty. Among its most ardent supporters were book publishers and the leading manufacturers of electrical appliances for consumer use. The latter were to spend millions of dollars thereafter in enforcement proceedings against discount-houses and other price-cutters.

From 1937 to 1951, Fair Trade seemed to be so firmly entrenched that even those who rebelled against it most strenuously came to regard further recourse to the courts as hopeless. Then, in 1951, the Fair Trade apple-cart was suddenly upset by a decision of the United States Supreme Court which was as unexpected as it was devastating.[7] That decision held that while the Miller-Tydings Act unquestionably gave federal sanction to certain price-maintenance agreements, it contained nothing which bound non-signers of such contracts to respect the minimum price they established!

The effect of that decision was to precipitate price-wars of such a sensational character that they made front-page news in the daily press for several weeks. The friends of Fair Trade were quick to capitalize the situation by demanding that Congress immediately pass new legislation to plug the hole which the Supreme Court had found in the Miller-Tydings Act. Such a law, the McGuire Act, was promptly passed. It

[7] Calvert Distillers Corp. v. Schwegmann, 341 U.S. 384 (1951).

was approved July 14, 1952. It looked as if Fair Trade had not only been restored but would thereafter be impregnable.

That, however, did not prove to be the case. Price-cutters who were taken to court took a new tack. They contended that the non-signer clause violated the guarantees contained in *State* constitutions. That contention was sustained in so many cases that by 1962 Fair Trade had become unenforceable against non-signers in no less than 24 of the 45 States under whose Fair Trade laws they had been specifically covered. This was in addition to the four States and the District of Columbia, in which no Fair Trade law had ever been enacted.

To remedy that situation, the friends of Fair Trade decided to appeal to Congress again—that the only course left was to put Fair Trade on a Federal rather than a State basis. They had an appropriate bill prepared accordingly and it was promptly introduced in both Houses in 1958. It got only as far, however, as the public hearing stage.

In 1961, a new tack was taken. Federal legislation based entirely on the right of trade-mark owners to protect their goodwill was introduced under the name of Quality Stabilization bills. They were approved by Committees of both Houses but did not reach a vote on the floor. Undoubtedly they will be reintroduced in the 1963 Congress. If they become law, they would enable trade-mark owners to prevent price-cutting without reliance upon any price-maintenance agreement and irrespective of the absence of State laws on the subject.

As of September 17, 1962, however, the effectiveness of Fair Trade was seriously diminished even in the 22 States in which it was still legally enforceable. Practically all of such States were contiguous to one or more States in which Fair Trade was unenforceable against non-signers. Thus, many retailers who would have preferred to have maintained Fair Trade prices in compliance with the laws of their own States found it impracticable to do so in the face of the competition of price-cutters in a contiguous State who were free to cut to their heart's content. In such cases, manufacturers were naturally reluctant to proceed against distributors who were disregarding Fair Trade only because they had no alternative if they were to remain competitive. The strength of the discount store development was unmistakably sounding the knell of Fair Trade some 30 years after its widespread adoption.[8]

But to get back to the days when the drug chains could and did cut prices without restraint, their aggressive competition incurred deep resentment on the part of their independent competitors and the wholesale druggists who supplied them.

How far this feeling had developed by 1914 is indicated by the comprehensive series of articles by Charles W. Hurd and M. M. Zimmerman, then of the editorial staff of *Printers' Ink*, published in successive issues of that weekly, beginning with that of September 10, 1914.

The first article in the series was entitled: "Why Advertisers Must Give Chain Store Growth Their Serious Attention."

[8] The 22 States in which Fair Trade was enforceable as of September 17, 1962 were:

1. Arizona	9. Maryland	17. N. Dakota
2. California	10. Massachusetts	18. Pennsylvania
3. Connecticut	11. Mississippi	19. Rhode Island
4. Delaware	12. Nevada	20. S. Dakota
5. Hawaii	13. New Hampshire	21. Virginia
6. Idaho	14. New Jersey	22. Wisconsin
7. Illinois	15. New York	
8. Maine	16. N. Carolina	

The 28 States in which Fair Trade was not enforceable as of that date were:

1. Alabama	10. Kentucky	19. Oklahoma
2. Alaska	11. Louisiana	20. Oregon
3. Arkansas	12. Michigan	21. S. Carolina
4. Colorado	13. Minnesota	22. Tennessee
5. Florida	14. Missouri	23. Texas
6. Georgia	15. Montana	24. Utah
7. Indiana	16. Nebraska	25. Vermont
8. Iowa	17. New Mexico	26. Washington
9. Kansas	18. *Ohio	27. W. Virginia
		28. Wyoming

The District of Columbia never had a Fair Trade Act.
* Conflicting decisions in the State courts must await action of higher court.

It pointed out that the system then consisted of no less than 2,000 chains with some 20,000 stores. Among them it listed United Cigar Stores Company with 900, Great Atlantic & Pacific Tea Company with 800, F. W. Woolworth Company with 774, and the Riker-Hegeman drug chain with 105 and "growing at the rate of more than three a month."

Why this development was believed to be "portentous to advertising" was thus explained:

"That the profound change in trade channels which these developments mark is portentous to advertising cannot be doubted. Consider them and their results. Unusual ability, no doubt, from the start; from that to system and standardization; thence to direct buying in quantity and special discounts; then on to price-cutting and the promotion of private brands—these are the undisputed means and methods of the majority of them."

Referring to the chains as a "new and formidable power in business," the authors pointed out that they had been strengthened by the rulings of the Supreme Court virtually forbidding price maintenance, and asserted that "there is no wonder it has swelled the uneasiness to alarm and sent the manufacturers, jobbers and independent retailers to Congress for relief. The legislation embodied in the Stevens bill, the Metz bill and perhaps the Clayton bill, to name no others, is a direct assault upon all types of concentrated retailing," by which they referred to the chains, department stores and mail-order houses.

In the second article, reference was made to a circular said to have been sent to grocery jobbers by one of the leading manufacturers of a nationally advertised breakfast cereal.

"Any jobber is blind who shuts his eyes to the increasing menace of the chains," it read, "a menace to your business far more than to ours.

"Think a moment. What has become of the old corner tobacconist? Answer: United Cigar Stores. What has become of the old 'home-cooking' restaurants in so many cities? Answer: Child's, $12,000,000 (backed by Standard Oil) and Thompson's, $6,000,000—to say nothing of several others. Big Business (United Drug Company and Riker-Hegeman) already dominates the drug stores of New York, Boston and Chicago."

And then the authors add that the bare possibility that the cereal company in question "may end its long fight against the price-cutting chain stores in the grocery field by throwing overboard its famous 'square deal' policy and surrendering to them is really momentous news. It gives us a measure of the growing strength of the chains, as well as the weakness or indifference of the jobbers, to say nothing of the other elements in the field."

But the efforts of leading grocery manufacturers to protect their traditional channels of distribution by refusing to sell direct to the chains persisted for many years thereafter. That their policy was dictated by the pressures exerted on them by wholesalers rather than by any desire on their part to handicap the chains is suggested clearly enough by some of the cases which grew out of the activities of wholesalers' associations in various parts of the country.

Thus, in 1922, the Federal Trade Commission ordered the Wholesale Grocers Association of El Paso to cease and desist from influencing manufacturers not to sell direct to Standard Grocery Co., which had been founded in 1916, and had a chain of six stores in El Paso besides running a regular wholesale grocery business. The order was sustained by the Court which pointed out that "the combining of wholesaling and retailing is not a novelty and is not unlawful." [9]

In Southern California, on April 2, 1924, the United States asked for an injunction against the Southern California Wholesale Grocers Association, a food-brokers' association, and others, alleging that for the preceding three years they

[9] Wholesale Groc. Assn. v. Fed. Trade Commn., 277 Fed. R. 657 (1922).

had influenced manufacturers to refuse to sell direct to chains. After a trial lasting four weeks, Federal Judge W. P. James granted the injunction, although he conceded that it might be true, as the defendants contended, that "the practice of the chain stores to attract business by advertising and selling certain lines at close to non-profit prices disturbed the system of retail business." [10]

Along the same lines was a complaint filed by the Federal Trade Commission against the Arkansas Wholesale Grocers Association on September 13, 1924. It charged that the wholesalers had designated "the channel of distribution commencing with the manufacturer or producer, flowing thence to the wholesaler, from the wholesaler to the retailer and from the retailer to the consuming public, as the only regular and legitimate channel of distribution," and had brought pressure to bear on manufacturers who dealt with "irregular" channels by threatened "boycott" and other coercive means.

Typical of the methods used was a bulletin of January 9, 1922, sent by the association to its members, containing the following suggestion:

"We hope that all wholesale grocers will look over their list of manufacturers from whom they buy and see the ones that are selling the chain stores at the same price they are selling the wholesale grocer. When you buy from them, you give them the club that they are pounding you with and the club that they pound the retailer with."

An earlier bulletin, November 3, 1921, referred to a list of "undesirables" published in a trade paper, *Duncan's Trade Register,* and added "that is what he terms the manufacturers who are selling the chain stores at the prices they sell the wholesaler," urging members to subscribe to the paper in order to get the list.

The Federal Trade Commission issued an order requiring

[10] U.S. *v.* So. Calif. Wholesale Grocers Assn., 7 Fed. (2nd) 944 (1925).

the wholesalers to cease and desist the activities in question, and the Court upheld it.[11]

But the chains did not rely upon the Government to fight their battles for them. Instead they took their case right to the manufacturers themselves.

The interesting story of this phase of their early struggles was told in some detail by the late Arthur C. Jones, back in 1925. At that time, he was the president of his own chain, The Piggly-Wiggly California Co., and also secretary and treasurer of the Western States Chain Grocers' Association.

"During the year 1921, the chain operators of Los Angeles seriously considered the matter of buying direct from manufacturers," he declared,[12] "but met with such a determined resistance from local wholesaler trade and brokers that it was thought that little could be done about the matter then.

"However, in September, 1921, J. A. Daley, president of Daley's, Inc., E. F. Stanton, president of Bay Cities Merc. Co., Sam Seelig, president of Sam Seelig Co. [predecessor of Safeway Stores], F. E. Chaffee, president of Chaffee's, Inc., and myself went in a body to San Francisco and Seattle and thence eastward to Chicago, Detroit and New York, stopping off at intermediate points wherever there was a manufacturer of importance."

This task force, as it would be called today, represented at the time about 200 stores doing about $10,000,000 a year. Four years later, the same group had 650 stores and was doing some $40,000,000 a year.

Altogether, the group called on 60 manufacturers, and Mr. Jones records that most of them reacted unfavorably. However five of them were won over and agreed to sell the chains direct and did so from that time on.

The arguments presented by the task force covered four main points:

[11] Arkansas Wholesale Grocers Assn. v. Fed. Trade Commn., 18 Fed. (2nd) 866.
[12] *Chain Store Age*, November, 1925, p. 11.

1. If the grocery chains grew as big as their early history indicated they would, no wholesale grocer could carry adequate warehouse stocks to meet the chains' requirements.

2. If the wholesaler did not actually warehouse the merchandise but had it delivered by manufacturers direct to the chains' own warehouses, why should the chains pay middlemen for doing something they did not do?

3. The chains had reached the point where it was essential that they could be assured of an uninterrupted supply at prices that were economically sound, but unless they bought direct, they were at the mercy of middlemen.

4. The consumer had a right to enjoy whatever savings the chain-store system of distribution made possible, and eventually the consumer must be served.

Of course, the chains did not fail to point out that if the manufacturers of national brands refused to heed these arguments, the chains would be forced to deal with smaller firms who *would* sell them direct, and the day would come when the chains could get along without the national brands or without being dependent upon them.

"In the case of a well-known dessert, where the manufacturer refused and still refuses to sell us direct," Mr. Jones illustrated, "the chains have fostered and established here a local product and it now ranks *ahead* of the national brand both with independent retailers and chains. And this national product is as well known all over the country as any product you can name."

Undismayed by the cool reception they got in 1921, in the fall of the following year the task force made the same trip again and the same visits. The result was that fifteen more manufacturers agreed to sell the chains direct.

Having achieved so much with the buying power of only five chains behind them, the group then called a meeting of the 26 chains operating at that time in the western states, and organized the Western State Chain Grocers' Association. It represented 685 stores.

From that time on, more and more manufacturers changed their policy regarding selling the chains direct and, although at the time Mr. Jones wrote the article in question, there were still some important manufacturers who refused to recognize the chains, it was not long before practically all of them fell into line.

A by-product of the chains' direct approach to the manufacturers was an investigation by the Federal authorities of the activities of the wholesalers and brokers which had brought it about. That investigation resulted in the suit against the wholesalers to which reference has previously been made.

Incidentally, Mr. Jones noted that the 26 members of the association then had 1,621 stores in operation, with a volume of more than $100,000,000 a year, compared with the 685 stores they had only three years earlier. He attributed the rapidity of their growth at that time to the fact that they were able to get the necessities of life to the consumer cheaper than had been possible before because they were able to "perform the functions of both wholesaler and retailer at one cost."

So much for the earlier reactions of the established order to the challenge of the chains. As has been shown, the first steps taken by the wholesalers in both the grocery and the drug fields were confined to entrenching themselves with manufacturers as the only "regular and legitimate" channel of distribution.[13] When the drug trade found that its efforts to halt price-cutting was nullified by the Supreme Court decision condemning price maintenance as illegal and the wholesale grocers found that they could not legally work on manufacturers to hold the line, other steps were naturally discussed.

In the second decade of the century, chain-store expansion in all lines had been so active that by the early '20s the move-

---

[13] Reminiscent of this attitude on the part of the "established order" of 35 years ago, is the current disposition in some quarters to refer to discount houses as "illegitimate" retailers.

ment was being widely discussed as a menace to the existing order. Without any legal means to curb price-cutting and with the chains' right to buy direct now beginning to be recognized by manufacturers and producers in almost all lines, about the only possible way left to check further chain-store growth would be through the legislatures. It is not surprising, therefore, that at the convention of the National Association of Retail Grocers, at Los Angeles, in 1922,[14] it was openly suggested that "there ought to be a law" to limit the number of chain stores permitted in any one community.

What followed that suggestion, whether as a result of it or not, made chain-store history for many years thereafter—a period which was to prove extremely difficult and costly to the chains but from which they were to emerge the stronger, perhaps, for their tribulation.

[14] Hayward and White, *Chain Stores* (McGraw-Hill Book Company, New York, 1925), 2nd Edition, p. 393.

CHAPTER VII

"THERE OUGHT TO BE A LAW"

THE HISTORY of retailing reveals that every innovation in distribution methods has been opposed by those fearful of its impact on the existing order. Department stores, mail-order houses, house-to-house sellers and, most recently, the supermarkets, each in turn ran into more or less organized opposition. Almost invariably the State legislatures were appealed to for special taxes or other restrictive measures designed to check the new method of distribution or to stop it altogether.[1]

But nothing of this kind ever approached in intensity or scope what the chains ran into. The rapidity of their growth between 1910 and 1920, coupled with the price-cutting which many of them practiced, made them the target for plenty of criticism from manufacturers, wholesalers and independent retailers, but no definite effort to check their progress other than indirectly seems to have been made before the early '20s.

True enough, the chain-store "menace" was given as one of the principal reasons for proposed legislation to end the predatory price-cutting evil, but nobody had gone so far as to suggest a more direct attack on the chains themselves.

In 1922, however, at the convention of the National Association of Retail Grocers at Los Angeles[2] it was openly sug-

[1] John P. Nichols, *The Chain Store Tells Its Story* (Institute of Distribution, New York, 1940) p. 127.
[2] See p. 124, *supra*.

gested that the number of chain stores in any community should be limited by law.

No doubt the idea appealed strongly to the grocers who heard it proposed, but how was it to be implemented?

Two approaches naturally presented themselves. The first would be a law flatly prohibiting the operation of more than one store, or more than some other specified number of stores, by a single owner. The second, less drastic but potentially as effective, would be to use the States' taxing power to impose special license taxes on chain stores severe enough to make the opening of additional stores too expensive to permit profitable operation.

The trouble with either approach, however, as the anti-chain forces must have been advised by their lawyers, was that such a law might be held unconstitutional.[3] The Fourteenth Amendment of the Constitution forbids any State to deprive any person of life, liberty or property without due process of law or to deny to any person the equal protection of the laws.

Obviously the chains would claim that a flat prohibition against operating more than a given number of stores would be a denial of their right to engage in a legitimate activity; and special taxes aimed at the chains alone would be assailed, in turn, on the ground that they violated the constitutional guarantee of the equal protection of the laws to all.

The only ground upon which such laws could possibly be sustained would be (1) that they represented a valid exercise of the State's police power—the power which every State has to take whatever measures are necessary to preserve the public health, security, morals or general welfare; and (2) although the equal protection of the laws demands that taxes shall be levied equally upon all who fall within the same classification, tax equality is not necessary as between those who

[3] See views expressed by Charles Wesley Dunn, general counsel for the National Association of Retail Grocers, 1928, p. 161 *post.*

fall within different classifications—and independent stores and chain stores might reasonably be classified differently for taxation purposes.

In any event, however, the suggestion made at the Los Angeles convention seems to have been taken seriously by at least one delegation. The Missouri grocers promptly secured the introduction of an anti-chain-store bill in the very next session of their legislature.[4]

This bill was a particularly vicious one, too. It provided for a tax of $50 on the third store (in the State), $100 on the fourth, $200 on the fifth, and so on. By that rate of geometric progression, the tax on the tenth store would have been $6,400!

The bill was disapproved by the House Committee by a vote of eight to two, but the Senate Committee approved it. Public hearings were held and testimony was offered showing that chain-store overhead and chain-store prices were both substantially lower than those of their competitors. Comparative prices of 32 well-known grocery items, as of February 20, 1923, were used to establish a substantial differential in favor of the chains.

The bill did not pass. If, however, its introduction gives Missouri the distinction of having been the first State to consider the enactment of such a law, it should not be overlooked that Missouri was likewise the first State to kill such a proposal. Furthermore, Missouri shares with nineteen other States the distinction of never having enacted an anti-chain measure of any kind.

The next year a milder type of anti-chain law was introduced in the Virginia legislature by Senator Saxon Holt of Newport News.[5] It provided that chain stores in communities of 2,500 population or more should pay a tax of $15 on every $1,000 worth of merchandise purchased, if only for two stores,

[4] Hayward and White, *Chain Stores*, op. cit., p. 363.
[5] *Retail Ledger*, Philadelphia, February 1, 1924.

and $20 for every $1,000 worth of merchandise purchased if three or more stores were operated. The fate of the bill is not recorded, but apparently it failed.

One anti-chain bill is reported to have been introduced in 1923,[6] another in 1924, two in 1925 and a fifth in 1926, but references to them do not identify the States involved. All five failed to pass.

Then in 1927, by which time the hue and cry against chain stores had gained rapidly in volume, no less than thirteen bills aimed at the chains were offered in various State legislatures, including Alabama, Arkansas, Illinois, Iowa, Georgia, Kansas, Maryland, North Carolina, Pennsylvania and Wisconsin. Three of them, Maryland, North Carolina and Georgia, passed bills aimed at chain stores in general. A fourth, Pennsylvania, passed one aimed only at chain drug stores.

The Maryland law is of special interest because it went after its objective head on. It flatly prohibited the operation of more than five chain stores in Allegany County by any individual or corporation and, for full measure, it also imposed a license fee of $500 on each chain store operated. The same type of bill was considered that year in Arkansas, Iowa, Kansas and Wisconsin, but only the Maryland bill was enacted.[7]

Obviously the Maryland law would have achieved its purpose effectively, and the chains could not permit it to stand unchallenged.

Accordingly an action was promptly started by the Keystone Grocery & Tea Co. in the Circuit Court of Allegany County to have the law declared unconstitutional.[8] Other chains, including the F. W. Woolworth Company, which filed

---

[6] All data relating to anti-chain-store legislation is drawn from the *Retailers Manual of Taxes and Regulations*, 1960-61 and earlier editions, compiled and published by the Institute of Distribution and Variety Stores Association, New York.

[7] *Chain Store Age*, June, 1927.

[8] Keystone Grocery & Tea Co. *v.* Huster, unreported, but appearing in the invaluable collection of cases entitled *Chain Stores in the Law Courts*, compiled by E. W. Simms, of White & Simms, for the Institute of Distribution, 1939, p. 1.

a brief, supported the proceeding, for a favorable outcome was obviously of the utmost importance if the chains were to continue to function.

The Keystone company had been established in 1917, and in the ten years of its existence had grown to the point where it had 210 stores in all, although only nine of them were in Allegany County. Under the law in question, it was confronted with the alternative of closing four stores and paying an annual tax of $500 on each of the five retained, or being found guilty of a misdemeanor.

On April 21, 1928, Judge Albert A. Doub handed down his decision. Recognizing the far-reaching significance of the issues involved, he wrote an extensive opinion. He declared:

"This seems to be the first case in which a statute dealing with the chain stores has been considered by any of the Courts of this country except the case of The Great Atlantic & Pacific Tea Company v. Doughton, Commissioner of Revenue of North Carolina, in the Superior Court of Wake County, North Carolina. The Act there passed on was one to impose a special license tax on owners of six stores or more, while such tax was not imposed on owners of five stores or less, and the Court held the act to be unconstitutional and void. No opinion was filed but the findings of facts showed the principles involved in the case before us, or most of them, were considered and the act was declared to be unconstitutional and void."

Considering the chain's claim that the law in question violated the Fourteenth Amendment of the Constitution, Judge Doub said:

"The plaintiff is engaged in an innocent, ordinary, useful and necessary business, permitted and authorized by the laws of this State and every other State. It has made substantial investments in merchandise, stock, legal obligations and commitments for leases and intangible property, in organizing its business and building up its good will. These investments, to the extent of all nine chain stores, will be substantially impaired by the provisions of this statute. As far as the five stores are concerned the effect of the license fee of five hundred dollars will be to impair the profits on the investment to a very material degree and the owners will evidently be deprived of property under the provisions of the first and second sections of the Act. One store in the city of Cumberland may pay a tax of twenty dollars [a tax levied on all retailers based on amount of inventory carried] while the chain store will be required to pay a license tax of five hundred and twenty dollars, although both of them are engaged in the same general business, conducting it in substantially the same manner, having the same amount of capital invested, subject to the same losses and perhaps able to secure, as a result of the business, similar profits. It is impossible to declare that both of them will receive, if this Act is to be enforced, the equal protection of the laws as required by the Fourteenth Amendment of the Constitution."

Judge Doub pointed out further that as "there is nothing characteristic of the chain store that makes it peculiarly and essentially different in organization, in plan or in method of doing business from other stores similarly organized but not classified as chain stores," the law represented an unreasonable and unjustifiable discrimination between the chain stores and other stores of the same general class.

Furthermore, the Court decided that a license tax of $500 was so out of line with customary mercantile license taxes that it was "unreasonable, oppressive and confiscatory," particularly as it was a flat charge without relation to locality, inventory value, sales or profits.

Of course it was contended in behalf of the law that, even though it did discriminate against chain stores, such discrimination was justified as an exercise by the State of its "police power."

But Judge Doub couldn't see it that way. Said he:

"What is there in terms of the Act that bears upon public order, security, health or morals? It is not directed against any of the practices alleged to be peculiar to the chain-store business and charged to be objectionable. It recites in the title that the object is to limit the number of chain stores and to provide an additional license fee and penalties. Its purpose is not regulation, not correction of abuses and not the prevention of monopoly, but reduction of certain classes of stores (and raising revenue) of any conceivable size, conducted under any conceivable plan, for one organization in Allegany County. It permits the five chain stores to indulge in all the practices said to be objectionable, provided only five are guilty of such alleged offenses. All of the five chain stores may be located in the city of Cumberland or of Frostburg. They may be permitted to monopolize all the retail grocery business of the city to the selfish profit of the owner and without making any charitable contributions to the community. They may undersell and eliminate competitors and send to other places their profits; and yet they are perfectly free to develop into a monopoly, if such a thing is possible, by underselling their competitors and driving them all out of business. The retail grocery business is not classified as a public service business, affected with any public interest or *quasi* public interest."

Turning to the other side of the picture, Judge Doub took judicial notice of the many ways in which chain stores serve the public interest. He said:

"By purchasing direct from the manufacturer and producer and eliminating the profits and expenses of the wholesaler, jobber and broker and the cost of delivery and selling for cash and thereby escaping the usual losses resulting from sales on credit the chains are more likely to give to the farmer, truckman and consumer part of the middle man's profit and so to become a blessing to society and the public generally. Indeed the very elements so earnestly insisted upon by the defendants as a justification for this extra license fee are the very elements that would seem to justify the development of the chain store.

"The testimony does not disclose that there is anything sinister about their practices foreboding any evil to the public which can be anticipated, but it does show that the chain stores are more cleanly and sanitary than others; that they are conducted with skill and efficiency; that they do not delude the buyer into purchasing goods by giving him credit when he is unable to pay for them; that they turn over their stock more rapidly than other stores and do not keep on their shelves goods long enough to deteriorate and become unwholesome or impaired in quality and that through them the tendency is to reduce the cost to the consumer. With the rapid development of means of transit and the increase in the number of automobiles, now owned by almost every family in the country, delivery of goods by the merchant is no longer so necessary, and the buyer can save something of the cost of operating his automobile by saving the expense of delivery. Moreover, chain stores help to insure regular rentals, furnish regular employment, stabilize the value of real estate and spend a large part of the proceeds of their sales in the community."

Concluding that there was nothing in the record that even remotely proved that the Act bore "any relation either directly or indirectly to the protection of the general public in their health, morals, good order, security or general welfare," Judge Doub found the law "repugnant to the Constitution" and issued a permanent injunction restraining its enforcement.

Judge Doub's reasoning has been quoted at such length not only because his opinion was the first to be handed down in a case involving anti-chain legislation, but because it presents many of the arguments the chains were to use again and again in support of their contention that anti-chain-store taxes were inescapably in conflict with the Constitution.

The decision was apparently accepted as final so far as the flat prohibition approach to the problem was concerned. No appeal was taken from it and no similar bill was ever passed by any other State legislature.

For a time it seemed that Judge Doub's line of reasoning might prove equally effective against laws which, masked as revenue measures, struck at the chains by imposing heavier taxes on them than on their single-store competitors, without putting a limit on the number of stores which could be operated.

The North Carolina decision to which Judge Doub referred had been made in a case challenging the constitutionality of a 1927 law which levied a license tax of $50 on each store operated by anyone with six or more.

The plaintiffs in the case included A&P, The David Pender Grocery Co., Rose's 5, 10, and 25¢ Stores, F. W. Woolworth Company, J. C. Penney Company, G. R. Kinney Company, Milner Stores, Carolina Stores, and M. Samuels Company. Each of them operated six or more stores in the State, each of them had paid the tax under protest, and each of them wanted its money back on the ground that the law was unconstitutional and void.

The case had been tried by Judge Cranmer, without a jury, and, in February, 1928, he had decided that the law was unconstitutional, but he had handed down no opinion.

However his decision was appealed and later that year the North Carolina Supreme Court affirmed it.[9]

The key point of the decision was that there was no "real and substantial difference" between a merchant who operates six or more stores and one who operates five or less stores. Judge Connor, who wrote the opinion for the Court, concluded therefore that treating them differently for taxation purposes was based on an arbitrary classification and resulted in depriving the taxed group of the equal protection of the laws.

Chief Justice Stacy and Judge Clarkson, who concurred in the decision, stressed the point that the vice in the law in question was that, whereas a chain of five stores paid no tax, a chain of six stores was taxed not only on its sixth store but on its first five stores as well. They thought that that was so arbitrary that the law had to be invalidated.

[9] Great A&P Tea Co. v. Doughton, 196 N.C. 145; 144 S.E. 701 (1928).

The Georgia law passed in 1927 followed the same pattern as the North Carolina law. It imposed a tax of $250 per store on chains operating five or more stores. It, too, was declared unconstitutional but, in any event, it was superseded by a new law passed at the 1929 session. The new law followed the identical pattern of the earlier one, except that the tax was set at $50 per store instead of $250, but it did introduce a new wrinkle which was apparently designed to meet the constitutional shortcomings of the 1927 law.

The new wrinkle was an express statement in the law itself that "under the police powers of this State, the business of conducting chain stores . . . hereby is classified as a business tending to foster monopoly."

The law was attacked by Woolworth and other chains. When the lower court refused to declare it unconstitutional, an appeal was taken to the Georgia Supreme Court. The decision was reversed.[10] The Court handed down only a short opinion. It did not have to pass on the question as to whether the business of conducting chain stores tends to foster monopoly, because it invalidated the law on the ground that "the classification attempted to be made is founded on the difference between one who owns or operates more than five stores on the one hand, and one who operates five or less on the other" and is "arbitrary and unreasonable."

In other words, the Court did not decide that a State could not classify chain stores separately for taxation purposes, but merely that if it did undertake to do so, it would have to treat *all* chains equally.

The fourth law passed in 1927, in Pennsylvania, which, as has been pointed out, was aimed only at the drug chains, followed the flat-prohibition approach although its objective was to be achieved in a devious way. It prohibited anyone from *owning* a drug store unless he was a registered pharmacist, and, in the case of a corporation, unless *all* the stockholders

[10] Woolworth v. Harrison, 171 Ga. 891; 156 S.E. 904 (1931).

were registered pharmacists, although it did permit a corporation to continue to own and operate the stores it had when the
act became effective even though its stockholders did not
meet the requirement.

The Louis K. Liggett Company promptly went into action.
An injunction was sought in a Federal court composed of
three judges. After all the arguments had been heard, the
court sustained the law! It decided that the Act was a valid
exercise of the police power, because there was a reasonable
relation between the *ownership* of a drug store and the safe-
guarding of the public health. That relation was found in the
fact that the *owners* of a drug store, rather than the pharmacist in charge of the prescription department, have the final
say as to what drugs shall be stocked, and the legislature may
reasonably have thought that a corporation whose stockholders were not all registered men might be tempted to buy
drugs on price rather than on quality!

The case was carried direct to the U.S. Supreme Court. Justice Sutherland, writing the opinion for the Court,[11] decided
that in view of the fact that the State's pharmacy laws provided ample safeguards against the improper compounding of
prescriptions or sale of drugs detrimental to the public safety,
the idea that it was necessary for the *owners* of a drug store to
be qualified pharmacists was based on "conjecture, unsup-
ported by anything of substance."

Pointing out that no evidence had been produced to show
that the operation of chain drug stores had been detrimental
to public health, he declared that the law could not be sustained as a valid exercise of the police power, and the lower
court's decision was reversed.

This was the first time an anti-chain law had reached the
highest court in the land. Its outcome was particularly encouraging to the chains because it was felt that if the police-
power doctrine could not be successfully invoked against the

[11] Liggett *v.* Baldridge, 278 U.S. 105 (1928).

drug chains, which had a direct relation to public health, the chains in other fields would have an even stronger case.

That the Pennsylvania Drug Store Ownership Law, as it was called, reflected an organized effort to stop the growth of the drug chains was evidenced, as George M. Gales, president of Liggett's, pointed out at the time, by the fact that similar bills had been introduced in sixteen other States as well, although most of them had died.

In 1928, only one of the four anti-chain bills introduced was passed. That was in South Carolina. It followed the same pattern as the North Carolina and Georgia laws, imposing a tax of $100 per store on chains operating five or more, and it met the same fate. On February 27, 1929, the Richland County Court of Common Pleas declared it unconstitutional, citing the decision of the North Carolina Supreme Court which had just been handed down.[12]

Notwithstanding these setbacks the anti-chain legislative barrage was maintained with increasing vigor. In 1929, no less than 62 more bills were introduced. Three of them passed: one in Georgia, which was invalidated, as previously pointed out, another in North Carolina and a third in Indiana.

These North Carolina and Indiana bills were destined to become extremely significant, for they introduced a new feature designed to correct the constitutional flaw in the earlier acts.

They both started the chain-store tax with the *second* store, thus laying the foundation for the contention that the single store merchant was different from a merchant with two or more stores not merely in *degree* but in *kind*—that he was essentially a different breed of cat!

The North Carolina law set a flat-rate tax of $50 per store on each store in excess of one. The chains challenged it in the Wake County Superior Court, the very Court which had pre-

---

[12] Southern Grocery Stores Inc. *v.* Query, unreported, but appearing in *Chain Stores in the Law Courts*, p. 18, *op. cit.*

viously declared the 1927 law unconstitutional. But this time it decided that a classification which distinguished chain stores from single stores was neither arbitrary nor unreasonable.

An appeal to the North Carolina Supreme Court availed nothing. Judge Connor, who had written the opinion invalidating the 1927 act, now wrote one sustaining the 1929 variation.[13]

"There is a real and substantial difference between merchants who exercise the privilege of carrying on their business in this State by means of two or more stores and those who maintain and operate only one store," he declared, adding that the former "have and exercise a more valuable privilege."

He pointed out that the trouble with the 1927 law was that the tax was not levied on chain-store operators *per se,* as was evidenced by the fact that it exempted the chains with five or less stores.

That decision was handed down in 1930. It was the first serious set-back the chains had had. They carried it to the U.S. Supreme Court, but by that time, that Court had already made its historic decision regarding the Indiana law, and the North Carolina Supreme Court's decision was automatically sustained.

The Indiana tax differed from the North Carolina tax in one important respect in that it was a graduated tax, which increased progressively with the number of stores operated. It imposed a license tax of $3 per year on single stores, $10 per year on each additional store up to five; $15 per year on each additional store up to ten; $20 per year on each additional store up to twenty; and $25 per year on each additional store in excess of twenty.

Although the tax was really nominal in amount, the chains opposed it vigorously not only because they disagreed with

[13] Great A&P Tea Co. *v.* Maxwell, 199 N.C. 433, 154 S.E. 838, affirmed without opinion, 284 U.S. 575.

the principle of special taxes against chain stores but because they knew that once such a pattern of taxation received judicial sanction, it would be only a question of time and conditions before it would be used to impose a greater toll. With most of the States at that time finding it increasingly difficult to balance their budgets, any new source of revenue which could be tapped without too much political danger would naturally have a strong appeal to legislators. Special taxes against chain stores certainly belonged in that category.

For the purpose of testing the constitutionality of the Indiana tax, a case was instituted in a special Federal Court of three judges sitting in Indianapolis.

The plaintiff was Lafayette Jackson, owner of a local grocery chain doing business as the Standard Grocery Co.

Mr. Jackson owned and operated 225 stores, all in the city of Indianapolis.

If his 225 stores had been owned and operated by 225 different individuals, the total tax paid by them would have been 225 times $3, or $675. But because all the stores were owned by a single individual the graduated formula employed in the law made Mr. Jackson's tax $5,443, or eight times as much as it would have been had the stores been separately owned.

Able lawyers were retained by Mr. Jackson and the other chains, who were all vitally interested in the outcome of the case. The trial lasted for more than a week, with both sides producing marketing experts to support their conflicting contentions. The chains contended, of course, that, as Judge Doub had decided in the Maryland case, the only difference between a chain and a single store was in the number of stores operated, and that that difference did not provide a legal basis on which to tax them unequally. The State, on the other hand, insisted that the chains enjoyed certain advantages inherent in their system which put them in a different class from single store merchants and justified the imposition of a higher tax.

The three-judge court decided for the chains, declaring the law unconstitutional.[14] The State appealed direct to the U.S. Supreme Court.

When the case was argued March 5, 1931, the only adverse decision that could be used against the chains was that of the North Carolina Supreme Court, which was itself being appealed to the U.S. Supreme Court. On the other hand, the chains could point to the decision of the Supreme Court itself invalidating the Pennsylvania Drug Store Ownership Law only a few months earlier.

Nevertheless, when the decision was handed down on May 18, the chain stores learned to their amazement that, so far as the Supreme Court was concerned, chain stores could lawfully be taxed differently from independent stores, and that the tax could be lawfully graduated according to the number of stores operated.[15]

True enough, the decision was a divided one, with Justices Roberts, Holmes, Brandeis, Stone and C. J. Hughes constituting the majority, and Justices Sutherland, Van Devanter, McReynolds and Butler dissenting.

Justice Roberts, who wrote the majority opinion, declared:

> "It is not the function of this Court in cases like the present to consider the propriety or justness of the tax, to seek for the motives or to criticize the public policy which prompted the adoption of the legislation. Our duty is to sustain the classification . . . if there are substantial differences between the occupations separately classified. Such differences need not be great."

In concluding that the classification was neither arbitrary nor unreasonable, the Justice argued that the astonishing growth of the chains was proof enough "that there are differences and advantages" in their favor.

[14] State Board v. Jackson, 38 Fed. (2nd) 652.
[15] State Board v. Jackson, 283 U.S. 527 (1931).

Furthermore, he said the Court below had erroneously assumed that the difference was solely one of ownership.

"It disregarded the differences shown by the record," he declared. "They consist not merely in ownership, but in organization, management and type of business transacted. The statute treats upon a similar basis all owners of chain stores similarly situated. . . . That is all that the Constitution requires."

Justice Sutherland, whose dissenting opinion was concurred in by three of his colleagues, took the position that whatever advantages the chain stores enjoyed stemmed from the fact that their operations were on a larger scale, and, as the State's own expert witness had conceded, were enjoyed equally by any large-scale operator even if he operated only one store, such as a large department store.

"It thus appears," he declared, "that the advantages attributed to the chain store lie not in the fact that it is one of a *NUMBER* of stores under the same management, supervision or ownership, but in the fact that it is one of the parts of a *LARGE BUSINESS.* . . . The classification should fall because it is made to depend . . . upon the mere circumstance —wholly irrelevant so far as any of the advantages claimed are concerned—that the business of one is carried on under many roofs, and that of the other under one only."

Conceding that the maximum tax of $25 might not in itself be considered excessive, he pointed out, prophetically enough, that:

"It will open the door of opportunity to the State to increase the amount to an oppressive extent. This Court has frequently said, and it cannot be too often repeated in cases of this character, that the power to tax is the power to destroy; and this constitutes a reason why that power, however moderately exercised in given instances, should be zealously confined to the limits set by the Constitution. . . . There does not seem to be any sure comfort in the suggestion, sometimes made, that this court may be expected to intervene whenever the tax reaches the point of destruction."

How correct the Justice was is reflected in the fact that within two years after this decision, Indiana raised its chain-store tax from $25 per store to $150 per store, in the top bracket. Furthermore, the Supreme Court was soon to declare specifically that chain-store taxes could be as drastic as a State saw fit to impose, even if the burden became prohibitive.

But whatever one may think of the conflicting viewpoints expressed in the majority and dissenting opinions, the majority opinion, of course, became the law of the land, even though by a five-to-four margin.

The decision was all that was necessary to release a regular epidemic of such proposals, and, as most of the States in that period were eagerly seeking new sources of revenue, the outlook for the chains was dark indeed.

What actually happened is indicated by the box score shown in Table 17. It reveals that, prior to 1931, the number of tax bills introduced against the chains had totalled 164 of which 10 had been enacted in seven different States. In 1931, however, 175 were introduced; in 1932, 125, and in 1933, 225! Of the 525 bills introduced in those three years, eighteen were enacted. From 1934 to 1941, inclusive, 500 more of such bills were introduced, of which 32 became law. Altogether, from 1923 to 1941, inclusive, 60 of these bills were enacted, although the majority of them merely superseded earlier enactments. In fact, all the 60 bills which became laws were enacted in 28 States. Today only 14 States impose such taxes, and one of these, North Carolina, materially modified its tax in 1949.

In the fourteen States which no longer impose such taxes, here is what happened: six were repealed; four were declared unconstitutional as being in conflict with State constitutions; two expired by their own limitation and were not re-enacted;

TABLE 17

ANTI-CHAIN-STORE TAX BILLS, 1923-1961

Source: Retailers Manual of Taxes and Regulations, 16th Edition, 1961, published by Variety Stores Association, Inc. and Institute of Distribution, Inc., edited by Gladys M. Kiernan, Editor, and Arthur Pite, Associate Editor.

YEAR	BILLS	ENACTED	STATES AND DISPOSITION*
1923	1	0	
1924	1	0	
1925	2	0	
1926	1	0	
1927	13	3	Ga. (A); Md. (A); N. C. (A).
1928	4	1	S. C. (A).
1929	62	3	Ga. (A); Ind. (B); N. C. (B).
1930	80	3	Ky. (A); Miss. (B); S. C. (I).
1931	175	3	Ala. (B); Ariz. (C); Fla. (A).
1932	125	2	La. (B); Wis. (B).
1933	225	13	Fla. (B); Ida. (C); Ind. (I); Me. (C); Md. (I); Mich. (B); Minn. (B); Mont. (B); N. M. (B); N. C. (B); Vt. (A); W. Va. (I); Wis. (A).
1934	40	4	Colo. (H); Ky. (A); La. (I); N. M. (A).
1935	163	9	Ala. (I); Calif. (D); Fla. (B); Ia. (I); Mich. (I); N. C. (B); S. D. (A); Tex. (I); Wis. (E).
1936	27	2	Ky. (A); Miss. (B).
1937	97	8	Ga. (C); Minn. (E); Mont. (A); N. C. (B); Pa. (A); S. D. (B); Tenn. (I); Wis. (E); Miss. (B).
1938	19	1	Miss. (B).
1939	99	4	Mont. (I); N. C. (F); S. D. (C); Tenn. (A).
1940	10	2	Ky. (A); Miss. (I).
1941	45	2	Fla. (C); Utah (D).
1942	7	0	
1943	20	0	
1944	4	0	
1945	10	0	
1946	1	0	
1947	12	0	
1948	3	0	
1949	16	1	N. C. (See 1939).
1950	4	0	
1951	8	0	
1952	0	0	
1953	3	0	
1954	2	0	
1955	9	0	
1956	1	0	
1957	8	1	W. Va. (J).
1958	1	0	
1959	8	0	
1960	2	0	
1961	4	0	
	1,312	62	

* KEY TO DISPOSITION. (A) Invalidated; (B) Superseded; (C) Repealed; (D) Rejected by Referendum; (E) Expired by limitation; (F) Graduated rates replaced by flat tax in 1949; (H) Retained by referendum; (I) In effect; (J) Increased tax enacted in 1933.

142

and two were rejected by the public through a referendum.

A breakdown of anti-chain-store tax legislation by States is provided in Table 18. Not included because of its different nature is the chain store warehouse tax enacted by the State of Washington in 1955. It imposes a tax of ¼ of 1% on the wholesale value of merchandise distributed by a chain of two or more stores from its own warehouse.

In addition to the taxes levied by the States, as disclosed in Table 17, a number of cities passed local ordinances along the same lines. The first of these municipal taxes was imposed by Portland, Ore., in 1931. A public referendum initiated by the chains failed, by a small margin, to upset it. A number of other cities throughout the country followed Portland's example. Many of these municipal chain-store taxes, however, were either repealed by the bodies which enacted them or were invalidated by the courts.[16] Of 68 cities still imposing such taxes, 64 are in North Carolina, and two in West Virginia, while South Carolina and Virginia each have one. In the majority of instances, the tax is on a flat-rate basis and amounts to $50 per year per store.[17]

Although, with the Indiana decision, the chains were licked so far as laws of the same type were concerned, they challenged the constitutionality of every *new* enactment which, because of some new feature, gave them a chance to go to bat again.

Thus, when Florida enacted a law in 1931 imposing a graduated tax on chain stores after the pattern of the Indiana law, but increasing the tax where the stores involved were located in more than one county, the chains promptly sought an injunction. The lower court denied it, the Supreme Court of Florida likewise agreed that the law was constitutional, and again the chains appealed to the U.S. Supreme Court.

[16] *The Chain Store Tells Its Story, op. cit.,* pp. 150, 151; *The Chain Store Problem, op. cit.,* pp. 261, 262.
[17] *Retailers Manual of Taxes and Regulations, op. cit.*

TABLE 18
ANTI-CHAIN-STORE LEGISLATION BY STATES*

NONE ENACTED	ENACTED BUT INOPERATIVE	STILL IN EFFECT
Alaska	Arizona*a*	Alabama
Arkansas	California*b*	Colorado
Connecticut	Florida*a*	Indiana
Delaware	Georgia*a*	Iowa
Hawaii	Idaho*a*	Louisiana
Illinois	Kentucky*c*	Maryland
Kansas	Maine*a*	Michigan
Massachusetts	Minnesota*d*	Mississippi
Missouri	New Mexico*c*	Montana
Nebraska	Pennsylvania*c*	North Carolina
Nevada	South Dakota*a*	South Carolina
New Hampshire	Utah*b*	Tennessee
New Jersey	Vermont*c*	Texas
New York	Wisconsin*d*	West Virginia
North Dakota		
Ohio		
Oklahoma		
Oregon		
Rhode Island		
Virginia		
Washington		
Wyoming		

a Repealed; *b* Rejected by referendum; *c* Invalidated by court decision; *d* Expired by its own terms.

* Source: *Retailers Manual of Taxes and Regulations, op. cit.* and Institute of Distribution files.

Justice Roberts, who had written the majority opinion in the Indiana case, wrote the majority opinion in this one also.[18] He agreed with the chains that it was arbitrary and unreasonable to levy a higher tax on a given number of stores if they were located in more than one county than if they were located all in one county.

The Court invalidated that section of the law but upheld the rest of it, taking advantage of the occasion to reaffirm its decision in the Indiana case. It emphasized its conviction that a chain was different from the ordinary individually operated small store, a department store or a co-operative or a voluntary chain (a group of individually owned stores banded to-

[18] Liggett v. Lee, 288 U.S. 517 (1933).

gether for their mutual benefit). Even though in some cases
and to some extent, the advantages stemming from the chain-
store system might likewise be enjoyed by other types of operation, the Court was firm in its belief that chain stores were
sufficiently different to warrant special tax treatment.

Furthermore, the Court upheld another section of the law
which boded no good for the chains if other States were led to
adopt it. It required each county to impose an additional tax
amounting to 25% of the State tax, graduated on the stores
within the county, and, for full measure, authorized each
incorporated municipality in the State to do the same thing!

A by-product of this decision was the lengthy dissenting
opinion of Justice Brandeis. With inimitable clarity, he spelled
out his philosophy regarding the menace of "big business."

He was for upholding the whole statute, including the extra
tax imposed on chains operating in more than one county.

Pointing out that all the plaintiffs in the case were corporations, he took the position that, as far as they were concerned
at least, the State could charge them anything it wanted for
the privilege of engaging in business. He declared:

> "As this privilege is one which a State may withhold or
> grant it may charge such compensation as it pleases. . . .
> Since the authority to operate many stores, or to operate in
> two or more counties, is certainly a broader privilege than
> to operate only one store, or in only one county, there is in
> this record no basis for finding that it is unreasonable to make
> the charge higher for the greater privilege."

Furthermore, he made the point that the law in question
was not merely a revenue measure—its main purpose was
social and economic. On that basis, he said, that "if the State
should conclude that bigness in retail merchandising as mani-
fested in corporate chain stores menaces the public welfare,
it might prohibit the excessive size or extent of that business
as it prohibits excessive size or weight in motor trucks or excessive height in the buildings of a city."

Justice Cardozo also wrote a dissenting opinion, with which Justice Stone concurred, but he did not cover as much territory as Justice Brandeis, whose reasons, he said, "had been stated with such a wealth of learning."

His view was that, in increasing the tax for chains operating in more than one county, the State might reasonably have felt that chains in that category had ceased to be local enterprises, and, for that reason, were less desirable socially. "Courts would be lacking in candor," he said, "if they were not to concede the presence of such a motive behind this chain-store legislation. But a purpose to bear more heavily on one class than another will not avail without more to condemn a tax as void. . . . The concept may be right or wrong. At least it corresponds to an intelligible belief, and one widely prevalent today among honest men and women. . . . With that our function ends."

Is a filling station a store?

That was the question which the Standard Oil Company of N.J. was primarily interested in having the courts answer when the West Virginia Tax Commissioner answered it in the affirmative. For the affirmative answer meant that under the chain-store license tax enacted in 1933, Standard Oil would have to pay a tax of $250 on each of its filling stations in excess of 75. As it operated 949 of them in the State, and more than half of them had shown an average profit of only $89.75, it was obviously a mighty heavy burden for such stations to carry.

A three-judge Federal Court decided that a filling station was not a store, within the meaning of the act and, in any event, the tax was so much harsher when applied to filling stations than when it was applied to other chains that it amounted to a denial to Standard Oil of the equal protection of the laws.

When the appeal reached the Supreme Court, Judge Cardozo wrote the majority opinion.[19] He disagreed with the lower court on both counts. Not only did he find that gasoline stations were well within the definition of "store" contained in the Act, but he confirmed what Justice Sutherland had predicted in the Indiana case—that even a prohibitive tax would be sustained.

Said Justice Cardozo: "When the power to tax exists, the extent of the burden is a matter for the discretion of the lawmakers," citing with approval the language used by the Court in connection with a different type of tax: "Even if the tax should destroy a business, it would not be made invalid or require compensation upon that ground alone. Those who enter upon a business take that risk." For whatever consolation it might offer, the Justice added that "the tax now assailed may have its roots in an erroneous conception of the ills of the body politic or of the efficacy of such a measure to bring about a cure. We have no thought in anything we have written to declare it expedient or even just, or, for that matter, to declare the contrary. We deal with power only."

Justices Van Devanter, McReynolds, Sutherland and Butler again dissented as they had in the Indiana case, but the majority, of course, prevailed. Thus the States were given free rein to tax the chains just as much as they pleased.

That decision was handed down January 14, 1935. A couple of months later, however, the Supreme Court handed down another decision in which the chains were to fare much better.

The case involved the constitutionality of another new type of law, passed in Kentucky in 1930, whose pattern had been followed by several other States before the Supreme Court finally passed on it.

This Kentucky law levied a graduated tax on *all* retailers, based on sales. It did not single out the chains but struck at them just as effectively by penalizing large volume however

[19] Fox v. Standard Oil of N.J., 294 U.S. 87 (1935).

attained—whether through a big department store or through
a number of smaller stores owned and operated by a single
individual or corporation.

The progression of the tax was painfully steep, ranging
from $\frac{1}{20}$th of 1 per cent on sales of $400,000 or less, to 1%
on sales in excess of $1,000,000.

How it would have worked can be illustrated by applying
the formula to (1) a department store with sales of $4,000,-
000; (2) a chain of ten stores with sales of $400,000 each;
and (3) ten independent stores each doing $400,000.

The department store's tax would have totalled $33,050,
made up as follows:

Sales	Rate	Tax
1st $400,000	$\frac{1}{20}$th of 1%	$200
Next 100,000	$\frac{2}{20}$ths of 1%	100
Next 100,000	$\frac{5}{20}$ths of 1%	250
Next 100,000	$\frac{8}{20}$ths of 1%	400
Next 100,000	$\frac{11}{20}$ths of 1%	550
Next 100,000	$\frac{14}{20}$ths of 1%	700
Next 100,000	$\frac{17}{20}$ths of 1%	850
Next 3,000,000	1%	30,000
Total		$33,050

The chain of ten stores having the same total sales would
have had to pay the same total tax of $33,050, or an average
of $3,305 per store.

But the ten individual stores, each doing $400,000, would
have had to pay only $200 each, or a total of $2,000.

As a matter of fact, the individual stores would have had
to pay nothing at all in most instances under this law, for
every merchant was allowed to take as a credit against the
tax whatever he had to pay under other laws. In the case of
most merchants doing less than $100,000 a year, which in-
cludes the vast majority of independents, the allowance would
have meant no tax on his sales at all.

Several department stores and chains attacked the law on the basis of its obvious inequality. A three-judge District Court dismissed the bill on ground of lack of jurisdiction. An appeal to the U.S. Supreme Court brought a reversal.[20] The District Court then tried the case on the merits and found the law valid. A second appeal to the U.S. Supreme Court again brought a reversal, the law being held unconstitutional by a six-to-three decision.[21] This double trip to the Supreme Court accounts for the time lag between the passage of the law in 1930 and the Court's decision in 1935.

Justice Roberts, who had written the majority opinion in the Indiana case upholding a graduated tax based on the number of *stores* operated, and also in the Florida case, in which the soundness of that principle was reaffirmed, now wrote the majority opinion condemning a graduated tax based on the volume of *sales* attained.

Here is how he reconciled what, on their face, might seem to be conflicting rulings. He said:

"In several recent cases we sustained the classification of chain stores for taxation at rates higher than those applicable to single stores and graduated upward on each store as the total number of units in one ownership increased. We found this classification reasonable because of advantages incident to the conduct of the multiple stores and obvious differences in chain methods of merchandising as contrasted with those practised in the operation of one store. The instant cases present a classification of quite another kind. The Kentucky statute ignores the form of organization and the method of conducting business. The taxable class is retail merchants, whether individuals, partnerships or corporations; those who sell in one store or many; those who offer but one sort of goods and those who, through departments, deal in many lines of merchandise. The law arbitrarily classified these vendors for the imposition of a varying rate of taxation, solely by reference to the volume of their transactions, disregarding the

[20] Stewart Dry Goods Co. *v.* Lewis, 287 U.S. 9 (1932).
[21] Stewart Dry Goods Co. *v.* Lewis, 294 U.S. 550 (1935).

absence of any reasonable relation between the chosen criterion of classification and the privilege the enjoyment of which is said to be the subject taxed. It exacts from two persons different amounts for the privilege of doing exactly similar acts because the one has performed the act oftener than the other."

Earlier in his opinion, the Justice had characterized the law as "unjustifiably unequal, whimsical and arbitrary, as much so as would be a tax on tangible personal property, say cattle, stepped up in rate on each additional animal owned by the taxpayer, or a tax on land similarly graduated according to the number of parcels owned."

Rejecting the argument that a merchant's net income and his consequent ability to pay increase as the volume of his sales grow, the Justice said:

"Argument is not needed, and indeed practical admission was made at the bar, that the gross sales of a merchant do not bear a constant relation to his net profits; that net profits vary from year to year in the same enterprise; that diverse kinds of merchandise yield differing rates of profit; and that gross and net profits vary with the character of the business as well as its volume. . . . Expert witnesses . . . endeavored to establish that net profits or net worth grow with increased sales. But their testimony not only indicated great variations within each class selected for comparison, but also showed that in some of the classes representing the greater amount of sales the net profit, or the addition to the net worth, is smaller than in a class having less aggregate sales. The best that can be said for this evidence is that, averaging the results of the concerns making the reports, it is true "generally speaking," as the court below put it, that profits increase with sales. The ratio of increase, however, differs in different lines of activity and even as between concerns carrying on the same business, and so many exceptions and reservations must be made that averages are misleading . . . We think the graduated rates imposed were not intended to bear any relation to net profits."

How Justice Roberts could have recognized these obvious

facts in condemning the Kentucky tax based on sales and have ignored them in the Indiana case where they applied with equal force is hard to understand.

That they do apply with equal force to a graduated tax based on the number of stores was made clear by Dr. Charles F. Phillips, now president of Bates College, in the course of a comprehensive discussion of "State Discriminatory Chain Store Taxation," as of 1936.[22]

He showed by convincing examples that the Indiana chain-store tax was every bit as "unequal, whimsical and arbitrary" as Justice Roberts said the Kentucky law was. He emphasized (1) that it hits small chains as well as big ones; (2) it ignores the great range of variation between the profits of different chains both within the same field of operation and in different fields, and even as between the stores operated by the same chain; and (3) it ignores the fact that chain-store profits are by no means constant from year to year.

In the case of the Indiana law, the Supreme Court held that the fact that "generally speaking" more *stores* means more profits justified a graduated tax based upon the number of stores, but in the case of the Kentucky law they held that the fact that "generally speaking" more *sales* means more profits did *not* justify a graduated tax based upon sales.

Perhaps if the Kentucky law had come up for consideration first, the Indiana law would never have been upheld; but, as it was, the chains must consider themselves fortunate that the decision in the Indiana case did not lead the Supreme Court to take the same action in the Kentucky case.

Another type of chain-store tax was involved in a Louisiana law passed in 1934. It was modeled after the Indiana law, except for one added feature. The tax was graduated on the basis of the total number of stores operated whether *within* the State or *outside*. The top bracket of $550 per store applied to all stores in excess of 500.

[22] *Harvard Business Review*, Spring Number, 1936.

A&P then had some 15,000 stores in all, but only 106 of them were in Louisiana. Nevertheless, by the terms of the law A&P would have to pay $550 on each of its Louisiana stores, whereas a chain with only 106 stores altogether, wherever located, would have had to pay considerably less tax on each store.

A&P and other chains applied to a special three-judge Federal Court for an injunction and, when that Court upheld the law, an appeal was taken to the U.S. Supreme Court.

Again Justice Roberts wrote the majority opinion, and the decision sustaining the law[23] was hardly a surprise. For, as the Court declared:

> "If the competitive advantages of a chain increase with the number of its component links, it is hard to see how these advantages cease at the state boundary. Under the findings, a store belonging to a chain of one hundred, all located in Louisiana, has not the same advantages as one of a hundred Louisiana stores belonging to a national chain of one thousand."

The Court had no trouble in distinguishing this case from the one in Florida. There the tax was increased if the chain had stores in more than one county. The increase was held arbitrary because it was unrelated to the *size* or *character* of the chain and was conditioned solely upon the *location* of one or more of the stores. Under the Louisiana law, however, the classification is not based upon the location of the stores, in fact the location of the stores is rendered immaterial, but upon the total number of stores in the chain which, according to the Court, measures its competitive advantages and economic results.

But more significant perhaps than any other feature of this decision was the Court's declaration that the law should be upheld on much broader considerations than those it had applied.

[23] Great A&P Tea Co. v. Grosjean, 301 U.S. 412 (1937).

"In the exercise of its police power the State may forbid, as inimical to the public welfare, the prosecution of a particular type of business, or regulate a business in such manner as to abate evils deemed to arise from its pursuit," Justice Roberts declared. "Whatever a State may forbid or regulate it may permit upon condition that a fee be paid in return for the privilege, and such a fee may be exacted to discourage the prosecution of a business or to adjust competitive or economic inequalities. Taxation may be made the implement of the exercise of the State's police power; and proper and reasonable discrimination between classes to promote fair competitive conditions and to equalize economic advantages is therefore lawful."

Applying those principles to the case at hand, the Justice went on to point out that:

"If, in the interest of the people of the State, the legislature deemed it necessary either to mitigate evils of competition as between single stores and chains or to neutralize disadvantages of small chains in their competition with larger ones, or to discourage merchandising within the state by chains grown so large as to become a menace to the general welfare, it was at liberty to regulate the matter directly or to resort to the type of taxation evidenced by the Act of 1934 as a means of regulation."

Justices Sutherland, McReynolds and Butler dissented. Neither Justice Van Devanter nor Justice Stone took any part in the consideration of the case or in the decision.

In his dissenting opinion, Justice Sutherland referred to the Indiana decision, which he still felt was wrongly decided, but which, accepting it as authoritative, went to the extreme verge of the law, adding: "it seems to us equally certain that the present decision goes far beyond the verge."

The key point raised by the Justice was that the advantage enjoyed by the stores located in Louisiana by reason of the fact that their owner operated a given number of stores in some other state or county was too vague and uncertain to justify the tax formula used in the statute. Referring to the decision in the Kentucky case and the grounds upon which it was based, he said the vices in the present statute were the same.

The net result of all this legislation and litigation may be summed up as follows:

1. Of the 28 States which, at one time or another, have had anti-chain-store taxes in effect, only 14 of them have them today. One of those, North Carolina, in 1949 eliminated the graduated type of tax, imposing a flat tax of $65 per store, irrespective of the total number operated.

2. No State has passed an anti-chain-store tax since 1941, although 123 bills have been introduced in that period, and in 1957 W. Virginia did increase the tax it had enacted in 1933.

3. Since 1941, on the other hand, four chain-store tax laws then in existence have been eliminated. In 1942, a public referendum rejected a Utah tax which had been passed in 1941; in 1946, the Kentucky Supreme Court invalidated a tax act passed in 1940; in 1949, Idaho repealed the chain-store tax it had enacted in 1933; and, in 1951, Georgia repealed its 1937 tax.

4. As a result of the decisions which have been reviewed in the preceding pages and which the U.S. Supreme Court has shown no disposition to disturb, anti-chain-store taxes are constitutional, as far as the Federal constitution is concerned. Even if a tax is drastic enough to put the chains out of business, that fact would not invalidate it.

Obviously, the barrage of adverse legislation which has been reviewed in the foregoing pages and which, as was shown in Table 17, page 142, involved the consideration of no less than 1,312 bills between 1923 and 1961, did not develop spontaneously in widely separated State capitols. It reflects rather the insistent demand for protection against the chain-store "menace" generated in the first place by wholesalers and independent merchants and later stimulated by professional agitators and others who championed their cause.

How this demand developed into a nationwide crusade against the chains which grew in intensity as the chains grew in number and size, and what came out of it, are covered in some detail in succeeding chapters.

CHAPTER VIII

THE HUE AND CRY GATHERS VOLUME

How FAR will this chain-store trend go? What is the secret of chain-store success? Is it all on the up and up, or does it stem from uneconomic, if not actually unlawful, practices? Even if the system is sound economically, is it desirable from a social standpoint? Is the independent merchant doomed? How would the public interest be affected if he were eliminated? How soon will it be before the chains monopolize distribution and, after that, how soon before they monopolize production too?

These were some of the questions which began to be asked and answered with increasing frequency as the chain-store movement gathered momentum and became increasingly evident to everyone with eyes to see. Long before 1925, the phenomenon had naturally received growing attention in the trade press because of its direct impact on established distribution channels. But, from that time on, the so-called "chain-store question" began to arouse interest on a broader front, with the financial and general business papers and even consumer periodicals devoting more attention to it.

The mere suggestion that chain-store expansion was leading us straight and swiftly into a state of unadulterated monopoly was enough, of course, to arouse the attention of politicians who never lost the opportunity to sound the tocsin whenever such an issue presented itself. But it went further than that. Economists delved into the subject objectively, government bureaus and officials undertook investigations to see whether existing laws were being violated or should be tightened, and governors, senators and congressmen, all over the country, began to take sides.

One of the first manifestations of the lively interest business men were taking in the chain-store issue was a public debate arranged by the Illinois Retail Clothiers' and Furnishers' Association as a feature of its eighteenth annual convention in Chicago, on February 9, 1928, between T. K. Kelly, "billed" as a banker and president of T. K. Kelly Sales System, of Minneapolis, and the author, as editor of *Chain Store Age*.

The question: Resolved, that the chain-store system is not to the public interest.

Although this debate was the first of its kind, its main significance lies in the facts that (1) it was arranged in a field which, at that time, had not felt the impact of chain-store competition to any great extent; and (2) it received far more space in the trade press than might have been expected, several publications printing both sides *in full*. As each side had been given an hour for the presentation of its case, the number of pages required for the full report was considerable.[1]

In the years which followed, the subject was to be debated over and over again, not only before audiences of business men[2] and in public forums but, more particularly, by high school and college debating teams all over the country. In a bibliography published in 1940,[3] no less than seven Debate Manuals are listed, including: the University Debaters' Man-

[1] *Daily News Record*, New York, February 10, 1928; *National Retail Clothier*, Chicago, March 1, 1928; *Retail Ledger*, Philadelphia, February 2, 1928; *Men's Wear*, February 22, 1928.

[2] On September 16, 1929, the Ad-Sell League, of Omaha, a business man's organization, staged a debate on the subject between J. Frank Grimes, founder of the Independent Grocers' Alliance, and the author. It is quoted in *The Chain Store —Boon or Bane?, op. cit.*, at page 122.

[3] *The Chain Store Tells Its Story, op. cit.*, p. 262.

ual, on the Chain Store System, issued by H. W. Wilson Publishing Co., New York, in 1930; a Handbook on Chain Stores for High School Debates, published by Albion College Debate Service, Albion, Mich.; and Debate Handbook, The Chain Store Question, by E. C. Buehler, University of Kansas, 1930.

Another bibliography on the chain-store question, issued by the Debaters' Information Bureau, Portland, Me., in 1930, listed fifteen other bibliographies on the subject; six organizations putting out material, pro or con; nineteen sources of information; three anti-chain-store publications; seven chainstore publications; 21 book references; 91 pamphlets and government documents; 473 periodical articles and 184 newspaper articles! The great majority of the periodical articles listed were published in 1928, 1929 and 1930, but the years 1925, 1926 and 1927 were well represented too.

Although the periodical articles were by no means all antichain in their approach, even those which reported chainstore progress objectively, or openly welcomed it, provided additional ammunition for those who viewed the situation with misgivings. The great number of men in public life who took up the cudgels against the chains, whether sincerely or for political advantage, materially strengthened the antichain-store case.

Probably the only reason anti-chain-store sentiment did not result in even more anti-chain-store tax bills than were actually introduced between 1927 and 1930, inclusive, was the fact that, until 1931, when the Supreme Court handed down its decision in the Indiana case, most lawyers were convinced that such legislation was hopelessly unconstitutional, as many of the lower courts had already decided.

Typical of the anti-chain viewpoint, as it was expressed by leading public figures and in the daily press, are the following observations which were quoted by the author in an earlier work on the subject.[4]

[4] *The Chain Store—Boon or Bane?, op. cit.,* pp. 1-3.

"The chain stores are undermining the foundation of our entire local happiness and prosperity. They have destroyed our home markets and merchants, paying a minimum to our local enterprises and charities, sapping the life-blood of prosperous communities and leaving about as much in return as a travelling band of gypsies."

Thus declared a former speaker of the Indiana House of Representatives in a letter addressed to some of his constituents.

In one of the "Letters from the People" on the editorial page of the *St. Louis Post Dispatch,* appeared the following observations:

"We have the greatest school system in the world to educate our youths to be future business men. What are their prospects for business if the chain stores continue to develop more and more every day? Do the mothers and fathers realize what will happen to their children when they have to go to work for chain stores at $20 per week, or less? The chain stores may appeal to some people as a very bright business, but our country is built on the foundation of live and let live. Economy is one thing, but eliminating that vast amount of people from work is another."

U.S. Senator Royal S. Copeland, of New York, was credited with the following contribution:

"When a chain enters a city block, ten other stores close up. In smaller cities and towns, the chain store contributes nothing to the community. Chain stores are parasites. I think they undermine the foundations of the country."

And Senator Hugo L. Black, of Alabama, later to become a Justice of the U.S. Supreme Court,[5] delivered himself of the following tirade which leaves little doubt where his sympathies would have been had he been a member of that court when the Indiana case was decided:

"Chain groceries, chain dry-goods stores, chain clothing stores, here today and merged tomorrow—grow in size and

[5] Appointed 1937.

power. We are rapidly becoming a nation of a few business masters and many clerks and servants. The local man and merchant is passing and his community loses his contribution to local affairs as an independent thinker and executive. A few of these useful citizens, thus supplanted, become clerks of the great chain machines, at inadequate salaries, while many enter the growing ranks of the unemployed. A wild craze for efficiency in production, sale and distribution has swept over the land, increasing the number of unemployed, building up a caste system, dangerous to any government." [6]

Another U.S. Senator, Burton Wheeler, of Montana, expressed a similar viewpoint over a radio network, declaring:

"The western Progressives are fighting against the domination of Congress by men who represent selfish corporate interests, because they believe sincerely that, unless the growing concentrations of wealth and power are checked, this nation will soon be converted into a plutocracy where a few supremely rich men will rule and the rights of the common men will be trampled under foot. We have seen the development of huge mergers and the rapid increase of chain banks and chain stores throughout the country until, today, the genuinely independent banker and independent business man are rapidly disappearing from our life. The type of men whose business built up the nation have been driven out of business in every State of the Union, and their places have been taken by the hired agents of the great mergers and chains which dominate and control the business of the entire country. We believe that these great aggregations of wealth must be subjected to effective government regulation if the people are to be protected from the inevitable evils of unregulated monopoly."

These viewpoints are quoted not for the purpose of refuting them at this point but merely to illustrate the kind of attack to which the chains were subjected day in and day out during the period of their greatest expansion. Certainly the bogy of monopoly could never have been pictured against a more

[6] *Congressional Record,* January 8, 1930.

favorable background than the chains offered at that time. The events of the past twenty years, as they are recorded in these pages, provide their own refutation of most of the anti-chain arguments raised when the crusade was at its height. But this point is as good as any other to put into the record a statement made in 1928 which, because of its source, as well as its own logic and obvious common sense, provides a refreshing antidote to some of the foregoing quotations.

Charles Wesley Dunn,[7] a leading member of the American bar, was counsel at that time for the National Association of Retail Grocers as well as the American Grocery Specialty Manufacturers' Association (now the Grocery Manufacturers of America). Discussing the so-called chain-store question, he said:[8]

"My position is essentially this:

"First: I believe that the principle of chain store retailing is economically sound and in due application progressively works for the constructive improvement of the retail business as a business and in its service to the consuming public; that in its elementary economic conception the chain store is but a natural, logical and inevitable evolutionary development of retailing, directed to introduce scientific merchandising into it and make it more effective to all concerned; that the success of the chain store is basically due to its economic soundness; that the permanency of the chain store is beyond question and the only economic question is how far it will go and how it will evolve.

"Second: I believe that what and all that can be objected to in the chain store business, as a business and as in the case of any business, is the use of wrongful or uneconomic practice in or incidental to its pursuit, or the development of illegal monopoly in it. That wrongful and uneconomic practices have been and are used in the business, cannot be denied. That such practices are detrimental to all concerned and should be eliminated, likewise cannot be denied. As to

[7] Died November 2, 1959.
[8] In a communication to the National Chain Store Grocers Association at its eighth annual meeting, Memphis, October 11, 1928.

an illegal chain grocery store monopoly, I see none. But I do see the use of methods in this business which have been heretofore and elsewhere used to create illegal monopoly. That such methods are detrimental to all concerned and should be eliminated, again cannot be denied. And in view of the size and concentration of the chain store business, such methods, if not eliminated, will continue to raise the monopoly question.

"Third: I believe that legislation directed to outlaw the chain store business or in any way unduly to discriminate against it is unsound in principle, unconstitutional in law and unjust in application."

That Mr. Dunn, like most other good lawyers, was wrong in his view that anti-chain-store laws were unconstitutional, became clear only when the Supreme Court so decided, but history has proved that he was right in most of his other observations regarding the economic basis for chain-store success. The "uneconomic practices" to which he referred (and which were used not only by the chains but by large-scale operators of all types) were to a large extent eliminated when they were made *unlawful*, whether they were uneconomic or not, by the Robinson-Patman Act of 1936.

But in 1928, the tide of criticism was so strong against the chains that neither Mr. Dunn's disinterested appraisal of what was happening in distribution nor the arguments of chain-store proponents proved of much avail.

One of the first concrete results of the anti-chain crusade was a resolution introduced in the U.S. Senate by Senator Smith W. Brookhart, of Iowa, and approved May 5, 1928, calling for an extensive chain-store inquiry by the Federal Trade Commission.

According to Mr. Dunn,[9] the resolution originated with the National Association of Retail Grocers, of which he was gen-

[9] *The Grocery and Drug Chain Store Business,* a lecture delivered by Charles Wesley Dunn at the Harvard Graduate School of Business Administration on May 17-18, 1928.

eral counsel, and was prepared for the association by John A. Cunningham, secretary, Iowa Retail Merchants Association,[10] and Mr. Cunningham "secured its introduction." Mr. Dunn, himself, thought the investigation was in order and desirable, because of charges of unfair practices which were widely made in the retail trade and because "the public is entitled and interested to know whether the charge is founded and, if so, whether the present laws are adequate in the circumstances." The chains had nothing to fear, he added, if their conduct was clear and should welcome the inquiry, because it afforded them an opportunity to answer the charges.

The resolution itself [11] is presented here in full because, in the light of its origin, it can be accepted as an accurate picture of what the chain-store problem looked like to the independent grocers. It read as follows:

"Whereas it is estimated that from 1921 to 1927 the retail sales of all chain stores have increased from approximately 4 per centum to 16 per centum of all retail sales; and

"Whereas there are estimated to be less than four thousand chain store systems with over one hundred thousand stores; and

"Whereas many of these chains operate from one hundred to several thousand stores; and

"Whereas there have been numerous consolidations of chain stores throughout the history of the movement, and particularly in the last few years; and

"Whereas these chain stores now control a substantial proportion of the distribution of certain commodities in certain cities, are rapidly increasing this proportion of control in these and other cities, and are beginning to extend this system of merchandising into country districts as well; and

"Whereas the continuance of the growth of chain store distribution and the consolidation of such chain stores may result in the development of monopolistic organizations in certain lines of retail distribution; and

[10] *N.Y. Journal of Commerce*, September 8, 1928, p. 9.
[11] Senate R. 224, 70th Congress, First Session.

"Whereas many of these concerns, though engaged in interstate commerce in buying, may not be engaged in interstate commerce in selling; and

"Whereas in consequence, the extent to which such consolidations are now, or should be made, amenable to the jurisdiction of the Federal anti-trust laws is a matter of serious concern to the public; Now, therefore, be it

"Resolved, that the Federal Trade Commission is hereby directed to undertake an inquiry into the chain store system of marketing and distribution as conducted by manufacturing, wholesaling, retailing, or other types of chain stores and to ascertain and report to the Senate:

"(1) The extent to which such consolidations have been effected in violation of the anti-trust laws, if at all;

"(2) The extent to which consolidations or combinations of such organizations are susceptible to regulation under the Federal Trade Commission Act or the anti-trust laws, if at all; and

"(3) What legislation, if any, should be enacted for the purpose of regulating and controlling chain store distribution.

"And for the information of the Senate in connection with the aforesaid subdivisions (1), (2) and (3) of this resolution the commission is directed to inquire into and report in full to the Senate:

"(a) The extent to which the chain store movement has tended to create a monopoly or concentration of control in the distribution of any commodity either locally or nationally;

"(b) Evidences indicating the existence of unfair methods of competition in commerce or agreements, conspiracies, or combinations in restraint of trade involving chain store distribution;

"(c) The advantages or disadvantages of chain store distribution in comparison with those of other types of distribution as shown by prices, costs, profits and margins, quality of goods and services rendered by chain stores and other distributors or resulting from integration, managerial efficiency, low overhead, or other similar causes;

"(d) How far the rapid increase in the chain store system of distribution is based upon actual savings in cost of management and operation and how far upon quantity prices available only to chain store distributors or any class of them;

"(e) Whether or not such quantity prices constitute a violation of either the Federal Trade Commission Act, the Clayton Act or any other statute and

"(f) What legislation, if any, should be enacted with reference to such quantity prices."

This was a major assignment handed to the Federal Trade Commission and, with the limited manpower at its disposal, it took the Commission six years before it was able to send the Senate its final report and conclusions. In the interim, it had submitted 33 separate reports on various phases of its study as the work progressed. Some idea of the scope of the inquiry may be gathered from the fact that the official report consists of some 2,694 printed pages and made a volume more than 5 inches thick.

Among the subjects covered were:

1. The growth and development of chain stores and their distribution by States.

2. Chain-store wages.

3. Short-weighing and over-weighing in chain and independent grocery stores.

4. Chain-store price policies.

5. Comparative prices of chains and independent stores in the grocery and drug fields in four different cities.

6. Chain-store manufacturing and sources of supply.

7. Special discounts and allowances received by chains in grocery, drug and tobacco fields.

8. Sales, margins, costs and profits of chains.

9. Voluntary chains in the drug, grocery and hardware fields.

10. Final report and conclusions.

The data collected by the Commission was obtained, for the most part, through schedules filed by the chains and others from whom information was desired. The chain-store schedule consisted of 36 printed pages. Field work by the Commission's staff and special investigators produced the additional data needed for the study.

What the Commission inquiry revealed with respect to the various subjects covered will not be discussed at length in these pages. On many of them the data compiled was inadequate to warrant conclusions of any real significance. Naturally, in the course of the investigation *some* evidence was found to support the familiar charges of chain-store short-weights, low wages, price-cutting and excessive discounts and allowances. On the other hand, the investigation revealed that such practices were by no means confined to the chains—that independent merchants and wholesalers indulged in them too.

But on the main question which the Senate had put to the Commission: "What legislation, if any, should be enacted for the purpose of regulating and controlling chain-store distribution?" this is what the Commission said:[12]

"To tax out of existence the advantages of chain stores over competitors is to tax out of existence the advantages which the consuming public have found in patronizing them, with a consequent addition to the cost of living for that section of the public. That portion of the public which is able to pay cash and is willing to forego delivery service in return for the advantage of lower prices will be deprived of that privilege, generally speaking, although there are exceptions both ways. It will also tend to an arbitrary frustration of whatever saving in cost of production and distribution results from integration of the functions of producer, wholesaler and retailer. So, on the whole, the number of people adversely affected by such a tax would constitute a very substantial percentage in comparison with the number adversely affected by present conditions. The graduated tax on chain

[12] 74th Congress, 1st Session, Senate Document No. 4, *Final Report on the Chain Store Investigation.*

stores cannot accomplish fully the social ends aimed at by such legislation without producing incidentally these results." [13]

And on the question of a possible monopoly, the Commission's conclusions were equally decisive. Not only did the Commission find no evidence of a chain-store monopoly at the time of its investigation, but it recommended that all danger from that direction in the future could be readily averted by a simple amendment of existing anti-trust laws. The amendment it suggested would prohibit one corporation from acquiring the assets of another corporation where the effect "may be substantially to lessen competition or to tend to create a monopoly." In 1950 such an amendment to Section 7 of the Clayton Act was actually enacted,[14] although, of course, it is aimed at mergers of all kinds and not merely at mergers of chain-store companies.

But, no doubt, the mere fact that the Federal Trade Commission was *investigating* chain stores was prejudicial to the chains. On the principle that there is no smoke without fire, many people believe that an indictment is only the initial step to a verdict of guilty, and an "investigation" has about the same significance. Why are the chains being investigated by the Federal Trade Commission if their success is on the up and up? was a question which the average layman was in no

---

[13] That authorities on public finance regarded special taxes to discourage chain stores with no greater favor than the Federal Trade Commission was revealed by two surveys made in 1935 and 1938, respectively. The first was made by Miss Mabel L. Walker, Executive Secretary, Tax Policy League (now Tax Institute, Inc.) and published in *Tax Systems of the World*, 6th Edition, Commerce Clearing House, Inc., Chicago, 1935. Of 52 senior professors of public finance in leading American colleges and universities, who responded to a questionnaire asking for their attitude on various types of taxes, 45, or 86%, disapproved "special taxes to discourage chain stores," 6 were non-committal and only one approved them.

The second study, made by the New York State Tax Commission in 1938, and reported in the 7th Edition of the above work, published in 1938, revealed that, of 127 Professors of Finance answering the same question, 114, or 89%, disapproved of such taxes, 8 favored them and 5 were non-committal.

[14] P.L. 899, December 29, 1950.

position to answer but which carried its own implications to any but the more logical.

One of the most aggravating features of the anti-chain crusade was the "trade-at-home" campaign sponsored by local merchants with or without the help of professional agitators. The publicity given to such a project in one community naturally prompted promotion-minded retailers in others to launch similar campaigns.

When such a campaign was organized in Petersburg, Va., early in 1926, *Chain Store Age*[15] pointed out that it was doomed to failure because, while the local merchants might support it financially, consumers would remain skeptical. In fact, "the more the independent merchants thunder against the menace of the chains," the editorial observed, "the more the consumer begins to realize their underlying virtues." A warning was offered that "about the very worst thing that could happen to cities like Petersburg, which raise war-chests to fight the chains, would be to have the chains take them at their word and leave them flat."

A few months later, *Chain Store Age*[16] reported that the Petersburg campaign was still on, "a high-powered speaker from New York" having been imported to promote it. Whether or not the "high-powered speaker from New York" was responsible was not made clear but the story quoted a chain-store manager in Petersburg as saying that his sales had *increased* 50% since the campaign had begun!

That same month the independent merchants of Jacksonville, Ill., ran a full-page advertisement in the local newspaper warning the public that "the future of the children" was jeopardized by chain-store growth.

This sort of thing spread throughout the country, gradually at first but gaining momentum in the years which followed,

[15] April, 1926.
[16] July, 1926.

especially when professional promoters saw in such campaigns a chance to profit by them. Among the trade-at-home campaigns which were being waged in 1929, was one in Springfield, Mo., under the auspices of the local Chamber of Commerce. Because it was more or less typical of similar campaigns elsewhere, some of the copy angles used in the local newspaper advertising will serve to reveal the appeal most commonly employed.

The slogan for the campaign in question was: "Keep Ozark Dollars in the Ozarks." Under the headline: "The Chain Store Menace," an advertisement in the Springfield *Leader*, May 13, 1929, read as follows:

"Too much cannot be said against certain chain stores and their methods. Their local managers are 'mechanical operators,' controlled entirely by a set formula. These local managers cannot participate in any action, cause or activity for the good of all Springfield. They are not permitted to 'give until it hurts' either of their time or of their company's money. Their duties, boiled down, are to 'get Springfield's money' and to send it to the Home Office.

"Cities are not built on this basis.

"Your loyalty to the Home Owned Stores—your patronage and friendliness to these stores—and your recognition of the Chain Store in its true light—that of a parasite upon legitimate business and a menace to our city's prosperity, will result in a CONTINUATION of that prosperity which has made Springfield so outstanding."

The advertisement carried the signature of the Chamber of Commerce, Community Building Bureau.

Another advertisement in the series[17] stressed the point that "not one of the executive heads of any chain store organization now opening up in this city, owns a residence here. Living in distant cities, we can hardly expect these chain-store

[17] May 6, 1929.

owners to have any other interest in Springfield and the Ozarks than to take what money they can out of the city. The owners of our home stores, together with you and all other loyal citizens, are boosters for Springfield. Our money has built up the city. Let's continue to stand together." Readers were urged to "Patronize Your Home-Owned Stores —the Money They Earn Stays in Springfield—for the Development of Springfield—not Chicago or New York."

The "absentee-ownership" theme was not, of course, the only one used but it was undoubtedly the one most commonly employed. The appeal for loyalty to the local merchant was based largely on the implication that the community was dependent upon him for the building and support of its schools, churches, public parks, libraries and other community institutions. Entirely ignored was the fact that most public activities are supported by public funds in the form of *taxes* to which *all* contribute in one way or another—the wage-earner and the tenant as well as the employer and the home-owner, the chain store as well as the single-store merchant, the manufacturer as well as the distributor and the professional man as well as the business man. So far as donations to churches, charities and other activities dependent largely upon voluntary contributions were concerned, the fact that the average independent merchant was in no position to make more than a token contribution, if any, to such projects was also lost sight of.

Nevertheless, these "trade-at-home" campaigns persisted. In the year ending October 1, 1930, the National Chain Store Association noted that they had been developed in more than 400 cities and towns throughout the United States.

What the situation was at that time was summarized by the late Robert W. Lyons, executive vice president of that association, as follows:

"Up to a year ago, the American public was conscious only

that something tremendous was taking place in the field of distribution. Anti-chain-store propaganda was so great that much genuine sympathy was aroused on behalf of the out-of-date and unsuccessful merchant. In more than 400 cities and towns throughout the United States, active local organizations were developed to fight the so-called 'chain-store menace.' United States senators, congressmen, governors, judges, State legislators, county and city officials, were being drawn into the ever-widening group who were opposed to the chain store. Local radio stations from coast to coast were being impressed with the profits to be made by selling their time to the enemies of the chain store. More than 100 newspapers had added their voice to this already noisy chorus."

Included in the ammunition used by the anti-chain interests were various pamphlets prepared and circulated by the American Wholesale Grocers' Association and other organized and individual sponsors. One of these pamphlets, whose title suggests its nature, was called: "Sons and Daughters for Sale"; it was the work of W. A. Masters, treasurer of an old-line dry-goods wholesale house. It was widely circulated through other jobbers, manufacturers and retailers.

The use of the radio against the chains on an extensive scale was probably initiated by W. K. ("Old Man") Henderson of Shreveport, La., who used his own station KWKH, Shreveport, for that purpose. Incorporating his project as the "Hello World Broadcasting Corporation"—named after the opening words of all his broadcasts, "Hello World"—"Old Man" Henderson, as he dubbed himself, discovered very quickly that attacking the chains in a vituperative way brought him country-wide attention which he lost no time in capitalizing.

His first step was to organize over the air the "Merchants' Minute Men," an organization to which any independent merchant could belong by merely sending Henderson $12. His appeal to those who felt the need for assistance against

"the chain-store octopus," which Henderson built up so ter-
rifyingly, was an effective one and money is said to have
flowed into his coffers from all corners of the country.[18]

To supplement that income, Henderson offered to sell his
own brand of coffee at $1 a pound to anyone who wanted
to contribute to the cause. As the best coffee was selling at
that time at less than half that price, Henderson's coffee sales
must have netted him a liberal profit.

How much Henderson collected in all from his campaign
only he knew, but the general impression was that he had
uncovered a "gold mine." At any rate, he could not keep this
new type of anti-chain racket to himself very long. Imitators
sprang up in various sections of the country and the air war
against the chains was extended to many fronts. In fact,
although Henderson dropped his campaign before the end of
1931 and turned his attention to other activities, the other
broadcasters maintained the air barrage for some time longer.

One interesting feature of the Henderson campaign was
a counterattack launched by Clarence Saunders, one of the
founders of the Piggly Wiggly system of self-service stores
but then operating individually as "Clarence Saunders, Sole
Owner of My Name." He used full-page advertisements in
the Memphis newspapers to lambaste the Shreveport traducer
of the chains. In such an advertisement in the Memphis *Commercial Appeal*, March 14, 1930, which was addressed to "Rat
Henderson," Saunders let loose a flood of personal vitupera-
tion which even Henderson must have found it difficult if not
impossible to match.

That many of the anti-chain-store projects were regarded
as "rackets" by the legitimate retailers' associations is evidenced by two bulletins in the author's possession.

One of them, dated February 14, 1930, was issued by C.H.

[18] "Henderson's Merchant Minute Men Challenge the Chains," *Printers' Ink*,
February 20, 1930.

Janssen, secretary-manager of the National Association of Retail Grocers. It read in part as follows:

"At the present time, there are in the United States literally thousands of individuals interesting themselves in anti-chain-store campaigns purely for the money they can make out of it for themselves. To the extent that any so-called anti-chain-store campaign is based purely on the educational grounds of acquainting the merchants and the public with the economic, social and civic benefits of the individual type of distribution, we have no criticism to offer, but we all know that every movement which has reached a momentum where it interests a large number of our people attracts what we may term 'camp followers' who attach themselves to such movements for the purpose of exploiting them to promote profits for themselves. . . .

"There are on my desk at the present time seven applications for financial assistance from newly born companies and individuals. . . . I have had inquiries from nearly every section of the country indicating that our self-appointed friends are numerous.

"Retail grocers and all merchants should be warned against parting with their money to support irresponsible parties or campaigns which promise no constructive results for the individual trade. A recent attempt to secure information about several such organizations clearly indicates that these organizations are set up to make money for their promoters."

The other bulletin, dated February 19, 1930, was issued by George V. Sheridan, director, Ohio Council of Retail Merchants, and, referring to one of the new anti-chain-store associations which were operating in Ohio, read in part as follows:

". . . We are receiving a number of inquiries from merchants and local secretaries as to whether we have indorsed or are affiliated with this 'movement' to fight the chain stores. In reply, we will state definitely that none of the organizations connected with the Council have indorsed or are connected with this organization in any way. So far as we have been able to learn, none of the existing state retail associations outside the Council have indorsed it. Several have definitely refused to approve the movement. . . .

"The Ohio Wholesale Grocers' Association and the Ohio Retail Grocers' Association, both of which have been active in the past in fighting the chain stores, have advised their members definitely to withhold financial support from . . . any of these movements originating in Ohio. . . .

"The Dayton Better Business Bureau has issued a confidential report calling attention to the fact that at least one-half of the $10 membership fee goes to the salesmen and promoters who are soliciting the memberships."

What were the chains doing all this time to offset the abuse to which they were being subjected on so many fronts?

As a matter of fact, not until the end of 1928, when the National Chain Store Association came into being, were the chains equipped to do anything at all in an over-all way. Prior to that, the chains had only two associations, both in the grocery field. One was the National Chain Store Grocers Association, organized in 1920, and the other a regional association, the Western States Chain Grocers Association, organized in 1922, to which reference has already been made.[19]

The national association, of which Alfred H. Beckmann had been one of the founders and had served as its executive director throughout its existence, fulfilled its purpose more or less effectively until it was succeeded in 1928 by the National Chain Store Association. Its annual meetings had brought together food-chain operators from all over the country. Many of them were destined to work together in the common interest for many years to follow. It was the only organization in its time which was equipped to keep an eye on the anti-chain movement which was then getting under way, particularly

[19] P. 122, *supra*.

on the anti-chain-store legislative measures which were then beginning to crop up.

However, as *Chain Store Age* had pointed out in its very first issue, which appeared in June, 1925, what the situation called for was a national chain-store association open to chains in all fields. Not only would all chains be affected by the wave of anti-chain bills which, even then, was indicated, but why should the food chains carry the burden of fighting them alone?

That proposal was slow to take root but, when in 1927 three anti-chain-store tax bills were actually enacted, as has been previously detailed, the first step in the proposed direction was taken. At its convention in 1927, the National Chain Store Grocers Association amended its constitution to provide for the admission of chains outside the food field as associate members. Furthermore, a large part of the meeting was devoted to a discussion of the problem and what could be done about it.

The final step was taken the following year in Memphis, when the old association met for its eighth and final convention. There it was dissolved and a new organization, the National Chain Store Association, open to chains in all fields, was simultaneously organized to take its place. Within a few months, as soon as they had had a chance to learn of the new organization, practically all the leading chains in all fields became affiliated with it.

Its first president was E. G. Yonker, Sanitary Grocery Co. (now Safeway), Washington, D.C.; first vice president, F. H. Massmann, National Tea Co., Chicago; second vice president, Edward Dale, Safeway Stores, Inc., Oakland, Calif.; third vice president, T. Harry Roulston, Thomas Roulston Inc., Brooklyn, N.Y.; treasurer, H. C. Bohack, H. C. Bohack Co., Brooklyn, N.Y.; and secretary and general manager *pro tem*, the author, who was the editor of *Chain Store Age*. The reason all the original officers came from the grocery field despite the general nature of the new organization was that few of the top men of the chains in other fields had been present at the organization meeting in Memphis. The following year, however, Paul H. Metzger, Washington Shirt Shops, Chicago, and Malcolm G. Gibbs, Peoples Drug Stores, Washington, D.C., were elected vice presidents in addition to Edward Dale, Safeway Stores, and William N. Haraway, Continental Food Stores. Ward Melville, Melville Shoe Corporation, New York, became treasurer, and other chains were well represented on the board of directors and the executive committee. Among the members of the board were George B. Everitt, Montgomery Ward & Co., Chicago; George M. Gales, Louis K. Liggett Co., New York; E. H. Krom, G. R. Kinney Co., New York; Frank Melville, Jr., Melville Shoe Corporation; J. C. Penney, J. C. Penney Company, New York; C. B. Van Dusen, S. S. Kresge Co., Detroit; Gen. R. E. Wood, Sears, Roebuck & Co., Chicago; C. R. Walgreen, Walgreen Company, Chicago; and Don Davis, Western Auto Supply Co., Kansas City, Mo.; besides four from the grocery field: C. F. Adams, First National Stores, Somerville, Mass.; Samuel Robinson, American Stores Co., Philadelphia; Ross McIntyre, MacMarr Stores, Portland, Ore.; and M. B. Skaggs, Safeway Stores.

The executive committee consisted of F. H. Massmann, National Tea Co., chairman; E. G. Yonker, Sanitary Grocery Co.; Alvin E. Dodd, Sears, Roebuck & Co.; Ward Melville, Melville Shoe Corp.; Roy H. Ott, J. C. Penney Company; T. H. Roulston, Thos. Roulston, Inc.; Wheeler Sammons, Walgreen Company; W. T. Grant, W. T. Grant Co., New York, and John B. Bonham, Kroger Grocery & Baking Co., Cincinnati.

Elected as president was William H. Albers, Kroger Grocery & Baking Company, but in May, 1930, when he resigned from that company, his successor, Albert H. Morrill, took over as president of that company and of the National Chain Store Association as well.

Reappointed as executive vice president was Robert W. Lyons, the young Indiana lawyer who had been selected to direct the association's activities a few months after its organization and who had demonstrated early that he was fully equal to the task.

With such a powerful and representative organization, the chains could hardly have been expected to remain silent and inactive in the face of the barrage of propaganda which was being unleashed against them—to allow their traducers to go unanswered. Nor could they have been expected to stay away from the State capitols where legislators were being urged to check their further progress by punitive and discriminatory taxes.

After all, did not the new type of distribution they had introduced represent a definite improvement over the one it was, to some extent, replacing? Had not the success they had achieved come legitimately? Did it not reflect public approval of the kind of stores they were operating? And if their growth had been extensive and rapid, especially in recent years, was that not in the public interest? If the public preferred chain stores, as their patronage indicated, why not establish them wherever needed as rapidly as possible? Furthermore, most of the charges levelled at the chains were false, exaggerated or irrelevant and the whole anti-chain movement was inspired and sustained by the selfish interests of those who felt the effects of chain-store competition or who sought to capitalize the resentment which resulted.

At least that was the way the chains felt about the situation. What they did about it is reflected in the annual report of Mr. Lyons, covering the work of the association in the year ending October 1, 1930.

In order to meet and counteract the growth of anti-chain-store propaganda, an organized educational campaign had been commenced shortly after October 1, 1929. Its purpose was to give to the public a clearer understanding of just what the chain stores meant in terms of superior merchandise at lower cost, to provide students in high schools and colleges with authoritative information about the chain-store system, to acquaint the farmer with the benefits he derives from more efficient distribution as represented by the chains, and inform Federal and State executives and legislators regarding the social and economic value of the chains and the danger involved in imposing unsound tax burdens on them.

One feature of the program was a monthly bulletin called *Chain Store Progress*. It presented a digest of current developments, editorial comment and addresses made regarding the chain-store question. More than 400,000 copies of it were distributed during the year. The bulk of the copies went to legislators, editors, teachers of marketing, State marketing officials, college libraries, debaters and a special list of more than 21,000 leading citizens.

Several hundred thousand pamphlets and reprints of speeches were also distributed and articles were supplied to leading periodicals.

Mr. Lyons, executives of member companies and two professional speakers addressed scores of meetings of business men and made radio broadcasts whenever the opportunity arose.

"One of the most interesting manifestations of the public interest in the chain-store question," Mr. Lyons pointed out, "has been the increasing frequency with which it has been selected as the topic for leading high school and college debates. More than 500 such debates have been held during the past year. In practically every case we have been asked to supply the data upon which the chain store could be adequately championed. We have supplied such material in ever-increasing quantities and, based upon our present information, we are anticipating almost 5,000 similar debates to be held throughout the United States during the coming year. We have prepared a comprehensive Debaters' Manual, covering every phase of the chain-store subject, and are prepared to distribute it wherever such information is required. It is gratifying to note that approximately 85 per cent of all the debates held this year were decided in favor of the teams which supported the chain stores in their arguments. We believe that our thorough-going preparation of debate material has been an important factor in contributing to this success."

The association set up a research department, with Dr. Paul C. Olsen, of Columbia University, as consulting director. It not only undertook to gather, analyze and interpret a vast quantity of data about chain stores issued by others, but made some important original studies itself.

One of the main functions of the association was to see that the flood of discriminatory tax legislation which was finding its way into almost every State legislature met with at least some resistance. Whenever and wherever such bills were introduced, the association arranged for representation by counsel and sent a member of its own staff to appraise the situation and decide what measures could be taken to defeat the proposal. How effective the association's effort was is indicated by the fact that of 142 bills introduced in 29 legislatures between January 1, 1929, and October 1, 1930, only six imposing chain-store taxes were passed.

If the association was proud of its work in the legislatures, as Mr. Lyons' report indicated, it had even more cause for gratification with the success the chains had so far achieved in the courts. Wherever they had challenged the constitutionality of anti-chain tax laws, they had won. The association was particularly pleased with the chains' latest victory in Indianapolis, where a three-judge Federal Court had declared the Indiana tax of 1929 unconstitutional. The association's research department had compiled the economic data and statistics used so effectively in the case. The whole case was built around the testimony of Mr. Lyons and Dr. Paul H. Nystrom, professor of marketing, Columbia University.

On the litigation front, indeed, the outlook then was bright enough for Mr. Lyons to express the hope that within the next two years, by careful preparation and guidance of litigation, such as had characterized the Indiana case, the association would be able "to establish the manifest unconstitutionality" of all these anti-chain tax laws.

Unfortunately, however, within a very few months after that expression of confidence, the whole picture was to change.

On May 18, 1931, the decision of the three-judge Court was reversed by the U.S. Supreme Court. In deciding that the Indiana chain-store tax was constitutional,[20] the Supreme Court validated not only that particular tax but *all* chain-store taxes of that type. It established the principle that chain stores were different in *kind* from independent stores and not merely *in degree,* and that the difference was great enough to justify different tax treatment. True enough, the decision was by a divided court, five to four, but it was just as decisive and as ominous, from a chain-store standpoint, as if it had been unanimous.

It was a heavy blow for the chains, coming as it did from a source which they had reasonably regarded as their one sure refuge. Furthermore, it came at a most unfortunate time— when the need for additional State revenue was almost universal throughout the country. With practically every State looking hungrily for new tax sources, how could the chains hope to avert a veritable avalanche of new levies for which the Supreme Court had not only cleared the way but had flood-lighted it?

However, the chains were fortunate in one respect. Most of the legislatures which had regular sessions scheduled for 1931 had already adjourned. Only eleven were still in session. Thus, the full effect of the decision would be deferred at least until the following year, when only nine States were scheduled to hold regular sessions, although at least fifteen more

[20] State Board *v.* Jackson, p. 132, *supra.*

were expected to call special sessions because of their revenue deficits.

To meet this crisis, the association advanced its annual meeting to June 22, 1931—to take immediate stock of the situation and decide what could be done about it.

What happened at that meeting was revealed in Mr. Lyons' report for the year ending September 30, 1931. Because of the summer meeting, it had been decided to forego the usual convention in October. To take its place, *Chain Store Age* devoted its October issue to what was designated as a "stay-at-home convention." Among the reports presented at that "convention" was that of Mr. Lyons. It revealed that, at the June meeting, the majority had favored an immediate, gigantic campaign to inform consumers of the true meaning of anti-chain-store taxes, stressing their effect on the general standard of living. Others, more conservative-minded, had felt that the launching of any such campaign might well be deferred until the leaders of the industry had had more time to weigh the various problems involved. One thing they had all agreed upon was that the budget for the year beginning October 1 should be double what it had previously been.[21] Most of the additional funds would be needed for the extra tax-defense work, which would certainly be necessary, and the educational and research programs would have to be stepped up even if an all-out educational campaign were not undertaken.

During the year, Mr. Lyons reported, more than 5,000 debates on the chain-store question had been staged before high-school and college audiences aggregating some 1,900,-000 persons.

Of the eleven legislatures still in session when the Supreme Court decision was handed down, Mr. Lyons reported that seven had lost no time in pressing anti-chain-store bills for passage. And some of them were far more severe than the relatively mild tax involved in the decision.

[21] The budget had previously been $250,000.

"In Florida," Mr. Lyons pointed out, "the tax proposed in the top bracket was $250 per store, but an Illinois bill set the maximum at $1,000."

"Fortunately for the chain-store industry," he observed, "only two chain-store bills were passed since the Supreme Court's decision—Florida and Alabama (a bill taxing chain stores was passed by both houses in Wisconsin but, owing to a technical error, Governor LaFollette returned it to the legislature where it was tabled until the next session).

"The year 1931-1932, however, with nine legislatures in regular session and fifteen in special session, may tell an entirely different story unless some sound, aggressive action is taken by the chain-store industry."

What actually happened in 1932, when 125 bills were introduced, is shown in Table 17, page 142, as is also the box-score for 1933, when 225 bills came up for consideration and thirteen of them were passed.

How many of the seventeen anti-chain-store tax laws passed in 1931, 1932 and 1933, after the Supreme Court decision, might have been enacted in any event cannot, of course, be known. The combined effect of sustained anti-chain propaganda and the widespread need for additional State revenue would probably have produced some of them even if their constitutionality had still remained in doubt. On the other hand, but for the decision, many of the laws in question would not have been enacted.

But the decision, unexpectedly enough, had some favorable consequences too. Among them was the reaction of the daily press. Almost unanimously it deprecated the decision, stressing the potential danger to the economy if it resulted in checking chain-store development. That the reaction was not just another case of sympathy for the under-dog was obvious from its extent and the reasons which accompanied it.

Chain Store Age,[22] commenting on it, declared:

[22] *Chain Store Age*, July, 1931.

"In the whole history of chain-store development, we doubt whether as much space has been devoted to the merits of the chain-store idea as has been used in the few weeks since the Supreme Court decision was handed down, and certainly the amount of *favorable* comm nt the chains have received in the public press was never a[roached before the Supreme Court declared that the chai s are the legitimate prey of every State which wants to mulct them.

"Why this belated recognition by the newspapers of the merits of the chain-store idea? Why this sudden awakening to the folly of penalizing the chain store for the benefit of those who serve the public less efficiently?

"The answer lies in the fact that for the first time the newspapers of the country have a clear idea of what the agitation against the chains really means. This decision of the Supreme Court has driven home the fact that the chains have grown because they represent a distinct improvement over the methods of distribution they are, to some extent, replacing. Unfavorable as this decision is from the chain-store standpoint in one respect, certain it is the chains themselves could issue no more effective propaganda in their own behalf. . . .

"We are convinced that the reason so many newspapers have revealed such a friendly attitude towards the chain-store idea since this decision was handed down is that, for the first time, their eyes have been opened to the truth.

"If that is a correct deduction, then the course of the chains is crystal clear. The simple truths set out by the Supreme Court must be repeated so frequently, so forcibly and so convincingly that not only the newspapers of the country but every man, woman and child will understand and appreciate them. Only in that way may the chains expect to escape the penalties of discriminatory taxation which the Supreme Court has declared the States are at liberty to impose even though, in the same opinion, the most cogent reasons are given why chain-store growth should be encouraged."

But no such all-out educational campaign developed. Although the association did set up a committee in 1931 [23] to discuss such a campaign and to make its recommendations, and various comprehensive plans were submitted by committeemen who favored the idea, that was as far as it went. Several factors combined to thwart further action along those lines, as will appear later.

Another favorable outcome of the Supreme Court decision was its effect on the more conservative element among the leaders in the independent field itself. Many of them believed that it might prove to be a boomerang which would eventually hurt the independent merchant as well as the chains.

In a speech to the National Retail Dry Goods Association, whose membership consisted primarily of independent retailers, George V. Sheridan, executive director of the Ohio Retailers' Council, another organization primarily interested in promoting the interests of independent retailers, pointed out that "a legislature which taxes chain stores today will tax all stores tomorrow." [24] He was particularly apprehensive of the effect on all retailers of a gross sales tax, such as was imposed by the Kentucky Act of 1930, if that type of tax should likewise be held constitutional by the Supreme Court. A decision from that Court was then expected momentarily, although when it was handed down in 1932, it was an abortive one. It merely required the lower court which, on technical grounds, had dismissed the case challenging the constitutionality of the law, to try the issues on the merits. The Supreme Court's final decision, declaring the Act unconstitutional, was not handed down until several years later. [25]

Mr. Sheridan stressed the fact that such a tax not only hurt the big department stores as well as chain stores, being based

[23] The committee consisted of Fred H. Massmann, National Tea Co.; Ward Melville, Melville Shoe Corporation; Roy Ott, J. C. Penney Company; Wheeler Sammons, Walgreen Company, and the author. *Chain Store Age*, October, 1931.

[24] *Chain Store Age*, March, 1932.

[25] P. 147, *supra*.

entirely on sales volume, but that even small independent stores could not expect to remain immune, even though the law as it then stood practically exempted the small-scale merchant. What was to prevent the legislature at any time from amending the law to bring even the small retailers into the tax-paying category?

In any event, the National Retail Dry Goods Association took a definite position against special chain-store taxes as did many individual champions of the independent merchant who openly advised against them.

So far as the chains themselves were concerned, although an all-out educational program appealed to many of their leaders as an obvious step to be taken, whatever it might cost, some of the factors which prevented it from ever getting beyond the planning stage may now be considered.

In the first place, the long-range benefits of an educational campaign seemed to many to be of secondary value compared with the immediate task of fighting the numerous anti-chain tax bills, already pending in the legislatures, or which were certain to be introduced later.

To the objection raised by some that lobbying against proposed legislation was a dangerous business, if not actually unethical, Mr. Lyons replied forcefully in a report to the executive committee in March, 1932. Because of the criticism which was later to be leveled at the tax-defense measures used by the chains, particularly with respect to their practice of retaining politically powerful representatives at State capitols, Mr. Lyons' observations on the "ethics" involved are worth preserving. He said:[26]

> "The problem concerning the wisdom and the ethics of our tax-defense program is one of profound significance. Any intelligent judgment of it must be based upon a broad understanding of the character and development of State government.

[26] From typewritten copy in author's possession.

"State legislatures throughout the United States, in the exercise of governmental functions, are considering proposals designed to drive chain stores out of existence, or to place them at a competitive disadvantage. The question, therefore, arises as to what the chain stores should do and have a right to do in opposing such legislation.

"In answering this question, I stand upon the time-honored premise that the governments of the various states are organized no less to protect the chain stores, the manufacturers from whom chain stores buy, and every business of every kind, than they are to protect the rights and prerogatives of the individual retailer and the individual citizen.

"It seems to me to follow that if proposed tax laws will injure chain-store operations, and thus curtail benefits heretofore made available to the consuming public, then the chain stores not only enjoy the right to oppose such legislation before the proper governmental bodies, but they owe an inescapable obligation of citizenship to make that opposition as effective as possible, while keeping it, in spirit and in fact, within the law. Furthermore, it seems to me that every manufacturer from whom we buy, and whose prosperity, together with that of his employes and his community, is involved in any pernicious or destructive tax scheme, owes an equally inescapable obligation to raise his voice and his influence in opposition to such corruption of governmental action. . . .

"If democratic government, administered under party systems, were perfect in integrity and wisdom, it would be unnecessary to meet this problem. Unfortunately, this is not the case. The history of party politics and of politicians has been the same the world over. Their activities have been developed as an expression of the will of the voters—but they are scarcely established until they sterilize self-government and actually restrain the average voter from having what he really wants. The ultimate status of political parties and politicians is to tell the people what they want, and to give it to them even when they want nothing at all. . . .

"To understand the problem which the chain stores face, it is necessary to realize that in every State there is a wet vote and a dry vote, a city vote and a rural vote, a radical vote and a conservative vote, the utility vote and the railroad vote, the farm vote and the soldier vote, the hoodlum vote and the church vote and so on without end.

"These organized and articulate minorities maintain extensive lobbies for the purpose of securing their legislative objectives, which mostly result in plundering the public treasury for some selfish end. Our State governments, far from being perfect, apparently worship but one god—legislation. The arts and sciences of administration and management, which sound government demands are totally ignored by the politician, for obvious reasons. Legislation fascinates because, under the cloak of law, special privilege is made legal. I maintain that it is no less the granting of a special privilege for a State legislature to tax chain stores and let their competitors go untaxed, than for it to give soldiers, or the Anti-Saloon League, or the farmer, a dole out of the public treasury.

"If I am right in my conclusions about this, then it follows that in the interest of sound government there needs to be a vigorous check upon those political systems which make it possible for organized minority groups to force destructive legislation through our State assemblies, with a resultant expense to the whole people.

"No one, I am sure, will suggest that the current flood of anti-chain-store tax legislation is a reflection of the will of the majority of our people. Nor will they suggest that it is being fostered by any save a selfish minority interest. Even so, unless the chain stores refuse to acquiesce in the feeble attitude that would have us abandon our defenses, they will find themselves the victims of those strong opposing forces which are already trying to organize party politics so as to loot them of their justly earned success. . . .

"The proposal that the chain stores give up their tax defense is in fact to urge the chain stores to resolve themselves into a sort of defenseless jelly, for which our enemies pray and upon which they hope to feed."

Another factor which worked against serious consideration of a major educational campaign was the discouraging depression under which the country was staggering. Although chain-store sales were not feeling the effect of reduced consumer buying power to the same degree as retail sales in general, chain-store sales, and profits, also, were definitely declining. Furthermore, the situation gave little hope for improvement in the foreseeable future. One direct effect of declining chain-store sales was a corresponding decline in the association's revenue, which was based on the sales of member companies. In the face of these conditions, the decision made in June, 1931, to double the budget for the following year was rescinded, and the 1931-1932 year began with less revenue in sight than had been budgeted the previous year, before the devastating Supreme Court decision.

Still another consideration was a feeling upon the part of many of the operators that perhaps the best approach to a solution of their problems would be to set up State associations in place of or to supplement the national organization. The tax problems, it was argued, were at the State level, and the support of local chains in opposing them might be gained more readily than had proved to be the case with the national association directing the effort. The idea found sufficient favor to bring about the organization of the Illinois Chain Store Association on February 3, 1932, although an attempt a month later to organize a similar association for New York made no headway.

On the top of this conflict of ideas among the chain-store leaders came the New Deal and the National Recovery Administration,[27] which provided the answer, so far as the National Chain Store Association was concerned. For at a special three-day meeting in Washington in June, 1933, called by the chains for the purpose of deciding their future course, it was quickly agreed that the national association would no longer meet their needs. Under NRA each industry and trade was required to develop a code for its own regulation. No code could be approved by the "Blue Eagle" Administrator unless the organization sponsoring it was "truly representa-

[27] The National Industrial Recovery Act, June 16, 1933.

tive" of the field affected. Obviously the N.C.S.A. would not have met that test for all the various kinds of chains affiliated with it. It did not have enough members in any individual field to make it "truly representative" of any of them.

Thus, in 1933, the N.C.S.A. followed the example of its predecessor and dissolved itself. It was succeeded by individual associations in each of the fields in which the chains played an important part. Thus came into being the Food and Grocery Chain Stores of America, Inc., whose unwieldy name was later changed to National Association of Food Chains; the Limited Price Variety Stores Association, whose name was similarly shortened in 1957 to Variety Stores Association; the National Association of Chain Drug Stores; the National Council of Shoe Retailers; and the Mail Order Association; and, later on, the Institute of Distribution.

With the new associations pre-occupied with the many new problems created by NRA, and the old association out of the picture, what became of the tax-defense program which Mr. Lyons had organized and directed so successfully from 1929 to 1932? Fortunately for the chains as a whole, it was salvaged by the action of fourteen of the larger companies who realized the necessity of keeping it going. They retained Mr. Lyons as counsel and he continued to function in that capacity until his death in 1949.

That the organization of separate chain-store associations in the various fields was a wise one, soon became apparent. No single association could have met the need for special technical guidance in each of the fields in which the chains were a factor. Certainly the National Chain Store Association, as it was set up in 1933, was in no way geared to provide that kind of leadership.

Throughout the relatively brief existence of NRA[28] the chains would have been hard put without a special trade

[28] The National Industrial Recovery Act was declared unconstitutional by the U.S. Supreme Court, May 27, 1935, in Schechter v. U.S., 295 U.S. 495.

association in each field to represent them. In the grocery field, for instance, not only did the food chains have to work out a code for their own regulation as grocery distributors, but it was necessary to follow closely the framing of 64 codes in other industries to make sure that none of them worked unfairly against the interest of the food chains or other food distributors.[29] The same was true, to a greater or lesser extent, in each of the other fields in which the chains had set up their own association.

But the usefulness of these separate chain-store associations did not end with the termination of NRA. On the contrary, it increased substantially in the years which followed and which brought with them even more serious problems. As is revealed in later chapters, the associations played a major role in improving the chains' public relations in the only sound way in which public relations can be improved—by helping the chains do a better all-round job.

In the meanwhile, however, several chains got themselves involved in the organization of another association which was to cause them plenty of adverse publicity and embarrassment and was to result indirectly in the passage of a Federal law designed to limit the buying advantages which large-scale operators had previously enjoyed. The story of the congressional inquiry into the organization and purposes of the American Retail Federation, its expansion into an investigation of large-scale buying, and its outcome—the passage of the Robinson-Patman Act of 1936—has a direct bearing on the subject-matter of this chapter but, because of its more general application, is covered in a special chapter of its own.

[29] See "Report on N.A.F.C.," *Chain Store Age*, Grocery Edition, October, 1948.

CHAPTER IX

THE "SUPERLOBBY"
INVESTIGATION

ONE OF THE MOST eventful chapters in chain-store history was the outcome of a bungled publicity release announcing the organization of a new retail association by a group of the country's outstanding merchants.

The unfortunate release not only nearly wrecked the association in question before it was a week old, but brought about a Congressional investigation of chain-store buying practices which, in turn, played its part in securing the passage of the Robinson-Patman Act and, incidentally, launched Congressman Wright Patman on an anti-chain crusade aimed at chain-store elimination.

The story can best be told as it actually unfolded.

On April 17, 1935, the *N.Y. Times* carried a front-page story with the following headlines;

MERCHANTS OF THE NATION ORGANIZE
TO ACT AS UNIT ON ECONOMIC ISSUES

"Unified Voice" on Legislative Problems to be Aim of Group of 1,000,000—All Leading Retailers Represented

Colonel Sherrill Will Direct Activities

"Formation of the American Retail Federation to serve as the 'unified voice' of the entire field of distribution on national legislation and economic problems," the story began, "was announced here yesterday by Louis E. Kirstein, of William Filene's Sons Company, Boston, who has played a leading role in the creation of the new group.

"The federation expects to have a membership of more than 1,000,000 merchants having an annual sales volume of approximately $20,000,000,000."

The story went on to point out:

1. Plans for the federation had been developed in the previous six months.

2. Col. Clarence O. Sherrill would direct it as president with an executive committee of ten, with headquarters in Washington, D.C.

3. Mr. Kirstein had emphasized that, just as the oil producers, steel and automobile manufacturers, railroads and farmers "have long organized into national associations truly representative of their industries," so the need for a single spokesman group for the entire retail field had become evident during the early days of NRA.

4. He had also declared that membership would be open to all merchants, whether large or small, and whether they are members of retail associations or not, and that the new association would not compete with existing organizations but would be supplemental to them.

5. Major features of the program were (a) cooperation with governmental and other agencies participating in movements for the national welfare; (b) coordination of all branches of retail distribution to improve it; (c) representation of the national associations affiliated with the federation in national public relations compatible with the program of policies laid down by the board of trustees; and (d) stimulation of greater appreciation on the part of retailers of the service given them by the national retail associations and

encouragement of the development of representative, well-organized and coordinated State councils.

6. A vital function would be to furnish statistics on retail distribution to government and other agencies.

7. Col. Sherrill would resign immediately as vice president of Kroger Grocery and Baking Company to take up his new post.

8. Herbert J. Tily, president of Strawbridge and Clothier, a Philadelphia department store, who had been one of the leaders in the formation of the federation, was president of the Retailer's National Council, an informal organization representing *thirteen leading retail associations*. "They, together with numerous other retail units, doing an extremely large volume of business," the story declared, "will become *the nucleus of the new federation*. These associations comprise the National Retail Dry Goods Association, National Association of Retail Clothiers, National Association of Retail Grocers, National Retail Furniture Association, National Retail Hardware Association, American National Retail Jewelers Association, National Association of Retail Druggists, National Shoe Retailers Association, Limited Price Variety Stores Association, Inc., Mail Order Association of America, National Council of Shoe Retailers, National Retail Association of Music Merchants and Food and Grocery Chain Stores of America."

9. Mr. Kirstein had explained that the membership set-up had been designed "to safeguard the interests of the smaller merchant by adequate representation on the governing body."

10. The executive committee consisted of Mr. Kirstein; Percy S. Straus, R. H. Macy & Co.; John S. Burke, B. Altman & Co.; George M. Gales, Liggett Drug Company; Claude W. Kress, S. H. Kress & Co.; Fred Lazarus, Jr., The F. & R. Lazarus & Co.; Albert H. Morrill, Kroger Grocery & Baking Co.; Lessing J. Rosenwald, Sears, Roebuck and Co.; Earl C. Sams, J. C. Penney Co.; and Herbert J. Tily.

11. Twenty other leading merchants had taken an active part in the formation of the federation. All were department store men except seven chain-store executives: W. T. Grant, W. T. Grant Co.; Joy H. Johnson, Walgreen Company; Ward Melville, Melville Shoe Corporation; Samuel Robinson, American Stores Co.; C. B. Van Dusen, S. S. Kresge Co.; E. G. Yonker, Safeway Stores; and Earl B. Puckett, Hahn Department Stores (now Allied Stores).

12. Temporary offices had been opened at the New Willard.

The newspaper stories followed rather closely a press release which had been issued by the organizers of the federation.

How the advent of the new association was greeted by the trade press is indicated by a signed article in *Women's Wear Daily*, one of the Fairchild publications, the same evening. W. D. Hart declared himself as follows:

> "At last it has come. Or perhaps it would be better to say that it is well on its way. What? A unified voice for the retail craft. The formation of the American Retail Federation is one of the most vital happenings in the retail industry in many a year. . . . Such an organization as is planned by the new group in regard to educating Government officials, manufacturers and consumers has unlimited possibilities. The true picture of the field of distribution can be developed by this group."

In the same issue, Col. Sherrill was featured as "the new Field Marshal of retail distribution."

Retailing, another Fairchild publication, a weekly, in its April 22 issue, hailed the federation enthusiastically. Under the heading: "At Last—National Organization," Earl W. Elhart declared editorially:

> "The business of retailing is about to be given a 'national voice.' Through the organization of the new American Retail Federation for the first time in American history unified

representation of more than one million retail stores is provided for. . . . This new association, launched with such impressive backing, should be indeed a New Deal for the merchants from one end of the country to another. . . . The need for just such an organization as has been created has been repeatedly pointed out on this page. . . ."

Chain Store Age, May, 1935, declared editorially under the head: "Retailing Finds Its Voice," in part, as follows:

"Retailing has long needed not merely a spokesman but a 'loud-speaker.' Now it has one in the shape of the newly organized American Retail Federation, an association of associations, designed to represent all types of retailing, and sponsored by most of the leading retail organizations already functioning in their individual spheres. The selection of Col. C. O. Sherrill as president of the federation is hardly less significant than the conception of the organization itself. No better choice could have been made. If the federation is to be successful, it is going to need just what Col. Sherrill can supply."

The editorial suggested that ARF would relieve retailers themselves of "the burden of watching the legislatures and of organizing the opposition" to undesirable legislation proposals, and pointed out that ARF's "political influence may be expected to grow as its scope becomes better understood."

Referring to the relation of ARF to the chains, the editorial said:

"The American Retail Federation is not a chain-store organization, but the important part the chains play in retail distribution is clearly recognized in the make-up of the executive committee, of whose ten members five are department-store men and the others are chain-store executives. Col. Sherrill, although connected with the Kroger Grocery & Baking Company for several years, has resigned from that company to give his full time to the Federation."

The editorial pointed out that "the thirteen national retail associations which have for many years been affiliated with the Retailers National Council are expected to become members of the new federation at once."

That is how the new federation appeared to those who had no reason to believe that it was anything other than it purported to be. How it appeared to others and what happened as a result of their adverse reactions provided the makings of one of the many sensational chapters in chain-store history. Before proceeding with it, however, a brief résumé of Col. Sherrill's record before he became "the Field Marshal of Retail Distribution" may be useful.

As it was described in the release upon which the *Times* story was based, "Col. Sherrill brings to his new duties a wealth of experience in the retail field, coupled with a broad viewpoint growing out of his West Point training, Army experience and various governmental, civic and business duties. He is a West Point graduate and has served in all grades of the Engineer Corps, from lieutenant to colonel, in the United States, Philippines and Canal Zone. During the World War he was Chief of Staff of the Seventy-seventh Division and served in France with distinction, as witnessed by his receiving the Distinguished Service Medal and the Croix de Guerre.

"Col. Sherrill's civic and governmental experience covers a wide field. He was in Washington as director of public buildings and parks. From this position he was drafted to become the first city manager of Cincinnati. His brilliant success is attested by the very able administration which he gave to Cincinnati, as that city has become almost the American ideal for city-manager operation. In 1930 he became vice-president of the Kroger Grocery & Baking Company of Cincinnati, and he has served as vice president of the Cincinnati Chamber of Commerce, president of the Cincinnati Better Business Bureau, chairman of the Ohio National Recovery Administration Advisory Committee and director of the Ohio Retail Council. Governor Davey, of Ohio, has called upon

Col. Sherrill to head a survey of all State governmental functions, with an organization being loaned by the larger industries of the State. This valuable public work will soon be completed."

But neither Col. Sherrill's reputation nor the standing of
the men responsible for the organization of the ARF availed
to save the project from a sneak attack as unprovoked and
as unexpected, if not as world-shaking, as the one which was
to lay Pearl Harbor low some six years later.

What happened, within a week after ARF had been
launched so auspiciously, was thus reported in the New York
Herald Tribune of April 25:

HOUSE INQUIRY

IS ORDERED ON

RETAIL GROUP

New Federation Headed by
Col. Sherrill is Called
a "Chain Store Lobby"

The story began:

"Congressional investigation of the newly created American Retail Federation on charges that it represents a 'superlobby' backed by chain store interests was ordered by the
House of Representatives today through the adoption of a
resolution presented by Representative John J. Cochran,
Democrat, of Missouri."

What had brought all that about? What could possibly
have happened in the short space of those few days to turn
the ARF dream into a nightmare, as one trade-paper editor
appropriately termed it?

Most of the blame must be put, strangely enough, on the
organizers of the ARF themselves! The seat of the trouble
was the release they had given to the newspapers. It was not
as clear as it might have been. It had led the newspapers to

say something that wasn't so. They had said categorically that the thirteen national associations affiliated with the Retailers' National Council, which were listed by name, would "form the nucleus" of ARF. The fact was not only that the associations in question had not pledged themselves to membership in the ARF but they had not even been invited to join! Furthermore, the story in the newspapers was the first information the rank-and-file members of these organizations had received regarding the ARF.

No doubt the ARF organizers had taken for granted that Dr. Tily's group would join the new association without question just because he himself had been one of its most enthusiastic sponsors. And, in giving the list of the associations to the newspapers, they had apparently failed to make clear the actual situation.

The resentment of the leaders of some of these associations had been immediate, direct and bitter. Some of them, such as the National Association of Retail Druggists, the National Association of Retail Grocers and the National Retail Hardware Association, whose membership consisted primarily of small independent retailers, were taking a major part in anti-chain activities. The mere suggestion that they were contemplating affiliating themselves with an organization in which the chains would be a key factor had made them "see red."

What happened was graphically described by John Guernsey, editor of the Philadelphia *Retail Ledger* in his May, 1935, issue. In a signed article headed: "Retail Federation Dream Becomes Nightmare," he said:

> "The National (sic) Retail Federation entered the roped arena of national politics last month, fell over its own feet, antagonized most of the fight fans and convulsed the rest by its bungling tactics and took some hard blows on the chin before it even shucked off its lounging robe."

Among the hard blows, he included the reactions of several leaders of associations whose names had been used in the press as forming "the nucleus" of the federation. He quoted Roscoe Rau, of the National Retail Furniture Association, as saying: "It is news to us. Not having been given any information, we cannot foretell the attitude of our board."

And John Dargavel, of the National Association of Retail Druggists, had said: "We emphatically deny any allegation or inference that we will affiliate with or be any part of the Retail Federation. We positively refuse to become catspaws for the big chain and department stores."

Robert Sheets, speaking for the National Retail Hardware Association, had declared:

"The National Retail Hardware Association has never been invited to have a part, has no knowledge of the basis for the statement by Kirstein that it will be one of the vertebra of such a new organization and has no intention of being associated therewith."

Rivers Peterson, also speaking for the Hardware Association, had been even more specific. "The Hardware Association will not join," he had said, "and from this day is out definitely to establish a cleavage between the predatory Goliaths personified by the mail-order houses, chains and big stores, such as this new federation represents, and the great body of smaller retailers whose best interests are directly opposed to those of the 'big fellows' who are traveling toward a desired destination concealed beneath the coat tails of the 'little fellows' who are politically powerful."

But, after quoting these reactions, John Guernsey deprecated them. "The men behind this new federation," he declared, "are among the ablest merchants and the finest type of American citizens in this country." Naming some of them, he went on: "Such men have no ulterior motive in setting up this organization nor would they stoop to any practices unfair to others." And then he added, prophetically enough, "the Congressional investigation will come to nothing, but meantime will prove embarrassing because it puts these unselfish men in a false light by innuendo and association of ideas."

Addressing himself to the "many capable national and local retail associations whose valuable work of years in the interest of the retail craft has been so slighted," he urged them "to avoid incriminations that you may later regret, and take steps to line up with the long-range objectives of the federation. By joining it you can control it, even if you think it is on the wrong track at present. You can prevent it from being used as a 'catspaw for the chains and mail-order houses.' "

But with so much resentment already engendered against the new organization, some of it was bound to spill over and reach the attention of anti-chain Congressmen. The result was the House Resolution which prompted the *Herald Tribune* story.

Numbered H.R. 203, it provided for the appointment of a special committee of seven "to investigate the American Retail Federation, its capitalization, its membership, its objectives, the sources of its funds, its financial connections and its officers and agents and to investigate the record of stock dividends, officers' salaries, profits, interlocking directorates and banking affiliations of all corporations directly affiliated with, or contributing to, the said American Retail Federation."

The resolution was preceded by ten "Whereas" clauses based on statements alleged to have been contained in the *N.Y. Times* story, but which, for the most part, were actually without any foundation whatever. Witness, for example, the opening preamble, which read as follows:

"Whereas the Associated Press on April 16, 1935 and the New York *Times* of April 17, 1935, reported that a super-lobby to be known as the 'American Retail Federation' was recently formed to promote the business of chain stores throughout the United States and to influence the action of Members of Congress with reference to legislation affecting chain stores and their holding companies!"

Witness also the questionable assumptions and misstatements in these additional preambles:

"Whereas it is apparent that said American Retail Federation is organized for the purpose of increasing the profits of big business, through lobbying tactics, designed to prevent small businesses from securing competitive opportunities equal to those enjoyed by corporations representing vast aggregations of capital; and . . .

"Whereas the said superlobby has already opened palatial headquarters in the city of Washington, District of Columbia, and has attempted and is now attempting, to force and coerce thousands of small retail merchants, dealing in the necessities of life, into the ranks of this superlobby, so that it may thereafter hold out to Members of Congress and to others in the Government that it represents a completely centralized and authentic voice for all retailers of the Nation; and . . .

"Whereas, it is further reported that this superlobby, the American Retail Federation, is now proceeding upon a plan designed to force the small independent retail merchants of America, engaged in the sale of the necessities of everyday life, to contribute an additional $2,000,000 annually to the funds available to the organization in its lobbying activities, and for the further purpose of permitting it to disseminate propaganda among the consumers and producers of the United States."

But the House was in no position to question the accuracy of any of the statements in the preambles, and the resolution was promptly adopted. The committee of seven originally appointed included its sponsor, Representative Cochran, as chairman, but when he withdrew, May 17, 1935, before the investigation got under way, Representative Wright Patman, of Texas, was named in his place. Considering the anti-chain animus which was behind the investigation, no more appropriate appointment could have been made. It launched Mr. Patman on an anti-chain crusade which was to subject the chains to untold expense and trouble in the years which followed and which, despite some major set-backs, he has not yet abandoned.[1]

To skip, for the moment, the many interesting facts brought out in the course of the investigation regarding the methods used by the chains in defending themselves against discriminatory taxes, some of the findings of the majority report[2] will suffice to show how baseless the investigation actually was. The report declares:

"While there is a slight difference of opinion from the witnesses as to the real purpose of the organization in question, there can be little doubt that this federation was organized primarily for the purposes of promoting not only the interests of chain stores throughout the United States but also to promote the interests of department stores which had a like financial responsibility with the large chains. The evidence shows beyond any question that those in charge of the federation will be primarily engaged in research work concerning retail distribution and other problems for the purpose of ultimately disseminating that information throughout the United States of America, and especially for the purpose of appearing before committees of Congress in order to influence legislation which the federation believes to be to the best interest of the various groups which the federation represents.

"It may be well to say, in passing, that there is a voluminous amount of testimony dealing with chain store activities from a State and National viewpoint prior to the formation of the American Retail Federation. It was the belief of the committee that through the submission of such evidence we might show an unbroken chain of factual circumstances which would prove conclusively that the American Retail Federation was organized for the purpose of carrying forward the unfair methods and practices of certain large chain

[1] The other members of the committee were Representatives Boileau, Bloom, Cole, Dockweiler, Lucas and McLean.

[2] 74th Congress, 2nd Session, H.R. Report No. 2373; it was filed by Representatives Patman, Dockweiler, Lucas and Boileau.

stores and other national organizations. However, the evidence upon this point wholly fails to make such connection."

Although that admission might seem to be generous enough, actually it was less than the truth. For the evidence showed positively that no such connection existed.

Referring to the charge in one of the preambles to the effect that the "superlobby" was attempting to force and coerce thousands of small retail merchants into its ranks, the report admits that while the rank-and-file membership of the Ohio Retail Council had been "persuaded to become members of and thereby add numerical strength to the support of the American Retail Federation . . . there is no evidence before the committee of actual force and coercion of any such members."

With respect to the further charge that the small independent retail merchants were to be forced to contribute $2,000,-000 annually to the "superlobby," the majority report admits that "there is no evidence in the record" to prove it.

Finally, the majority report admitted that there was no evidence to support a further contention as to "the coercion of hundreds of thousands of underpaid employes throughout the Nation to flood the respective Members of the United States Congress with letters, petitions and propaganda designed to improperly and untruthfully represent the public sentiment of the respective constituencies of said Members of Congress."

The minority report,[3] as might have been expected, gave the ARF a clean bill of health. Conceding that the organization's own publicity at the outset might have conveyed the impression that its purpose was to organize a superlobby to protect the chains, the minority pointed out that "such a conclusion is not justified by the testimony adduced by the committee at its hearings when given the weight it is entitled to by reason of the character, standing and attainments of the

[3] Filed by Representatives Bloom, McLean and Cole.

gentlemen who organized the American Retail Federation, its declared objects and purposes."

After quoting some of the testimony of Messrs. Kirstein and Lazarus and referring to that of Col. Sherrill, the minority arrived at the following significant conclusion:

> "In the judgment of the undersigned, the American Retail Federation, as organized, is similar to many other existing organizations, except that it has for its purpose the coordination of all retailers, whereas previously existing organizations have been confined to particular trades. The individuals who head the movement are men of high standing, who have attained wide success as American businessmen, and their objectives and purposes, as explained in their testimony, may well serve a laudable purpose. We find nothing to indicate an intention to trespass beyond ethical limitations in the presentation to Congress and the Members thereof their views as to pending legislation or to the Government departments in the interpretation of the law and the regulations made pursuant thereof."

But, gratifying as this report must have been to the sponsors of the ARF when it was finally presented to the House, on April 7, 1936, it could not undo the damage the organization had already suffered.

Many of the associations which had definitely planned to join the ARF because they were in complete accord with its purposes and realized the need for such an organization naturally deferred taking any steps in that direction while the investigation continued. Nor could ARF itself solicit memberships under such conditions. Thus a whole year was lost before ARF was free to pursue the program it had laid out for itself.

Nevertheless, under the energetic leadership of Col. Sherrill, ARF was soon making up for lost time. One by one, all the important national retail associations became members of the ARF in the next few years. What must have been particularly gratifying to the organizers was the fact that by 1942 every one of the thirteen national associations which they had confidently expected from the start would enter the fold had done so, including, of course, even those which had been so antagonistic then. Furthermore, it may be said at this point that the ARF is a stronger and more influential organization today than at any time since its eventful arrival on the scene. Its record to date has not only completely vindicated the good faith of its organizers but has demonstrated that their judgment was sound and their vision true. The ARF did indeed become the "unified voice" of retailing. As of Sept. 17, 1962, it spoke for 31 national and 43 state retail associations, representing retail outlets across the nation. Since its organization, it has had five presidents—Col. Sherrill who, after two years of service, yielded to a demand that he return to the job which had earned him nation-wide recognition and respect, that of city manager of Cincinnati; Dr. David R. Craig, who served from 1937 to 1941; the late Walter Morrow, who died in office in 1948; his successor, Rowland Jones, Jr., who had previously made an enviable record as the Washington representative of the National Association of Retail Druggists and who served most effectively until his retirement in 1961; and the present incumbent, Calvin K. Snyder.

That retailing needs a "unified voice" today as much as it did when the federation was first conceived was made clear by Mr. Jones in the course of his second annual report as its president, presented April 3, 1950.

"We have become, as a nation," he declared, "a conglomeration of pressure groups—good, bad and in between—all clamoring for attention and demanding all shades and varieties of government action and intervention into the everyday lives of all our people.

"The segments of our economy which would be affected adversely, were many of the demands of these groups to be granted, must of stark necessity organize themselves for defensive political action or resign themselves to becoming the eunuchs of our economic and political system, passive and helpless to protect their legitimate interests and freedom of action and decision.[4]

"My conception of the federation is a retail-industry fire department, adequately equipped and ready to go into action when danger threatens. And like all good fire departments, it should utilize the interim periods in fire-prevention work. Brought to its full potential in membership, influence and good repute, it may extinguish many fires in their incipiency. Through the nurturing of government and public understanding of the functions and needs of the retail industry and its prime importance to the economy, the major cause of fires— misunderstandings and misinformation—can be eliminated over the long pull."

By 1958, the need for an organization like the ARF to speak for all retailing had become greater than ever. Among other threats on the legislative front, a persistent effort to extend the coverage of the Federal Wage-Hour law to retailing was in itself sufficient reason for unified opposition. Unfortunately, despite the Federation's leadership in this fight, when the Fair Labor Standards Act was amended in 1961, the "retail exemption" went by the boards!

In January, 1958, Mr. Jones declared that "the need of the hour is an American Retail Federation solidly financed to do the things that cry to be done, supported by a strong rise in interest and dedication to the idea that only the retail industry itself with all its facets and organizations can defend the legitimate interests of the industry."

So much for the American Retail Federation. It finds a place in these pages only because the Congressional investigation which its birth precipitated brought the chains most conspicuously into the limelight. Furthermore, some of the testimony adduced at the hearings played an important part in the debates which resulted in the Robinson-Patman Act.

[4] Compare with observations of Robert W. Lyons, p. 185, *supra*.

Keeping in mind the fact that the investigation was premised on the charge that the new ARF was nothing but a "false front" propaganda device conceived by the chains to help them in their struggle against discriminatory anti-chain taxes, the course the hearings took was what might have been expected. Headed by Representative Patman, a former district attorney, whose hostility to the chains was to become his main political stock-in-trade, the committee, with its power of subpoena, was well equipped to expose whatever shortcomings the chain-store system might involve and to show up, in their worst possible light, whatever mistakes or indiscretions individual chain-store men might have committed.

Certainly the anti-chain interests must have smacked their lips with anticipation as the committee came into possession of such promising food for scandal as the private files of leading chain-store figures and organizations. Although in most cases access was freely given, the committee's agents were armed with subpoenas which would have enabled them to seize the files in question if they had not been made available.

Among the files used by the committee were those of the organizers of the ARF, of the Food and Grocery Chain Stores of America and of Robert W. Lyons, formerly executive secretary of the dissolved National Chain Store Association, who was then representing fourteen leading chains as counsel in charge of their lobbying activities against discriminatory legislation.

What the committee actually uncovered is dealt with in the next chapter.

CHAPTER X

WHAT THE INVESTIGATION DISCLOSED

THE RECORD of the hearings consists of more than 1,200 pages. It covers not only the testimony regarding the ARF but the additional testimony concerning the trade practices of companies engaged in large-scale buying, the scope of the originally authorized investigation having been extended by another resolution, H.R. No. 239, to authorize a broader probe.

Although only eighteen days in all were required for the taking of the testimony, they were spread through June, July, August and December, 1935, and January, February and March, 1936.

Without attempting even to summarize all the testimony the hearings produced, comment will be confined to that part of it which might fairly be regarded as most damaging to the chains. Mr. Patman's own "index-digest" of the record, which was printed by the committee, is not particularly useful for that purpose because of its obvious unfairness.[1] One example will suffice to show how unreliable a digester Mr. Patman is.

On page 1 of his "index-digest," he declares:

"Col. Clarence C. Sherrill has testified that as president of the American Retail Federation he still holds to the chain

[1] Index Digest of Record of Hearings before Special Committee on Investigation American Retail Federation &c., 74th Congress, First Session.

store theory that it is the best policy to eliminate as many as possible from the retail trade."

In support of that statement, on page 17, Mr. Patman digests Col. Sherrill's testimony as follows:

"Sherrill stated that he still holds to the chain store theory that it is the best policy to eliminate as many people as possible between producer and consumer and that he has not, since he left Kroger Co. and became president of American Retail Federation, changed his views (vol. 4, No. 2, p. 40)."

Is that what Col. Sherrill actually said or even intimated? Here is the record itself:

THE CHAIRMAN. Of course, Colonel Sherrill, we give you credit for believing that the chain story theory is the right theory; that chain stores should be encouraged and promoted rather than retarded.

MR. SHERRILL. You say you give me credit for that?

THE CHAIRMAN. Are we right in giving you credit for that?

MR. SHERRILL. I was of the opinion, when I was employed by the chain store company, that the chain store method of distribution is a sound one and that it has economies that are valuable both for the chain store operators and for the consumer; yes.

THE CHAIRMAN. That is, to eliminate as many people between the producer and consumer as possible?

MR. SHERRILL. To eliminate as many people between the producer and consumer as possible, except where they were doing a real valuable service.

The main facts revealed by the investigation which would seem to call for explanation on the part of the chains may be considered under the following heads:

1. Publication of a medium to carry chain-store propaganda to farm leaders.

2. "Espionage" of an anti-chain-store association.

3. Invoking an NRA regulation to block the showing of an anti-chain film.

4. Legislative tactics used to combat discriminatory chain-store taxes.

5. Receipt by the chains of discounts and allowances not available to independent retailers.

1. Publication of a medium to carry chain-store propaganda to farm leaders.

The propaganda medium which came under fire was a mimeographed bulletin called "Farm to Market News." The evidence showed that it had been conceived by a former representative of the American Farm Bureau Federation who was well-known to farm leaders and who planned to issue it under his own name and as reflecting his own convictions if the chains would finance it. Three food chains had agreed to underwrite the project and the bulletin was accordingly issued for about a year.

Nobody contended that an effort by the chains, or by a group of them, to influence farm opinion in their favor through the medium of a bulletin was in itself objectionable in any way. The only criticism raised against the "Farm to Market News" was that its backers were purposely concealed. Albert H. Morrill, president of the Kroger Grocery & Baking Co., one of the sponsors of the bulletin, who was interrogated about it, frankly conceded that the failure to disclose its actual sponsorship had been a mistake, but he pointed out that it was the kind of mistake that anybody might have made under similar conditions.

In any event, the questionable bulletin was not published long enough to do the chains much good or anyone else much harm. It had been discontinued long before the committee investigating the ARF had come into existence.

2. "Espionage" of an anti-chain-store association.

Among the many organizations which were set up to fight the chains and, incidentally, in most cases, to enrich the promoters, as pointed out earlier in these pages, was one called the National Anti-Chain Stores League. The evidence dis-

closed that in March, 1935, a John E. Barr, one of its employes, had approached John A. Logan, executive vice president of Food and Grocery Chain Stores of America, with an
offer to keep him posted on the anti-chain-store association's
activities. He had explained to Mr. Logan that the journal the
organization was planning to issue to independent retailers
would not only attack the chains but would carry Nazi propaganda, and as he was a veteran of World War I, he thought
that was "going a bit too far."

Mr. Logan testified that he had submitted the whole matter
to his executive committee and they had authorized him to
pay Barr $50 a week. The arrangement lasted for a short time,
during which period, Mr. Logan testified, he received ample
evidence from Barr to convince him that "the organization
was conceived for personal profits and personal gains for the
men who organized it." Barr testified to the same effect.

The only question of propriety raised by Mr. Patman with
respect to the arrangement with Barr was whether it was "ethical." Mr. Logan conceded that if the league had been an association established for legitimate purposes, he would not have
considered paying Barr for information concerning its activities—even though they were directed against the chains—but
that was not the situation as he saw it. On the contrary, he was
convinced that the league was a "racket" and it had among its
objectives the spreading of Nazi propaganda through the journal that was to be widely circulated among retail merchants.
Under such conditions, he could not see that any question of
"ethics" was involved.

*3. Invoking an NRA regulation to block the showing of an
anti-chain film.*

The film in question was a five-reel talking picture called
"Forward America." It was produced by a Frank R. Wilson,
formerly with NRA, with the idea of "dramatizing the arguments against syndicate chain stores and showing the eco-

nomic effect on American communities of the operations of
chain stores and mail-order houses." [2]

The nature of the picture is indicated more specifically in a
circular used to promote the film and which was referred to
by Mr. Patman and read into the record as follows:

> "At last here is the dynamite that will blast the chain stores
> and mail-order houses from your community. Mr. Independ-
> ent Merchant, here is your opportunity to recapture your
> birthright and regain your former prosperity. . . .
>
> "This picture . . . is being shown with telling effect in
> many American cities, with resultant decrease in chain and
> mail-order business and a corresponding increase in the busi-
> ness of independent local merchants. . . .
>
> "If you want to know the truth about the depression, see
> 'Forward America.' If you want to know who is to blame,
> see 'Forward America.' If you want to know how it was
> started and how it is being continued, see 'Forward America.'
> Independent Merchants, organize and appoint a live local
> man to get in touch with us and we will show him how to pro-
> ceed. You can help solve America's greatest illness by having
> 'Forward America' shown in your community."

What, if anything, could the chains do to protect themselves against a picture of this kind, a picture which, as they
saw it, accused them unjustly of almost every crime on the
calendar?

At that time NRA was still in command of the economy.
Every industry and trade was governed by a code. The Code
of Fair Competition for the Retail Food and Grocery Trade
contained a provision that "no food and grocery retailer shall
use advertising . . . of any . . . nature, which is inaccurate in any material particular or misrepresents . . . credit
terms . . . policies or services; and no food and grocer retailer shall use advertising and/or selling methods which tend
to deceive or mislead the customer." Another provision read:

[2] Hearings before Special Committee on Investigation of American Retail Federation, Vol. 1, p. 333.

"No food and grocery retailer shall use advertising which refers inaccurately in any material particular to any competitor or his merchandise, prices, values, credit, terms, policies or services."

Could it be that either of these provisions were violated by retail grocers who purchased tickets from the sponsors of "Forward America" at 25 cents each and distributed them to their customers and others, admitting them to the theater where the picture was showing?

Certainly nothing could be lost by trying. And so in various cities where the picture was shown complaints were filed with the local food and grocery code authority. Several of these local authorities appealed to C. H. Janssen, the chairman of the National Food and Grocery Distributors Code Authority, for a ruling. Hector Lazo, assistant to Mr. Janssen, a witness at the hearing, was questioned at great length by Mr. Patman and another member of the committee in an obvious attempt to establish that the film was condemned, through the connivance of the chains, without giving its sponsor an opportunity to be heard in its defense.

What actually happened is revealed in a letter of February 16, 1935, from Mr. Janssen to J. Neumann, the secretary of the local food and grocery Code Authority in Cincinnati, who had asked for a ruling regarding the film.[3]

After quoting the facts which Mr. Neumann had presented and the provisions of the Code applicable to them, Mr. Janssen said:

> "In response to your request, The National Food and Grocery Distributors Code Authority gave due and careful consideration to the same, and preparatory to stating an opinion, invited a private showing and hearing of the film and its accompanying lecture, following which it unanimously expressed the following opinion:
>
> "It is the opinion of the members of the National Food

[3] *Ibid.*, p. 335.

and Grocery Distributors Code Authority that the talking film as shown to the members in New York on February 7, 1935, (1) refers inaccurately in material particulars to a competitor and/or a class of competitors in retail food and grocery distribution in a number of respects; (2) that it tends to deceive or mislead the customers.

"On the basis of the foregoing, it is my opinion that any member of the food and grocery trade participating in the distribution of tickets to a showing of such film or its message does therein also become a party to the dissemination of its inaccuracies or its misrepresentation of policies or services and tendency to deceive or mislead customers, and so forth, as such prohibitions are specifically stated in article IX, section 1, paragraphs (a) and (b) in the Code of Fair Competition for the Food and Grocery Trade."

That this ruling was used effectively by the chains to discourage the showing of the film can hardly be doubted. Mr. Logan had written to Mr. Janssen on January 3,[4] calling attention to the film, expressing his view that the showing of the film by wholesale and retail grocers was a violation of the code, asking that local and State code authorities in Kansas, and elsewhere, where the film was being shown, be advised of the code provisions, and also requesting information on the proper procedure for "obtaining prompt action against wholesale and retail grocers who violate the code by participating in and dissemination of unfair and inaccurate advertising of the character of 'Forward America.' " When the ruling in question was handed down on February 16, the chains would have had no reason for not taking full advantage of it.

What happened was probably accurately described in a letter sent by Mr. Wilson, the producer of the film, to Mr. Patman, a paragraph from which he read into the record as follows:

"Just to show how effective this chain store lobby was in your State, the home-owned merchants of Amarillo, Texas,

[4] *Ibid.*, p. 330.

appointed a committee to raise $1,200 for the sale of tickets to merchants for distribution to the public, so that an auditorium could be engaged for the showing of 'Forward America.' On the very day that the solicitors started out to collect the money for this ticket distribution the chain store representatives placed in the hands of every home-owned business of Amarillo a copy of this Code Authority opinion. The result was that many of the dealers of Amarillo who were enthusiastic about the picture failed to participate in its sponsorship because of the fear of Federal prosecution."

Now what did Mr. Patman find to criticize in the efforts of the chains to discourage the showing of "Forward America"?

His main complaint, according to his own "index-digest" of the record, was that "at no time was Frank R. Wilson, the owner of the film, offered an opportunity by the chain store interests to appear before the code authorities or NRA for the purpose of showing that his film did not misrepresent chain stores or unduly disparage them."

What Mr. Patman overlooked was that Mr. Wilson was given an opportunity to exhibit the film itself to the National Authority and the film, of course, spoke for itself.

Who constituted the National Code Authority?

Mr. Lazo testified that it consisted of the representatives elected by the boards of directors of the six national trade associations sponsoring the codes. At the time they were: C. H. Janssen, executive chairman, the head of the executive staff and representing no one; C. M. D. Miller, representing the retailer-owned wholesale cooperatives; Asa Strause, representing the voluntary groups; Milton W. Griggs, representing the National-American Wholesale Grocers Association; C. Y. Early, representing the United States Wholesale Grocers Association; F. H. Massmann, representing the Food and Grocery Chain Stores of America; and H. C. Petersen, representing the National Association of Retail Grocers.

When Mr. Lazo pointed out that the only question was whether or not the film contained, in the opinion of the National Code Authority, inaccurate references to competition, he was asked how they could give an opinion without hearing both sides of the case. He answered: "These men have spent their entire lifetime in food distribution."

Challenged by Mr. Patman to name "one instance of false advertising" in the film, Mr. Lazo mentioned that it charged "the chain stores directly with being the only ones guilty of short-weighting, for example . . . saying specifically: 'this is the reason why chain stores can sell more cheaply to you,' then they show the short-weights."

The testimony continued:

THE CHAIRMAN. And you say that is wrong?

MR. LAZO. I say that it is wrong to charge any one particular factor with all the vices.

THE CHAIRMAN. Suppose that the fact was that Mr. Wilson could have come in and shown you proof, sworn testimony, to the effect that that is true. Would it still be possible to show the truth?

MR. LAZO. Yes.

THE CHAIRMAN. All right; why don't [sic] they listen to Mr. Wilson's side and let him attempt to show you that it was true?

MR. LAZO. We know that short-weighting exists in the trade. Our contention was that it was not limited to chain stores.

THE CHAIRMAN. I know, but what if there was proof before the Federal Trade Commission under oath—

MR. LAZO. That it was limited to chain stores?

THE CHAIRMAN. Yes.

MR. LAZO. I don't believe there was any such proof, sir. . . . The impression that was given in the film is that all these vices that we were attempting to correct through the codes were limited to chain-store type of distribution. Now our contention was and our contention is that we were cognizant of these vices in the trade, but they were not limited to any one factor.

Other questions brought out that, where a formal complaint was lodged with a local code authority, the procedure called for the citing of the merchant, against whom the complaint was lodged, to appear at a hearing. In this case, however, the opinion or ruling of the National Code Authority was not based on such a complaint at all. It was given to a local code authority, with whom such a complaint had apparently been lodged, and who had appealed to the national body for guidance. What procedure the local authority followed in his handling of the complaint before him, does not appear in the record. In any event, however, it would hardly seem that the national authority was called upon to do more than it actually did—to view the film to see whether or not it referred inaccurately in material particulars to a competitor or tended to deceive or mislead customers. If these leaders of all types of food and grocery distribution concluded unanimously, as they did, that the film did not accurately portray trade practices and was deceptive and misleading to the public, Mr. Janssen's action would seem to have rested on a sound foundation. If it resulted in stopping or limiting the circulation of the film, wasn't that the effect the provisions in the code were designed to achieve?

4. Legislative tactics used to combat discriminatory chain-store taxes.

If the chains had stepped out of bounds in the course of their lobbying activities against discriminatory legislation, the investigation certainly provided ample opportunity to find out just what they had been up to. For who could know more about what had been done than one of the witnesses who came before the committee—Robert W. Lyons? Here was the man who had directed the tax-defense work of the National Chain Store Association from 1929 to 1934 and had thereafter continued it for fourteen leading non-food chains, as has already been related.[5] Furthermore he had given the commit-

---

[5] See p. 189, *supra.*

tee's agents free access to his files so that they could confront him with actual letters he had written and received.

True enough, Mr. Lyons at first refused to answer a number of questions, although he had appeared before the committee voluntarily. He based his refusal on two grounds: (1) the information requested was privileged by reason of the professional relation which existed between him and his clients; and (2) the questions went into matters which, he claimed, a Congressional committee could not legally explore since its inquisitorial power extended only to matters on which Congress could legislate. He claimed that activities in State capitols could hardly be a matter for Federal legislation.

Nevertheless, whatever legal ground Mr. Lyons might have had and maintained for refusing to answer the committee's questions, he did not stick to it. He answered enough questions to give the committee a clear picture of the scope of his lobbying activities for the chains and the policies and principles he followed in pursuing them. Supplemented by testimony on the same subject from Mr. Logan, Albert W. Hughes, assistant to the president of the J. C. Penney Company (later to become president and in 1958, chairman of the board), and other witnesses, and innumerable letters selected by the committee from the files of Mr. Lyons and the food-chain association, the picture was about as complete, if not as devastating, as the committee could have wished.

What did it show?

Mr. Lyons testified that for the year commencing October 1, 1934, as counsel for fourteen leading chains, he had a tax-defense budget of $175,000. That was the same amount, incidentally, which the National Chain Store Association had set up for its annual legislative tax-defense budget in 1931 when Mr. Lyons had been in charge of it as executive vice president. After the dissolution of that association, Mr. Lyons had continued the task as counsel for the fourteen chains who shared the expense of it on the basis of their relative sales. His fourteen clients, he told the committee, were: F. W. Woolworth Co., S. S. Kresge Co., W. T. Grant Co., S. H. Kress & Co., J. J. Newberry Co., H. L. Green Co., G. C. Murphy Co., Neisner Bros., Scott-Burr Stores Corp., Charles Stores Co. and M. H. Fishman Co., all members of the Limited Price Variety Stores Association, and J. C. Penney Company, Melville Shoe Corporation and Walgreen Co.

How was the fund used?

None of it was spent for anything but counsel fees, Mr. Lyons testified. Local counsel was engaged in every State capitol where legislation discriminating against chain stores was introduced. The general practice was for Mr. Lyons to send one of the three legislative experts on his staff to the seat of the trouble. His function was to size up the situation, arrange for the employment of competent legal counsel and report to Mr. Lyons.

As to the type of men Mr. Lyons selected as local counsel, he testified as follows:

"I have employed counsel with two things in mind, first, to let us have an opinion as to whether an important proposition was legal, constitutional, serious, or otherwise . . . and secondly, of necessity, to measure whether the threat of that legislation is serious. As a practical matter, that lawyer must have contacts with members of the various committees with whom he can frankly, honestly and honorably discuss the problems. So, in every case, I attempt to hire an attorney who has public experience and is able to measure these matters with good conscience and good judgment and who is able as a lawyer, to give us a sound, intelligent opinion as to both our legal, constitutional and political problems."

He never employed a legislator as counsel while he was in office.

Asked whether he ever hired local counsel on a contingent basis, paying a small retainer fee and later a substantial additional fee if no discriminatory chain-store legislation was adopted, Mr. Lyons said he did in some instances in States where contingent fee arrangements were lawful. He saw nothing unethical in it.

The following extract from the record, revealing a phase of legislative strategy sometimes used in desperate cases, speaks for itself:

THE CHAIRMAN. Have you not had correspondence with your lawyers in which you have said, "If we cannot stop this bill we will have it so amended so it will be unconstitutional"?

MR. LYONS. I would not be at all surprised if I had.

THE CHAIRMAN. You advised them to get that done?

MR. LYONS. I advised them to do everything they legally and properly could.

THE CHAIRMAN. You felt that it was ethical?

MR. LYONS. Yes, sir. . . .

THE CHAIRMAN. If you go before a legislative body and you misrepresent to those legislators as to what the law is and lead them to believe that they should have a better bill or a different bill, when that bill is not unconstitutional [sic] would not that be unethical?

MR. LYONS. Neither I nor my lawyers have ever so represented.

THE CHAIRMAN. It would be all right if they did do that and get an unconstitutional bill through?

MR. LYONS. If you mean would I approve a program, if that were the only alternative of preventing an unjust law being enacted, to amend the bill and make it unconstitutional, I say to you that I would want them to make every effort to do that . . .

THE CHAIRMAN. You would try to persuade the legislators to vote for such a bill and would not tell them it was unconstitutional?

MR. LYONS. I would certainly tell them—

THE CHAIRMAN. And lead them to believe it was a better bill, in order to get an unconstitutional bill through?

MR. LYONS. It is not necessary for us to be naïve about these things.

When Mr. Hughes, of the Penney Company, was asked whether he approved of his lawyer pursuing such tactics, he replied: "I would say that if somebody was going to sandbag me I would be entitled to grab any weapon that I could get hold of to hit him."

And to Mr. Patman's comment that "legislators are presumed not to be in the sandbagging business," Mr. Hughes continued: "That is no reflection on legislators at all, sir. The only reflection was in the fact that, in studying chain-store bills pretty carefully for the last six or eight years, it is my definite, sober judgment that the demand for most of them does not emanate from legislators at all. It comes either from a wholesaler or an independent who thinks he can subsidize himself by getting a law passed; and that is what I meant by sandbagging. I am not reflecting upon the legislators in any way whatsoever."

When anti-chain-store bills were under consideration, an important angle from the chains' standpoint was the extent of their coverage. Were the definitions in the bill broad enough, for instance, to include voluntary chains as well, and filling-stations? If they were, the chains could count on their co-operation in opposing the bills. If they were not, efforts were made by the chains' legislative representatives to have the bills amended accordingly. So far as the voluntary chains were concerned, it was argued that since they enjoyed many of the advantages of the regular chains, they ought to bear the same tax burden; and, so far as the chain filling-stations were concerned, it was pointed out that they were in fact "stores" even though they were called "stations." That, indeed, was what the U.S. Supreme Court decided in the case of Fox v. Standard Oil of N.J. (See page 147, *supra*.) But, in order to cover the point, before that decision was handed down, the chains naturally tried to have the bills include filling-stations specifically.

Much of the correspondence revealed clearly enough that these efforts to broaden the coverage of pending bills were frequently made, and the witnesses, who were interrogated on the point, saw nothing to apologize for in such tactics.

Although the very word "lobbying" has a sinister connotation in general usage, none of the members of the committee questioned the right of the chains to engage in such activities, provided they refrained from deception and subterfuge.

"The chains have a perfect right to lobby," declared Mr. Patman at one point where Mr. Logan turned questioner. "It is just as proper for them to lobby in defense of or to sponsor legislation as it is for me to advocate or to oppose legislation . . . the only thing in my mind is that they should do it openly and above board and not try to use a front, or not try to deceive people."

But if it is proper, as it is, for the chains to oppose legislation which they deem discriminatory or unsound in any other respect, why is it not equally proper for them to suggest the amendment of a bill to broaden its coverage for the dual purpose of (a) augmenting opposition to it, and (b) making it more equitable if it should be adopted?

Whether the chains' representatives went beyond the bounds of propriety when, in a desperate case, they sought to introduce a clause in an objectionable bill which they believed would render it unconstitutional, presents a nice question of ethics. But, as Mr. Lyons reminded Mr. Patman, why do we have to be naïve about these things? If the chains had attempted to defend themselves and their legitimate interests in the legislative arena without the aid of experts versed in legislative strategy, where would they have been? Marquis of Queensbury rules are all right when both sides can be made to abide by them, but everything goes in a roughhouse. And if, as Mr. Hughes put it, the chains knew they were being sandbagged, they can hardly be criticized for taking any lawful measures needed to outwit or defeat their aggressors.

5. Receipt by the chains of discounts and allowances not available to independent retailers.

On July 9, 1935, the committee turned its attention to the subject of "trade practices of big-scale retail and wholesale buying and selling organizations" which it had been directed to investigate.

In compliance with an offer from A&P to give the committee any information it wanted, Charles W. Parr appeared as a witness. Mr. Parr was assistant to David T. Bofinger, who was in charge of the company's buying activities at the national level.

Mr. Parr testified that A&P received approximately $6,000,-000 in advertising allowances and $2,000,000 as brokerage in 1934. It spent approximately $6,000,000 for advertising. He presented to the committee a complete list of the manufacturers from whom A&P received such allowances, with the basis for the allowance in each case.

The manufacturers listed numbered nearly 300 and Mr. Parr explained that they constituted what the company referred to as its "preferred list" of suppliers. What that signified was thus made clear:

"We have never laid down any arbitrary rules which prohibit any of our individual warehouses from buying any brand of merchandise which they wish to handle or for which they have a demand, but we do have a preferred list at headquarters to which we ask them to give support wherever possible . . . the people with whom we have advertising contracts, quantity price arrangements or brokerage arrangements."

The following extract from the record gives some typical examples of the arrangements made with manufacturers on the preferred list:

"Armour & Co., regular line, 3 to 7 per cent on canned meats advertising allowance; fresh meats, one-half per cent quantity if purchases total $10,000,000.

"California Packing Corporation, Del Monte, 5 per cent purchasing contract.

"General Foods Corporation, line, $30,000 flat for advertising; Baker's Chocolate, $0.066 per carton, quantity discount (entire trade).

"Standard Brands, foil yeast, $144,000 a year advertising allowance, 10 per cent quantity discount; Chase & Sanborn's coffee, $97,164 per year advertising allowance; Tenderleaf Tea, $394 per 1,000 advertising allowance; Royal Gelatine, $38,004 per year advertising allowance; Royal Baking Powder, $15,000 per year advertising allowance; Dr. Price Baking Powder, $996 per year advertising allowance.

"Swift & Co., canned meats, 3 to 5 per cent on 200,000 pounds to over 300,000 pounds, quantity discount.

"Wilson & Co., canned meats, 5 per cent brokerage."

Now what was the significance of such allowances as these, which, in the aggregate, amounted to $8,000,000 in 1934?

In the first place, to provide a yardstick by which to measure the relative importance of such allowances in the case of A&P, the company's total sales for the year ending February 28, 1935, were $842,015,871, and its net profits, after depreciation and Federal taxes, were $16,709,000.

Secondly, such allowances were not confined to A&P. As the committee was to learn later from "lists" supplied by other chains, including two voluntary chains, all large-scale buyers who had a service to render at the retail level and were in a position to render it, likewise received allowances, although, of course, no single company or organization received as much in the aggregate as A&P. Lists of allowances received were filed by Safeway, Kroger, First National, National Tea, Gristede Bros., D. Pender Groc. Co., Independent Grocers Alliance (a voluntary chain), National Retailer-Owned Grocers (a co-operative group), Liggett's, Walgreen, Woolworth and Kress.

To what extent such allowances reached even small independent retailers was not explored to any extent, but some evidence on that point came out when executives of General Foods and Standard Brands explained the scope of their respective sales-promotion activities.

Thirdly, although A&P's allowances when stacked up represented a sizable total, they came from many sources. The largest single item, $360,000 from General Foods, covered that company's complete line of products, which numbered 80.

Testifying regarding that allowance, Mr. Parr pointed out that the $360,000 was actually an estimate of the amount to be paid for the full year, as the obligation was to pay 5% of total purchases which, he believed, that year would amount to $9,000,000. The difference would be met by a year-end adjustment. A contract prepared by the manufacturer specified the advertising and special promotion activities A&P was to provide in behalf of General Foods products in return for the allowance. But A&P was not required to render proof of actual advertising or promotion service. The advertising allowance was in addition to whatever regular quantity discount was shown on the invoice as a deduction from the sales price.

Mr. Parr also pointed out that, in connection with advertising-allowance contracts, his company usually agreed to cooperate with the manufacturer by running special sales in which the items would be featured below regular prices.

How manufacturers benefited from the advertising allowances and brokerage they paid to A&P was well illustrated, indirectly, by one item of evidence which revealed what happened when such allowances were *not* made. A letter to Mr. Parr from J. V. Beckmann, A&P's representative on the West Coast, pointed out that "F. E. Booth & Co. formerly did a fair business with us throughout the country, which has fallen off to almost nothing since the California Sardine Code became effective, have come and offered to restore the regular 5 per cent brokerage on sardines. They will pay this money to us in cash monthly. I have accepted this and advised them we will remove the restriction on Booth sardines and would like to have you advise me just how you want this information put out to the directors."

The following extract from the record sheds some light on the significance of that communication:

THE CHAIRMAN. Now, what does he mean when he says, "We will remove the restriction on Booth sardines"? Did you have some stop order on the sale of Booth sardines?

MR. PARR. No. What he refers to there is that the company and the individual warehouses—45 to 50 warehouses are kept informed on all arrangements, as far as possible, that we have—and when the sardine code, which prohibited the payment of brokerage, went into effect they automatically knew that, because it was common knowledge. When they knew that they were not to receive the usual credit of 5 per cent we did not tell them to discontinue handling Booth sardines, but they lost interest in it.

THE CHAIRMAN. They lost interest in it and put them back where they were not so conspicuous?

MR. PARR. No; they just did not feature them and did not advertise.

Explaining the reference to the "directors," Mr. Parr said: "Our company is divided into six divisions and in each division there is a purchasing director, a man who supervises the purchasing for the division under headquarters."

Whether the sardine packer in question was violating the code in restoring the brokerage at that time, was a question raised by Mr. Patman, but Mr. Parr insisted that, in any event, it would have been a violation by the seller and not by the buyer as the buyer was not bound by the sardine code. But, be that as it may, the incident shows clearly enough how valuable to the manufacturer was the advertising and merchandising cooperation a company like A&P could furnish and how costly if withheld. About the only way a manufacturer could increase his sales through A&P stores in the face of such a loss of interest as resulted in the case of Booth sardines would be by stimulating consumer demand through national advertising. That, of course, might cost the manufacturer far more than the cooperation he could buy from

A&P and other large-scale distributors by means of advertising allowances.

The complete service rendered by A&P, Mr. Parr declared, went far beyond newspaper advertising. It included window signs, window displays, store displays, counter displays, radio advertising, circular mail, and all sorts of promotional work, involving printing, all of which the company did at its own expense.

How the allowances received from suppliers were handled by A&P was thus explained by Mr. Parr: "We have an account known as the advertising account. That account is No. 702. . . . All receipts from manufacturers go into account No. 702, and the appropriation for advertising, for special sales, for sales promotion work, for signs, for circulars, for lithographic work and everything of that kind . . . are made from that account."

Admitting that the allowances which went into Account No. 702 paid also for the advertising of some products on which no allowance was received, Mr. Parr pointed out that, on the other hand, newspaper advertising was only part of the service A&P gave manufacturers who paid such allowances. As one example, he mentioned that the contract with California Packing Corporation specifically provided for a big general national sale on their entire line every month. A tremendous amount of effort and expense went into these promotions of the Del Monte line, he explained, and involved, as well, lower than regular prices.

But despite A&P's special interest in Del Monte, upon which the company received a 5% allowance, consumer demand for Dole's, upon which no allowance was received, compelled A&P to stock that line too. As Mr. Parr explained the situation in a letter which was read into the record: "There is no doubt an insistent consumer demand for Dole's in certain markets, and the only thing we can do, under the circumstances, is to fill these orders as specified. We know the situation to be true right here in New York, for instance, where everything possible has been done to prevent the necessity of handling Dole's pack, but consumer trade here insists upon this brand."

But even though advertising allowances would seem to have a sound basis, how about brokerage? Did it not give A&P an advantage over competitors who did not get it?

How Mr. Parr answered those questions is revealed in the following extract from the record:

MR. BLOOM. But who gets the 5 per cent eventually?

MR. PAAR. It goes to the A&P Tea Co.

MR. BLOOM. Is that not an advantage over the other fellow?

MR. PARR. It could be construed as such, probably, in the same way that we have an advantage when we buy goods in car lots as compared with the fellow who buys goods in less than car lots.

MR. BLOOM. No; that is a legitimate discount or price, where people buy car lots or buy at wholesale or in gross lots, or contract for a certain amount of goods during the year. That is legitimate business. But where a concern receives a special advertising allowance or special discount, or has its own brokers, it naturally has the advantage over the other fellow. As a merchant I would think that is the case.

MR. PARR. Well, we have the advantage to this extent: In the same way that, a great many years ago, we might have had an advantage over the small independent when we started buying goods in car lots. In other words, when we started to do that we started to perform the function of a wholesale grocery. We opened our own warehouses and, instead of buying goods from a wholesale grocer, we started buying direct from the manufacturer.

MR. BLOOM. Don't you have to do that, Mr. Parr? Where you have, we will say, in this district 256 stores, you would naturally have to have your own warehouse, where you could distribute your goods to your stores and get them as you want them and when you want them.

MR. PARR. That is right. In other words in our warehousing operations we perform a legitimate wholesale function. That is, we bring our goods in car lots and distribute them around to our retail stores. Now, in the last 10 or 12 years we have attempted to do the same thing, or to follow the same principle, in regard to operating our own brokerage offices instead of dealing with an outsider. In other words, we are attempting every day to deal more directly with the producer. We believe it is more satisfactory for everybody concerned when the transaction is confined to just as few people as possible. The more direct line we can establish between the producer and consumer, the more satisfactory it is for all three of us.

MR. BLOOM. Then you believe that the farmer would be benefited if he could deal directly in that way, too, do you not?

MR. PARR. Oh, I certainly do. I think the more direct the transaction can be made, the more satisfactory it is for the producer, distributor and consumer.

What Mr. Parr had in mind, of course, was that where a distributor can bypass a broker and, by dealing direct with the producer or manufacturer, earn the brokerage himself, his price to the consumer can be correspondingly lower, which will mean that the consumer's buying power will be to that extent increased. So that while the producer gains nothing by paying the brokerage to the distributor instead of to a broker, he benefits indirectly because he helps to increase consumption by helping to lower retail prices.

Of course, Mr. Parr was able to tell the story of advertising allowances from the standpoint only of what his own company received. What other companies received, he didn't know, although he expressed a belief that, according to the Federal Trade Commission, "the average allowances that we receive are no greater than those received by other purchasers, and in many cases the small dealer got better allowances than we did."

But the manufacturers themselves knew to whom they were paying these allowances, and how much, and the evidence on that point speaks for itself.

Austin S. Igleheart, president of General Food Sales Company, whose allowance to A&P loomed so large, pointed out that the contract providing for that payment did not stand alone. On the contrary, similar contracts, although providing for substantially lower payments in most cases, numbered, as of August 9, 1934, 1,714. They were made with all types of distributors who could render a service in return. He broke them down as follows:

324 contracts with corporate chains operating 45,698 stores.
547 with voluntary chains, embracing 66,587 stores.
843 with retailers not identified with voluntary chains and operating collectively 2,039 stores.

This made a total of 114,324 retail stores obligated to render a service for which the company had agreed to pay them. Asked why no wholesale grocers appeared in his enumeration, Mr. Igleheart pointed out that, unless they were affiliated with voluntary chains, they would have no way to render the service for which such allowances were made.

Traver Smith, vice president of Standard Brands, testified that the only allowances his company made were for what they called "cooperation service."

How much they paid for the service depended upon its value. In the case of A&P, the "preferred list" showed, it totalled approximately $300,000 a year. A written contract specified what was to be done by the customer in each case to earn a sum inserted in the contract. Such contracts were made only with customers who had something to sell in the way of service. As Standard Brands sold direct to the retailer and its salesmen called on its 250,000 outlets every four days, they used their judgment whether or not the cooperation of particular customers was worth buying.

The way it worked, Mr. Smith explained, was that if a customer was not selling enough Chase & Sanborn coffee, for instance, the salesman would suggest how the situation might be improved by a handbill, a poster in the window, a mention in the newspaper advertising, if any, a counter display or some other type of cooperation. If the grocer agreed to cooperate in the way suggested, they would agree, then and there, how much would be paid for it. If the service was given the payment would be made. In the case of A&P and four other chains, such arrangements were made on a chain-wide basis at headquarters level instead of with the individual store managers.

Asked why only A&P and Kroger received an advertising allowance on Fleischman's yeast, Mr. Smith declared:

"Naturally, with a two and one-half cent item you cannot give advertising allowances all through the country. The only way you can possibly consider an advertising allowance is on a large-scale operation. Now any discounts or payments that we make to A&P or Kroger for cooperation are due to the fact that they are the two accounts in the country that can give us a broad market operation in promoting the sales of our yeast, and we have contracts with both those accounts for a specific service to be rendered in promoting the sale of our yeasts." They paid A&P $12,000 a month and Kroger $500 a month for the cooperation they contracted for and nothing to any other chain or other organization.

Further explaining the A&P arrangement, Mr. Smith continued:

"We give them $12,000 a month, or $144,000 a year, purely for the promotional service which they render us, which is this: They give us distribution in 14,000 or more stores; they allow us to put up package displays, as we call them, with little signs, because yeast is usually tucked away in a refrigerator where nobody can see it. I have seen large posters they have gotten out . . . about 6 feet by 2 or 3. They have mentioned it at frequent intervals in their newspaper advertising and they have really given us a very comprehensive service to try to promote the sale of our yeast."

Asked why he couldn't buy the same service from independents, he found great difficulty in getting committee members to appreciate that a payment of less than $1 a month to an independent grocer, which was what the payment to A&P averaged per store per month, would hardly buy much co-operation of any kind and certainly very little advertising! In other words, he insisted, it had to be a mass proposition. Even if an independent store in a given case did as much business as an A&P store across the street, he pointed out, the independent's operation would end there, whereas the A&P store's would be multiplied by some 15,000.

What was the effect of this testimony?

Its immediate effect was to create quite a sensation in the grocery trade. For, although everybody was familiar with the fact that advertising allowances were in common use, the details of individual arrangements were, of course, known only to the parties involved. Since the allowance varied with the kind and amount of cooperation contracted for in each case, such arrangements were considered and kept more or less confidential.

When, therefore, A&P's "preferred list" was read into the record at the hearing and thus became public property, the trade press had one of the hottest stories it had been able to pick up in many a long day. One publication, *Sales Management*, which was just going to press, ran the complete list in its July 15 issue in a special four-page section printed on pink paper. For some time thereafter the list was usually referred to in the trade as the "pink supplement."

Manufacturers on the list were naturally interested to see how the allowances they were offering compared with those of their competitors.[6] On the other hand, chains and other large-scale organizations were equally interested to see whether A&P was getting more, or less, than they were.

Advertising allowances were generally regarded at that time, and still are, as a useful and legitimate feature of any

---

[6] Similar lists were subsequently provided by a number of other chains and became part of the official record, but they did not receive the publicity given to A&P's list.

well-coordinated sales plan, provided they were used solely to
secure dealer cooperation. As Neil H. Borden, professor of
advertising, Harvard University, pointed out in his authoritative study, *The Economic Effects of Advertising*,[7] "most
manufacturers, even when they have a strong pull resulting
from space advertising, strive at the same time to get active
dealer support in the stocking and display of products, in the
use of counter and window displays, in the offering of selling
suggestions by sales clerks and in the mention of products in
the retailers' direct-action advertising."

Manufacturers found that the most effective, if not the only,
way to secure that kind of cooperation was to pay for it. Provided they got what they paid for, advertising allowances
were considered well worth what they cost. They came in for
condemnation in many quarters only because they could so
easily be used as a mask for discriminatory price concessions.

Such price concessions were, of course, illegal. Ever since
1914, they had been prohibited in interstate commerce by the
Clayton Act. However, the Clayton Act prohibition was inadequate in two respects which left the door open, or at least
ajar, for those who wanted to bypass it. One was the proviso
permitting quantity discounts, without limiting them in any
way. Thus it sanctioned a scale of discounts rigged to favor
large-scale purchasers who alone would be in a position to
earn the top-bracket discounts. The other was a proviso specifically permitting price concessions when made "in good
faith to meet competition" which, too, was obviously subject
to abuse.

The Clayton Act did not attempt to regulate or restrict advertising allowances. Although they were offered to some customers and not to others and were, to that extent, discriminatory, they did not run foul of the Clayton Act because that
prohibited only discriminations in *price*. Legally, therefore, a

---

[7] *The Economic Effects of Advertising*, Neil H. Borden (Richard D. Irwin, Inc.,
Chicago, 1942).

manufacturer had as much right to buy his dealer-coopera-
tion where it would do him the most good as he had, in setting
up his advertising program, to put some publications on his
schedule and to ignore others, or to use time rather than
space, or, in short, to select the particular advertising media
which he felt would serve his purpose best. Nobody had ever
suggested that an advertising appropriation should be divided
proportionately among all available media—that it wasn't fair
or in the public interest to use only the big and successful
publications, for instance, and pass up the smaller and less
important ones. Why shouldn't dealer cooperation be bought
on the same principle?

Of course, the two situations are not identical. When a
manufacturer buys advertising space or time from an organization which buys nothing from *him,* neither the temptation
nor the opportunity to grant a price concession exists. But
when a manufacturer buys *anything* from a *customer* the
story is quite different. Then the opportunity to pay more
than its fair value is always present. Whether the danger of
such an abuse is great enough to warrant banning all advertising allowances or limiting them to the point where they
would become impracticable was, and still is, the real problem.

In any event, the publication of A&P's "preferred list"
naturally stirred up plenty of interest in the whole subject of
the buying advantages enjoyed by large-scale distributors. It
revealed for the first time not only that some manufacturers
were paying large sums to individual companies, but that
such allowances, in the aggregate, could stack up to a stupendous figure—in the case of A&P to $8,000,000 in a single
year.

That these disclosures helped to secure the enactment of
the Robinson-Patman Act, which was then in the hands of the
House Committee on the Judiciary, is quite clear. Indeed, on
July 10, 1935, the very next day after the "preferred list" had

been filed with his committee, Mr. Patman was able to make effective use of it in that connection. Appearing that day before the Judiciary Committee in support of the proposed legislation, including his own bill, H.R. 8442, he referred to the list and described its significance, as he saw it.[8] The following day, when he appeared again, he arranged to supply each member of the committee with a copy of the printed record containing the testimony relating to it. Furthermore, H. B. Teegarden, general counsel of the United States Wholesale Grocers Association, who had prepared the bill in the first place, filed a brief at the close of the hearing in which he directed the committee's attention specifically to all the testimony relating to A&P's advertising allowances.

The Robinson-Patman Act took effect June 19, 1936. It might have been enacted, of course, even if the investigation of the ARF had never been undertaken. As it was, however, the investigation must certainly be credited with having helped to secure its passage—if any credit can be claimed for having helped to put such an ambiguous and impractical piece of legislation on the books.

For whatever may be said of some of the objectives of the Robinson-Patman Act, few statutes have created more confusion and litigation. Today, 26 years after its passage, the courts are still struggling with its ambiguities and nobody can be certain whether a particular practice violates the law or not.

What the Act actually did was to amend the Clayton Act in several particulars and to introduce some innovations of its own.

The main amendments related to quantity discounts which were limited in two important respects: (a) they were permitted only to the extent that they reflected actual savings to the vendor; and (b) even when they reflected such sav-

[8] Hearing, Committee on the Judiciary, 74th Congress, 1st Session, July 10, 1935, p. 6.

ings, they could be forbidden by the Federal Trade Commission, after a hearing, to the extent that the maximum discounts could be earned by *too few* of the vendor's customers.

One of the new angles introduced was a provision which, in effect, prohibited advertising allowances or other payments to a customer unless they were made available to all customers on "proportionately equal terms."

Another new provision prohibited the payment of "brokerage" or a payment "in lieu of brokerage" to purchasers, even in cases where the vendor saved the brokerage by dealing directly with the purchaser.

How ambiguous some of the provisions of the Act are is perhaps best attested by the action of Mr. Patman himself. In 1938, he wrote a 400-page book to help clarify it.[9] In the preface he declared that it was prepared "in response to more than a thousand requests for information, received from manufacturers, sales managers, advertising men, retailers, wholesalers and others affected by the Act. . . . The repetition of certain questions indicates a misconception of the intent of the Act, particularly as to what it *does not* prohibit. The first wave of opinions and comments from economists and lawyers, volunteered in the press or requested from counsel, was critical, deprecatory or downright destructive in tone. . . . As a result, many perfectly sound practices were abandoned, some confusion followed for a few months, and the first reaction of business was unfavorable. Price lists were suspended, advertising allowances were withdrawn, and pricing policies were revised. Most of this was unnecessary, as subsequent events proved."

But although Mr. Patman added that "confusion ultimately gave way to common sense," he still felt, apparently, that a 400-page book was needed to "clarify" the Act.

Furthermore, eight years later, Federal Judge Walter C. Lindley declared in a case which involved the Robinson-

[9] *The Robinson-Patman Act*, Wright Patman (Ronald Press, New York, 1938).

Patman Act only incidentally: "Sometimes I doubt whether we ever needed the Robinson-Patman law, with all its elusive uncertainty. I have thought that the Sherman Act, properly interpreted and administered, would have remedied all the ills meant to be cured. . . . I doubt if any judge would assert that he knows exactly what does or does not amount to violation of the Robinson-Patman Act in any and all instances." [10]

As to the impracticability of the provision requiring that advertising allowances and other payments be made available to all customers on "proportionately equal terms," Beckman and Nolen, in *The Chain Store Problem,* had this to say:

> "In many cases, the difficulties in attempting to apportion allowances among small as well as large buyers will make their use impossible. For example, if an advertising allowance of $8 per 100 cases is offered to chain stores, what should the manufacturer offer the small retailer who buys but one case? Obviously, 8 cents would buy very little in the way of advertising. The obstacles in the path of a legal application of allowances will force many to abandon their use entirely, as has already been done in a number of cases." [11]

The Federal Trade Commission is still issuing complaints against reputable manufacturers whose advertising allowances are allegedly in violation of the provision in question.

Summarizing the results of the ill-conceived investigation of the American Retail Federation, the following points stand out:

1. It failed absolutely in its prime purpose of branding that organization as a "superlobby" designed to promote the interest of the chains. On the contrary, the evidence established that chain-store men had had no part in the conception of the federation but had become interested in it because they were in accord with its only purpose—to serve as the voice of retailing in general.

[10] U.S. v. Great A&P Tea Co., 67 Fed. Supp. 626.
[11] *The Chain Store Problem, op. cit.,* p. 282.

2. It slowed up the development of ARF for a year but did not prevent the organization thereafter from achieving the original aims of its organizers.

3. It provided some of the momentum which led to the passage of the Robinson-Patman Act.

4. It brought out considerable material which could be used by the anti-chain interests, fairly or unfairly, to stir up prejudice and create resentment against the chains.

One of its direct fruits, for instance, was an anti-chain book carrying Mr. Patman's endorsement.[12] Its reliability may be judged from the fact that the author declares in the preface: "There probably would have been no congressional investigation of the chain store if the chain-store people had not overstepped themselves in seeking to set up a powerful national lobbying agency known as the American Retail Federation. Their flagrant attempt to put over the organization as a set-up to 'protect the small retailer' attracted the attention of members of Congress and indicated the need of an investigation."

Although the author claimed to have made an "intense study" of the entire record—and, indeed, the book consists mainly of selected extracts from it—his study apparently stopped short of the committee's final report—or did it? For in that report, it will be recalled, the majority definitely admitted that their "chain-store superlobby" theory wholly failed to stand up!

One conclusion which may be fairly drawn from an analysis of the record is that, considering the opportunity the anti-chain interest had to pry into the private files of the chains' most active defenders, surprisingly little, if anything, was revealed to the discredit of the chain-store system.

[12] *Wells of Discontent*, Charles G. Daughters (Daughters, 1937).

CHAPTER XI

IN THE COURT OF
PUBLIC OPINION

WHILE THE investigation of the American Retail Federation was producing newspaper headlines and centering the attention of most chain-store men on Washington, another front in the anti-chain war was opening in California.

Encouraged, no doubt, by the growing agitation against "big business" in general, a California group which called itself the Anti-Monopoly League was urging drastic action against the chains. Among various anti-chain-store bills introduced at the 1935 session of the State legislature was one, called the Retail Store License bill, which the league was actively sponsoring. The "license" it proposed was $1 a year for a single store, $2 for a second store, $4 for a third store and so on progressively up to $256 for the ninth store, with all stores in excess of nine paying $500 each.

The pressure behind the bill was overwhelming. Legislators could hardly have failed to be impressed by the claim that 80,000 California independent merchants demanded its passage—frankly admitting that the purpose of the tax was to drive the chains out of California.

Nothing the chains could say or do at Sacramento could prevail against that kind of pressure—despite all the "influence" they were supposed to have built up for themselves in State capitols, according to what the Patman committee was claiming at the Washington hearings. The Senate passed the bill by a vote of 34 to 4 and the Assembly by a vote of 68 to 8—a showing which revealed clearly enough the helplessness of the chains in such a situation and explains why they felt justified in resorting sometimes to any lawful measure called for in self-defense.

Realizing the destructive character of the tax, Governor Merriam held a public hearing before deciding whether to sign or veto it. The chains put up the best case they could, marshalling all the arguments they could muster against its unfairness and economic shortcomings. No doubt they were able to make out a strong case. But their opponents resorted to a different technique, which was thus described in a detailed report covering the story of this legislation issued by the advertising agency which was later retained by the chains to direct their fight against it.[1]

> "Close to a thousand independent merchants, militant and noisy, arrived on special trains on the day of the hearing and staged an impressive 'March on Sacramento.' Brass bands led them with martial music; flying banners proclaimed their demands that the bill be signed; gay buttons in their lapels identified them as crusaders for a cause; and they marched and countermarched through the capital city, swarming into the Assembly Chamber to take their places four hours before the hearing was scheduled to begin."

The main argument used by their representatives was that the tax was needed to protect the small merchant against the competition of the big chains.

The Governor delayed his decision for ten days, but on July 21 he approved the Act, saying: "the chain-store operators feel that this legislation will prove discriminatory in its application. If so, the opportunity is theirs to prevent this act from becoming effective by invoking the referendum and submitting the question directly to the people."

[1] *Discrimination vs. Business,* Lord & Thomas, p. 4.

And that, of course, was what the chains proceeded to do. To invoke the referendum, under the California law, the chains needed 116,487 signatures of qualified voters to a petition demanding it. The number had to equal 5% of all the votes cast for governor at the previous general election. By September 14 they had more than enough and the referendum was officially certified by the Secretary of State. It meant that the chains had until the next general election, November 3, 1936, a little more than thirteen months, in which to convince the voters of California that the chain-store tax was against their interests.

As the Lord & Thomas report points out, the chains had several obstacles to overcome besides their own weaknesses from a public-relations standpoint. "The enemies of the chains had timed their attack with shrewd foresight," the report observes. "The year was a Presidential year, in which it would be hard to arouse public sentiment on collateral issues; the chain-store tax would be simply one of 23 measures on a formidable and confusing California ballot; the contest would come at a time when conspicuous figures like Wright Patman were breathing fire and brimstone from Washington against the chains and all their works."

Furthermore, the battleground favored the anti-chain interests. "California, in 1936," the report declares, "was a field presenting special handicaps to any attempt at interpreting business sympathetically. It was a stronghold for all sorts of political doctrines based on discontent. Its State treasury was embarrassed by a big deficit which lent a powerful appeal to any proposal to tax the other fellow. Finally, neither the time nor the place was auspicious for any effort based on reason and intelligent analysis; both were ideal for a campaign of emotional, inflammatory character."

The first thing the chains did was to organize the California Chain Stores Association to ensure unified action. Some 65 chains with stores in California were represented in it and were committed to share the costs of the campaign proportionately among them.

The next thing, and probably the smartest thing they could have done, was to recognize their own inability to shape up the kind of campaign the situation called for, or to carry it through. They realized that they were in the position of a man who was desperately sick and needed the attention of the best doctor he could get. Self-medication, in a case like that, was likely to prove fatal. Their deliberations on the choice of a doctor resulted in their selection of one of the leading advertising agencies, Lord & Thomas, from whose final report on the campaign many of the details contained in this chapter were drawn.

Lord & Thomas, in turn, assigned its executive vice president, Don Francisco,[2] to be the campaign director. The chains wisely decided that he should be the supreme commander in fact as well as in name, for, as he himself pointed out in a speech describing the campaign, the position of the campaign director had to be like that of a quarterback on a football team.

"No successful coach would let his team go on the field with several of the players authorized to call the signals," he declared. "No successful quarterback would call a signal until he had first surveyed the position of his teammates and opponents on the field of battle. The choice of plays and the exact timing are rarely determined far in advance."

In a political campaign, he pointed out, the final decision and the authority to make quick decisions on important matters must rest with the campaign director. "In the California campaign," he said, "committees and conferences were avoided. Events moved too rapidly for meetings. I had the ablest advisers on every hand and I used them constantly. Most of the ideas we used were suggested to me by my asso-

[2] Later to become vice president of J. Walter Thompson Co., New York. He retired in 1956.

ciates. But in the conduct of the campaign, even the chain-store executives let us 'call the signals.' Never have I worked with the advantage of such full confidence and complete co-operation."

That the confidence the chains put in Don Francisco as their quarterback was fully justified, the outcome of the campaign was to demonstrate unmistakably. But he gave the chains more than a victory—he gave them a course in public relations which they were never after to forget. The campaign which he and his associates mapped out and which was carried out under his leadership not only achieved its immediate objective, but provided the basis for a permanent policy which was to yield the chains tremendous returns in the years which followed.

Some of the principles he laid down are best revealed in his own language, taken from one of his speeches relating to the campaign.

"Business cannot proceed on the assumption that customers are friends," he declared. "Motorists may buy at your service station but damn you because they think you are a monopoly. They may go out of their way to save a few pennies at your chain store and then denounce you for paying low wages. Making friends and making customers are two different jobs —separate though related.

"Without friends, without enlightened public opinion based upon self-interest, a business with a million customers can be crucified by a militant minority.

"Thus public relations has come to be of prime importance. Public relations is neither press agentry nor institution advertising. It is not sending out press releases after the show is produced. It begins while the show is being planned. It starts on the inside with a realization that *the best private relations make the best public relations.* Just as the advertising man strives to get his product and package right before he shouts about it, so the public-relations man starts by seeking the deep-rooted weaknesses of a business and correcting them. He starts with an effort to mold or modify events in order to create favorable news and make friends. And, finally, successful public relations recognize that *it is not enough for policies to be right—they must also seem right.* The real public-relations men are the top executives who make policies."

Although the chains suffered from the antagonism to all "big business," Mr. Francisco was quick to point out to his clients that their troubles also stemmed from certain handicaps of their own making. *First,* they had made some mistakes, although it is probable that the chain stores had made no more mistakes than other businesses. In view of their quick growth, he thought it remarkable that they had not made more. *Second,* in their rapid development they had stepped on a lot of toes. Furthermore, he explained, they had not stopped to say "pardon me" or "I couldn't help it, I was in a terrible hurry." They had stepped not only on the toes of wholesalers and independent retailers but on those of local bankers, attorneys, insurance agents, appliance salesmen and others.

This was a new slant to chain-store executives, for although they were familiar with criticisms based on their failure to patronize local services, such as those supplied by banks, insurance men and others, they had always felt it was a sufficient answer to explain why the chain-store system did not need such services. Now they were told that, although economically, legally and in every other way, their practices may have been justified, their public relations had suffered just the same. Finally, they had not told their story. They had believed that any business which could sell for less and attract millions of customers would be welcomed as a friend in any community. They had overlooked that customers are not necessarily friends.

As Mr. Francisco put it: "Those with injured toes formed a militant organization and had been at work for many years.

Their activities had undermined confidence in the chains by harping constantly on their mistakes and by raising doubts as to their desirability as a social institution. The general antagonism to big business created a most favorable background for such a crusade."

So much publicity had been given to the real and fancied shortcomings of the chains that their virtues were overshadowed. "Apparently forgotten," Mr. Francisco pointed out, "were the important services which chains rendered as prime outlets for the farmer's produce, the opportunity offered to deserving employes to climb to positions of responsibility, and the service performed for the average family by providing convenience, cleanliness, better merchandise and lower prices. In the face of this abuse the chains had been singularly inarticulate, or, at most, had contented themselves with defensively debating the damaging thrusts of their opponents."

The basic program was worked out before the campaign started. Although it was kept more or less flexible, several fundamental policies were adhered to throughout.

The first policy was to *get off the defensive* as soon as possible and launch an offensive. Mr. Francisco held that there were only two kinds of effective defense in a campaign such as the chains had to wage. First, total silence, a complete disregard of the opponent's charges; and second, a counterattack that is so vigorous that the opponents are put on the defensive. Until they had built their organization and laid their plans, they were advised to ignore the accusations of their enemies. Then, instead of attempting to answer false accusations and thereby give them greater publicity, the chains featured the advantages of their system.

Another important policy was to refrain from attacking the independent merchant. To have done so would have served to arouse sympathy for him as the "under dog."

"Since we never attacked the independents," Mr. Francisco pointed out, "the rank and file were very lukewarm about contributing money or enlisting in the crusade against us. Thus their efforts were materially weakened. We exposed the tax as a scheme engineered by selfish middlemen who sought to place a severe handicap on their chain-store competitors at public expense. We did not hesitate to attack the professional organizers, racketeering money-raisers and self-seeking politicians who worked against us. But toward other retailers we were always tolerant. We gave them no reason for fighting us.

"Our opponents had made it appear that all chains were national monopolies controlled by Wall Street. One of our jobs was to make clear that a majority of the chains that would be hit by the tax were relatively small California-owned organizations that operated a few stores within the state."

Fundamentally the campaign was built on the belief that the most effective attack against the tax could and would be made not by the chains themselves but by those who would be affected by it indirectly—the farmer, the manufacturer, the property-owner and, most important of all, the consumer.

The overall plan consisted actually of two separate campaigns. The first, of ten months' duration, was designed to make friends for chain stores by (a) finding and correcting mistakes; (b) healing sore spots and explaining misunderstandings; and (c) telling the chains' story of service. The second, of less than two months' duration, was an all-out, hard-hitting attack against the chain-store tax itself.

One fortunate break the chains got was an opportunity early in the campaign to cooperate with agricultural producers, and thus to create better relations with a group for whom they were already rendering a vital service but whose attitude towards the chains was openly critical. On February 26, 1936, the California Canning Peach Growers wrote to Mr. Francisco, pointing out that the entire California Cling Peach Industry was suffering from an under-consumption of canned peaches. Because of his "very close touch" with the chain stores, he was asked to secure the cooperation of the food chains in putting on a drive whereby consumption of the product in question could be greatly increased and thereby benefit "the most important canning operation in the State of California." [3]

Naturally the chains acted quickly and effectively. Through their national association, a nationwide drive was launched at once. It absorbed the surplus and enabled the peach growers to dispose of their new crop at a substantial profit instead of suffering the disaster which had previously seemed inevitable.

In that effort, food chains all over the country cooperated. Later on, when the price of beef was dropping so fast because of the abnormal slaughter brought about by the drought that the livestock growers were panic-stricken, the chains received another opportunity to demonstrate what organized distribution could do. The nationwide drive they put on again saved a critical situation.

Finally, only two weeks before the election, the food chains received another opportunity, in connection with a surplus crop of California dried fruits. Once again they earned the admiration and gratitude of an important group of California producers by moving an unprecedented volume of the product into consumption.

These drives showed in a concrete way the important part the chain-store system played in our national economy. They did more to command the friendship and respect of California farmers and producers than all the economic arguments, however sound, the chains could possibly have presented.

Following their California experience, the grocery chains developed a permanent agricultural relief program which, in the years to follow, was to move many a surplus crop into consumption all over the country. That "practical farm relief" program, as it has been called, will be discussed in greater detail in a later chapter.

In getting across the story of the service the chain stores

[3] *Discrimination vs. Business, supra,* p. 5a.

were rendering, which was one of the main efforts during the first ten months of the campaign, every suitable medium and device was used. Included were radio programs, newspaper advertising, booklets, posters, speeches, essay contests. Throughout it all, however, the approach was educational and informative rather than argumentative and no reference was made to the tax at any time.

Not until six weeks before Election Day was the direct attack on the tax unleashed. By that time, the proposition as it was to appear on the ballot had been assigned a number, 22. The number itself gave the chains a chance to fashion an effective slogan against it: "22 Is a Tax on You!" Because it rhymed, it helped voters remember the number of the proposal. Because it was "a Tax on You" it helped voters remember that the answer was "No." That slogan, repeated over and over again in every type of medium for 30 days, was a potent factor in crystallizing the issue and in simplifying the voter's task on election day.

"When the zero hour came," Mr. Francisco related some time later, "every worker and medium changed from public relations to anti-tax activity. 'California's Hour' [4] commercials assailed the tax, the California Consumer's Conference released posters and newspaper advertisements attacking it. Resolutions against the tax were passed or taken out of files and publicized. Chain-store employes and workers wore buttons on their lapels and signs on their automobile bumpers reading '22 Is a Tax on You.' On a score of radio stations, lawyers, property owners, business men, women and farmers spoke against the tax. During the last three days prior to the election, the California Chain Stores Association itself finally spoke. Over the association's signature three large advertisements appeared on successive days summarizing the editorials that had appeared against the tax, the prominent organizations that had passed resolutions against it and the small Cali-

[4] A weekly radio program of entertainment, sponsored by the chains throughout the campaign but which, up to that time, had not even mentioned the tax.

fornia-owned organizations that would be injured if it passed. There were meetings by the score, frenzied activity everywhere—at last the battle was on."

Once the drive opened it never let up. Every step had been carefully timed so that the peak was reached at the exact moment when it would prove most effective. Furthermore, an extremely vital factor if all the effort was not to prove in vain —getting out the vote—was never lost sight of. An elaborate organization had been set up to organize employes for precinct work. The residence of every chain-store employe in the large cities was pin-pointed on a map and each one who volunteered for service was cataloged and assigned certain voters to call on. Some were assigned to get out the vote and others to watch the polls on election day.

"This was a very vital part of the program," Mr. Francisco pointed out, "for poor precinct work can win or lose elections. We adopted the standard technique for organizing precinct workers and applied it to chain-store employes. The job of interviewing voters throughout the state and making sure that those who planned to vote 'No' would do so on Election Day was a tremendous one, but we were able to achieve it by breaking it down into many little jobs through a military type of organization."

What was the outcome?

As has been intimated, the chains won a decisive victory.

The voters rejected the discriminatory chain-store tax by a vote of 1,369,778 to 1,067,443, a majority against the tax of 302,335.

Furthermore, that result reflected the views of voters all over the State, for 57 out of California's 58 counties voted "No" to the proposal.

Although the campaign had undoubtedly been expensive to the chains, the total cost was far less than they would have had to pay for the privilege of staying in business had the tax prevailed.

But the pecuniary benefits of their victory, great as they were, were small compared with some of the other results—most important of which were the lessons it taught. What they were are best described in the language of the "supreme commander."

"By their campaign the chain stores of California not only defeated the chain-store tax," Mr. Francisco declared, "but they improved their relations with employes, farmers and customers, made themselves better understood and increased their sales. Today they have more friends as well as more customers.

"The tax on California chain stores was not defeated because a majority of voters were unwilling to soak the chains, but because many were unwilling to soak themselves. The job of the chain stores was to interpret the effect of the tax to various groups of voters from the viewpoint of their self-interest. The employe saw the tax as a threat to his job. The farmer saw it as a measure that would cripple an important outlet for his produce. The businessman saw it as a discriminatory misuse of the tax power that might be extended to his business. The consumer saw it as a retail tax that would raise prices.

"In the last analysis, each citizen votes for himself. He has little sympathy for the problems of chain stores, railroads, utilities or other businesses. What he wants to know about laws and taxes is how they affect him. That is the opportunity and the safeguard of business.

"People know that businesses are big, successful and profitable. . . . People do not know what business has done for them—to create jobs, to effect economies, to perfect service, to save time and money, to reduce the cost of living and to raise the standard of living.

"Business needs a favorable public opinion as well as a consumer demand for its products. . . . Business can protect itself by first demonstrating and telling how it serves America, and then by showing how unfair legislation handicaps its ability to render that service."

The detailed story of the strategy and tactics employed so effectively in the California referendum campaign makes fascinating reading besides attesting the scope of the "know how" needed to produce such a result. But the full story belongs rather to the annals of public relations than in a history of chain stores. Before leaving it, however, a word or two should be said about the strength of the opposition. What did the chains have to beat to win?

In the first place, the Anti-Monopoly League, which had successfully sponsored the chain-store tax originally, could hardly have been expected to give back the fruits of its victory without a struggle. It certainly showed no disposition to do so.

The league, which was a federation of anti-chain interests, started out to raise a war-chest of $2,500,000. How much was actually obtained or how much of what was raised actually went into the campaign is not known. A court action by one of the field men who became disgruntled because the "exclusive" area assigned to him had already been worked revealed that the principal fund-raiser had a contract giving him 40 per cent of all money collected.

Be that as it may, the league was able to finance a program substantial enough to give the chains considerable concern.

"Their strategy, before the electorate as before the legislature," the Lord & Thomas report declares, "was to make the chains defendants in a court of popular prejudice, rather than to explain or support the proposed tax. . . . Their favored campaign documents were 'horror' cartoons, such as those picturing the chains as an octopus strangling California in its greedy tentacles, or as a cow, complacently browsing on the state's wealth, while top-hatted Wall Street, tugging at her udders, drained that wealth into guilty New York. . . .

"During the early months of the campaign, the Anti-Monopoly League's radio programs and advertisements stressed a vital secondary message; along with their condemnation of the greed of the chains, they urged generous contributions to the support of the league as a 'non-profit organization,' whose leaders were 'unselfishly sacrificing in behalf of the program!' "

According to Mr. Francisco, their most telling argument was that the tax amounted to only $1.37 per day per store. "However," he pointed out, "they used this in a major way only in San Francisco and the Bay cities."

The Corner Store Philosopher was their most effective radio program and, Mr. Francisco confesses, it "had us worried. The 'Philosopher' disregarded facts and played entirely on the emotions. In a kindly drawl he told of his experiences with chain-store employes, farmers and neighbors. The stories were pure fiction but they dramatized all the arguments used against us. We were glad when lack of funds brought about the substitution of some of the opposing generals in place of the insidious 'Corner Store Philosopher.' "

The "lack of funds" referred to was attributed to the damaging publicity the league suffered as a result of the court exposure of its fund-raising activities. The president of the Anti-Monopoly League, himself, testified that 40% of all the funds raised were to be turned over to the man who had the contract to gather them in. That revelation undoubtedly lost the league a lot of supporters. Contributions did not come in as freely as at first.

Nevertheless, although the campaign in behalf of the tax failed, some gauge of its force is provided in the fact that it did at least roll up a total of 1,067,443 votes. Had it been even 15 per cent more effective than it was, the outstanding efforts of the chains would have been in vain.

The California referendum was not the first trial of the so-called chain-store question in the court of public opinion, although it was the first successful one.

The first attempt of the kind involved a local ordinance

passed in the city of Portland, Ore., in the fall of 1931.[5] It imposed only a modest tax, ranging from $6 on the first store to $50 on all stores in excess of 50. Nevertheless the chains decided to test it through the referendum process. At the 1932 election, the issue polled a vote of 105,653, of which 53,871 favored the tax and 51,782 opposed it. In view of the moderate character of the tax, the voters could hardly have been expected to get too excited about it. Such a small tax, however unfair, would hardly put any of the chains out of business or require them to raise their prices enough for anyone to notice it. In the light of that fact the chains had some reason for gratification. The margin of their defeat, only 2,089 votes, was slim enough to suggest that under different conditions they would have better luck. However, if they had any such hopes, they were shortly to be rather roughly disillusioned.

For in 1934, in Colorado, they had to fight what was the first and only attempt ever made to enact a chain-store tax by popular vote through the medium of an "initiative" petition. The proposal was voted on at the general election that year and was adopted by a vote of 132,160 to 106,359. And it was no small tax either, ranging from $2 on a single store up to $300 on stores in excess of 24.

The chains did nothing much about it until their success in California suggested that an appeal to the public in Colorado might prove equally effective. The necessary steps were accordingly taken and at the 1938 election a proposal to repeal the chain-store tax appeared on the ballot.

Unfortunately for the chains, the ballot carried another proposal as well—a proposal to repeal the old-age pension plan which had been adopted in 1936 and under which everyone over 60 was entitled to $45 a month. Inasmuch as the State then faced a $2,000,000 deficit, those who favored the retention of the pension plan could see no sense in voting for a repeal of the chain-store tax or any other revenue-producing

[5] *The Chain Store Tells the Story, op. cit.,* p. 151.

measure. The proposal to repeal the chain-store tax was defeated by a vote of 240,000 to 160,000.

Four years later, however, the application of some of the California techniques proved more successful in Utah. A law passed by the 1941 legislature not only imposed a severe tax, of the Louisiana type, on existing stores, the scale ranging from $50 per store on less than 100 stores to $500 per store on stores in excess of 500, the particular bracket being determined by the number of stores operated *anywhere,* but it introduced a new feature. On all stores added or relocated in Utah after July 1, 1941, the tax would be $500 per store if less than 100 were operated, while chains with 500 or more stores would have to pay $5,000 for each new store or old one relocated!

The chains again invoked the referendum process and put on an all-out program. The proposal on the ballot being number 2, the slogan "No. 2 Is a Tax on You!" was a logical choice. At the annual election on November 3, 1942, the chains prevailed by a vote of 85,188 to 38,504, with every county in the State voting against the tax.

In achieving that decisive result, the chains were able to make much of the fact that the tax was actually a "death sentence" for chain stores in Utah; that there were only 123 chain stores compared with 6,000 independents in the State; that the independents accounted for seven-eighths of the total retail sales; that the bill exempted service-station chains and voluntary chains; and that the elimination of chain-store competition would inevitably mean higher prices for Utah housewives.

But, powerful as these arguments undoubtedly were, much of the credit for the chains' victory must be given to a definite swing in public attitude in favor of the chains which had begun to develop a couple of years earlier. Ironically enough, Congressman Patman's supreme effort to end the chain-store problem once and for all by his so-called Federal "Death Sentence" bill, which was the subject of an extensive public hearing in the spring of 1940, actually proved the salvation of the chains. In one sense it did, indeed, end the chain-store problem, for the supporters of the chains turned out in such overwhelming numbers and strength that the anti-chain politicians must have realized, then and there, that the open season for chain-killing was over.

Not only was the "Death Sentence" bill, sponsored by Mr. Patman, completely discredited, but no State passed a discriminatory chain-store tax after 1941; the Utah law, as we have seen, was rejected by popular vote in 1942; an Idaho tax was repealed in 1949; and, that same year, the graduated feature of the North Carolina statute was replaced by a modest flat-rate tax without reference to the number of stores operated. In 1951, the Georgia tax was repealed.

Commenting on the result of the Utah referendum a few days after the election in 1942, the New York *Herald Tribune* declared editorially:

> "One of the unspectacular but none the less pleasing episodes of Tuesday's balloting occurred in Utah, where the voters of the state repudiated, by a count of more than two to one, a law passed last year which would have placed a punitive tax on chain stores. . . .
>
> "There seems to be good reason to believe that this movement to drive the chain store out of existence by taxation reached its high-water mark in the hearings on the Patman bill, which would have nationalized this debasement of the tax function. . . . What happened in Utah this week indicates that the educational value of those hearings was not wasted. Unfortunately for the Patmans and their kind, the public today has a better grasp on the economics of the chain-store tax than it had a decade ago."

Certainly the story of the Patman "death sentence" bill rates a chapter of its own.

CHAPTER XII

THE "DEATH SENTENCE" BILL

THE FIRST ATTEMPT to impose a punitive tax against chain stores on a national basis came in February, 1938, in the shape of a bill introduced by Representative Wright Patman, of Texas. It carried the names of more than 70 other Congressmen as "co-framers, co-authors and co-sponsors."

The bill, which was designated as H.R. 9464, was aimed primarily at the chains which operated in a number of States, but its provisions were drastic enough to have put many a chain out of business even though all its stores were located in a single State.

The tax imposed started at $50 a store on the tenth to the fifteenth store and increased progressively until all stores in excess of 500 would have to pay $1,000 each annually. But that was only the beginning! After the tax had been calculated on that basis, the amount was to be *multiplied* by the number of States in which the taxpayer operated.

Just by way of example, the tax on the Woolworth Company in 1938 would have amounted to some $81,000,000 although its net profits that year amounted to only $28,000,000! With 1,864 stores in operation in 48 States and the District of Columbia, the tax would have amounted to $1,650,000 if all the stores had been operated in a single State, but because they were scattered all over the union, that sum had to be multiplied by 49, giving the tidy sum of $81,070,000. In the case of the A&P, with approximately 12,000 stores in 40 States at that time, the tax would have totalled more than $471,000,-000!

How the tax would have hit some of the other chains is shown in Table 19, but its impact on a relatively small chain which happened to operate in a number of states is well illustrated by the case of Mangel Stores, an apparel chain, with 106 stores scattered over 27 states. The tax on the 106 stores, if all had been located in one state, would have amounted to

TABLE 19

IMPACT OF PATMAN "DEATH SENTENCE" BILL
ON 24 CHAINS AS OF 1938*

COMPANY	NUMBER OF STORES	NUMBER OF STATES	1938 EARNINGS	H.R. 1 TAX
American Stores	2,416	8	$ 57,627	$ 17,652,000
A&P[1]	12,000	40	9,119,114	471,620,000
Bickford's	106	4	558,924	92,800
Bohack, H. C.	488	1	(179,741)	279,700
Dixie Home Stores	172	2	189,197	105,800
Edison Bros.	123	29	919,323	894,650
Fanny Farmer	237	15	904,009	1,315,500
First Nat'l Stores	2,350	7	2,705,191	14,983,500
Gamble-Skogmo	247	18	278,538	1,686,600
Grant Co., W. T.	491	38	2,766,424	10,731,200
Kinney, G. R.	328	37	151,503	5,420,500
Kresge[2]	679	27	8,997,051	12,676,500
Kress, S. H.	235	29	3,668,216	2,508,500
Kroger Co.	3,992	19	3,741,569	71,867,500
Lerner Stores	164	39	1,299,231	1,922,700
Liggett	552	36	518,432	12,330,000
Mangel Stores	106	27	18,674	626,400
Melville Shoe Corp.	639	40	1,484,061	17,180,000
Newberry	476	45	1,792,741	12,100,500
Penney, J. C.	1,541	48	13,739,160	63,912,000
Safeway[2]	2,873	22	4,206,781	58,597,000
Schiff Co.	277	28	265,180	3,127,600
Walgreen Co.	510	37	2,067,846	11,118,500
Woolworth Co.[3]	1,864	48	28,584,944	81,070,500

[1] Estimated U.S. stores; earnings include Canadian stores.
[2] Includes Canadian stores and earnings.
[3] Includes Canadian and Cuban stores and earnings.
* From Appendix B, "Keep Market Street Open," a brief filed by chains opposing Patman bill, appearing in record of hearing at page 652.

approximately $23,000, but, multiplied by 27, it would have come to $626,000, quite a burden for a chain whose profits that year amounted to only $18,674!

But recognizing that these taxes amounted practically to a death sentence for most of the chains which had achieved even a moderate degree of success, the bill did graciously provide an escape for those who desired to take advantage of it. The full impact of the tax was deferred for two years during which period the affected chains could liquidate voluntarily. In other words, they could escape the death penalty by committing suicide!

As might have been expected, the general reaction to such a drastic measure was condemnation.

Typical of the immediate comment on the bill was an editorial in *Business Week*, February 5, 1938, headed "Killing Chain Stores."

"Would you believe it," the editorial asked, "if you were told that a congressman, and an influential congressman at that, had proposed that the federal Government tax the F. W. Woolworth Co. about $90,000,000 a year? And that it tax the A&P $600,000,000?

"Yet that is the meaning of Rep. Patman's new bill. . . . Destruction is the object. For since the chains cannot stand such enormous taxes, they would be forced out of business, to the delight of many competitors. . . . A mighty effort is under way to smash the chains.

"Upon this effort the public must render judgment. It must make up its mind whether all the benefits of mass buying, mass distribution and mass retailing shall be destroyed in order to ensure that a multitude of small retailers, who are for the most part bad merchants, poorly financed, and ill equipped to give service, shall be subsidized at the expense of the ultimate consumer; or whether the government shall permit some progress to be made in the direction of efficiency and cost reduction for the benefit of the people who go into stores every day and pay in pennies and nickels for the necessities of life."

Retailing, in its issue of February 21, 1938, carried an editorial headed: "Death Sentence."

"Chain stores are now confronted with the executioner's axe," it declared. "If the bill just introduced by Representative Wright Patman is passed in anything like its present form, chain stores, as we know them, will pass out of the business picture within two years. . . . While the chain stores have not been blameless in their buying and competitive methods, it is incredible to think that they should be wiped out. . . . This is a fight which concerns every branch of retailing, big and little. The chains may need further regulation, but not destruction. The National Retail Dry Goods Association and other groups should help to defeat this measure."

From the very day of its introduction, a ground swell of opposition started to develop against the Patman bill which was eventually to reach overwhelming proportions.

But the almost universal condemnation his proposal was receiving did little to dampen Mr. Patman's ardor. When, in September of that year, he was invited by the National Conference of Business Paper Editors to debate the merits of his bill at the annual convention of its affiliated association, Associated Business Papers, he jumped at the chance.

"I look upon this meeting," he wrote, in accepting the invitation, "as a wonderful opportunity to sell a good cause to people who really have more to do with molding public opinion in this country than any other group. If I am right in this fight, I should win and will win, if the people get the truth. If I do not have the right side, I am not entitled to win. It is pleasing to me to know that the fight has at last been brought out into the open. It is the first time." [1]

It devolved upon the author to oppose Mr. Patman in that debate which was held at the Union League Club, Chicago. The debate appears in full in *Chain Stores and Legislation*,[2] and no purpose will be served by considering it at length in these pages, particularly as all the arguments Mr. Patman

[1] Letter from Hon. Wright Patman, Texarkana, Tex., dated September 23, 1938, to Bascom N. Timmons, Washington, D.C., from copy in author's files.
[2] By Daniel Bloomfield (New York: H. W. Wilson Co., 1939).

used then in favor of his measure were repeated in amplified form in the long public hearing which is to be discussed in some detail in this chapter.

However, one of Mr. Patman's most fantastic claims, which he had made in Congress in 1937 and reiterated in the course of the debate deserves treatment at this point because he persisted in using it thereafter even after its invalidity had been demonstrated to him.

On June 17, 1937, Mr. Patman had declared in Congress[3] that "a study has just been completed which shows that *the cost of food is higher in cities where chain stores predominate.*"

He based that contention on a study of intercity living costs made by the Works Progress Administration, which he had tied up with Census figures showing how the chains stood in the cities in question as compared with the independents.

Our own comment on Mr. Patman's astounding claim, as it appeared in *Chain Store Age*[4] at that time, will serve to set up the basic facts. Our editorial said:

> "Because of his reference to official data, the Congressman's argument had a decidedly genuine ring, but an examination of the sources themselves reveals that he handed his colleagues a gold brick. To achieve his purpose he resorted to a method which even a high school debater might scorn to employ—the use of *selected* instances. He used the figures which served him and completely ignored the rest, a treatment which no one who was trying to paint a *fair* picture would ever employ.
>
> "The living-cost study he quoted covered 59 cities, but Patman used only twenty. Not only did he ignore the others, but he deliberately intimated that they all pointed the same way, when the fact is that many of them pointed in just the opposite direction.
>
> " 'I can name you cities all over this nation,' he declared, 'and prove to you that where the chains have control in any

---

[3] *Congressional Record,* June 17, 1937, p. 5914.
[4] August, 1937

line of business prices are higher than in cities where the independents have control of similar lines of business.'

"But not a word did he say about the cities which indicated just the opposite and which he had right in front of him in the study from which he drew his statistics.

"Now what were the facts?

"The Division of Social Research of the WPA in 1936 made a comparative study of the cost of living in 59 different cities. Using Washington, D.C. as the base and calling it 100, a relative figure was established for each of the others. The *median* figure for the cost of food was 93.9. In other words, of the 59 cities, 27 show a food cost index higher than 93.9, 29 a lower index, and three stand exactly at the median level.

"In the group of cities in which the index is *higher* than 93.9 are nine 'chain' cities and eighteen 'independent' cities, while in the group in which the index is *lower* than 93.9 will be found nine 'chain' cities and twenty 'independent' cities. Exactly at the median level are one 'chain' city and two 'independent' cities.

"Obviously an accurate interpretation of these figures lends no support whatever to the Patman contention, but in the way he used them he conveyed an entirely different picture. He pointed out, for instance, that in Houston, an 'independent' city, the index was 90.7 and in El Paso, another 'independent' city, it was 92.5, whereas in Dallas, a 'chain' city, it was 95. In the same way, he paired various other cities, always selecting for his unfair comparisons only 'chain' cities in which the cost of living happened to be high and only 'independent' cities in which the cost of living happened to be low.

"Of course, anyone who would be willing to adopt the same tactics, could use Patman's own authority to confound his argument. One could show, for instance, that Detroit, a 'chain' city, has an index of 93.2, whereas Bridgeport, Conn., an 'independent' city, has the highest food index in the whole list—102.3; that Dallas, the 'chain' city to which Patman referred as having a comparatively high index of 95, compares quite favorably with New York, an 'independent' city, with an index of 100.1; that Cleveland, a 'chain' city, has an index of 93.3, whereas Newark, N.J., an 'independent' city has an index of 99.5; and Los Angeles, a 'chain' city, has an index of only 92.8 compared with San Francisco, an 'independent' city, whose index is 96.3.

"But that, of course, is a criminal way to distort evidence and anyone who would resort to it deliberately would be guilty of intellectual dishonesty of the rankest kind. Whether or not Congressman Patman *deliberately* juggled the data in the manner indicated cannot, of course, be inferred from the facts available, but even though he be acquitted of the suspicion of downright chicanery, he can hardly hope to escape the charge of a carelessness so gross as to be almost as culpable.

"The truth is that inter-city living costs vary for *many* different reasons, of which the prevailing type of distribution is only one. The fact that the cost of living is comparatively high in a particular city in which the chains do the bulk of the business provides no justification whatever for the conclusion that food costs are high there because of the chains. On the contrary, ordinary common sense and available data on the subject would suggest rather that the *high* cost of living in such a city must be *despite* the chains and not because of them—that the cost of living would be *even higher* but for the competitive effect of chain-store prices.

"And nobody should realize that fact more clearly than Congressman Patman himself, for has not his whole chain-baiting campaign of the last couple of years been based on his complaint that the chains are driving the independents out of business *by underselling them?* . . .

"The fact is, as has frequently been demonstrated by impartial investigators, . . . that the grocery chains not only *can* but *do* undersell their independent competitors, and if the blame for the high cost of living in a given city can fairly be placed on the shoulders of the one factor which tends to keep prices down then Congressman Patman is a public benefactor and the chains are a public menace. Otherwise, Wright Patman is wrong!"

Whether or not Mr. Patman had ever seen that editorial before that night is not known, although reprints of it had been widely circulated in Washington and throughout the country, but it certainly was brought to his attention in the course of the debate. It came up in the course of the rebuttal arguments.

Said Mr. Patman: "I also say to you (I have facts and figures to support this statement of mine. I myself placed them in the *Congressional Record* on June 17, 1937, where they will be found on page 7708)[5] and I believe conclusively that these figures and facts show that the price of food is higher in chain-controlled towns and cities than it is in those communities which are not controlled by chain outfits."

In reply, the author offered to rest his whole case on the truth or falsity of that statement. After pointing out its obvious fallacies and flaws as had been done in the editorial previously quoted, he handed Mr. Patman a reprint of it, with the suggestion that if he "is fair-minded enough to withdraw a statement which has no justification he will never make it again."

But the effect on Mr. Patman was apparently not lasting. In a radio speech delivered on February 21, 1939,[6] only three months after that debate, he included among his objections to the interstate chain system: "It causes the cost of food to be higher in towns and communities controlled by it."

And, in an extension of remarks reported in the *Congressional Record* a few days later,[7] he made the statement that "cost of food is higher in chain-controlled towns and communities."

That the erroneous and illogical notion remained with Mr. Patman throughout the years was evidenced eleven years later, when he and the author appeared once again on opposite sides of the old question. This time it was on a television program called "Court of Current Issues."[8] Mr. Patman put the following question to Prof. O. Glenn Saxon, one of the chain-store "witnesses":

[5] Actually the page is 5914.
[6] *Congressional Record*, Vol. 84, Part 11, p. 667.
[7] *Ibid.*, p. 761.
[8] Reported in *Chain Store Age*, November, 1949.

"Don't these same statistics prove that in cities where the chains have control, the cost of food is always higher?"

When the witness answered in the negative, the matter was not pursued, but if a thousand qualified witnesses had all answered in the same way, Mr. Patman would probably have remained unconvinced judging by the persistency with which he had stuck to his baseless contention for so long.

Of course much of Mr. Patman's muddy thinking on this point stemmed from his misleading use of the word *control* in connection with the division of a city's food business among chains and independents. Perhaps in a parliamentary body, a majority of 51 per cent may give *control*, because the other 49 per cent is as hopelessly beaten as if it were only 1 per cent.

But control of a parliamentary body and control of the cost of living under competitive conditions are two entirely different things. The fact that the chains may *enjoy* 51% or 61% or even 70% of a city's business gives them no power to raise prices at will, as Mr. Patman naïvely suggested, for the public is still a free agent and can buy from whom it likes. Indeed, the only way in which the chains could hope to maintain the favorable position they commanded would be by keeping their prices *down*.

The Patman bill made no progress whatever in Congress in 1938.

Early the following year it was reintroduced, this time as H.R. 1. It was referred to the Committee on Ways and Means. But although no action was taken on it that year, the mere fact that it was pending precipitated nationwide discussion of the chain-store system. Nearly 350 national organizations representing all lines of activity—agricultural, industrial, commercial, labor and consumer—not only discussed the bill but passed resolutions condemning it.

Because of the widespread hostility to the bill, the chains missed no opportunity to discuss its shortcomings on the air, from the platform, or through any other medium that offered.

In December, 1939, John A. Logan, president of the National Association of Food Chains, debated the issues over the air with Hector Lazo, and other chain-store spokesmen welcomed similar opportunities.

After all, the chains realized that this bill was to give them the best opportunity they had ever had to show where the chain stores stood not only in popular esteem but in the thinking of all important groups, save only those with whom they were in direct competition—the wholesalers and retailers. And, because of the long lag between the introduction of the first bill and the public hearing on H.R. 1, they had all the time they wanted to prepare for the conflict.

In March of 1940, a sub-committee was appointed by the Ways and Means Committee to conduct a public hearing on the measure. It consisted of Representatives John W. McCormack, Massachusetts, chairman; John W. Boehne, Jr., Indiana; Richard M. Duncan, Missouri; John D. Dingell, Michigan; Frank Crowther, New York; Harold Knutson, Minnesota; and Roy O. Woodruff, Michigan.

The hearings started March 27 and continued daily until May 16. Each session, however, was only two hours long. Nevertheless, before the hearings were over nearly 200 witnesses were heard, some at great length, and numerous exhibits and briefs were put into the record by both sides. The printed record of the hearing comprises 2,257 pages! [9]

As is usual, those who favored the bill were heard first. As its author, Mr. Patman took all of the first session to present his argument for it and all of the second to answer the questions put to him by the committee.

Before commencing his argument, Mr. Patman offered certain amendments to the bill to modify its effect. He asked the committee to cut the proposed tax in half. He also offered to

[9] Hearings before a sub-committee of the Committee of Ways and Means, House of Representatives, 76th Cong., 3rd Sess., on H.R. 1, a bill providing for an excise tax on chain stores.

exempt entirely all chains operating no more than 50 stores in the State in which the principal place of business was located or within a radius of 100 miles of the city or town in which such place of business was located. Finally, he offered to give the interstate chains, against which the bill was mainly directed, *seven* years in which to liquidate instead of the *two* years allowed in the original bill. But this seven years "breathing spell"—which Congressman Knutson characterized as "purgatory"—would be denied to any chain operating more than 50 stores which increased their number or which changed the location of any store during the seven-year period. He also offered to include filling stations, which had been exempted in the original bill.

Right at the start of his argument, Mr. Patman took up the question of the constitutionality of the proposal.

"The object of H.R. 1," he declared, "is to restrict interstate chain stores to the boundaries of one State, or to a smaller area than some of them now cover.

"The question is asked: 'If that is the object, why not leave out the tax provision and offer a bill that says an interstate [sic] chain cannot operate in more than one State?'

"My answer is that such a proposal, if enacted, would probably be held unconstitutional, whereas, if we use the taxing power of Congress to reach the same objective, there will be no doubt of the constitutionality of the law, when enacted.

"Why did Congress place a 10% tax on the State bank currency after the war between the States? Was it in order to raise revenue? Not at all."

Elaborating on that historical incident a little later, he said:

"I invite your attention to the fact that during President Grant's administration we had all kinds of State banks all over the country that were issuing so-called wildcat currency. Congress wanted to pass a law that would stop these banks from issuing the wildcat currency. . . . But Congress decided that they could not pass a law that would be constitutional that would have that effect. But someone suggested, 'We can tax them and that will do the same thing'; so they passed a law taxing this currency issued by State banks 10 per cent. That destroyed many State banks but it served a more worthy purpose of preserving our great currency system of this country. So that in President Grant's time the taxing power was used as a vehicle to correct an evil that could not be reached in any other manner in a constitutional way."

But Mr. Patman's implication that the taxing power may be used constitutionally to achieve indirectly what Congress has no constitutional power to achieve directly was his own constitutional philosophy. It was just the opposite of the philosophy of the U.S. Supreme Court, as had appeared in the very case he used as his principal authority—the case involving the constitutionality of an act of Congress imposing a prohibitive tax against State banknotes.

Such a law *was* passed, as Mr. Patman declared, and it *was* held constitutional, as he stated, but if he really thought that the court held in the case in question that Congress could use its taxing power to achieve unconstitutional objectives, he missed the point completely.

The case in question was Veazie Bank *v*. Fenno, 8 Wallace 533. What the Court held was that as Congress is empowered by the Constitution to protect its own currency, it could constitutionally forbid the States to issue banknotes which circulated as money; and because it *could legally forbid* the issue of such banknotes, it could achieve the same constitutional result through the exercise of its taxing power.

That, of course, is a very different proposition from Mr. Patman's version of it. It was not a case, as he contended, of using the taxing power "as a vehicle to correct an evil that could *not* be reached in any other manner in a constitutional way," but of using it to correct an evil which *might* have been reached constitutionally by a flat prohibition.

What Mr. Patman overlooked was that when Chief Justice

Marshall uttered his famous dictum, back in 1819, that "the power to tax involves the power to destroy" he did not say, or imply, that the power to tax involves the *right* to destroy. On the contrary, in the very case in which the dictum was offered, the Chief Justice held that the power to tax did *not* involve the right to destroy.

In that historic case[10] Maryland had passed a prohibitive tax against a branch of the United States Bank. In that respect, it might be regarded perhaps as the first chain-store case to reach the United States Supreme Court, although it related to branch banks rather than branch stores. Having first decided that the Federal Government had a right to establish the bank itself, and could set up branches wherever it saw fit, the Chief Justice easily reached the conclusion that no State had the right to destroy what the Federal Government had the right to create. And as the States had no right to destroy the branch banks directly, they had no right to use their taxing power to achieve the same result indirectly.

Applying that sound principle to Mr. Patman's own bill, the use of the Federal taxing power to destroy interstate chain stores would obviously be constitutional *only* if a Federal law flatly prohibiting the operation of such stores would be constitutional. But on that point Mr. Patman himself said that he had been advised that *such* a law would *not* be constitutional. On that basis, H.R. 1 could have no constitutional validity, despite Mr. Patman's blithe assumption that the power to tax is subject to no limitations.

The committee did not interrogate Mr. Patman on his unique position regarding basic constitutional principles, nor were they challenged by any of the witnesses for the chains. That, however, was rendered unnecessary because, at the end of his statement, the committee inserted in the record a mem-

---

[10] McCulloch *v.* Maryland, 4 Wheaton 316 (1819). See *The American Constitution,* Alfred H. Kelly and Winfred A. Harbison (New York: Norton & Co., 1948) p. 290.

orandum prepared by the staff of the Joint Committee on Internal Revenue Taxation at the committee's request. In that memorandum, the attorney for the Joint Committee advised that H.R. 1 would "clearly violate" the Federal Constitution.[11]

Continuing with his argument, Mr. Patman offered the committee some elaborate-looking charts. They showed that four of the largest banks in the country and seven of the leading private banking firms were represented on the directorates of some of the leading chain-store companies. Another chart showed that one large private banking firm was represented on the directorate of half a dozen or more leading chains as well as on the boards of many large manufacturing companies.

The purpose of that testimony, apparently, was to support Mr. Patman's theory that the fact that large chains and some large manufacturing companies have the same banking affiliations results in the refusal of the latter to sell their products to competitors of the chains!

But the committee did not seem to be deeply impressed with either the exhibits or the implications Mr. Patman saw in them. On the contrary, they seemed to think it a perfectly natural thing for banks to be represented on the boards of companies with which they had extensive financial dealings. One committeeman pointed out that when the R.F.C. makes a loan to a corporation it secures representation on the borrower's board of directors. Another observed that probably in

---

[11] That ex-Governor Christianson had a better grasp of the constitutional principles involved than his colleague is indicated by the following exchange between him and a member of the committee which took place at the end of the hearing: "Mr. Dingell. Governor, speaking about whether it could be done or not, the tax club to bring about the abatement or the reduction or the elimination of the chain-store system could be used only if the purpose of the bill were constitutional; that is the elimination of the chain-store system. If that were constitutional then rightfully the Congress could use the tax club to bring that about. I think we will agree on that.
"Mr. Christianson. That is right.
"Mr. Dingell. On the other hand, if that is an unconstitutional move, then of course the taxing power of Congress could not be used to bring that about.
"Mr. Christianson. That is true." (Hearing Record, p. 1967.)

many cases the connection between the bank and the chain was merely that of transfer agent.

Mr. Patman's main objections to the interstate chains, he said, were:

1. They tend to concentrate money power and credit in the hands of a few banks, mostly in the East.

2. They destroy local communities.

3. They depress farm prices.

4. They will eventually attain a monopoly in distribution if not checked.

5. They limit the opportunity for the young man of to-morrow.

Typical of the fallacies which characterized his whole argument and which seemed at times to strain the patience of the committee was his contention that as 53% of the banks had failed between 1921 and 1933, and as that was the period in which the chain stores had their greatest growth, the chain-store system must have been responsible for the bank failures!

Similarly he argued that as the farmer got a smaller share of the consumer's dollar than he did twenty years earlier, before the chain stores became an important factor in distribution, the chain stores must be responsible for the farmer's ills. He estimated that total farm income would have been $3,000,000,000 a year greater if there were no chain stores!

He also blamed the depression and unemployment on chain stores and, in answer to a question, insisted that if his bill became a law, we would have national prosperity within a year or two years!

Of course the committee did not allow these and other wild statements to go unchallenged. They wanted to know, for instance, whether he really believed the chains were solely responsible for the appalling succession of bank failures between 1921 and 1933, for the economic changes in our community life, for the depression and the decline in farm income. Was it not true that bank failures were greatest in areas where chain stores were fewest? Hadn't good roads and the development of the automobile been chiefly responsible for the changes which had overcome the smaller communities? Would not retail business have gravitated to the larger towns and cities, because of good roads and automobiles, even if we had no chain stores? Didn't the war have something to do with the depression?

While Mr. Patman stood by his original statements as long as he could, he was finally forced to admit that many other factors might have been responsible for the results he attributed entirely to chain stores, and to content himself with the consoling observation that the chain stores had been a contributing factor also.

The contention that the chains depress farm prices led Congressman Knutson to put into the record a letter he had received from the dairy farmers in Minnesota. It said they were marketing some 20,000,000 pounds of butter through chain stores, were receiving a premium price for it, that they had been doing business with chains for twenty years or more, and that the chains not only provide a ready market but, because of their economies, reduce the spread between producer and consumer. Subsequently, similar testimony was offered by numerous witnesses representing almost every branch of agriculture.

But perhaps the most killing blow suffered by the supporters of the bill in the early days of the hearing was a letter received from Secretary of Agriculture Wallace. The committee had asked him for his official viewpoint regarding the Patman bill.

Secretary Wallace condemned the bill in no uncertain terms. "In our opinion," he said, "sound public policy requires that we promote efficient methods of marketing and distribution rather than discourage or prevent them by taxes such as those provided in this bill."

The Secretary did go on to say that his department was not

"insensible to the dangers associated with the growth of larger corporations, whether they are engaged in the handling of food or in any other kind of business," and that some chains are so large that "their methods and practices need some regulation to prevent the misuse of bargaining power and to enforce fair methods of competition." But he pointed out that "it should be possible to provide suitable regulations which will prevent abuses and dishonest practices by chain stores" and that the department "would be in favor of any such regulations."

"However," he concluded, "we think it would be unwise and unnecessary to give up the economies which have been brought about by chain-store distribution in order to prevent certain practices which may not be in the public interest."

Altogether some twenty witnesses appeared in favor of the bill. They occupied eleven full sessions, or 22 hours in all. The larger part of their burden was carried by Mr. Patman himself, ex-Governor Theodore H. Christianson, president of the Freedom of Opportunity Foundation and public relations director for the National Association of Retail Druggists; George Schulte, publisher of *Interstate Merchant*, St. Louis; Gerrit Vander Hooning, president, National Association of Retail Grocers; J. H. McLaurin, president, United States Wholesale Grocers Association; Rowland Jones, Jr., Washington representative of the National Association of Retail Druggists; Rivers Peterson, Indianapolis, managing director of the National Retail Hardware Association; and Frank G. Stewart, vice president of Freedom of Opportunity Foundation and president of Motor Equipment Wholesalers Association.

The only other witnesses consisted of a couple of manufacturers of work clothes who sold their output to wholesalers exclusively, a small-town banker who organized the Independent Bankers Association to fight against branch banking, a lawyer, an organizer of a Louisiana Farmers Protective

Union, consisting of strawberry growers, and five Congress-men.

The significant fact about this list is that it consisted almost entirely of *wholesalers* and *retailers,* or their association spokesmen—all *interested* witnesses who admittedly expected to fall heir to the business then being done by the chains if the chains were eliminated from the picture. That these witnesses favored the bill was not the least bit surprising. Particularly noteworthy is the fact that the list included no spokesman for the *public* interest, despite Mr. Patman's far-reaching claims that the very future of the nation depended on its passage.

The fact that this measure was able to command support at the hearing of no representative labor group, no representative consumer group, no representative newspaper group, no representative real-estate group, no representative manufacturing group, could hardly have been overlooked by the committee. Nothing better illustrates the real character and purpose of legislation of this kind than the line-up of those who appear in favor of it—and against it.

Ex-Gov. Christianson confined his argument in favor of the bill to a single point—the danger of monopoly. He reviewed the growth of some of the chains via the merger process in the late '20's and suggested that if the formula were continued indefinitely we would eventually have a single chain in each field.

Existing anti-monopoly laws did not provide adequate protection against this threat, he contended, because they could be invoked only against actual monopolies—not against monopoly in the making. The only effective way to prevent a potential monopoly from developing into an actual monopoly, he pointed out, was by legislation imposing a tax heavy enough to make further growth unprofitable.

When he said that it was not so much the present position of the chains that he feared but the potential danger inherent in their further expansion, Congressman Knutson put a question which was to be asked thereafter of every witness who appeared for the bill: "Would you be satisfied with legislation to freeze the present situation?"

Gov. Christianson thought that would be adequate, but when Chairman McCormack pursued the point and asked to whom the freezing process should be applied—the man with only a few stores now as well as to the man with hundreds or thousands of stores, the suggested remedy did not appear so simple.

Finally, however, the witness suggested that all expansion should be prohibited except by the man with less than 50 stores and he should be permitted to grow only to that extent. The witness also expressed the view that future expansion within the suggested limitation should be confined to one State or at least to a reasonable area. He doubted that these results could be achieved by any type of legislation other than a tax.

The chief witness in favor of the bill was George Schulte, of St. Louis, publisher of *Interstate Merchant,* a weekly grocery paper, which for the previous fifteen years had devoted most of its space to a continuous and vituperative attack on the chain stores.

Mr. Schulte's contribution, which took the best part of three sessions, was devoted largely to an attempt to prove the obviously contradictory proposition that while chain stores allegedly paid lower wages than independents, employed fewer people, acquired their merchandise cheaper, paid less taxes, made fewer contributions to local charities and other activities, extended no credit and made no deliveries, their operating costs were nevertheless higher than the combined operating costs of wholesaler and retailer, and their prices to the consumer were higher too.

Just why the independent merchant was being driven out of business by the chains if he actually sold for less and gave credit and made deliveries in the bargain, Mr. Schulte failed to make clear.

Nor was it apparent from Mr. Schulte's argument why any special tax to check chain-store growth was needed if, because of their higher operating costs, the chains were compelled to charge the consumer more and yet give less in the way of service.

Mr. Schulte repeated Mr. Patman's statistics showing that 53% of the banks failed between 1921 and 1933, and when he was asked by Chairman McCormack what inference he drew from the figures he quoted, he replied: "The decrease in the number of banks is due to the decrease in the volume of independent business."

But when Congressman Boehne pressed the point and wanted to know whether the witness contended that the growth of chain stores was responsible for the bank failures, he admitted that chain stores were "not entirely responsible." The admission led the Congressman to remark that, of course, there were many other factors to account for bank failures during the period in question. Chairman McCormack indicated what the principal reason was when he asked Mr. Schulte if he had read the report of the Comptroller of the Currency on the main cause of the failure of banks. When the witness said he had not read the report, he was informed that "the main reason was poor management."

Mr. Schulte devoted a lot of time to fragments of the voluminous reports of the Federal Trade Commission in connection with its six-year investigation of chain stores. Naturally he picked out whatever he could find that tended to back up his claims of chain-store shortcomings. But the effect of all his testimony regarding the F.T.C. study was completely negated when Congressman Crowther read into the record the following paragraph from the Commission's final report on its investigation:

"To tax out of existence the advantages of chain stores over competitors is to tax out of existence the advantages which the consuming public have found in patronizing them with a consequent addition to the cost of living for that section of the public. That portion of the public which is able to pay cash and is willing to forego delivery service in return for the advantage of lower prices will be deprived of that privilege, generally speaking, although there are exceptions both ways."

Mr. Schulte made the usual claim that chain stores were guilty of giving customers short weight. He introduced into the record the fact that in 1935 a number of chain-store managers in the city of Washington had been found guilty of giving short weight on chickens purchased by inspectors of the Department of Weights and Measures. But again the effect of the testimony was badly shattered when Congressman Knutson put into the record an official report he had just received showing that during the past three years in the District of Columbia 67 short-weight cases had been found in grocery and meat stores, and that of these 65 were found in independent stores and only two in chain stores.

Mr. Schulte's presentation, as a whole, was characterized by the trade magazine *Tide* as "a jungle of contradictions."

Gerrit Vander Hooning, president of the National Association of Retail Grocers, insisted that his principal objection to chain stores was based on their power to exact lower prices from producers, on the one hand, and to engage in "loss-leader" merchandising, on the other.

But when he was subjected to questioning by the committee, he frankly admitted that independent grocers use "loss leaders" also, that the consumer is mainly interested in getting the most for his money and that if the trend were toward consumer cooperatives, then neither the chain nor the independent merchant would be entitled to protection.

Asked whether he would approve of legislation "that would undertake to freeze the present set-up," he replied that it would be a step in the right direction—but a man with the ambition to open a number of stores should not be stopped, nor should his operation of stores be confined to a single State, and that he would prefer to see the abuses in chain-store operation eliminated rather than the chain stores themselves. When the witness insisted that his main fear was the effect of chain-store growth on the farmer, Chairman McCormack put into the record a letter received from Secretary of Agriculture Wallace, to which reference has already been made.

J. H. McLaurin, president of the United States Wholesale Grocers Association, the organization which had been mainly responsible for the passage of the Robinson-Patman Act, and which had always worked aggressively for the elimination of chain-store competition, emphasized the action the courts had taken in the case of the packers twenty years before.

In that case, he pointed out, the Federal Government had curbed the growing power of the big meat packers by frustrating their plan to operate retail grocery and meat stores and prohibited them from processing, wholesaling or retailing any food product not connected with packing house commodities. That result had been achieved by a consent decree.

Why, he asked, shouldn't the big grocery chains be checked as the packers were checked? And then he answered his own question thus:

> "The reason that we come to Congress for relief and not to the courts, as in the case of the packers, is that we have no evidence of conspiracy or combination among the interstate chain-store systems, such as existed among the Big Five meat packers."

The statement of Rowland Jones, Jr., then Washington representative of the National Association of Retail Druggists, who appeared for the bill, is particularly interesting not so much for what he said as for the fact that only eight years later he was to be elected president of the American Retail

Federation—the organization which the chains had at one time been accused of dominating.

Mr. Jones devoted himself mainly to the social aspects of the issue before the committee. He struck a new note when he elaborated on his claim that the horse-and-buggy era represented "the nearest thing to Utopia ever achieved."

Chairman McCormack took issue with his implication that the chain stores were responsible for the changes in our economic and social life which had followed the transition from "the horse-and-buggy days" to our present streamlined mode of living. On the contrary, he pointed out, the social changes of the previous 30 years had been due largely to the introduction of good roads and the wider use of automobiles, improvements in transportation and communications generally and many other achievements of science and industry. The "self-contained community," he intimated, was doomed with the passing of the "horse and buggy" as the principal means of transportation.

Rivers Peterson, managing director of the National Retail Hardware Association, argued principally against the greater buying power of the big chains which enabled them, he claimed, to exact lower prices from their suppliers than other distributors enjoyed. He had little hope that the Robinson-Patman Act would correct the situation. He attributed the decline in the number of independent hardware stores to the competition of the mail-order chain stores, the variety chains, automotive supply chains, and even the grocery chains, which in some cases were handling aluminum ware.

But various members of the committee raised the point that chain-store competition was only one of the factors responsible for the decline of the independent hardware store. They mentioned the slump in the building trades. "The slump in building during the past ten years," said Congressman Dingell, "is responsible for 40% of our unemployment directly and probably another 30% indirectly. With such a slump in building activity, wouldn't carpenters and artisans naturally buy less hardware and tools, and is that not the real reason for the passing of so many hardware stores in recent years?"

Mr. Peterson conceded that that was undoubtedly a factor but insisted that, because of the chains, the independents got less of the business that remained.

Chairman McCormack, too, reminded the witness that the depression was likewise a factor in the decline in the number of hardware stores, and inefficiency in management. And, referring to the testimony of Rowland Jones, he went on to say:

"The other day one gentleman made a very powerful argument about the self-contained community and community life decades ago. And it was a very beautiful picture. I enjoyed listening to it. As I was listening to it, the thought ran through my mind that the first flight of the airplane was only in 1906 and for about ten seconds. And there have been such inventions as the telephone and wireless, the radio and other improvements in means of communication and transportation. You cannot have all that and have the community life of 50 years ago. . . . We have got to have a self-contained community life, as much as possible, consistent with those changes. Either that, or we have got to say to the human mind, 'You can't invent,' which, of course we cannot do and would not want to do. In other words, from these improvements have come great benefits, but there have also arisen problems."

Five Congressmen appeared in favor of the bill. In view of the fact that more than 70 had joined Mr. Patman as co-sponsors of the bill when it had been originally introduced in 1938, a greater turn-out than five might have been expected. Even though some of the co-sponsors of 1938 had lost their seats, what about the rest of them? Could it have been that the widespread opposition the bill had developed in the two years prior to the hearing had caused most of the sponsors to change their minds about it?

On April 10, 1940, those who were opposed to the bill

started to tell their story. Before they were through, a month later, more than 150 of them had had their say. Among them were included representatives of almost every important economic and social group which comprised the nation's framework—agriculture, manufacturers, organized labor, marketing authorities, consumers, and, of course, the chains themselves. Although only ten chain-store operators appeared as witnesses, the reason for not having more was more or less obvious—the time available could be put to more effective use by presenting the testimony of others who were not interested so directly as the chains in the defeat of the bill. Then, too, the story told by the chain-store men who did appear would merely have been re-told over and over again had more of them made an appearance.

The chain-store men who did appear included Charles F. Adams, First National Stores; Thomas N. Beavers, Peoples Drug Stores; Ralph F. Burkard, First National Stores; Lewis W. Cole, Steiden Stores, Louisville; Rilea W. Doe, Safeway Stores; Earl R. French, Atlantic Commission Co.; W. T. Grant, W. T. Grant Co.; Van H. Priest, Van H. Priest Co., Madison, Fla.; Earl C. Sams, J. C. Penney Company; and Lingan A. Warren, Safeway Stores.

The first witness in opposition was Earl C. Sams, president of the J. C. Penney Company. He told the inspiring story of that company's outstanding growth, from microscopic beginnings in 1902 to 1,554 stores in 1939, with stores in 48 states, 30,000 employes and sales that year of $282,000,000.

He then gave five main reasons for his opposition to the bill, as follows:

"1. It would destroy the Penney company or any other similar company.

"2. It would destroy the finest field of opportunity that has ever existed in retailing for the young ambitious man born without family means.

"3. It would add to the cost of living for every American

family of limited means and would lower the American standard of living.

"4. It would deal a staggering blow to the entire economic
life of this country and would be especially destructive of
the smaller cities and towns for the benefit of the larger
cities.

"5. It would hurt and tax this entire nation for the protection and enrichment of a small minority group of self-
interested middlemen and of another small minority group of
ill-advised marginal retailers."

Mr. Sams proceeded to support each of these propositions
with a wealth of facts which seemed to be well received by
the committee.

Taking up the plight of small communities and the familiar
charge that chain-store growth was responsible for it, Mr.
Sams said:

> "If the national chains were wiped out, it would remove the
> most substantial bulwark which these small trading centers
> have against the pull of the big cities. It has been said that
> chain stores were ruining the smaller communities. Chain
> stores didn't ruin them. The automobile and the good roads
> naturally caused the people to turn to larger centers to do
> their trading. No law, no human mandate can breathe life
> back in the very small trading center which formerly sup-
> ported a couple of general stores. Those stores existed only
> because without automobiles or good roads the customer
> couldn't get to the city. Because of horse-and-buggy transpor-
> tation and because of mud roads the customer bought what
> the general store offered at its own prices or she ordered by
> mail."

Pointing out that, between 1920 and 1939, hard surface
roads increased from 350,000 miles to 1,100,000 and the number of registered automobiles increased from 8,255,000 to
26,250,000, he said that the chain stores had served as a check
on the drying up of towns and small cities in the face of these
two factors. That had been achieved because "the national
chains have brought to these small centers the same values,

the same reliable merchandise and the same prices, the same crisp new styles, and the same modern stores that were available in the bigger cities. And the customers know it."

Regarding the suggestion which had been made to "freeze" the existing situation, Mr. Sams said it would be wrong because it would deprive many sections of the country of the services that chains had not yet brought to them.

At the conclusion of his testimony, Mr. Sams offered for the record a printed study called *Keep Market Street Open*,[12] which had been prepared as of March, 1940, and was presented for the chains as a group in opposition to the bill under consideration.

The brief was replete with statistics and facts to refute all the claims made by Congressman Patman, Gov. Christianson and George Schulte and to establish affirmatively that:

1. Chain stores raise the scale of living.
2. Chain stores keep business and purchasing power in the towns.
3. They were the product of local enterprise.
4. The ownership of chain-store stocks is widely dispersed.
5. Chain headquarters are distributed all over the nation.
6. Chains have no interlocking directorates.
7. Chain stores pay better wages.
8. Employes stay with chain stores.
9. Chain stores bring capital into town.
10. Chain stores pay higher rents.
11. Chain stores widen markets and improve farm income.
12. Chain stores invest in community welfare.
13. Chain stores set high standards for all retailing.
14. Chain stores respond to disaster needs.
15. They pay more taxes.
16. They are a minor factor in the toll of retail mortality.

[12] Hearing Record, *op. cit.*, pp. 602-671.

17. They improve the young man's opportunity.

18. They enlarge the opportunities for competitors.

19. They offer equality of opportunity to consumers.

The brief provided a fitting background for the personal testimony of the witnesses to follow. They included 53 spokesmen for the farm interests; 56 for manufacturers and processors; eight for organized labor; six for real estate interests; seven for consumer organizations; three economists; fifteen for various miscellaneous interests; and ten chain-store operators.

Summarizing the reasons given by each of these interests for their opposition to the bill, consider first the farmer's viewpoint.

In addition to the condemnation of the measure by the Secretary of Agriculture, referred to earlier, the three leading national farm organizations—the American Farm Bureau Federation, the National Grange and the National Council of Farm Cooperatives—all came out unequivocally against the bill. Other farm representatives speaking for hundreds of thousands of producers and processors in individual branches of agriculture joined their national leaders in condemning the bill for the following reasons:

1. The charge that the large food chains use their great buying power to depress farm prices, as so frequently charged by Mr. Patman, was false.

2. No type of distribution available to the farmer was more valuable than the chain store under normal conditions and, under abnormal conditions, such as arise from surplus crops or natural catastrophes, the cooperation of the chains was vital to the farmer.

3. The farmer valued the chain-store system not only because it enabled him to sell his products to better advantage but because it enabled him to satisfy his own requirements more economically.

4. The farmer realized that his own welfare depended upon

lowering the cost of distribution and he was convinced that the chain-store system provided one of the best means toward that end.

What did Mr. Patman have to say about all that? After sitting in the committee room day after day for a month and hearing the farmers declare their unqualified faith in chain stores and their dependence upon the chain store system, what did he say when he summed up the case in behalf of his bill?

He still insisted that the chains depress farm prices, contending that nobody had answered the charges he had made to that effect on the opening day of the hearing. He completely overlooked the devastating answer given by Edward A. O'Neal, president of the American Farm Bureau Federation.[13] For the express purpose of getting an official explanation of why in 1913 the farmer received 53% of the consumer's dollar, but in 1939 only 40.5%, he had written the Secretary of Agriculture on April 4 asking whether it "was the result of chain-store operation." He had put the Secretary's answer in the record. After referring to the many factors affecting the spread between farm and consumer prices, the Secretary had concluded:

"It is impossible to place any statistical reliance upon a conclusion based upon these trends in marketing changes and chain-store growth. These comparisons merely denote *contemporary* developments and do not demonstrate *cause* and *effect*." In other words, just because two things happen at the same time, one is not necessarily the result of the other.

As in the case of so many of Mr. Patman's other contentions, the statistics he used, correct in themselves, provided no basis whatever for the conclusions he blithely drew from them. The fact that 53% of the banks failed between 1921 and 1933, which was also the period of greatest chain-store growth, was proof enough for him that the chains were responsible for the bank failures. The fact that in some cities where the chains do

[13] *Ibid.,* p. 776.

more than 50% of the grocery business the cost of living is higher than in some cities where the independents do more than 50% of the grocery business, was proof enough for him that the chains were responsible for the higher cost of living in the case of the cities he selected. Because the farmer's share of the consumer's food dollar declined between 1913 and 1939, chain-store growth during that period was the culprit! Little wonder that Congressman Knutson at one stage of the hearing lost his temper enough to exclaim to Mr. Patman:

. . . "The way you answered Dr. Crowther convinces me that you questioned the fact that this committee had ordinary intelligence."

The attitude of organized labor was revealed by a number of outstanding union leaders, although the American Federation of Labor had taken no official position on the bill.

According to Patrick E. Gorman, president of the Amalgamated Meat Cutters and Butcher Workers, A.F. of L., with a membership of 120,000, and other union spokesmen, organized labor's opposition was based on the following key points:

1. Chain stores are easier for organized labor to work with than independent merchants.

2. Chain stores pay higher wages for comparable work than independents, and chain-store hours are shorter.

3. Union members are consumers as well as workers. Chain stores make for lower living costs.

4. The elimination of chain stores would be a step in the direction of a return to "cottage industry" which would mean more proprietors but fewer employers—hence fewer employes.

5. Special taxes against multiple stores are a direct threat against the unions themselves since "the largest operator of the chain-unit system in the world is organized labor itself."

Although A.F. of L. had taken no official position on the bill, State federations, with a combined membership of well over 1,000,000, filed resolutions with the committee condemning it. The States in question were Alabama, Florida, Georgia, Iowa, Kansas, Kentucky, Louisiana, Michigan, New Jersey, Pennsylvania and Texas.

The viewpoint of real-estate men and property owners was presented by Walter S. Schmidt, past president of the National Association of Real Estate Boards, who appeared as spokesman for that organization. Also representing the association was Frank S. Slosson, who also spoke for the National Association of Building Owners and Managers, of which he was a past president.

Real-estate interests opposed the bill mainly for the following reasons:

1. Chain stores make the most desirable tenants of business property.

2. The future of the better business districts in many cities is threatened by the trend towards decentralization. The elimination of chain stores would accelerate that trend to the detriment of real-estate values and would reduce the tax revenue from business properties on which cities largely depend.

3. Chain stores set the pace in store modernization and enhance the drawing power of the trading area to the advantage of the whole community.

4. Banks, trust companies, insurance companies, colleges and charitable institutions have large investments in mortgages on properties occupied by chains. Such investments would be seriously endangered if the chains were compelled to abandon such locations.

5. Chain stores contribute to the stability of community life beyond the business area. Their elimination would hurt residential real estate as well as business property.

More than 50 witnesses appeared to express the viewpoint of manufacturers and processors, either as individuals or as spokesmen for manufacturers' associations, or both.

Many of the witnesses distributed only part of their output

through the chains, the remainder going to the wholesaler or direct to the independent retailer. Even in the case of those who sold all their output to the chains, or the major part of it, earlier experiences with other channels of distribution were almost invariably reported. Thus, in almost every instance, whatever they said was based on actual experience with both types of distribution.

They opposed the bill for the following main reasons:

1. Selling through the chain cuts selling costs substantially.

2. It cuts production costs, too, not only because of quantity purchases but because the orders are placed so as to permit of uninterrupted production schedules, which is particularly valuable in the case of seasonable merchandise.

3. It eliminates collection costs and credit losses.

4. It reduces the risk of inventory losses because merchandise is produced only on firm orders.

5. It requires less working capital because of the prompt payment of invoices on short terms.

6. It reduces labor turnover by making for steadier employment.

7. It increases the "real" wages of workers because the chains' lower prices reduce the cost of living.

8. It makes possible the production of many items which could not be marketed at all through less efficient channels.

9. It offers manufacturers the benefit of the skill, experience and information of keen buyers who are in direct contact with the consuming public, as compared with the indirect contact of the wholesaler.

10. It offers manufacturers an opportunity to test new items quickly and economically in various parts of the country through the retail laboratories represented by the units of the interstate chains.

11. It enables manufacturers to reduce the price of their products to all the channels through which they sell.

12. It increases the total volume of production because lower retail prices mean enlarged consumer buying power.

They also emphasized the social havoc which would result from the elimination of the large interstate chains. Many of the factories and mills supplying them provided the principal payroll in the communities in which they were located. Many of them were so geared to mass production for mass distribution that other channels of distribution would not suffice to keep them in operation.

How would the public interest be affected by the passage of the proposed bill?

Members of the committee had repeatedly asked the question. Mr. Patman had agreed that that was the real issue involved.

The viewpoint of the consumer was presented by six women —all outstanding figures in women's organizations and recognized authorities on consumer problems. They were Mrs. Ernest W. Howard, department chairman of legislation, District of Columbia Federation of Women's Clubs; Mrs. Mary D. Learned, chairman of the Massachusetts Committee on Consumer Legislation; Mrs. Harriet R. Howe, representing the American Home Economics Association; Mrs. Gustav Ketterer, chairman, Philadelphia Consumers Advisory Council; Dr. Caroline F. Ware, chairman of social studies, American Association of University Women; and Mrs. Andrew J. Noe, former president, New York City Federation of Women's Clubs.

All of them opposed the bill, Mrs. Howard characterizing it as "the most vicious, inhuman bill ever to come before Congress."

The main point these witnesses stressed was that the economies offered by the chain-store system of distribution were of supreme economic and social importance to people of limited income—in which category they placed two-thirds of all the families in the country.

"Women today know," declared Mrs. Howard, "how acute is the present problem of providing food, clothing and shelter for themselves, their husbands and their children out of their present income. When food prices rise, it is not a question of paying more for the same food, but simply this, they do not have the money with which to pay—therefore they must buy less and eat less and pay the doctor more."

That an excise tax on chain stores would be paid by the customers of the stores was obvious, according to Mrs. Learned, "for how else does a storekeeper get the money to pay taxes?" That prices would be raised in independent stores as well as in chain stores was likewise pointed out by Mrs. Learned. "I, as a consumer, say," she declared, "that it is just human nature that if you raise prices by taxation in one kind of store, then these untaxed stores will raise their prices too."

Dr. Ware's presentation was a notable contribution. Among the reasons she gave for the opposition of her organization, which was composed of 67,000 university women affiliated with 870 branches, were the following:

1. The bill proposes a punitive tax on agencies of distribution which serve the consumer well.

2. It is special-interest legislation to support a particular business group, regardless of the service which that group renders to the consuming public.

3. It is based on a misconception of the nature of the modern American economy and, in the presence of this modern economy, constitutes a threat to American democratic institutions.

Four outstanding marketing authorities appeared in opposition to the bill and supported their attitude with extensive and carefully prepared arguments.

Daniel Bloomfield, manager of the Retail Trade Board of the Boston Chamber of Commerce for seventeen years; Malcolm P. McNair, professor of marketing, Graduate School of Business Administration, Harvard University, and for many years director of the Harvard Bureau of Business Research; Joseph M. Klamon, associate professor of commerce, Washington University, St. Louis; and Roland S. Vaile, professor of economics and marketing, University of Minnesota, and editor-in-chief of the *Journal of Marketing*, constituted the group.

These men spoke as individuals, but they quoted freely from the studies made by other marketing authorities. If their attitude was not representative of the general feeling in their specialized field, it was not revealed at the hearing.

On the question of monopoly in retailing all were firm in the opinion that it was out of the question.

Asked by Representative Crowther whether he thought it was "within the realm of possibility that three or four, or even half a dozen of these corporate chains might within a reasonable time get complete control of distribution and price control of food products," Dr. Vaile replied:

> "I think that it is entirely impossible, and I am supported in that by every member of the editorial board of the *Journal of Marketing*. When I found I could appear before this committee, I wrote to the editorial board of the *Journal of Marketing*, seven of whom are teachers of marketing in the leading universities, five of whom are in marketing research lines, private lines, and two of whom are in retail stores, and all of them replied to that question that there was no danger of monopolistic control by chain stores."

At the conclusion of the evidence in opposition to the bill, Congressman Patman was given two days for rebuttal, although that admittedly was a concession to him not usually accorded at hearings before committees.

The time thus allotted was divided among the three men who had carried most of the burden of supporting it in the first place—Congressman Patman, himself, Gov. Christianson and George Schulte. Their concluding arguments consisted mainly of a reiteration of the claims made in their original statements.

The chains were given two days for rebuttal, too, but only one was needed. The task was assigned to Ralph F. Burkard, controller, First National Stores. He did a masterful job. He showed how the evidence offered in opposition to the bill effectively refuted all the claims that had been made in its behalf.

The day following the closing of the hearing, Hon. Robert L. Doughton, chairman of the Ways and Means Committee, announced that, in answer to its request, the Department of Commerce had appraised the proposed legislation and had unqualifiedly condemned it.

The reasons given by Acting Secretary of Commerce Edward J. Noble[14] for the position he took with respect to the Patman bill were:

1. It proposes the most extreme use yet suggested for the taxing power, not to raise revenue, not as an incentive, not as a regulator but to prohibit interstate business.

2. It would add a most vicious barrier to interstate trade of a legitimate character.

3. It would raise the cost and thereby lower the standard of living of the consumers with the lowest incomes.

4. It is designed to destroy the business and the livelihood of investors and their employes who have promoted short cuts in distribution, without reference to their having engaged in any unfair or oppressive practice.

5. It is fallaciously supposed to increase employment, whereas at best it would merely shift employment from one class of establishments to an older and apparently less efficient type, resulting probably in less continuity and lower standards of employment.

6. It prevents mass production from yielding its greatest benefit through mass distribution on a national scale.

[14] *Chain Store Age*, June, 1940.

That the Secretary of Commerce was not unmindful of the competitive plight of the small independent merchant was revealed in the following observations:

"The Department recognizes the severe competitive pressure on small independent merchants resulting from the growth of mass distribution with multiple outlets under one ownership and management. Business mortalities and unemployment resulting from increased efficiencies and lowered cost of distribution in competitive enterprises create social problems which are the just concern of government but whose solution does not lie in legislation penalizing efficiency.

"Failures due to unfair competition can find relief in laws already on the statute books prohibiting discriminatory selling practices, misleading advertising and other unethical methods of doing business . . . The primary public interest is served only when our distributing machinery operates at lowest cost, thereby bringing to the producer a larger share of the consumer's dollar, besides making that dollar go further than it does now. The displacements of labor and obsolescence of capital that are caused by new methods of distribution are on a par with all other problems of unemployment caused by technological advance."

The most significant and decisive fact about the hearing was not the high caliber of the numerous witnesses who appeared against the bill, the broad scope of the interests they represented and the convincing character of their testimony, but the failure of a single witness of the same caliber to appear in favor of it. Conceding that the chains were far better equipped financially to marshall their forces against the bill than their opponents were to support it, why was it that spokesmen for the farmer, for labor, for manufacturers and for consumers did not come forward of their own accord to support the bill if it really meant as much to them and their welfare as Mr. Patman contended?

Undoubtedly that is the way the committee must have sized up the case. On June 17, Chairman McCormack announced that his sub-committee had voted not to report the bill favorably either in its original form or with the amendment which had been submitted designed to "freeze" the chains at their existing size and locations. The effect of that decision was to kill the Patman bill forever, for, as Representative McCormack pointed out, if there were danger of monopoly in the chain-store field, the proper way to avert it would be by regulatory legislation rather than by punitive taxation.

Thus the chain-store "Death Sentence" bill suffered the death sentence itself. But although the bill itself was dead, the benefits the chains had gained from the public hearing were to live and multiply for many years to come.

Never before had the economic and social value of the chain-store system of distribution been so effectively demonstrated. On the other hand, the chains had been reminded of the shortcomings of the system too.

The elimination of the Patman bill marked a definite end to the period of struggle which had started some fifteen years earlier when the rapidity of chain-store expansion had awakened widespread concern among wholesalers and independent retailers. It opened the way for a new era in which the chains, freed from the need of defending themselves against efforts to put them out of business or to saddle discriminatory taxes on them, could devote their attention to doing a better job of retailing, assuming a greater share of their civic responsibilities in the cities in which their stores were located, and improving the working conditions and security of their employes.

To what extent the chains were able to fortify their position as an important economic and social feature of our national set-up in the years which followed forms the subject matter of Part III—the period of chain-store maturity.

PART III

MATURITY

CHAPTER XIII

THE CHAINS AND THE
COMMUNITY

ONE OF THE inherent differences between independent stores and chain stores is that whereas the former are typically home-owned, the latter are typically absentee-owned.

Critics of the chain-store system have always made a great point of that difference, but they built it up far beyond its actual significance. A chain which operated in a number of communities obviously could not have the same natural ties to each of them as the local merchant would have to his own community—the place where probably he was born and brought up, where he and his family knew everybody and in which he had developed a lifelong sentimental interest quite apart from his business interest. The result was, it was contended, that whereas the local merchant was part and parcel of his community, the chain store was merely *in* it and not *of* it.

To a large extent, of course, that was true, but how significant it was is another matter. Conceding that the chains had no sentimental interest in any of the communities in which their stores were located, it would not necessarily follow that they could not contribute as much to the community's welfare as the local merchant, or considerably more, provided *other* reasons impelled them to such a course.

And, as a matter of fact, as will be shown in this chapter,

that is exactly what happened. Although in the early days of their development and throughout the period of their active expansion they were so engrossed in their immediate problems that they gave little or no thought to their community responsibilities, later on they awoke to the realities of the situation. Today they are not merely holding up their end in the community but they are supplying a brand of leadership which only exceptional independent merchants can match.

If we analyze the basis of a merchant's interest in his community, we find that it is made up of three elements: (1) local pride; (2) self-interest; and (3) social duty.

As a general proposition, a man is more interested in his home town than in any other community. Certainly if he sticks to his home town and establishes a business there, he may be expected to have a greater interest in that community than in any other place on earth.

Such an interest is based primarily on sentiment. It is the same kind of sentiment that led Scott to ask: "Breathes there a man with soul so dead, Who never to himself has said: 'This is my own, my native land!'"

In the case of the country at large, we call it national pride or patriotism. In the case of a community, we call it local pride. But it is the same thing.

In addition to this sentimental tie, a merchant has also a material stake in the welfare of the community. If it prospers his business may be expected to prosper too. If it fails to keep pace with the times, his business must expect to suffer.

Then, too, in many cases the local merchant has relatives and friends who are also engaged in business or professional activities in the home town. Their welfare, too, depends upon the progress of the community. His natural interest in the welfare of his family and friends thus gives the local merchant an additional stake in the community's progress.

Finally, the home merchant's community interest is stimulated to a greater or lesser degree by his sense of social obligation—the feeling we all have to do our part or hold up our end in connection with undertakings from which we derive a benefit.

In the case of the chain stores, of course, the sentimental interest in the communities in which they are located is lacking. If the chains have any reason for participating in community activities, therefore, it must be found in the other two factors—self-interest, on the one hand, and the sense of social obligation, on the other.

From the standpoint of self-interest, the chains have at least as much at stake in the community as any other merchant, and more than most of them. For if the chain operates more than one unit in the town, its interest will be proportionately greater than that of the merchant who has only one store. So far as self-interest is concerned, therefore, a chain store operated by an absentee-owner might be expected to take as much interest in the community's welfare as an independent store.

The same thing applies to the remaining factor—social duty. Some people are undoubtedly influenced by their moral obligations to a greater degree than others. Some always do their part. Others never do. If a merchant is under a moral obligation to support community activities because he derives benefit from community development, that obligation applies to every store no matter where its owner lives. Whether the obligation will be met depends upon the owner's *principles* rather than upon his *residence*.

The comparison here, however, must be made between the independent merchant, on the one hand, and the man or men who control the policies of the chains, on the other—not between the independent merchant and the store manager. For the measure of the store manager's activities will depend entirely upon the policies established at his headquarters. This is a highly important distincton because, no matter how civic-minded a store manager may be compared with the average independent merchant, he will not follow his natural inclinations unless he knows that his headquarters will approve of whatever contribution of time or money he finds it desirable to make. On the other hand, even though some store managers will undoubtedly be below average in their own personal sense of civic responsibility, the community will not suffer provided the company itself *requires* all managers to contribute in reasonable measure.

Summing up the essential differences between independent merchants and chain stores with respect to community spirit and cooperation, in only one respect can a community expect more from a local man than from a chain-store manager and that is from the angle of sentiment or local pride. In that respect, the chain-store system must necessarily be at a disadvantage, and yet the question still remains as to how important that difference is. Can it be offset in other ways?

After all, it doesn't make much difference how actively the feeling of local pride surges in the breast of the local merchant unless he is *able* as well as willing to heed its call—and the statistics presented earlier in these pages show how difficult it must be for the great majority of independent merchants even to make both ends meet.

On the other hand, it doesn't matter how lacking the absentee-owner may be in this element of local pride, provided he is able and willing to do his fair share in promoting community welfare for other reasons. In other words, what inspires a merchant to contribute to the Community Chest, to take an active part in Chamber of Commerce work or to participate in similar activities is relatively unimportant. He may do it from local pride, or because he thinks it will help his business or just because he thinks it is the right thing to do. So long as he does his part, the community can ask or expect no more.

The fact is that whatever may have been the case in the early days of chain-store development, the chains did eventually recognize their duty to the communities in which they operated. Once they had decided that sound policy demanded that they do their part, they took the necessary steps to see that their store managers cooperated adequately. The fact that the chains were both willing and *able* to do their part meant far more to the communities than the natural inclinations of independent merchants who were unable to back up their local pride effectively.

That considerations of public relations undoubtedly prompted the chains to take this more active interest in community affairs detracts in no way from the value of the contribution they are making. Perhaps in that respect lies a factor which is lacking in the case of the independent merchant, or, which is at least less potent with him than it is in the case of the chains. The chains learned the value of maintaining public relations the hard way, but they learned it. They are not apt to forget it. Certainly one of the fundamental features of a sound public-relations program for any absentee-owned project is to earn and maintain the good will of the communities in which they are located.

That is something the critics of chain stores, and chain stores themselves, overlooked in the days when the only important factor in community cooperation was *assumed* to be the local pride of the home-town merchant. That community life might benefit far more from the contributions of absentee-owners, even though they were activated by considerations of public relations, than by the offerings of those who were moved solely by sentiment, was not generally realized, but it was a fact.

Of course the part the independent merchant played in this sphere was always exaggerated. As this author pointed out in 1932,[1] when the hue and cry against the chains was at a high point, "anybody would think, from the criticism to which the chains have been subjected in this connection, that all independent merchants are paragons of civic virtue and that most

[1] *The Chain Store—Boon or Bane?, op. cit.,* pp. 94-96.

of our public institutions—our churches, our schools, our concert halls, our highways, our parks, our museums, our hospitals, our libraries and our playgrounds—reflect their generosity. The truth of the matter is that the majority of our independent merchants have such a hard struggle to make both ends meet that it is out of the question for them to contribute to community projects in any substantial way, no matter how civic-minded they may be, and if our cities and towns had to depend upon the financial support received from such sources, we should have to get along without schools, without churches, without concert halls, without highways, without parks, without museums, without hospitals, without libraries and without playgrounds. . . .

"What many people overlook is the fact that the wherewithal to build schools and highways and parks and playgrounds and other public projects comes almost entirely from *taxation* rather than from *voluntary contributions* and the part the local merchant plays—or fails to play—in developing his community through voluntary contributions is not nearly so serious a matter as might be supposed."

But what has been said of the average independent merchant did not apply to the chains. The average unit of a national or sectional chain, even in 1932, was a successful proposition and was in a position to pay its just share of whatever might be required in the way of voluntary contributions toward community welfare work. As the author pointed out at that time,[2] "the duty of the foreign-owned store to contribute is just as clear and just as definite as that of the locally owned establishment. This duty arises from the fact that the owner of a store in a community, just the same as the owner of a home, or any other resident, must share, willy-nilly, in the fruits of such projects and, by all standards of social ethics, should be willing to contribute his pro-rata share of the expense of establishing or maintaining them."

[2] *Ibid.*, p. 98.

Conceding then that the chains had both the obligation and the ability to participate in community projects, how were they actually behaving?

One answer to that question was given by A. S. Dudley, president of the National Association of Commercial Organization Secretaries, an organization which included in its membership most of the local Chambers of Commerce throughout the country. In an address before the National Chain Store Association in October, 1930,[3] he said:

"Early in 1928 our National Association of Commercial Organization Secretaries approached the management of 344 chains operating 25 or more stores—asked for an expression of attitude towards Chambers of Commerce. . . . Within three months, 266 secretaries out of our active membership of approximately 700, reported a total increase in chain-store subscriptions amounting to $636,825.

"The organization of the National Chain Store Association which was perfected about this time established a common meeting ground. From the moment of your adoption of your Code of Ethics on the 12th of October, 1928, pledging yourselves to promote all worthy local civic enterprises and any movements looking towards the betterment of the communities in which you engaged in business, there has been reported by our members a vast increase in the financial subscriptions and in the cooperative attitude of chains towards chambers of commerce.

"In July of this year we began another survey to ascertain the present situation. Thirty days after starting the survey, 43 per cent of the Chambers of Commerce, represented by our membership, had filed reports. The summary shows that 594 chain stores began their financial support to Chambers of Commerce since 1928. With but one exception, every member of the National Chain Store Association is represented in the report.

"In comparing the actual number of dollars subscribed by chains with those of the independent merchants, approximately two-thirds of the secretaries reporting stated that the

[3] *Chain Store Age,* November, 1930.

amounts given by the chains were satisfactory. In other words, the subscriptions approximately equalled those of the independent merchants; while comparatively few secretaries reported no support whatever from the chains.

"Reports received are not 100 per cent in an affirmative vein, but independent merchants are far, far from the mark of perfection in living up to their civic duties."

That presents probably a fair picture of the situation which existed 30 years ago, when the chains were only just beginning to realize not only what their social duty was with respect to community cooperation but where their interest lay, from the standpoint of public relations.

In 1932, as had been pointed out on page 188, the Illinois Chain Store Council was formed for the express purpose of crystallizing chain-store cooperation in local community and agricultural activities and, before very long, similar councils were organized in other States and regions throughout the country. By 1942, approximately 30 of these State councils were functioning. In between those years, the chains had received an intensive course in public relations in connection with the California referendum, as has been previously related in Chapter XI.

The character of the contribution which chain-store managers can make in the field of community building was concretely illustrated by the Community Builder Awards which *Chain Store Age* initiated in 1939.

Announced in January, 1939, the objective was to select and honor as the "Community Builder of the Year" the chain-store manager who, in 1938, had performed the most outstanding services for his community.

"Throughout the country important service is being rendered to communities every day by chain-store managers who put their energy, training and experience to work to build the communities in which they live and work," the announcement related. "Often the extent of these signal services is lost sight of because of the modesty of these men or because the services are rendered 'in line of duty' and are seldom publicized outside of the communities which benefit.

"Contributions which these chain-store managers make to their communities should receive wider recognition, not only to acknowledge the services of these men but to disprove the fallacious arguments advanced by critics of chain stores.

"Therefore, *Chain Store Age* is undertaking the task of compiling an Honor Roll of Community Builders of 1938. This roll will consist of managers of stores in all types of chains who, during the past year, made worth-while contributions in the form of services to their communities. From the Honor Roll of Community Builders a committee will select the 'Community Builder of the Year.'" A permanent bronze plaque and $100 in cash were to be awarded to him by the publication. All the other managers who made the Honor Roll were to receive scrolls designating them as Community Builders.

Nomination for the Honor Roll could be made either by the manager's district manager or his headquarters or by a local newspaper editor, an officer of a chamber of commerce or service club, a minister or a city official. The nomination period remained open for ten weeks. From the nominations received, 303 were selected as worthy of a place on the Roll of Honor of Community Builders. The nominating letters describing the achievements of the men who seemed to rate consideration for the top award, that of the Community Builder of the Year, were submitted to three judges for their independent appraisal. The judges were D. Hodson Lewis, of Little Rock, Ark., president of the National Association of Commercial Organization Secretaries; Walter F. Dexter, of Sacramento, Calif., president of Lions International; and Howard P. Jones, of New York, executive director of the National Municipal League.

Emery E. Freeman, manager of the J. C. Penney Company's store in Mount Pleasant, Mich., was the man selected as the Community Builder of the Year.

What were the community activities that prompted the judges to select Mr. Freeman for that distinction?

He was president of the Chamber of Commerce.

As chairman of a chapter of the American Red Cross, he headed up a membership drive which resulted in a 33% increase over the previous year.

He worked with others to secure finances for a $50,000 building to house a garage for the State Highway Department, thereby retaining for Mount Pleasant a State activity employing 25 men.

He headed the financing of the citywide Santa Claus Sales event to promote Christmas shopping, bringing thousands to Mount Pleasant to do their Christmas shopping.

He provided work in his own store for fourteen college students by planning hours of employment to meet their study schedules wherever possible. Other students were given part-time extra work.

He served on a committee to raise funds for the Boy Scout budget, supporting the campaign with cash, window displays and as a solicitor of funds.

He served as rehabilitation officer of the American Legion.

He assisted the Methodist Church drive for a building fund and personally contributed $250. Other churches received his personal financial support.

He furnished free movies to three schools during a campaign to raise funds for the Parent-Teacher Association.

He was a director of the Exchange Savings Bank.

The foregoing list does not include all the activities mentioned in Mr. Freeman's nomination. But they are typical of the kind of services which not only Mr. Freeman but a great number of other store managers were equipped to perform and which many of them were actually performing. The fact that only 303 names appeared on the Honor Roll was by no means an indication that these were the only managers who deserved the honor. On the contrary, they represented but a small fraction of those who undoubtedly would have made the Honor Roll had they been nominated.

It must be remembered that relatively little publicity was given to the award except in the pages of the magazine sponsoring it and that the period for nominations was relatively short. As local organizations familiar with the services rendered by chain-store managers could hear of the awards only through store managers themselves, many who might have submitted nominations remained unaware of their opportunity to do so. Although the chains themselves were privileged to nominate their own managers, not all the companies realized the desirability of doing so.

Qualitatively if not quantitatively, this first Honor Roll was highly illuminating. Not every one of the men on the Roll did as much as Mr. Freeman, by any means, but they all did enough at least to indicate that the observation that chain-store managers are *in* a community but not *of* it, even if true, is not particularly significant.

A glance, at random, at some of the community contributions made by men on the Honor Roll will suffice to show the wide range they covered.

One manager, Dan Worth Bradley, Sears Roebuck and Co., Durham, N.C., served as director of his Kiwanis Club and of the Junior Chamber of Commerce, which he helped to organize, served on the Community Chest committee, was third among 150 in number of new members obtained for the Y.M.C.A., and broadcasted over a local radio station in behalf of the community, besides being active in church and Sunday School doings.

Another, O. S. Hillman, H. L. Green Co., Columbia, S.C., was president of the Merchant's Association, a member of the City Council, finance chairman of the advisory board of the

Salvation Army, director of children's clinic, orphan's home and day nursery, and member of the Boy Scout Council.

Frank C. Collins, Great Atlantic & Pacific Tea Co., Grafton, W. Va., as chairman of the county chapter of American Red Cross, had put over its first successful home-service campaign in eight years. He was a director of his Rotary Club, a member of the county board of trade and the Y.M.C.A., and a soloist in his church and organizer of a club for the boys of his church.

William E. Berry, Montgomery Ward & Co., Minot, N.D., was president of his Kiwanis Club, vice president and fund-drive chairman of Community Chest, which was over-subscribed, chairman of the Retail Merchants group of the Association of Commerce, chairman of a city recreation council which sponsored playgrounds and other youth activities, director of the Salvation Army advisory board and co-chairman of a campaign to stimulate business and relieve unemployment.

The fact that chain-store managers all over the country were engaging in the same kinds of community activities tells its own story. This kind of work must be headed up by somebody. Chain-store managers are well equipped to handle it. The general policy of so-called national companies, including the interstate chains, is to have their managers do their part. The result is that no community in which the chains operate need ever lack leadership of a high order. The chains are both able and willing to supply it.

The following year, the Community Builder Award was announced again. This time the nominations were limited to local organizations—commercial, civic, service, religious, charitable or educational. The chains themselves could not nominate managers. Furthermore the cash award was eliminated, as the honor of recognition as an outstanding Community Builder was believed to be the only reward required. To acquaint local organizations with the conditions of the award, announcements were sent to all members of the National Association of Commercial Organization Secretaries. The judges were Ormond F. Lyman, Peoria, Ill., president of that organization; Dr. Minnie L. Maffett, Dallas, Tex., president of the National Federation of Business and Professional Women's Clubs; and Howard W. Palmer, Greenwich, Conn., president of the National Editorial Association.

From the nominations received, 344 were selected for the Roll of Honor. The highest award of Community Builder of the Year went to Walter S. Small, J. C. Penney Company manager at La Crosse, Wis. He was awarded that title for all types of chains, and also for the Department Store Division. In the Variety Store Division, the outstanding manager was Forrest G. Weese, S. S. Kresge Co., Zanesville, Ohio. In the Grocery Store Division, Paul A. Kunkle, The Kroger Grocery & Baking Co., Trenton, Mich., was selected as the Community Builder of the Year, and in the Drug Store Division, that honor went to H. C. James, Peoples Drug Stores, Fredericksburg, Va.

Mr. Small had been nominated by the La Crosse Chamber of Commerce; Mr. Weese by the Zanesville Chamber of Commerce; Mr. Kunkle by the Trenton (Mich.) *Times*; and Mr. James by the Fredericksburg *Free Lance-Star*.

To list the many noteworthy achievements of these men and of the 340 others who made up the 1939 Honor Roll would be merely to duplicate what has already been said of the Community Builders of 1938. But Mr. Small's own observations on being notified of his selection are enlightening as a revelation of the store manager's own viewpoint.[4]

"I wish to thank *Chain Store Age* for selecting me for this honor," he wrote, "but I wish more to commend you for placing a high value on the discharge of community responsibility by chain-store managers.

"In La Crosse most chain-store managers respond readily

[4] *Ibid.*, July, 1940.

to community calls. Many are very active in civic affairs. There is a steadily increasing interest and cooperation in community building on the part of the chains.

"When there is a call for support of most any local cause there is a very gratifying response from chain-store men. We never hesitate to solicit the chains to do their part, financially or physically. In fact, the foreign-corporation list, as it was designated in Community Chest campaigns, was always considered a plum for the team that was lucky enough to get it.

"Those multiple organizations who do not encourage and insist on community interest, both financially and in manpower, on the part of their local representatives are working a hardship on all chains. . . .

"I do not necessarily deserve medals for discharging a responsibility which is definitely in my lap; to do less would be to miss an opportunity, but I thank you just the same. In my case I must admit that my community interest is a result of the teaching and the policy of the J. C. Penney Co."

The third Community Builder project, which proved to be the final one, was announced in January, 1941, to some 2,400 Chambers of Commerce and other local organizations. It produced the greatest number of nominations of the three, yielding 524 names for the 1940 Honor Roll. No top awards were made as had been the case in the two previous years. The decision to abandon these special awards was made with the idea of avoiding any suggestion of a contest. It was felt that that could be best achieved by awarding a single type of recognition available to all who qualified for it—a Scroll of Honor attesting the recipient's qualification as a Community Builder by reason of outstanding service performed in 1940.

Among the Honor Roll men announced in May, 1941, were thirteen who had received the honor twice before and 77 who had received it once, either in 1940 or 1939. Eliminating these duplications, the project had brought out the names of more than 1,000 store managers located in probably more than 750 different communities, who had distinguished themselves for their leadership in community activities as part and parcel of their jobs as chain-store managers, with or without any sentimental ties to the communities in which they were located, and with no expectation of any reward other than that which comes from the satisfaction of meeting one's responsibilities.

Obviously, this group of Community Builders did not begin to include all who might equally have qualified for that title. More than 73 different interstate chains were represented on the 1940 Honor Roll, an indication that the policy of encouraging store managers to accept their community responsibilities was by no means confined to just a few broadminded and public-spirited organizations.

The fact is that chain-store managers today have become the leading merchants in many of our communities. Unless they and the representatives of other kinds of absentee-owned enterprises recognize the responsibility which has fallen into their laps, as Mr. Small put it, such communities will suffer accordingly.

The situation was well described by a Chamber of Commerce man in the course of an address to the Pennsylvania Chain Store Council at Hershey, Pa., January 22, 1941.[5] Earl D. Bacon, the speaker, was president of the Pennsylvania Commercial Secretaries' Association and executive secretary of the Sharon, Pa., Chamber of Commerce, a field in which he had been engaged for eighteen years.

"Quite a change has been taking place in communities during the past several years," he declared. "Surely, everyone can remember some men in the towns where we grew up (we'd call them economic royalists now) who were responsible for the growth and well-being of the community. In many cases they were merchants. In others they were bankers or the proprietors of the leading industries, the power company or other leading enterprises. In every case, however, they were

[5] *Ibid.* (Administration Edition) March, 1941.

men of outstanding leadership who were vitally concerned
with the future of the town, for the simple reason that everything they had was invested right there at home. They were
willing to expend any reasonable amount of time, energy or
money to secure community development.

"We all know what has happened. The utilities were combined years ago. Gradually the industries have been sold to
national companies, and chain stores are constantly increasing in numbers and importance. The old entrepreneurs of
former generations have been replaced by a generation of
managers, running businesses for groups of stockholders who
are distributed far and wide. Some of these managers have
the same abilities of leadership and the same community spirit
that the former local leaders had. Generally speaking, however, and through no fault of their own, they do not have the
same vital personal interest in the affairs of the community.
Their first allegiance is to their bosses in New York, Philadelphia, Pittsburgh and other cities, or to an impersonal group
of stockholders. Their support of local community projects
is necessarily secondary to those allegiances."

Of course, what Mr. Bacon overlooked in that connection,
was that even in the days when community leadership was
largely in the hands of local merchants and other business
men, their support of local community projects, too, was
"necessarily secondary" to their major interest represented by
their own business. The first duty of *any* merchant, obviously
is to make a success of his own business, for if he neglects that
in order to give an undue measure of his time and attention
to public affairs, the net result must be prejudicial both to his
business and the community as well.

Using his own city of Sharon as an example of the extent
to which the changes in question had taken place, Mr. Bacon
declared that 94% of the industrial workers were dependent
upon absentee owners for their jobs. The chains were accounting for between 25% and 50% of the retail business. He con-

cluded that "to a greater and greater extent, more and more cities must rely upon 'outsiders' in many types of business for the things they used to do themselves. We secretaries in the smaller cities of the country are firmly of the belief that additional help from national firms is not only desirable—it is absolutely essential if our towns are to prosper."

How close were the chains in Pennsylvania coming to what was expected of them?

So far as their contributions to the operating budgets of civic and welfare organizations were concerned, Mr. Bacon said that most secretaries agreed that the support given by the members of the Pennsylvania Chain Store Council was "fairly adequate." So far as non-member chains were concerned, they were not, as a rule, doing their part. However, as most of the important national and sectional chains operating in Pennsylvania were members of the council, the fact that a few were not did not change the general picture materially.

So far as contributions to capital investments were concerned—the occasional capital for hospital buildings, for instance—the response of even the member-companies, Mr. Bacon said, had not been entirely satisfactory. Conceding that the national industries and utilities and many of the chains already saw the community problem and were responding to it generously, he declared that the chains would not be doing their full part until they subscribed to capital funds as regularly as they were doing to current operating budgets of local institutions.

Turning to the remaining problem of personal service, Mr. Bacon pointed out that the smaller communities were no longer self-sufficient. "We must rely upon the chains and other national firms," he said, "to supply the manpower once available at home."

To improve the situation then existing, he recommended that (1) shifting managers from one city to another should be restricted as much as possible with the community aspect in mind, pointing out that a manager must be in a town for several years at least before he can do his part as a civic leader; (2) managers should be relieved of as much store-detail work as possible in order to give them more time for community work; and (3) top executives of the chains should remind managers from time to time that they were expected to cooperate in community affairs as part of their job.

Mr. Bacon's frank appraisal of the situation was regarded by the chains at the time as constructive. It was published in full in *Chain Store Age*, March, 1941. By that time the changes in the make-up of our smaller communities, which have been noted, had about run their course. The transition from the so-called "horse-and-buggy" days to the streamlined era that superseded it was complete. So far as the chains were concerned, the era of their active expansion had ended ten years earlier. It was not to be resumed in the ten years that followed.

Nevertheless the need for chain-store participation and leadership in community activities definitely remained. It still exists.

That the chains have never lost sight of it is evidenced by their maintenance of the State councils they established for the express purpose of stimulating the interest of their store managers in local activities and putting their cooperation on an organized basis.

Although Chain Store Councils exist today under that designation in only six states, most of the national and regional chains as well as many of the larger local chains are now members of state retail organizations which are open to retailers of all kinds and types.

Judging from the monthly reports issued by the directors of these State councils, chain-store managers are filling responsible positions of leadership in communities all over the country. If the Community Builder awards initiated by *Chain Store Age* 20 years ago but discontinued in 1942, as has already been related, were to be revived, the resulting Honor Roll would include a representative from almost every community in which units of the national or regional chains are located. In 1954, the National Association of Food Chains launched an annual store-manager citizenship campaign with the same basic objective. Each year since then a dozen or more managers have been selected as the outstanding managers of the year from the standpoint of exceptional participation in community activities. Screened from thousands nominated by their own companies for the distinction, the successful nominees have been publicly honored and acclaimed by the National Association. This project, although confined to managers of chain food stores, serves not only to inspire them to take their civic responsibilities seriously but to demonstrate how any chain store manager can be a good citizen as well as a good merchant.

To summarize the underlying considerations involved in the relations of the chains to their communities, the first point to note is that the greatest contribution they can make lies, of course, in the economic sphere.

Their primary job is to give the community the most efficient kind of retail service their particular system makes possible. In doing that they help not only to keep the cost of living down and thus to raise the community's standard of living, but they stimulate the business and the life of the community by making it unnecessary for its residents to go elsewhere to satisfy their needs.

The second point is that chain stores have an opportunity to serve their communities in the social sphere too. They share it with independent merchants and other fellow townsmen, irrespective of business or professional connections.

It arises from the fact that many of the activities required to promote the welfare of the community depend upon voluntary support and direction. The duty to provide such support and direction falls ethically upon those who are best equipped to furnish them. The chains definitely belong in that category.

Conceding, therefore, that native-born townspeople may have greater *sentimental* reason for rallying to the support of the home town, that fact is of little practical value unless it is accompanied by both the ability and the will to make such contributions. On the other hand, the fact that chain-store managers may lack any sentimental interest whatever in the community is likewise of little practical significance, provided that their contributions are forthcoming for other valid reasons.

That such valid reasons do indeed exist would seem to insure that the chains will continue to play a major role in community leadership.

CHAPTER XIV

THE CHAINS AND THE FARMER

OF THE SCORES of thousands of consumer items which line the shelves and counters of retail stores, those which are not of agricultural origin, either wholly or partially, are relatively few.

That applies particularly, of course, to the things we eat, but it applies also to most of the things we wear or use in other ways. In the case of foodstuffs, some of them reach the stores and the consumer in the same shape they left the farm. Others first go through various phases of processing. In the case of clothing and many other consumer items, the agricultural products entering their construction usually have lost all resemblance to their original form, but they are there just the same. Cotton, for example, goes through many processes before it emerges in a retail store as a woman's dress or a man's shirt, but the price the farmer gets for his cotton depends in the last analysis under normal conditions on how many things made of cotton are moved into consumption.

Thus the relation of retailing to agriculture is a vital one, even though it may be indirect in most cases. The significant fact is that retail stores provide the outlets through which many agricultural products move into consumption.

What has been said applies to all kinds of stores—independent stores as well as chain stores. But when the chain stores became an important factor in retailing, particularly in the grocery field, something was added to the relation of farmer and retailer which had never existed before.

317

In the first place, because the chains were big enough to buy from the farmer direct, they brought into sharp contrast the disadvantages the farmer had traditionally suffered in disposing of his output through commission men. The difference was clearly explained by a number of agricultural witnesses in the Patman bill hearing. One of them, S. M. Jones, of New Bern, N.C., whose company packed and distributed the output of some 500 vegetable growers, said at the hearing:[1]

"Prior to the time the chain stores became an important factor in the distribution of fresh vegetables, most of our produce was shipped to distant markets to be handled on a commission basis by the local merchants. The grower had little or no opportunity to sell at shipping point and know in advance what he was going to receive. His returns on his consignment were very uncertain and oftentimes were disappointing. As a matter of fact, it was only too frequent that he did not get anything at all, the freight and selling costs having eaten up the proceeds of the sale. In recent years, largely by means of the support of chain buyers, markets have been established in shipping sections, either auction or private sale. Today most of the supplies are sold at shipping point, either for cash or at stated prices, rather than going forward under consignment. By this means the growers have immediate contact with the pulse of the market, know what they are receiving, and can often regulate their shipments to a degree in keeping with demand requirements. Greater market stability has followed the introduction of this method of selling, which, obviously, has been of direct benefit to the growers."

But the chains brought something else into retailing which meant even more to the farmer—lower distribution costs. How badly that was needed was stressed by Edward A. O'Neal, president of the American Farm Bureau Federation,

[1] Patman Bill Hearing, *op. cit.*, Vol. 2, p. 1468.

who declared when he appeared before the Patman bill committee on April 13, 1940:[2]

"Our distribution system has grown up like Topsy, in helter-skelter fashion. We have built up a costly, inefficient system of distribution which takes a heavy toll from both farmers and consumers. All too often farmers receive too little for their products and consumers pay too much. The cost of distribution is one of the great barriers that we must surmount between the farmers and the consumers. We must seek any and all improvements in our distribution system. . . .

"This great mass-producing industry of agriculture needs an efficient mass-distributing system close to consumers, to carry commodities to the doors of millions of consumers at the least necessary cost. Furthermore, it must be a system that can act quickly and on a nationwide basis in order to handle perishable products produced long distances from the points of consumption. Delay in getting to market may mean the loss of a year's farm income. The chain stores' system has supplied not only these local outlets on a nationwide basis, but also the centralized purchasing agencies which deal directly with the farmers' cooperative marketing organizations.

"Thus the chain-store system affords an opportunity to shorten the route between the farmer and the consumer by means of direct bargaining between farmers' cooperative organizations and chain store organizations which sell directly to consumers, thereby eliminating unnecessary transportation and handling costs and the losses resulting from glutting of markets and inefficient distribution."

The chains' lower distribution costs meant nothing to the farmer, of course, unless they were translated into better returns to the farmer or lower prices to the consumer, or both. That the chains did reduce retail prices on fruit and vegetables was generally recognized. The savings thus brought about meant that the consumer could buy more and the

[2] *Ibid.*, Vol. 2, pp. 775, 784.

farmer shared the benefit of the consumer's increased buying power.

But the chains helped to expand the market for farm products in another way. They pioneered in displaying and merchandising fresh fruit and vegetables more extensively and more effectively than had been the practice in the grocery field before they came into the picture.

Strangely enough, despite the substantial benefits the farmers derived from these marketing innovations, many years elapsed before they were fully recognized and appreciated. In the meanwhile, anti-chain interests were busy developing the thought that the chains were actually hurting the farmers more than they were helping them. By lowering the retail price of fruits and produce, it was contended, the chains were depressing farm prices. Using farm products as "loss leaders" might indeed increase their consumption, it was urged, but how did that help the farmer if he could not get his cost of production back?

Irrespective of the facts in the case, many farmers undoubtedly came to believe that chain-store merchandising methods were actually harmful to them. When, from time to time, a bountiful harvest of a particular farm crop resulted in a supply exceeding the demand and prices declined accordingly, the plight of the farmers affected called for a scapegoat. It was easy enough then to say that the chains' low prices were largely responsible for "depressing" the market, even though the blame was obviously not theirs at all.

The result was that by 1935, at which time the chains were moving about 35% of the total output of fruit and vegetables into consumption, the farmers had mixed feelings regarding the chains. That attitude might have continued indefinitely but for one of the most remarkable developments in the whole history of marketing which changed the picture in a most constructive way.

It happened in 1936. As the year opened, the California peach growers were faced with one of agriculture's frequently recurring problems—the prospect of a bigger crop than could be marketed profitably.

The trouble in this case was that the carryover of canned peaches from 1935 amounted to 6,400,000 cases, as against a normal carryover of only 4,200,000 cases. Under such conditions, the canners would not be interested in packing more than four or five million additional cases. That would be equivalent to only about half of the new crop and would mean that the grower's return on his crop would be cut from $30 per ton, which he needed to show a profit, to $20 or even $15 per ton, which would not cover his cost of production.

Instead of letting nature take its course, as had been the general practice theretofore, the leading peach growers got together and organized the Canning Peach Stabilization Committee, with H. C. Merritt, Jr., as its chairman. Obviously, the problem was to cut down the carryover in the early months of the year to make way for the new crop, and somebody got the bright idea that if the chains would organize a sales promotion drive on a nationwide basis maybe the situation could be saved.

The idea was not entirely new. Many of the food chains individually had aided farmers in the past in their own operating areas by putting on local campaigns designed to move a surplus crop into consumption. But this was the first time anybody had thought of asking all the chains to combine in a nationwide campaign to achieve such a result. The proposal was made to the Food and Grocery Chain Stores of America—which a few months later changed its name to National Association of Food Chains—and was promptly accepted. As has been pointed out earlier, the chains in California were engaged at that time in a campaign to defeat a drastic chain-store-tax proposal which the public was to pass on at the next general election. The plight of the peach growers provided an excellent opportunity to demonstrate just what organized distribution, as represented by the chain-store system, could do to help solve the farmer's constant problem of moving seasonable surpluses into consumption. The chains jumped at the chance.

What happened can be told in a few words. In April and May of that year, the chains put on a four weeks canned-peach campaign in which 34,000 stores throughout the nation participated. These stores increased their sales of canned peaches in April-May, 1936 by 171% compared with their sales for the corresponding period in 1935.

What a dent it made in the carryover was thus reported by Mr. Merritt in a letter to the chain-store association dated July 6, 1936.[3]

"Now that efforts of the chain stores of the nation to save the canned-peach industry from a ruinous surplus have been crowned with success," the letter said, "it is fitting that our committee make due acknowledgment of your participation in the four California Canned Peach Events. . . .

"The figures reveal a reduction in canned-peach stocks of 3,143,387 cases in the five months period from January to June. The withdrawals averaged 670,000 cases per month, as against an average of 381,000 cases per month in 1935. . . ."

What is more to the point, the growers received $30 per ton for their 1936 crop instead of the $15 which was all they had originally expected.

At the very time the details of this first epoch-making national campaign were being worked out by John A. Logan, then the executive vice president of the food-chain association, and its agricultural committee, something much bigger was in the making, although its full possibilities may not have been realized at the time by those who were organizing it.

As has been pointed out earlier, a large number of farmers at that time believed that certain practices of long standing

[3] *Practical Farm Relief*, National Association of Food Chains, April, 1937.

in distribution were inimical to agriculture and, rightly or wrongly, the chains were believed largely responsible for them. On the other hand, it was realized that many food-chain operators did not fully understand the farmers' problems.

Why not get together around a table and discuss their mutual problems in the hope that cooperation might perhaps be substituted for misunderstanding and ill-feeling?

Mr. Logan accordingly arranged such a conference to be held in New York between outstanding agricultural leaders and representatives of the food chains.[4] The farmers were represented by a special committee appointed by the National Cooperative Council, an association consisting of 51 agricultural cooperative organizations, with a membership of 1,500,-000 farmers.

Representing the chains in what turned out to be an historic meeting were Hunter C. Phelan, D. Pender Grocery Co. (now Colonial Stores); Charles F. Adams and B. F. McGoldrick, First National Stores; Lewis W. Cole, Steiden Stores; Thomas F. Cauley, Danahy-Faxon Stores; F. H. Massman, National Tea Company; W. L. McEachran, E. S. Burgan & Sons; Albert H. Morrill and Warren H. Clark, Kroger Grocery & Baking Co.; William Park, Fred W. Johnson and H. D. Williamson, American Stores Co., L. A. Warren and Frederick W. Williamson, Safeway Stores, Inc.; E. G. Yonker, Sanitary Grocery Co. (now Safeway Stores), and Mr. Logan.

Over and beyond this desire to clear the atmosphere between the farmers and the chains was the hope that the meeting might lead to a practical program for farm relief which would go far to set their relations on a solid and substantial basis.

As Mr. Logan was to point out later in reporting on what actually happened at the conference, chain-store leaders real-

[4] *The Chain Store Cooperates with Agriculture,* memorandum filed with California State Senate Interim Committee by Frederick W. Williamson for California Chain Store Association, December 7, 1936.

ized that one of the most pressing problems of agriculture had to do with seasonal surplus crops. Why couldn't the chains use their facilities and their know-how to move these surplus crops into consumption on a nationwide basis as these situations arose?

The conference was presided over by C. C. Teague, vice president of the National Cooperative Council and president of the California Fruit Growers Exchange.[5] Among the practices which were responsible, he believed, for whatever ill-will farmers felt towards the chains, he listed five which he thought ought to be eliminated:

1. Unethical brokerage payment.
2. Unearned advertising allowances.
3. The use of agricultural products as loss-leaders.
4. Unreasonable quantity discounts.
5. The control of supplies by direct or indirect financing.

In the discussion which followed, several of the farm leaders made clear that the practices complained of were by no means peculiar to chain-store operations. In fact many of them had been initiated and were followed by all manner of jobbers, commission men, wholesalers and other middlemen.

None of the chain representatives defended any of the practices complained of and the upshot of that phase of the meeting was that the chains formally pledged themselves to aid in elimination of those practices from all branches of the industry.

But most important of all was a resolution adopted at the conference by the food chains which read as follows:

"Further resolved: That the members of this organization will endeavor to cooperate with the producers through their cooperative organizations, wherever available, or through other established producer agencies, in the effective marketing of excess seasonal production and surpluses, giving due recognition in the course of such efforts to the laws of supply and demand. . . ."

[5] *Ibid.*

That understanding was variously described thereafter as "an economic landmark," "the most forward-looking step ever taken, both for agriculture and for the distribution of food products" and "the dawn of a new day for the farmer."

This meeting took place in May. Within the next twelve months no less than eight Producer-Consumer Campaigns, as they were called, had been staged by the food chains, with most gratifying results to all concerned.

The canned-peach campaign has already been covered.

The second campaign was to promote the sale of beef. Drought that summer had so reduced feed facilities that cattle were rushed to market in unprecedented numbers, with the result that the beef market was glutted. Cattlemen asked the food chains to put on a campaign to avert the threatened catastrophe.

The campaign the chains put on was singularly successful. Mr. Logan reported a year later that the chains increased their beef sales in August 34.7%—more than twice the increase in the August slaughter; and increased per capita beef consumption 11.1%. "Prices to cattle raisers, which had started down, steadied, actually advanced during August," he reported,[6] "and continued to advance in the following months. Cattlemen received 6% higher price and 37% more dollar income from August sales than the previous five-year average for the month. The Federal Government, which bought 2,500,000 head of cattle in the 1934 drought, and which was ready to buy again in 1936, actually bought only 5,000 head to prevent a livestock market collapse."

In October the chains got behind a campaign to sell dried fruit which had backed up on the producers because of a maritime strike which reduced exports. A two weeks' campaign staged by the chains increased their sales 79.1% over the previous year's sales for the period, and moved millions of pounds of dried fruits into domestic consumption. It prevented complete demoralization of the dried-fruit market.

[6] *Practical Farm Relief, op. cit.,* p. 6.

An abnormal crop of 20,000,000 turkeys that fall, 33% above 1935, again brought the chains into action. They increased their own sales 46% and sales generally were increased 26.6%. The net result was that most producing areas sold out and showed a profit instead of the serious loss they had expected.

The next campaign was the most sensational of all. A bumper grapefruit crop, 46.6% in excess of the previous year's, resulted in what the U.S. Department of Agriculture called "the nation's number one surplus problem." [7] The campaign staged by the chains in January and February increased their sales 284.7%! Surplus stocks were cleared and the growers realized from 25 to 45 cents more per box than they had expected. Again a severe loss was converted into a substantial profit.

At the same time the chains put on a campaign to boost lamb sales, which had declined as a result of the competition from the heavy turkey crop, aggravated by an increased slaughter as a result of the drought. The chains moved 59 per cent more lamb into consumption as compared with their sales in the same two months in 1935 and prices to producers rose from $8.40 per cwt. in December to $10.50 in January and $13 in March, although *retail prices* remained stable throughout the campaign.

Another turkey campaign was staged in February and a canned-pear campaign in April, with consistently satisfactory results.

These early campaigns set the pattern for a permanent farm-relief program which has been followed ever since. In March, 1951, in a talk before the Sales Executives Club,[8] Mr. Logan pointed out that since the program was started in 1936 more than 350 campaigns and promotions, covering almost every agricultural product, had cleared through the association's office. In addition, similar cooperation has been fre-

[7] *Ibid.*, p. 8.
[8] *Food Distribution Is Different,* an address before Sales Executives Club, Hotel Roosevelt, N.Y., March 13, 1951.

quently extended by A&P, which is not a member of the association, acting independently.

Although the program was initiated by the food chains, the chains in other fields were quick to recognize its underlying merit and to tie in with such promotions wherever the nature of the agricultural product involved enabled them to cooperate in a practical way.

Thus, in 1938, the Institute of Distribution mobilized its members, including variety-store chains and other types handling consumer items in which cotton figured, to cooperate with cotton growers and processors to promote the consumption of cotton products. They all staged special promotions tying in with National Cotton Week. Even the grocery chains participated in a modest way because some of their items were derived from cotton or cotton seed.

Then, too, when the dairy interests felt they could use chain-store cooperation to increase the consumption of milk in the summertime, when the supply was at its peak, practically all types of chains responded year after year in a month-long promotion. The drug chains and the variety chains joined the grocery chains and restaurant chains in promoting milk as a beverage at their soda fountains or for consumption in the shape of dairy dishes, and even chains which had no interest in selling dairy products in any form, such as the shoe chains, the hat chains and wearing apparel chains found ways to cooperate by displaying "Drink Milk" posters in their windows and stores.

What was behind this all-out effort of the chains to help solve the farmer's problem? Did they do it out of sheer altruism? If not, what did they expect to gain by it?

Rilea W. Doe, vice president of Safeway Stores, Inc., answered those questions and several others related to them when he appeared before the Patman bill committee to tell the story of the food chains' agricultural program.[9]

---

[9] Patman Bill Hearing, *op. cit.*, Vol. 2, p. 885.

In the first place, he pointed out, although the chains conceived and organized the program, they are not "the whole show." Other organized distribution groups were likewise cooperating to the best of their ability in many of the programs and the chains welcomed their participation.

Turning to the reasons for the chains' interest in promoting the welfare of the farmer, he said they were three, as follows:

"First, the chains need a dependable supply of dependable quality merchandise and, therefore, are interested in a stabilized agricultural market—a market that maintains an even keel through regular daily purchases of normal supplies.

"Second, farmers are a very large class of customers of chain food stores, and if they—the farmers—have more money it means more business for the chain-store companies, as well as other business men.

"Third, farmers represent such a large proportion of the population of the entire country, and are so important economically, that the entire nation's prosperity is interwoven with the prosperity of agriculture.

"Obviously, then, it is good business—we call it enlightened selfishness—for the food chains to concern themselves with the welfare of agriculture and to assist continually to improve and stabilize the market for farm products. Such a policy is founded upon sound economic and social principles. This farm program has proven to be a practical form of working, economic, democracy."

"Enlightened selfishness" on the part of the chains undoubtedly supplied another reason for their well-conceived and most effective agricultural program. By demonstrating to the farmer in this practical way the unique facilities the chains commanded for moving seasonal surpluses into consumption as well as for expanding the market for farm products in their regular day-in and day-out merchandising, they established a unity of interest which the farmer would not be apt to overlook.

That the farmers did not overlook it was apparent enough

whenever and wherever discriminatory anti-chain-store taxes were under consideration. Invariably their spokesmen took a firm and positive stand against such taxes. Typical of what was to happen over and over again in such situations was the appearance before a New York Senate Committee on March 2, 1938 of G. A. Jeffreys, secretary of the New York State Turkey Growers Association. Under consideration was a proposed special tax against chain stores. In opposing it, Mr. Jeffreys stressed what a big job the food chains had done in moving an unusually heavy crop of turkeys into consumption. And when the anti-chain spokesman interjected sarcastically that he supposed the American people would have to get along without turkeys if we had no chain stores, Mr. Jeffreys replied:

"Not at all. Of course we would have turkeys, with or without chain stores; but because of the chain stores *more* people can have turkey!"

But the position of farmers with respect to the economic value of the chain-store system was shown most convincingly two years later at the public hearing on the Patman "Death Sentence" bill. Spokesmen for farm group after farm group appeared at the hearing to testify in person why they were interested in the defeat of the bill. One after another they testified how vital to their prosperity the chain-store system had become, and rejected almost unanimously Mr. Patman's contention that the chains were responsible for depressing farm prices. No important agricultural group failed either to appear in person in opposition to the bill or to file formal resolutions condemning it.

Typical of the testimony was that of M. J. Duer, Exmore, Va., a grower and shipper, who shipped about 4,000 cars a year of potatoes, cabbage, onions, strawberries and beans, for his own account and that of 1,200 other growers. He declared:[10]

[10] *Ibid.*, pp. 1374, 1375.

"We sell about 50 per cent of our output to the corporate food chains. We sell practically all of our produce on an f.o.b. shipping point basis. The food chains buy almost entirely on that basis. I can safely say that our sales to the food chains net at least as much to us—and possibly a little more—than do sales to other classes of buyers, especially in declining markets.

"The reason for this is that the food-chain buyer is in the market day-in and day-out in the crop season. They do not speculate, so that if the market is declining their daily purchases have a considerable stabilizing effect, whereas other classes of buyers are inclined to speculate, and in the case of a declining market they may wait a few days, which, of course, results in a further drop. The charge has been made that the chain stores use farm produce as loss-leader items, with a depressing effect on prices. In our experience we know of no instance where this is so.

"The production of fruits and vegetables on the eastern shore has become a real volume business, progressing far beyond the stage of the small farmer taking a load of produce to market and selling it for what he can get. In order to properly market this volume, we must have distribution organized on a volume basis also. This is the only way we can keep our selling overhead down and be sure of selling the large quantities that we raise and which must be distributed over a very wide area. I may say right here that one of the reasons why we are so anxious to protect our chain-store distribution is that we have no credit worries with these buyers —we get our money promptly and we do not have to worry about getting it. Furthermore one of the worst abuses in the produce business has been the rejection of merchandise on arrival—often for no better reason than that the market was declining. We have never had such experience with our chain-store buyers. We always feel that a sale to a chain-store buyer is a final one and that, regardless of the trend or the market, it will stick. . . .

"It is my opinion that chain stores have a very definite place in our economic system—particularly in the distribution of fruits and vegetables to the consumers of this country —and can continue to be of great service in reducing the spread between the producer price and the consumer price."

Need one go any further than that for an explanation of the cordial relations which exist today between the chains and the farmer compared with the less favorable situation which prevailed 30 years ago?

The fact is that their present-day relations rest upon a solid foundation of interdependence and mutual understanding. Both in their everyday operations and the special campaigns they are geared to stage, when occasion calls for them, the chains offer agriculture a system of organized distribution which provides a practical solution to the farmer's main problem—how to increase the farmer's share of the consumer's dollar without reducing its purchasing power. So long as the chains retain their interest in cutting distribution costs, they may expect to retain the complete approval and cooperation of the farm interests.

CHAPTER XV

THE CHAINS AS EMPLOYERS

SOME 2,900,000 full and part time employes were required to operate the 183,000 stores the chains had in 1958, including in that category all firms with two or more stores.[1] That includes those employed in the headquarters and district offices of the chains, in their warehouses and in the field as well as those who work in the stores themselves.

What kind of jobs do the chains offer?

They range in responsibility and compensation all the way from that of the beginner behind the variety-store counter or the youngster learning the grocery business in the supermarket to that of the top man of the company—the president of the chain. Between these two extremes are many kinds of jobs involving manual or clerical work in the lower levels and varying degrees of merchandising and administrative experience in the higher levels.

Most of the jobs the chains provide are not materially different in character from those offered by retailing in general. Basically, retailing involves the same principles of buying and selling, display and promotion, store layout, personnel training and management, financing and public relations whether the operation be conducted under one roof or many separate roofs.

But the chains have one kind of job which is seldom found in single-store operation but which is inherent in chain-store

[1] Retail Census, 1958.

operation—that of store manager. With 114,000 stores, chains with four stores or more require 114,000 store managers, and two or three times as many assistant store managers and trainees on their way up. Store managers are needed, of course, even by the smallest chains. But when the number of stores gets to the point where proper supervision calls for field men to devote all their time to that task, another kind of job, that of supervisor, found only in the chain-store field, comes into the picture. These field supervisors may be responsible for a small group of stores or a large group, depending upon the kind of stores involved and the distance between them. They are recruited generally from the ranks of the managers themselves, the promotion meaning more pay and a chance to share in the profits of the stores they supervise through various forms of bonus arrangement based on improved operating results.

Before the chains came into the retail picture, the field consisted entirely of so many separately owned single stores. Some of them were large, but the great majority were small. Retailing as a career offered only one major incentive under such circumstances—the possibility of one day having a store of your own.

To be the owner of even a small store in those days was a considerable incentive to the young man who was really serious about sticking to retailing as a livelihood. For one thing, it would mean a measure of security—an escape from the employe's ever-present danger of losing his job. The worst thing about any job was that you could lose it through no fault of your own, as, for instance, if your boss failed. The employe had reason to worry about the hazards of retailing as well as the proprietor.

Then, of course, if you had a store of your own and it proved successful, what was to stop you from enlarging it or moving it to a bigger and better location? To become the biggest merchant in town was certainly a legitimate objective for the ambitious retail clerk to shoot at even though relatively few could hope to achieve it.

One big obstacle stood between the great majority of retail clerks and the desire to have stores of their own. That was lack of capital. It took money, of course, to open, equip and stock a store. The number of retail employes who could save enough out of their meager earnings to go into business for themselves was relatively small. Even those who were thrifty enough to accumulate a nest-egg were more apt to keep it for a rainy day than to risk it in a venture which might fail, especially as such a step involved giving up a paying job in the bargain.

The same considerations undoubtedly deterred many from taking the leap even if they could borrow the needed capital. Why give up a job to go into business on borrowed capital when, in the event of failure, you would be left with no business and no job and an indebtedness you would have to repay some day by the sweat of your brow?

These were and are natural reactions. Little wonder, then, that most new stores were opened not by men with actual retailing experience, most of whom lacked the capital or the courage to risk it in such ventures, but by individuals who had the capital but lacked the experience and know-how necessary to make such ventures successful.

But with the coming of the chains, an entirely new avenue to a successful career in retailing was opened. As every chain store must have a manager, here was a chance for any young man who wanted to get somewhere in retailing to secure the necessary training and eventually to have a store of his own, in effect, without investing or risking a single cent of his own money in the venture.

True enough, managing a store owned by somebody else is not the same as owning it yourself. But to assume that the difference favors ownership is to overlook many of the factors involved. Probably the most important of them are security, compensation, responsibility and opportunity. Consider each of them in turn.

1. *Security.* Although a chain-store manager is an employe and *can* lose his job, the risk of that is relatively slight as long as he applies his experience and ability in the company's interest. The company has a substantial investment in each of its managers. The longer they remain with the chain, generally speaking, the more valuable they become. They provide the manpower from which the company must draw when positions of greater responsibility have to be filled. At any rate, a chain-store manager is not apt to lose his job through failure of the company. Although some chains have failed, such disasters have been extremely rare. In most cases, the operation of a number of stores provides a degree of stability which makes for continued successful operation. On the other hand, the high mortality rate which has always prevailed among single-store retailers reflects a degree of insecurity which may not be ignored. Although the turnover among chain-store employes generally may be as high as it is in other types of retailing, and for the same reasons, that applies, in the chain-store field, only to the rank and file of selling and non-selling help. Once a man reaches the level of store manager, he has a lifetime job, generally speaking, if he does his part. That gives him a measure of security which few of those who engage in retailing on their own can fairly claim.

2. *Compensation.* A store manager's salary varies, of course, with the kind of store he manages, its size, its sales and its operating results and the caliber and ability of the manager himself. In most cases his compensation is at least equal to what the owner of a store, comparable in size and sales, would draw as salary. In addition, the owner would, of course, expect a return on his invested capital. What kind

of return he would get would depend upon how successful his store was. To the extent that his income is augmented by the store's profits, he might seem to be in a better financial position than a store manager whose main source of income is his basic salary. But the comparison is hardly a fair one for it overlooks two important facts. In the first place, most store managers receive, in addition to their basic salary, a bonus based on the store's profit. In the second place, a store manager's savings earn a return too. If instead of putting them into a store of his own, as the independent retailer did, he invested them in stocks and bonds or other securities, the income he derives from such sources must similarly be taken into the equation before comparing his financial status with that of a store owner.

In addition to his salary and bonus, the store manager usually enjoys such benefits as group insurance, a pension or retirement plan, and various other company-supplied privileges for which the owner of a similar store has to pay out of his own pocket.

3. *Responsibility.* The store manager is responsible for the success of his store, with all which that involves. Nevertheless, he is relieved of many of the major problems which fall upon a store owner. When he becomes a store manager he falls heir to a ready-made store owned by an established company with a set of operating policies based on extensive experience and know-how. Behind him he has a buying organization which provides him with the merchandise to stock his store, a sales-promotion department to help him merchandise his store, and a central control system to help him keep his store on the beam. The individual store owner, on the other hand, must attend to all these things himself in addition to the responsibilities which he and the store manager share in common. Even with their limited responsibilities, store managers suffer plenty of headaches, but the worries of a store owner who must bear the full brunt of all the

problems involved in successful retailing must be infinitely greater.

So far as actual working conditions are concerned, a store manager's responsibility for his store calls for a high degree of diligence and vigilance. Until he has developed assistants to the point where he can trust them to carry on in his absence, the store manager must stick pretty close to his store from opening to closing. But all that is true of the store owner too if he wants to run a successful store. True enough, the store owner has to answer to nobody but himself if, through his own indifference or neglect, his store shows a loss instead of a profit, whereas similar conduct on the part of the store manager would mean the loss of his job. But if the comparison between managership and ownership be confined to those managers and owners who are equally interested in being successful, little difference will be found between them so far as hard work is concerned.

4. *Opportunity.* The store manager does not have to remain a manager all his life. As has already been indicated, promotions to positions of higher responsibility in the field or at headquarters are always possibilities. The number of store managers who, having started at the bottom, have climbed all the rungs of the ladder to become top executives and even presidents of their companies is literally legion. Such companies as the A&P, and Woolworth, and Penney, to name only three of the biggest chains in their respective fields, are manned almost exclusively, so far as the thousands of key positions are concerned, by men who were picked from the ranks of store managers for promotion up the line. And that is true of practically *all* the other national and regional chains in all fields, with only the smaller and younger companies still being directed by their founders and owners.

The need for trained manpower of executive caliber is regarded by the chains in all fields as one of their greatest problems. In line with the universal policy of promoting from within the organization, the top executives of tomorrow will inevitably be drawn mainly from the ranks of today's store managers and their assistants.

To provide a means for such men to qualify for the bigger jobs they may one day have a chance to fill, the National Association of Food Chains envisioned in 1951 an educational program at college level that would do for distribution what the law schools and the medical schools do for the legal and medical professions.

The idea was implemented by the establishment of a four-year curriculum in food distribution set up at Michigan State University. In the seven years of its operation, it proved so successful that in 1958 it was duplicated at Cornell University, and 1959 was to see a similar curriculum set up at the University of Southern California. Thanks to the generous cooperation of suppliers and others, hundreds of scholarships have been made available for deserving applicants from any branch of the food industry. Thus these college courses, and others which are expected to be set up eventually, will provide the additional training which store managers and other employes may require to fit them for the bigger jobs which the chains will constantly be required to fill.

The outlook for the store owner, on the other hand, presents no such equivalent opportunities as a general rule. No matter how good a merchant is, as long as he confines himself to a single store his opportunities for any great measure of success are necessarily limited. He can, of course, enlarge his store or move it to a better location, or even become a chain-store operator himself, but the fact is that the great majority of independent retailers do none of these things. Whatever opportunities the independent merchant may find in that direction are open equally to the store manager. For, if after a successful experience as a store manager, a chain-store man decides to put his accumulated capital into a store of his own, nothing need stop him. Because of his training and experience as a store manager under expert direction, he will be far better equipped, in most cases, to engage in business on his own account than the average entrant into retailing who lacks such experience.

To become a really successful merchant offers certain additional satisfactions in the shape of local prestige and community leadership. The percentage of independent retailers who are successful enough to achieve such distinction, however, is exceedingly small. On the other hand, as has been shown in a preceding chapter, such satisfactions are realized by a large percentage of store managers. The fact that they do not own the successful stores they manage in no way disqualifies them for important positions of leadership in the community. On the contrary, the very fact that big and successful companies have selected them for the responsibilities of store management is proof in itself that they have what it takes to carry their share of community responsibilities as well.

The unique vocational opportunities in retailing offered by the chain-store system as compared with those offered outside of the chain-store field were aptly described by the late Hubert T. Parson, when he was president of the F. W. Woolworth Company:[2]

> "What is there about retailing that makes ownership such an important feature? One does not have to own a railroad in order to work out a successful career in the railroad field. You don't have to own a bank in order to achieve success in the financial field. By far the greater number of successful men in every line of industry and commerce are but 'employes' of the companies with which they are connected, no matter how exalted may be the positions they occupy.
>
> "The idea that it is necessary to own a store in order to achieve success in the retail field has absolutely nothing to support it. Compared with the uncertainty which confronts the average storekeeper, the many risks he runs and the obvious limitations of his vocation, the opportunity offered by a

[2] *Chain Store Age,* January, 1928.

strong corporate retail enterprise, whether it be in the chain-store field, the department-store field, the mail-order field, or any other branch of business would seem to be far superior.

"Of course, if a man lacks ability or character or persever-ance or ambition or any of the other basic qualities that are essential to success, he can't expect to go very far, no matter what line of endeavor he follows. Certainly he could hope for little in the chain-store field, while if he accumulates sufficient capital to open a store of his own it would be only a question of time before his own shortcomings would put him out of the picture—another failure added to the long list which exacts such a heavy toll from the public.

"But if a man has in him the stuff that success is made of, I can think of no form of retailing that offers better prospects than the chain-store field."

How true that is is indicated, as has already been pointed out, by the fact that virtually all the men occupying key exec-utive positions in the chain-store field today, started at or near the bottom. That statement could be readily documented, if space permitted, by listing the scores of thousands of chain-store executives by name and company and showing how they rose to their present high positions of responsibility step by step on the basis of merit alone. They did not have to own a store either by purchase or inheritance, or be related to the owner, nor did they have to invest a single dollar in the stock of the companies for whom they worked. And long as such a list would be, it would not include the names of thousands of other chain-store men who had the same kind of experience but who have either passed on or retired from active work.

The late Lansing P. Shield, president of the Grand Union Company, once exposed the fallacy that being an "employe" of a big retailing company is a disadvantage as compared with having a store of your own. Mr. Shield had started as a young man, when he came out of World War I, with the A&P. Work-ing his way up to an executive position in the accounting and auditing department of that chain, he resigned to take a similar position with Grand Union, a much smaller chain but one which, he figured, offered him a greater opportunity.

He was right. He rose step by step until he became general manager of the chain, and, in 1946, was made its president. The company operated 496 supermarkets as of January, 1963 and its sales in 1962 totalled $624,647,000.

On October 4, 1949, Mr. Shield appeared on the television program which was mentioned earlier.[3] It involved a "trial" of the issue: Are national retail chain stores a benefit or a detriment to our country? Mr. Shield appeared, naturally, as a "witness" for the chains. Congressman Patman appeared as "counsel" against the chains.

"Which would you rather see," asked Mr. Patman, "a nation of clerks or a nation of independent owners and independent business men?"

To which Mr. Shield replied:

"The chain store provides opportunities at every level. There are hundreds of executive positions even in a company of our size, and there's a great opportunity there for any boy who wants to come in and try to do a job."

And when Mr. Patman interjected: "To work for somebody else," Mr. Shield answered: "I work for somebody else, Mr. Congressman, and I don't mind it a bit."

Of course, Mr. Patman's implication that the chain-store system tended to make of us a nation of "clerks" whereas the old wholesaler-retailer system would make us "a nation of independent owners" was as fallacious as it could be. It was a relic of the days when the so-called "chain-store question" was a live issue and was being debated by colleges and high-school teams from one end of the country to the other. It was one of the stock arguments invariably raised by the anti-chain-store side.

The main trouble with the contention was that it applied

[3] See p. 254.

the term "clerks" to *all* chain-store employes—to the executives and the store managers as well as to the real clerks—which was obviously false, and implied that *all* the employes of other types of retailing were "independent owners," which was equally false. True enough, as was shown earlier, a large percentage of independent stores are too small to employ even a single clerk, but that is not true of the bigger and more successful ones which collectively employ some 7,000,000 men and women, the great majority of whom are "clerks" and none of whom could be described as "independent owners." So long as we have any large number of the kind of stores the public wants, whether they are independently owned or chain owned, an army of "clerks" will be needed to operate them, but the total number of "clerks" would be no greater than it now is even if all retail stores were owned by chains, which is, of course, out of the question.

The only plausible basis for the "nation of clerks" argument lies in the fact that 1,000 stores, separately owned, give us 1,000 "independent owners," whereas 1,000 stores owned by a chain gives us only one owner. But to imply that the chain of 1,000 stores would be run exclusively by "clerks" is to ignore the significant function performed by the 1,000 store managers not to say anything of the hundreds of higher-ranking executives which such a chain would also require for its successful operation.

The fact is, as this chapter has attempted to bring out, that the chain-store manager is at least as successful, from his own standpoint, and at least as useful, from a social and economic standpoint, as the average independent retailer. Indeed, if it were possible to make an accurate comparison of store managers as a class with store owners as a class on the basis of their relative ability as merchants and their social status as individuals, the difference should easily favor the store managers.

That can be said with some confidence because the ranks of independent retailers necessarily include many who fail to measure up to even minimum requirements. That results from the fact that anyone can become a retailer. You don't have to ask anybody's permission to open a store.

Would-be storekeepers do not have to demonstrate their ability to operate successfully. They do not have to satisfy anyone of their character and integrity—except perhaps the landlord and the wholesaler, neither of whom is always as critical as he ought to be even for his own protection. The doors are wide open to everyone—to the man with individuality and to the man without it, to the man of initiative and to the man who lacks it, to the man who seeks responsibility and to the man who would prefer to escape it, to the strong and self-reliant and to the weak and dependent, and ample evidence attests that retailing attracts all kinds with the preponderance, if the truth be told, on the side of the deficient.

But store managers do not come into being so easily. Store managers are *selected* by others; they cannot appoint themselves. Because a chain must intrust not only its property in the shape of the store and its equipment, merchandise and cash, but also the good-will of the enterprise to its store managers, it must select them deliberately and carefully. It may be taken for granted, therefore, that the mere fact that a man has been selected to manage a chain store is evidence that, in the opinion of those who are in the best position to know and whose interests require them to decide correctly, he is qualified in every respect for the job assigned to him.

Thus, if one were required to recruit hastily a group of 100 men possessing the qualities that make for good merchants and good citizens, he could not accomplish the task in any quicker way than by selecting the first 100 chain-store managers he could lay his hands on. Would anyone undertake to assemble as worthy a group out of the first 100 store *owners* he could lay his hands on?

The possibility that a minor employe in a large organization may be lost sight of—that his merit may go unrecognized and

others, less deserving, may pass him on the way up the ladder
—is often cited in criticism of such jobs. Whatever may be the
case so far as big companies in other fields are concerned, the
criticism has little basis in the chain-store field. There the big
companies make a very real effort to see that no man who is
doing a good job is overlooked, not only in fairness to the man
himself but in the companies' own interest.

Such a policy follows from the almost universal rule among
the chains of promotion from within. To fill vacancies in the
higher ranks as they occur, adequate personnel records are an
essential feature in chain-store administration.

Some years ago, Raymond H. Fogler, then the personnel
director of the W. T. Grant Co., described in detail in *Chain
Store Age*[4] the elaborate system that chain had developed to
keep an accurate and up-to-date record of the progress each
of its men was making.

"To every ambitious man in any chain store," he said, "the
question most frequently uppermost in his mind is undoubtedly 'Does the home office know about me and my work?'

"The answer should always be 'Yes,' and in every case it
could be substantiated by records, which are accurate, complete and up-to-date. Such records are absolutely essential if
a company in which the personnel is scattered, as in chain-
store organizations, is to be able to determine with a fair
degree of accuracy those men who, on the basis of demonstrated qualifications, are most deserving of promotion and
those best fitted for special work."

And then he went on to describe the various forms his company was using and how the information they provided was
put to effective use. How vital to the company's progress they
were to prove in the years of extremely rapid expansion which
followed, not even Mr. Fogler, himself, could have foreseen.

But the most interesting thing about that article, which appeared in August, 1925, was that its author's own case history

[4] August, 1925.

provides one of the outstanding examples of the opportunities the chain-store field offers.

Graduating from the University of Maine in 1915 with a B.S. degree, he had taken a post-graduate course at Princeton. There he got his M.S. two years later. Returning to the University of Maine in an administrative capacity, he decided, in 1919, to enter the business field. That was when he joined the W. T. Grant Co., which was then a chain of 25 stores.

Before very long he was put in charge of the personnel department. There he developed the system described in the article referred to. By 1925 the company had 70 stores but it was expanding at such a rapid rate that only four years later its stores numbered 280! As it was Mr. Fogler's responsibility, as personnel director, to find competent men in the organization for the many new jobs thus created, his "system" was certainly put to a most severe test.

In 1929, he was transferred to another extremely active department—real estate and construction. How active it was is indicated by the company's further expansion from 280 stores in 1929 to 446 in 1932.

Then something most unusual happened. Another company, Montgomery Ward & Co., a Johnny-come-lately in the chain-store field, was in dire trouble. Having confined itself strictly to the mail-order business, in which field it was the second-largest company, until 1926, that year it had decided to operate retail stores as well. Having reached that decision, it had moved so fast that by the end of 1927 it had 36 stores in operation. The next year it opened 208 additional stores. And, in 1929, it added 288 more. By 1931, this chain which had sprung from nothing in 1926, had 610 stores in operation and that year it had shown a deficit of $8,700,000. Some 450 of its stores were "in the red." [5]

Obviously something drastic had to be done. Sewell L. Avery, chairman of the successful U.S. Gypsum Co., was

[5] The Stores and the Catalogue, *Fortune*, January, 1935.

invited to take over. He accepted the assignment, tough as it looked at the time. His skillful analysis revealed quickly what was wrong; the mail-order house had done splendidly in its time in its own field, but when it had plunged headlong into the chain-store business without either the know-how or the manpower to direct it, trouble was inevitable.

One of the first steps to be taken was to find the best chain-store man available to head up Ward's retail stores. The choice finally fell upon Mr. Fogler and, though he was not exactly available, he was just the kind of man Mr. Avery was looking for. Naturally Mr. Fogler was reluctant to leave the company which had given him the opportunity to learn all he knew about chain-store operation. But the offer was so flattering and so attractive, that Mr. Grant decided the problem for him. He took the job.

At first his responsibility was confined entirely to the retail stores but before very long he was made vice president in charge of the entire operation. Then in November, 1938, after six years of hard work, during which the company had made a spectacular recovery, Mr. Fogler, then 46 years old, was made president of the company, with an annual salary of $103,350.

In 1939, Mr. Fogler's first full year as president, the company rang up sales of $475,000,000, a substantial increase over the $176,000,000 recorded in 1932, the year he had joined the company to direct the retail stores. Throughout the entire period, sales and profits had increased each year. Profits in 1939 amounted to $27,000,000 compared with a *deficit* of $5,700,000 in 1932. That the increase in sales did not reflect merely the general recovery from the depression is indicated by the fact that during the same period Sears, Roebuck and Co.'s sales increased from $275,000,000 to $617,000,000, a gain of only 124% compared with Ward's gain of 170%.

Nevertheless, despite the outstanding contribution Mr. Fogler had made to Montgomery Ward & Co.'s rehabilitation and improved operating picture, in April, 1940, he decided to resign! Apparently he could no longer see eye to eye with Mr. Avery, the chairman of the board, and rather than follow the course which Mr. Avery favored but which he felt was unsound, he gave up his job.

But that is not the end of Mr. Fogler's remarkable success story. Within a week after the announcement of his resignation as president of Montgomery Ward & Co., another announcement made the headlines: he had been appointed president of another important chain. That chain was the W. T. Grant Co., the company which had given him his first job 21 years earlier when, as a young man of 27, he had decided to enter the retail field.

Thus, in the relatively short period of 21 years, Mr. Fogler had the unique experience of attaining the topmost rung in *two* of the leading chains in the country. What more evidence is needed of the broad opportunities which this field offers to those who measure up to them?

Of course, many men achieve great success in the chain-store field without duplicating Mr. Fogler's exceptional double-top. Each chain has only one president at a time, but it has many other key executives, all of whom occupy responsible and well-paid positions and are eligible for further promotion. But one need look no further than the army of successful store managers, without whom the chains could not operate, for proof of the main theme of this chapter—that you do not have to *own* a store in order to work out a successful career in retailing. The chains offer an ideal training ground for all who have retail ambitions—for those who may dream of having one day a store or chain of their own as well as for those who, like Mr. Shield, see the advantages of working "for somebody else."

CHAPTER XVI

THE CHAINS TODAY—
AND TOMORROW

WHERE THE CHAINS stand today as an element in our over-all distribution set-up is indicated statistically by the Retail Census of 1958, as summarized in earlier chapters. Although that enumeration is now four years old, such subsequent changes as have occurred are negligible so far as the chains' statistical standing is concerned. However, certain recent trends and developments in retailing which the statistics do not reveal call for consideration here because of their bearing on the chains in the immediate future.

Particularly significant are (1) the continued growth of shopping centers; (2) the mushrooming interest in low-margin retailing generated by the growth and success of discount stores; and (3) the stepped up activity of Federal agencies against the chains to check their alleged progress towards monopoly.

1. *Shopping Centers and the Chains*

The growth of shopping centers in the past decade has been fittingly described as a revolution in retailing—a revolution which has not yet run its course.

For more than a century, our retail set-up had been based solidly on the Main Streets of the country and the downtown areas of the big cities. Then, hardly more than ten years ago, we began to be faced with an entirely new set of conditions. With millions of city dwellers having migrated to the suburbs since World War II, and the parking problem in traditional shopping sections having reached serious proportions, far-sighted real estate developers had seen the need for a new kind of retail facility—the suburban shopping center.

That their vision was sound has been unmistakably demonstrated. The movement has spread from one end of the country to the other. Wherever the population of suburban areas had grown or was growing to the point where retail facilities of the area were inadequate, a new shopping center was indicated. Very soon a new vocation arose in the real estate field—that of shopping-center developer. To assemble suitable acreage for such a project, to evaluate its potential from the standpoint of its prospective tenants, to lay it out in a way that would provide attractive stores, easy access and ample parking space, to sign up enough of the right kind of tenants to satisfy the institutions from whom the developer would seek the necessary financial backing, required special abilities. It offered substantial rewards to those whose imagination and skill enabled them to convert their surveys and plans into thriving retail centers.

In any event, shopping centers have multiplied so rapidly all over the country in the past few years that they are currently believed to account for 25% of total retail sales, or more than $50 billion a year. That is the estimate provided by Samuel O. Kaylin, editor of *Shopping Center Age* and of the Executive Editions of *Chain Store Age*. Mr. Kaylin, a close observer of the shopping center movement right from the start, has covered its progress continuously in the publications he edits.

To what extent shopping center sales have been developed at the expense of retailers operating in traditional locations would be difficult, if not impossible, to calculate. Without any question, Main Street and downtown stores have felt the

impact of this new competitive factor. Indeed, during the
period in question, many important downtown department
stores have closed their doors at such locations because of the
changed conditions which led to the development of shopping
centers.

How many of the casualties among smaller merchants may
be attributed to the same factor is more difficult to say because
of the many other mortal ills to which small retailers have
always been particularly vulnerable. Nevertheless, any merchant within a shopping center's sphere must have felt the
impact of its competition to a greater or lesser degree. In the
case of small-scale merchants, any such loss of volume would
be apt to have serious consequences.

On the other hand, to conclude that the tremendous volume
done by shopping centers reflects an equivalent volume of
sales lost to other retailers would be erroneous for several
reasons. In the first place, much of it undoubtedly represents
additional sales—sales which would have been made by no
retailer but for the persuasive merchandising and superior
facilities offered by center stores. In the second place, much
of it reflects the substantial growth of population in the new
areas served by shopping centers which, in any event, would
hardly have gone to the merchants who remained at their old
locations.

What is more to the point, perhaps, is that the retailers
remaining in traditional locations did not take the new competition lying down. On the contrary, in many sections of the
country, urban renewal and downtown rehabilitation projects,
aggressive merchandising campaigns and other constructive
measures were undertaken to meet the new competition. Such
measures have been successful enough to develop new business to offset, in part at least, the sales lost to shopping centers.
The future may see a state of more or less peaceful coexistence
of urban and suburban retailing.

The benefits the chains have enjoyed, on net balance, as a

result of the shopping center revolution can hardly be over-estimated. Although the chains did not originate the move-ment and, indeed, were less than enthusiastic about it in its early days, their participation was vital to its success. With all their stores located on the Main Streets of the country or in downtown sections of big cities, the chains were as much concerned as the independents about the future of such tradi-tional shopping areas. If, as expected, the new shopping centers siphoned off sales from such stores, the chains would suffer along with their smaller competitors.

The one big difference, however, was that the chains were in a position to offset such losses by opening their own units in shopping centers. While to some extent that would mean competing with their own stores outside of the centers, that would obviously be less costly than letting someone else get the benefit of the center's potential volume. The small-scale merchant, on the other hand, usually lacked the resources to expand his operation by moving into a shopping center even if given the opportunity to do so.

But the chains came to play a major role in the development of shopping centers in another way. Whereas they might con-ceivably have worked out their own salvation without com-mitting themselves to shopping center locations, the shopping centers would never have got to first base if the chains had refused to play ball with them. Certainly that is true of the larger centers, which depend for their success upon having the kind of stores that would draw customers from five or more miles away. This meant that such stores would have to be operated by established department stores and other retailers, whose names, like those of the chains, were already household words to everyone in the trading area. Thus, the well-known chains in each field became the prime prospects for shopping center developers.

Furthermore, if the units were to be big enough and im-pressive enough to command the necessary following, a larger capital investment and operating budget would be required than any but an already successful merchant could command.

Finally, the developers had an even more pressing reason for turning to the chains and other well-established retailers as prospective tenants for such projects. To finance the building of the centers, developers had to depend upon life insurance companies and other financial institutions to provide the wherewithal.

Applications for such financing had little chance of acceptance unless they were backed up by lease commitments by AAA-1 companies. Until quite recently, the rule-of-thumb formula applied by such financial institutions required at least 70% of the available space to be leased to such high-rating companies. Today the tendency is to relax that requirement somewhat, with a somewhat greater share of the space going to local merchants. Experience has shown that a greater diversity of shopping facilities in a center pays off.

In any event, the preference the chains have enjoyed in this new retail area had not gone unnoticed by the political champions of small business. Thus the Small Business Committees of the Senate and the House, respectively, have conducted hearings to ascertain what, if anything, could be done to make it easier for a small merchant to set up shop in a center.

"The chains and the department stores have no trouble locating in shopping centers because of their Triple-A rating," the small retailers have complained. "Why couldn't the Small Business Administration, or some other governmental agency, set up some sort of insurance plan that would make the small merchant as good a credit risk as a Triple-A concern?"

The trouble with that suggestion is that it would not quite meet the situation. For Triple-A companies are sought as prime tenants not merely because of their credit rating, but, just as importantly, because their established following and merchandising know-how will be most likely to produce a successful operation. The more business each shopping center unit can do, the better it is for all concerned—for the tenant himself, for the landlord whose rental is based on a percentage of sales, and for the other tenants of the center who benefit by the combined traffic all units draw. A retailer who couldn't be depended upon to realize the maximum possibilities of the space he occupied would not make a satisfactory tenant no matter how strong his credit was. Nevertheless, small stores can make desirable tenants as well as big ones, and, as has been pointed out before, the present tendency is to make shopping-center space more readily available to small-scale merchants. The chains, as well as financing institutions, believe that the drawing-power of centers can be increased in that way.[1]

How many shopping centers are currently in operation?

According to Mr. Kaylin's latest survey, 5,500 were in operation at the beginning of 1962. Of these, 1,000 had been opened in 1961. An additional 1,100, the survey showed, were scheduled to be opened in 1962.

What constitutes a shopping center has not been officially defined, but Mr. Kaylin's count includes only those possessing the following characteristics: (1) a minimum of five stores, usually including a supermarket, a variety store and a drug store; (2) ample, planned parking space; and (3) a single landlord.

Minimum-size centers are relatively few. The great majority of those included in the count provide for 20 to 50 stores, with parking space for several thousand cars, and naturally a much greater diversity of tenants than is possible in smaller centers. At the top of the scale are hundreds of mammoth centers throughout the country which combine stores of every kind and description with office facilities for banks, doctors, etc., amusement features, and service units of various kinds. Parking space for upwards of 3,000 cars is an essential feature.

[1] See "Essentials to Center Success," *Chain Store Age*, Executive Editions, September, 1962.

Although, at the inception of the shopping center movement, the chains were by no means sure that it would benefit
them because of their major commitments in traditional areas,
they soon realized that they had little choice but to go along
with it. This viewpoint is clearly reflected in the fact that in
recent years the chains have been opening more new stores
in shopping centers than out of them. In 1961, for instance,
of 9,200 new stores opened by the chains, 4,850, or 52%, were
located in shopping centers, with the chains in some fields
exceeding that proportion substantially.

Thus, while only 4,700, or 48%, of the 9,300 new stores
scheduled to be opened in 1962 were to be in shopping
centers, 625 of the 650 new stores projected by the variety
store chains, or 96%, were to be so located, as were 87% of the
new general merchandise and department stores, 77% of the
new chain drug stores, 75% of the new chain shoe stores and
66% of the new chain apparel stores.[2]

The present evaluation of shopping center locations by the
chains is further indicated by the fact that several leading
department store and supermarket chains have gone into the
development of shopping centers themselves. Rather than run
the risk of being shut out in a promising area, they have set
up subsidiary companies to develop centers in such areas
themselves.

Although the number of shopping centers has increased
fantastically in the past few years, the movement clearly still
has far to go. At the present rate of growth, we shall have
10,000 of them within a very few years. How many more than
that will be required to meet the needs of our ever-growing
and constantly shifting population would be difficult to esti-
mate, particularly in view of such countervailing factors as
the urban renewal movement.

In any event, the indicated growth of shopping centers is
particularly significant to the chains because more centers

[2] See *Chain Store Age*, Executive Editions, January, 1962.

inevitably means more chain stores. To the extent that the centers increase their share of total retail sales, the chains may figure on corresponding gains. Actually it means even more to the chains than additional sales. It means that the chains of the future will be firmly intrenched in what may easily become retailing's major front.

2. Discount Stores and the Chains

Discount stores became an important factor in retailing only a few years ago, but their development had been in the making long before it reached the point where it was referred to in trade circles as the "discount store explosion."

In their earlier days, discount stores were relatively few, were found mainly in the larger cities, occupied unimpressive quarters, and concentrated mainly on "hard" lines, such as electrical appliances, household wares, luggage and furniture. Under such conditions, they had little impact on retailing as a whole.[3]

Their sole appeal to the consumer, but a potent one, was that they offered standard products at less than standard prices. Ironically enough, the Fair Trade laws, which had been relied upon to make such merchandising impossible, had just the opposite effect. For wherever Fair Trade prices prevailed, the discounters had a ready-made, authentic yardstick by which to demonstrate to the consumer how much lower their prices were than those charged for the identical items in other kinds of stores. Such savings, ranging from 15% to 25%, made a great appeal to those who knew where they were available and the word "discount" began to have significance for more and more people. But without Fair Trade, the discount store might never have been born, and the major

[3] Indicative of the humble beginnings of discounting is the fact that Eugene Ferkauf, the founder of E. J. Korvette, Inc., today's largest discount store operation, got his start, in 1948, in an upstairs loft on East 46th Street, New York, where he concentrated on luggage and appliances, at "less than list prices." (See *Fortune*, April, 1962.)

changes it was eventually to bring about in retailing might never have occurred.

Naturally enough, leading manufacturers of Fair Traded products did not take this open defiance of their legal rights lying down. On the contrary, companies like General Electric, Westinghouse and Sunbeam got to the point where they were spending millions of dollars a year on injunctions and other legal proceedings against Fair Trade "scofflaws."

But while those who fought to preserve Fair Trade won many an individual battle, they eventually lost the war.

For one thing, they found that the cost of such litigation was becoming prohibitive. More significantly, the number of States in which Fair Trade laws could be invoked was rapidly dwindling, as one State after another declared its own law unconstitutional so far, at least, as it applied to non-signers of Fair Trade contracts.

Under such conditions, many of the most loyal supporters of Fair Trade took their products off Fair Trade. This permitted retailers of such items to set their own resale prices. As far as such items were concerned, discounters no longer had a standard price to shoot at.

As it was, however, Fair Trade had remained in force long enough not only to give discounting its original impetus but to enable it to pick up considerable momentum. The collapse of Fair Trade laws came too late to check the progress of the juggernaut.

What the pioneer discounters had made clear was that you didn't need the long margins most retailers had previously considered indispensable, provided you streamlined your operation to eliminate customer services and other operating features which were not indispensable. By cutting their operating costs, they could pass the benefit of resulting economies on to their customers in the shape of lower prices.

Actually, "low margin retailing," as utilized by discount stores represented no new concept in retailing. Fifty years ago, the grocery chains, led by A&P, with its "economy stores," had employed it effectively. The "cash and carry" system and other operating economies made possible by a multiunit operation laid the foundation for such later innovations as self-service and the supermarket concept.

With this exception, however, retailers generally, chains as well as independents, have consistently operated on what, by comparison with discount store margins, are now seen to be vulnerably high margins. The reference here is to an overall margin of 35% to 40% compared with less than 25% for discount stores.

This does not mean that the higher margins are unjustified or even avoidable as long as operating expenses remain at prevailing levels. It means only that the pioneer discount stores demonstrated, as the grocery chains had done before them, that profitable operation is feasible with lower margins providing operating costs are cut to pave the way for them. Furthermore, they demonstrated that the additional volume generated by lower prices may produce more gross margin *dollars* notwithstanding lower gross margin *percentages*.

Nevertheless, the merchandising lesson provided by the success of the early discount stores might have gone unheeded but for the impressive momentum the development began to gain about 1958.

Not only were new discount stores being opened rapidly throughout the country, but most of them were of a size and type to create local excitement wherever they made their appearance. Ranging in size from 30,000 to 150,000 square feet, these specially built stores were strategically located, offered adequate parking space, carried a wide assortment of both hard and soft lines, and were aggressively merchandised on a minimum-service, low-margin basis. Drawing traffic from far beyond their immediate vicinity, they gave traditional retailers in all fields growing cause for alarm.

Among the companies which were making conspicuous

headway at this stage were E. J. Korvette, Masters, Arlan's, Two Guys from Harrison, GEM, Towers, Grand Union's Grand-Way Centers, Spartan, Fed-Mart, Barker's, Bargain City, U.S.A., Zayre's, Consumers Mart of America, King's Department Stores and Atlantic Mills. They included "closed door" operations—open only to card-carrying members—and the open door variety, accessible to all who were ready to respond to the magic of the discount store appeal.

How they continued to expand thereafter is indicated by the fact that 2,590 operated by 428 chains were listed in the 1962 Discount Store Directory published by *Chain Store Guide*. Analyzing the data in that Directory, *Discount Store News*[4] estimated that the 2,025 discount department stores listed (including only those which carried a reasonable mix of hard and soft lines) occupied a total of 107 million square feet of space. Of these, 1,903 were open door stores and occupied 96 million square feet, averaging 50,445 square feet each, while the 122 closed-door units occupied 11 million square feet and averaged 91,147 square feet each!

Another measure of the rapid growth of discount stores is their estimated volume in 1961 of $4.25 billion—an average of $2.5 million per store. Sales in 1962, reflecting the opening of additional units, were expected to exceed $6 billion. *Fortune* magazine, in a comprehensive study of discounting appearing, under the title: "The Distribution Upheaval," in its April, May, July and August, 1962, issues, estimated that by 1970 "the discounters may have captured a larger share of the market than department stores now have." In 1961, department store sales totalled some $15 billion.

What gave the discount store movement general acceptance as a major development in retailing was the decision of

---

[4] August 27, 1962. In the same issue, *Discount Store News* estimated that of 1,903 open-door stores, 27.9% occupied less than 20,000 square feet each; 26.5% between 30,000 and 60,000; and 45.6% exceeded 60,000 square feet each.

many outstanding chains and leading independent merchants in other fields to get into discounting themselves.

Not all followed the same course. Some, notably Woolworth and Kresge, decided to set up separate discount store divisions and to open a substantial number of units, under a name other than their own, as rapidly as possible.

Others proceeded at a more leisurely pace, contenting themselves with opening just one or two units to get the feel of it. Still others endeavored to make up for lost time by acquiring existing discount store chains. Many saw their best opportunity in operating leased departments in discount stores owned by others.

By the middle of 1962, chains which had gone into discounting in one way or another included:

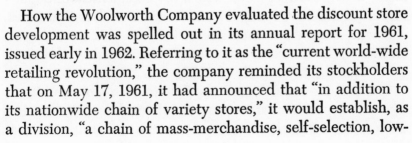

Variety Store Chains: Fishman, Grant, Kresge, Kress, Kuhn Bros., Murphy, Neisner, Sterling and Woolworth.

Supermarket Chains: Borman Foods, Food Fair, Food Giant, Grand Union, Jewel Tea, Kroger, National Tea, Penn Fruit, Red Owl, Safeway, Stop and Shop and Thriftimart.

Apparel Chains: Diana, Grayson-Robinson, Holly, Lane Bryant, Mangel, Miller-Wohl and Virginia Dare.

Shoe Chains: Edison, Endicott-Johnson, Genesco, Melville, and Shoe Corp. of America.

Drug Chains: Cunningham, Gray, Katz, Parkview, Thrift, Walgreen and Whelan.

Department Store Chains: Allied Stores and Interstate Department Stores.

Jewelry Chains: Kay and Zale.

How the Woolworth Company evaluated the discount store development was spelled out in its annual report for 1961, issued early in 1962. Referring to it as the "current world-wide retailing revolution," the company reminded its stockholders that on May 17, 1961, it had announced that "in addition to its nationwide chain of variety stores," it would establish, as a division, "a chain of mass-merchandise, self-selection, low-margin, high quality Woolco Department Stores." That division had now been organized, it went on, "to operate in the United States and Canada with the objective of becoming a dominant chain, after the first units are opened in the Spring of 1962."

"The current version of the retailing revolution," the report continued, "reveals consumer willingness to dispense with certain services in exchange for cash savings and the comforts of shopping for all manner of goods under a single roof, with self-selection and check-out counters.

"As long as consumers reap benefits, the retailing revolution will extend itself in directions which the company has been exploring and charting over a long period. Consumers have demonstrated enthusiasm over mass-merchandising of high-quality items at low prices in department store surroundings, as well as larger, community-oriented variety stores conveniently located.

"With the conviction that mass-merchandising of high-quality items at low prices in spacious, modern shopping facilities, is here to stay, the full force of the Company's resources and buying experience will be made available to Woolco."

The kind of store Woolworth had in mind was indicated in the report by a description of the first Woolco unit, to be opened in the Great Southern Shopping Center, Columbus, Ohio. It would be a one-story, 100,000 square-feet establishment, with a 480-foot front, with a full complement of departments emphasizing many lines of nationally advertised items, and with some departments leased. When this unit opened, on June 6, the Company announced that it would be followed by 17 more by the middle of 1963.

The S. S. Kresge Co. embarked on an even more ambitious discount department store program about the same time, but accompanied it with another project of a different nature. It decided to convert some of its unprofitable downtown and outlying stores to a special type of discount store operation, in which only a limited number of lines and items would be carried. They would be handled on a self-service basis at a drastically lowered mark-up.

These stores, under the name of Jupiter, of which 26 were in operation early in 1962, proved extremely successful. Furthermore, according to Harry B. Cunningham, the Company's president, in a speech reported in *Chain Store Age,* Variety Store Editions, July, 1962, they had provided a pattern of operation of which an adaptation, he believed, might have tremendous possibilities for all Kresge stores.

But Kresge's real plunge into the discount store field took the form of full-fledged discount department stores, 60,000 to 133,000 square feet in size, operated under the name of K-marts. With three in operation early in 1962, 14 more were scheduled to be opened that year, and 31 more in 1963.

Mr. Cunningham pointed out that "a firm decision to move importantly into the discount department store field was made in early 1961 after intensive research had convinced us that there was a tremendous opportunity in this area for our company." He emphasized his conviction, however, that "good variety stores will remain a highly important segment of general merchandise retailing," although he felt that their character would "reflect continued adjustments to current trends."

In the department store field, which was perhaps the most vulnerable to the discount challenge, Allied Stores, the third largest chain in the field, decided to meet fire with fire. For that purpose, it set up its own separate discount store operation under the name of Almart Stores.

The advantage of taking over an existing discount store operation instead of building one from the ground up is illustrated by the experience of Interstate Department Stores.

In 1958, when that chain was operating 47 junior department stores, its sales totalled $65 million. In its fiscal year ending January 31, 1962, its sales totalled $165 million! This tremendous increase reflected its acquisition in April, 1859, of White Front Stores, Inc., a two-store discount operation on the Coast; the sales of the first few units of a new chain it opened in the Midwest under the name Family Fair; and finally its acquisition of Topps Stores, an 8-store chain, in 1960.

In the supermarket, drug and apparel fields, many chains chose the leased department approach, although three notable exceptions were provided in the supermarket field by Grand Union, Food Fair and Stop and Shop, respectively, and in the drug field, several important chains met the challenge head on by establishing separate discount operations under a different name.

Grand Union was one of the first chains in any field to foresee what was happening. It took positive and courageous steps to meet the situation by engaging in a combined food and general merchandise operation itself. In 1956, accordingly, Grand Union converted a big supermarket at Keansburg, N.J. into such an operation on an experimental basis. It proved so promising that the company decided to go ahead at once with its program. Experienced executives from the general merchandise field were secured to direct that side of the business. The second unit, in Albany, N.Y., 37,000 square feet in size was to be followed rapidly by nine others, many of them considerably larger.[5] By 1962, Grand Union had 21 Grand-Way discount units in operation and was planning still more.

Food Fair, on the other hand, chose the acquisition route to get into discounting. In 1961 it acquired the J. M. Fields chain of 33 units. Thirteen more were scheduled to be opened in 1962. Stop & Shop followed the same pattern when it acquired the 13-store Bradlee chain in 1961. It continued to operate the added stores as Bradlee's.

[5] *Chain Store Age,* Grocery Editions, November, 1957.

In the drug field, a number of chains felt that the best way to meet discount competition on drug store products, which was becoming too strong to be ignored, was to set up separate chains of what might be called "fighting stores."

The main features of these new units, which were conceived as a permanent addition to the chains' existing operations, were:

(1) Very small selling area—from 2,000 to 4,000 square feet.

(2) High foot-traffic locations, often in old chain downtown units.

(3) Limited assortments—between 2,000 to 4,000 items and sizes of fast-turn drugs, vitamins and toiletries.

(4) Low operating costs—through lower rentals, low-cost self-service fixtures and reduced payroll.

(5) Across-the-board discount prices—usually 20% to 25% lower than suggested prices.

(6) Expected volume of $350,000 to $1,000,000 a year—depending on size of unit and whether or not it includes a Rx department.[6]

Within a very short time Cunningham had eight such units in Detroit and Cleveland, where they were operated as DOT Discount Stores; Gray's, of Cleveland, had opened several such units under the name of King's; and Sun-Ray in Philadelphia had three units under the name of Franklin. One of the biggest discount operations in the drug field, however, was that of Revco, developed by Regal Drug Co., of Detroit. Of the 58 units in operation in 1962 under the Revco name, 41 were the stores formerly owned by Standard Drug Co., of Cleveland. Most of them, therefore, are large-size units which have been converted to a discount drug store basis.

Although the operation of discount drug stores by chains with regular drug stores in the same area would seem to pose some special problems, the chains responsible for them pro-

[6] *Chain Store Age*, Druggist Editions, December, 1961.

fessed to be quite happy with the results and enthusiastic about their future.[7]

How great has the impact of the discount store development been on retailing in general and on the chains in particular?

In the first place, it has added 2,590 additional chain stores, operated by 428 companies. That was the count in the *1962 Discount Store Directory* previously referred to. Actually the *number* of the additional stores is no longer particularly meaningful for, as has been pointed out before, the trend towards ever bigger stores would have increased retail capacity materially even if the number of stores had remained the same or even if it declined. This is particularly true of the additional stores in the discount field, which are typically much larger than the average retail outlet.

Furthermore, with the momentum the development has already attained and the strength it will gain from its newest and most powerful converts—the traditional chains—it must inevitably enlarge the chains' share of total retail sales.

Obviously the dollars spent in discount stores do not represent additional consumer purchases, except to a minor extent. For the most part they are sales diverted from other stores. Which kind and type of stores will be affected most by the growth of discounting remains to be seen, but certainly those traditional retailers who have gone into discounting themselves or may do so in the future would seem to be in the most favored position. Through their own discount operations, whatever form they may take, they will offset whatever losses their regular stores may suffer, or, at least, reduce them. And since discounting is essentially a large-scale operation, it benefits from a multiunit set-up. Thus the chains, as a group, are likely to feel the impact of discounting less than the independents, as a group.

From a broader angle, the discounters have made a sub-

[7] *Chain Store Age,* Druggist Editions, December, 1961.

stantial contribution to the general welfare by establishing both the need and the feasibility of low-margin merchandising. Their example, as well as their competition, has led retailers in many fields to retreat from some of the fixations which have characterized their operations through the years. The result has been to make a wide range of merchandise available to the consumer at lower prices not only in discount stores but in other stores as well.

To the extent that this result tends to narrow the competitive advantages discount stores enjoyed initially, their further growth will presumably be slowed down. They will likewise suffer competitively if they make the mistake of restoring services which they eliminated to reduce their operating costs. Although a tendency in that direction has made its appearance, most discounters must recognize the danger they run in yielding to it, and, for that reason, it will probably be checked before it does too much harm.

Finally, in evaluating the impact of discounting on retailing in general, sight must not be lost of the fact that price appeal is not the only factor which influences retail purchases. Consumers in the higher income brackets, while in the minority, nevertheless provide a substantial market for those in a position to cater to it. Such customers are both able and willing to pay a premium for the kind of retail service they prefer. Many department stores, for instance, will bypass the discount challenge, in part at least, by emphasizing the lines and services which a substantial number of their customers will still demand and which they won't find in discount stores.

3. *The Chains and "Bigness"*

As was revealed in the Census figures for 1958 (Table 15, page 74), the chains in several important fields account for a substantial share of the available business.

What the Census figures do not show, however, is the status of the biggest chains in each field relative to that of the others.

With four food chains, A&P, Safeway, Kroger and Acme (formerly American Stores) now in the billion-dollar class and several others soon to join them, and four chains in the general merchandise field (Sears, Roebuck, Montgomery Ward, J. C. Penney and Woolworth) in the same exalted group, with several more just about to make the grade, to what extent do these leaders dominate their fields? Furthermore, as these big chains continue to expand, what monopolistic threat do they pose?

A look at the situation which prevailed in two important fields, variety stores and food, in 1958, the year of the latest Census, provides a logical starting point for a consideration of the topic to be covered in this section.

In 1958, variety store chains (those operating four stores or more) operated 38% of all variety stores but accounted for 81% of their combined sales. The biggest among them was the pioneer, the F. W. Woolworth Co. Although its sales passed the billion-dollar mark in 1960, in 1958 they totalled $865 million. How did Woolworth stack up against the rest of the field, and against its less direct competitors in other fields?

As appears from the tabulation which follows, Woolworth operated 10.2% of all variety stores and accounted for 23.8% of their combined sales.

The significant fact to note, however, is that Woolworth stores were in direct competition with those of nine other relatively big chains in the same field. With Woolworth they constituted what was sometimes referred to as "the Big Ten." Collectively, the nine chains operated 16.4% of the stores and accounted for 49.1% of the sales—more than twice those of Woolworth's. The rest of the field consisted of some 15,000 stores, or 73% of the total, and accounted for 27% of total sales. Thus, Woolworth's direct competition came from nine times as many other variety stores, which accounted for 76% of the field's total sales.

But Woolworth's direct competition as covered by the table

does not begin to tell the whole story. In addition, the big company has to meet the indirect competition of department stores (both traditional and discount), dry goods and general merchandise stores, as well as that of drug stores, apparel stores and supermarkets so far as particular lines of merchan-

VARIETY STORE GROUP, STORES AND SALES, 1958
(Based on 1958 Census and Company reports)

GROUP	STORES	%	SALES (MILLIONS)	%
ALL VARIETY STORES	21,017	100.0	$3,621.0	100.0
Woolworth Company	2,152	10.2	864.6	23.8
9 next largest chains[1]	3,456	16.4	1,777.6	49.1
All other chains[2]	2,399	11.4	290.0	8.0
Independents, etc.	13,010	62.0	689.0	19.1

[1] In order of sales, they were Grant, Kresge, Newberry, Murphy, Kress, Green, Neisner and McLellan. Green and McLellan were later merged with McCrory.

[2] With four stores or more.

dise are concerned. This competition is becoming more serious every day as stores in other fields stock more and more of the items which play an important role in variety-store merchandising.

In the light of these facts, the top company in the variety store field, big and successful as it is, would seem to occupy no dominating position as far as its competitors are concerned. On the contrary, it must keep constantly on its toes to hold its own against numerous and aggressive competitors, both chain and independent, who are big enough and strong enough to give a good account of themselves. This is especially true, in the independent ranks, of the stores affiliated with the large voluntary chain sponsored by Butler Brothers, under the name of Ben Franklin Stores, and the large group serviced by the Consolidated Merchants Syndicate. And, of course, as has already been detailed, Woolworth recently found it necessary to establish a separate chain of stores to cope with the discount store challenge.

What has been said of the biggest company in the field applies, of course, with even greater force to the other members of the "Big Ten." Big and successful as they are, as individual companies go, they are in no position to throw their weight around to the detriment of small business.

In the grocery field, the chains in 1958 accounted for 44% of the sales of the entire food group (Table 15, page 74). In this field, we have not only the biggest chain but the biggest retail organization of any kind, in the shape of A&P.

A&P's sales have exceeded $5 billion annually ever since 1958. In that year they amounted to $5,095 million. What did that mean with reference to the food field as a whole?

The entire food group consisted of 355,508 stores, with sales of some $49 billion in 1958. The chains (only those with four or more stores) had 25,005, or 7% of the stores, and accounted for some 21 billion, or 44%, of the sales.

How the four biggest chains compared with each other, with the rest of the chain store group and with the retail food field as a whole, is shown in the tabulation which follows.

FOOD GROUP, STORES AND SALES, 1958
(Based on 1958 Census and Company reports)

GROUP	STORES	%	SALES (MILLIONS)	%
ALL FOOD STORES	355,508	100.0	$49,022	100.0
A&P	4,252	1.2	5,095	10.4
Safeway	2,117	.6	2,225	4.5
Kroger	1,428	.4	1,776	3.6
Acme (formerly American)	823	.2	875	1.8
Other chains[1]	16,385	4.6	11,621	23.7
Independents, &c.	330,503	93.0	27,430	56.0

[1] With four or more stores.

Looking at the foregoing table statistically, A&P would hardly seem to be the economic menace its critics might like to prove it to be. Operating but one per cent of the stores and enjoying only 10% of total retail food sales, it would seem to be outnumbered and outweighed by its competitors collectively.

Although the big company enjoys only 10 per cent of the total food trade, however, it enjoys a greater percentage in some areas. Indeed, in some instances, it may enjoy as much as 20% of the available trade, or even more. That is true likewise of some of the other chains, small as well as large, and even of some of the more successful affiliated independents. Many an individual store may be particularly strong in its home town or, in the case of a chain store, in a community where it has been fortunate enough to develop a proportionately large and loyal following.

But to conclude that such a situation is necessarily bad or against the public interest is to ignore entirely the basic realities of retail trade—to assume that somehow a retailer can compel people to trade with him instead of having to win their trade by superior service and to retain it in the same way.

The fact is, of course, that neither the A&P nor any other retailer *controls* a single dollar's worth of business anywhere. Whatever share of the available business A&P, or any other retailer, enjoys, it holds only during good behavior. The foregoing table shows only how competitive the grocery business is quantitatively. It does not show, what is even more significant, the quality of the competition which every chain, from A&P down, has to meet. Not only do the bigger chains have to meet the competition of chains of their own caliber in almost every community in which they operate, but they find just as great a challenge in the competition of successful independents and small local chains.[8]

With competition as extensive in the food field as it is, no company is big enough to exploit the public by raising prices or in any other way. Big business may be sufficiently entrenched in some lines of production to disregard the public interest by raising prices unduly, but that has never been true of big business in distribution.

[8] See "Those Hardy Independents," *Chain Store Age*, Grocery Editions, July, 1960, p. 35.

Two other criticisms levelled at big business, however, are just as applicable to distribution as they are to production. One of them relates to the ability of big companies to use their resources to eliminate competition, either by acquisition or destruction. The other relates to the buying advantages which accrue to them by reason of their large-scale purchases.

So far as the elimination of competition by acquisition is concerned, a big company is obviously in a better financial position to buy out a competitor than a small company would be. Many of the leading companies in various lines of industry have attained at least part of their present size and power by mergers and acquisitions. In the chain-store field, too, some of the bigger companies have followed the same course to a greater or lesser degree. In the late '20's, when chain-store expansion was at its peak, several of the companies which now head the list in their respective fields accelerated their growth via the merger process. As it happens, that was not true of the biggest chain of all. A&P attained its major growth by the simple process of opening additional stores of its own, as has been related in an earlier chapter. Mergers and acquisitions have, however, played no small part in the development of other big chains.

In any event, the ability of big companies to become even bigger in this way no longer presents much of a problem from the standpoint of the public interest. For the Federal Trade Commission is now equipped with ample power to nullify any merger or acquisition which tends to restrain competition unduly.[9]

That a big company can use its resources to drive weaker companies out of business as well as to buy them out is, of course, of greater concern to small business. Undoubtedly it has been done in many lines of industry. Drastic price-cutting and other devices have been employed for the express purpose of eliminating competitors. In retailing, however, no such

[9] See p. 167, *supra,* and also p. 377, *post.*

destructive policy could achieve more than temporary success owing to the depth of the competitive set-up. Profitless selling cannot be maintained forever even by the biggest companies, and to suffer operating losses for the purpose of eliminating one competitor with the certainty that he would be replaced by another, perhaps by a stronger one, would not make much sense.

Conceding that the big chains have sufficient resources to make life miserable if not unendurable for their weaker competitors by drastic price-cutting, the futility of such tactics, if nothing else, argues against such a policy. Furthermore, in addition to the Federal anti-trust acts which prohibit all conduct in restraint of trade, many States have what are known as "Unfair Trade" statutes aimed specifically against predatory price-cutting. These acts are not to be confused with the Fair Trade laws which many States have enacted to legalize price maintenance—to permit the manufacturers of branded products to establish a minimum resale price binding on all retailers.

Nevertheless, one of the many charges made against A&P in a criminal anti-trust case some years ago was that it had deliberately operated many of its stores "in the red" for the purpose of driving competitors out of business.

The case[10] was tried in Danville, Ill. in 1945 before U.S. District Court Judge Walter C. Lindley without a jury.[11] The evidence on the issue in question did indeed establish that several of A&P's Divisions had operated "in the red" at various times, sometimes for protracted periods. But the real question, of course, was whether they were operated "in the red" for

[10] See United States v. N.Y. Great Atlantic & Pacific Tea Co., 173 F. 2d 79 (1949), affirming 67 F. Supp. 626 (1946). For comment on these decisions, see "The A&P Case: A Study in Applied Economic Theory," by M. A. Adelman, *The Quarterly Journal of Economics*, Harvard University, May, 1949; "The Great A&P Muddle," by the same author, *Fortune*, December, 1949; and "What the A&P Case Is All About," by the present author, Journal of Retailing, New York University, Spring, 1950.

[11] Later promoted to the U.S. Circuit Court of Appeals. He died in 1957.

the sinister purpose of putting competitors out of business, as the Government insisted, or whether, as the company undertook to prove, the losses occurred despite the measures A&P took to avert them.

A&P's top executives testified categorically that *no* store was ever operated at a loss for the purpose alleged or indeed for any purpose other than the legitimate one of attempting to develop additional *volume* through lower *prices* so that it would not have to operate "in the red" any longer.

My own opinion is that the company's contention was not refuted by the Government. How Judge Lindley felt about it is not revealed in his decision, since he found the defendants guilty on other grounds—the practices of the Atlantic Commission Co., one of A&P's important subsidiaries.

Even if the company's "manipulation of gross profit rates" or any of the other actions of which the Government complained "might not amount to a violation of the law standing alone," he declared, they nevertheless amounted to undue restraint of trade when coupled with the unlawful activities of the Atlantic Commission Co.

An appeal from Judge Lindley's decision resulted in an affirmance by the Circuit Court of Appeals. On the basis of that decision, the Government promptly filed a civil suit against A&P, reiterating all the charges it had made in the criminal proceeding, and asking that the company be split into seven separate retail units and five manufacturing units, each of them separately owned and managed, without any interlocking ownership or operating connection.

That suit never came to trial, a consent decree ending it on January 19, 1954.[12] The only structural change in the company's organization required by the decree was the dissolution of the Atlantic Commission Company. The four manufacturing subsidiaries and the vast retail set-up remained intact.

But the decree's most interesting provision for our present

[12] Trade Cases, 1954, Commerce Clearing House, Par. 67,658.

purpose was one relating to the Company's power to put competitors out of business by operating particular stores at a loss to achieve that purpose.

The provision enjoins A&P from "assigning a gross profit rate for any Division, knowing that such an assigned gross profit will result in the operation of any such Division at a loss, for the purpose of or with the intent of destroying or eliminating competition. . . . The purpose or intent prohibited in this section shall not be presumed merely by reason of the operation of a Division at a loss."

That provision, it would seem, gives A&P the only freedom it had ever claimed in this connection—the right to set its prices at any level it desired (in keeping with State or local laws) whether such prices resulted in an operating loss or not, and irrespective of the impact of such prices on competition, provided only that its purpose was not to destroy competition.

My own comment on this consent-decree at that time seemed even more appropriate five years later. "With A&P approaching its 100th birthday and doing a superlative job in serving the public—we are mighty glad that it may now expect to celebrate its centenary all in one piece." [13]

Unquestionably a big company in any field *can* use its resources in a variety of undesirable ways, including putting weaker competitors out of business, but, for the reasons already given, retailing provides a poor field in which to engage in such an undertaking.

What about the tremendous purchasing power commanded by big business in general and the big chains in particular? Does that involve competitive advantages which are not in the public interest?

Discounts based on quantities purchased have been a feature of American business from time immemorial. They have been in almost universal use. The greater the purchase the better the discount and, in effect, the lower the price. The

[13] Chain Store Age, Grocery Editions, February, 1954, page 67.

principle has been applied at every level—from the purchaser of raw materials down to the consumer, who may not recognize a 2-for-25-cent price as a quantity discount but enjoys it just the same. The quantity discount, like the quality of mercy, is "twice blessed: it blesseth him that gives and him that takes." It tends to promote trade—the foundation of our economy—and for that reason has always been legal. It has never been seriously questioned even by those whose purchases may not be big enough to earn the larger discounts available. What *is* questioned are the extra price concessions big buyers may receive from suppliers who are naturally tempted to favor their best customers or may be afraid not to do so.

That such extra price concessions to big buyers of all kinds were prevalent before the passage of the Robinson-Patman Act in 1936 is not to be denied. All buyers, small as well as big, try to buy as cheaply as possible and if loopholes in the laws against price discrimination permitted manufacturers and other suppliers to favor their bigger customers, such concessions were inevitable.

But, as has been pointed out in an earlier chapter, the Robinson-Patman Act plugged the loopholes in the Clayton Act. No longer was it legal for a manufacturer to shape his price structure to favor the bigger buyers unduly. Discounts based on quantity were still permitted, but only to the extent that they reflected actual cost savings to the manufacturer or other supplier. Price concessions masquerading as advertising allowances were prohibited, and even legitimate advertising allowances and special services or facilities which manufacturers had previously offered to favored customers were required to be offered to all customers on "proportionately equal terms."

How did these required changes in marketing practices affect the chains? Because of their relatively large buying power and the desirability of their business in other respects, the chains had undoubtedly benefited by the more flexible system which had previously prevailed. Indeed, according to some of their critics, their phenomenal growth and success could be attributed largely to the special discounts and allowances which were available prior to the Robinson-Patman Act.

The fact is, however, that the chains were never dependent upon such special allowances. That is clearly indicated by what has happened since they were outlawed. After all, the Robinson-Patman Act has now been in effect for more than 26 years, and yet the chains have maintained their competitive position and operated profitably throughout that entire period without the benefit of the banned allowances which are supposed to have meant so much to them.

The truth of the matter is that these allowances which ended with the Robinson-Patman Act were never important enough to signify competitively. The real advantages which the chains enjoyed and which alone accounted for their growth and success were inherent in their system and were not affected by the Act in question. These advantages have been discussed in detail in earlier chapters, but fundamentally they all stem from the operation of more than a single store.

On that basic principle the chain-store system grew to its present size and importance and produced thousands of successful companies. Among them today are more than 50 with sales in excess of $100 million a year, with 8 of them already in the billion-dollar a year category[14] and others headed in that direction.

That companies of this magnitude belong in the category of "big business"—whatever that term may connote to those who use it—can hardly be doubted. But whatever the term may

[14] A&P, Sears Roebuck, Montgomery Ward, Safeway, Kroger, Acme Stores, J. C. Penney and Woolworth.

connote to others, in the author's view, when a retail company, whether chain or independent, achieves "big business" status it can mean only one thing—outstanding merit.

For when the public chooses to spend millions of dollars a year in the stores of a single company in the face of the keen competition provided by other stores and other claimants for the consumer dollar, the public is saying to that company in the most convincing way: "We like your stores, we like your wares, we like your service and we like your prices." Here is no case of a monopoly situation which the public must accept or go without. Here, on the contrary, is the result of the free exercise of the public's selection from a wide range of alternative choices.

What has been said here of the biggest companies in the chain-store field applies equally to all chains which are operating successfully, whether they have achieved "big business" stature or not. The mere fact that they are operating a group of retail stores successfully—that they are not only selling a lot of merchandise but are selling it *profitably*—is evidence that they are rendering a useful service under our economic system. In such a competitive field as retailing, every company, large or small, which operates profitably merits the plaudits of a nation in which profits and competition are the two vital elements of its economy.

No useful purpose would be served by listing all the chains whose success indicates that they have merited public favor, even if it were practicable to do so. A clear indication of the important part the chain-store system has come to play in our retail distribution set-up is provided when the 50 or the 100 largest firms in the field are listed. In its August, 1962 issue, *Fortune* magazine, for instance, listed the 50 leading merchandising firms in 1961. Each of them had sales in excess of $200 million. Their combined sales totalled $37.3 billion, or an average of $746 million each. Of these outstanding companies, which included wholesalers as well as retailers, no less than 35, or 70%, were chains, and since the eight companies at the top of the list, each with sales in excess of $1 billion were all chains, as were the next seven on the list, the group obviously accounted for an even larger percentage of total sales.

A similar list but covering the 100 largest companies whose sales for 1961 were publicly reported was compiled by the First National City Bank. The 50 additional companies thus brought into the picture included those with sales in excess of $85 million. The number of *chains* in the list was 75.

Without any question such companies as these rate as big companies, but if the foregoing observations are sound, the question raised earlier as to whether some of the chains may have grown *too big* for the common good would seem to be answered definitely in the negative.

But the antitrust laws are designed to safeguard the economy against *incipient* monopoly as well as actual monopoly. Accordingly, both the Department of Justice and the Federal Trade Commission have challenged the validity of a number of mergers in recent years on the ground that their effect "may be substantially to lessen competition or to tend to create a monopoly."

Among the chains whose mergers have been challenged on this basis are the Kroger Co., National Tea Co., Grand Union Co. and Von's, in the grocery field, and Cunningham Drug Stores and Thrifty Drug Stores Co., in the drug field— although in the last instance the mere ownership of a block of stock in another chain was the basis of the complaint. In each instance, the government is demanding that the defendants divest themselves of one or more recent acquisitions, and, in some cases, of acquisitions made a number of years ago. In the shoe field, the Brown Shoe Company's acquisition of G. R. Kinney Co. in 1956 was attacked by the government, and was held, in 1959, to be illegal as monopolistic. The U.S. Supreme Court affirmed that decision and ordered divestiture in an opinion which will have an important bearing on the outcome of cases based on comparable situations.[15]

Besides the mergers currently under attack in the food field, many others have been effected in recent years. Indeed some chains own a considerable part of their present standing to such acquisitions. Nevertheless, a study by the author of the food chain field as it existed in 1961 compared with its make-up in 1953 revealed that such mergers had resulted in no significant change in the picture.[16] Indeed, it showed that more chains were in operation in 1961 than eight years earlier, despite the fact that a number of medium-sized chains which were operating in 1953 no longer existed as separate entities as a result of mergers, liquidations or other factors. Although the increase was accounted for almost entirely by a substantial gain in the number of two- and three-store companies, the number of companies with four or more stores showed a slight gain too.

With all food chains broken down by size-groups, the picture the study produced is shown in the following table:

TABLE 20

NUMBER OF FOOD CHAINS, 1953 AND 1961

(By size of company)

	GROUP	COMPANIES			STORES OPERATED		
		1953	1961	CHANGE	1953	1961	CHANGE
(I)	2 and 3 stores	2,013	2,516	+503	4,654	5,645	+991
(II)	4 to 9 stores	587	593	+6	3,040	3,129	+89
(III)	10 to 25 stores	171	169	−2	2,620	2,457	−163
(IV)	26 to 99 stores	85	84	−1	3,449	3,947	+498
(V)	100 or more stores	23	25	+2	14,115	14,987	+872
		2,879	3,387	+508	27,878	30,165	+2,287

One fact not revealed in the foregoing table but which was established by other data was that while the *number of chains*

[15] Brown Shoe Co. vs. United States, Commerce Clearing House Trade Cases, p. 76, 479, June 28, 1962.
[16] "Small Chain Virility a Bar to Monopoly," Chain Store Age, Executive Editions, January, 1962.

in the major categories remained surprisingly constant, the figures did not necessarily represent the same chains. Actually, a company-by-company inventory of the chains composing the groups in question in 1953 and thereafter, revealed a substantial movement of companies from one category to another, either by growth, merger or reduction in number of units. Despite these internal changes the number of companies remained substantially the same. This reflected, the author felt, "the virility and growing-power of the smaller chains and suggests that therein lies an effective bar against potential monopoly."

The chains owe the favorable position they occupy today to many factors. Among the most important, however, are (1) the underlying merit of the system itself; (2) the caliber of the men who became chain-store operators; (3) their readiness to adjust their operations to changing conditions; and (4) the effectiveness of their trade associations.

As to the merits of the system itself, they have already been covered at length in earlier chapters. Suffice it to say here that if the economic history of the past 50 years has established anything, it is that the chain-store system of distribution provides an effective basis for low-cost distribution. That is one of the things most needed if our vast facilities for mass production are to be effectively employed for the common good.

That basic fact, long conceded by virtually all economists and marketing authorities, must undoubtedly be given the major credit for the final triumph of the chains over those who used every available means to check their progress, if not to destroy them altogether.

A clear exposition of the vital role played by mass distribution in an economy of plenty is given by J. Frederic Dewhurst, Executive Director of the Twentieth Century Fund, and his associates in their revised edition of *America's Needs and Resources*, published in 1955.

Referring to the close interdependence in the American economy between producing goods and selling them, the authors declare that "the high degree of specialization in American industry, simplification of design, and the lavish use of automatic power-driven machinery in turning out low-cost standardized goods would be impossible without the means of assuring mass consumption in a mass market."

Noting that foreign observers who praise our industrial efficiency nevertheless condemn our "wasteful" selling and advertising methods, the authors observe that "it implies neither praise nor criticism of such methods to recognize that only by their use can the great advantages and economies of mass production be achieved. The distribution institutions and methods which make this possible—the mail order house, the chain store, the supermarket, instalment buying, market analysis, national advertising and, whether we like it or not, even the singing commercial—are just as much a part of American technology as are radioisotopes and fork-lift trucks."

"The true significance of technology in raising the American standard of living," the authors conclude, "is apparent only when production and distribution are viewed as a unified process. Then it is clear that technological progress has brought over the years and decades a steady lowering of the real costs of supplying the consumer with an ever wider range of useful goods and services."

The second factor to play a major role in chain store development was the caliber of the men who became involved in it. That chain-store operators, generally speaking, are different in certain respects from the general run of retail merchants is more or less obvious. The fact that they were *able* to open a second store indicates that their first ventures had been more or less successful, which, unfortunately, has not been universally true of retail merchants. On the contrary, the great majority of retail stores, the Census figures show, develop barely enough volume to sustain them, much less to provide the means for expansion.

Then, too, the decision to open a second store, which every chain-store operator has to make, indicates a degree of ambition, vision and courage which relatively few single-store merchants possess.

Finally, the success achieved by so many of the men who did not stop with a second store but went on to develop the chains which make up the system as it is today is perhaps the best proof of their special qualifications as merchants and as organizers.

The third factor contributing to the continuous growth of the chains in the face of ever-changing conditions has undoubtedly been their flexibility.

Typical of this flexibility was the adoption of the self-service principle, first by the food chains, and eventually by chains in other fields to which it was applicable, notably the variety-store and drug chains. The readiness of the chains to install any innovation which offers operating economies or better service to customers has been repeatedly demonstrated.

A prime example is furnished in the way the chains in the food field embraced the supermarket idea when its merits became apparent some twenty-five years ago. How the trend towards bigger stores in all fields was recognized and accepted by the chains is disclosed concretely by the substantial increase in their sales per store. On the basis of the Census data presented in Table 15, average sales per store for the chain store field as a whole rose from $68,000 a year in 1929 to $468,000 in 1958 and Table 14, page 62, shows how the trend towards bigger stores carried average sales per store still further by 1961.

How quickly even the biggest chains can change direction once they are convinced that the change is desirable is well illustrated by the major changes the Woolworth Company has made in recent years. When conditions necessitated abandoning the "Nothing over 10 Cents" slogan upon which the company's success had been founded, that step was taken. Although variety stores are still referred to by many as "the five and tens" no such limitation has prevailed for more than a score of years.

Then, when the application of self-service to variety store operation loomed up as a distinct possibility, Woolworth tried it out experimentally in three of its stores. That was in 1952. Today no less than 1,702 of the 2,502 stores operated by the chain and its subsidiaries are full-fledged self-service stores.

During this period, too, the widespread development of planned shopping centers found all the chains quick to sense the possibilities. As a result the great majority of new stores opened by leading chains in recent years have been located in such projects, as has already been pointed out.

And now, as we have seen, the Woolworth Company, in common with many other chains, has decided to enter the discount store field in a big way.

Among the many other ways in which the chains have demonstrated their flexibility should be mentioned their readiness to extend credit, to offer trading stamps and to add entirely new lines and departments. Whether such changes were introduced as a constructive step towards bigger sales or were adopted purely as a defensive measure to cope with aggressive competition, the point to be made is that the chains have demonstrated their readiness to abandon traditional policies, no matter how fundamental they may have seemed at one time, when changing conditions favored such steps.

But successful as so many of the chains proved to be, they realized 30 years ago that they could go only so far acting individually. For their common protection and for the development of their system in the public interest they needed the additional strength and stimulation to be gained by mutual cooperation through trade associations.

How the first national association was organized by the chains in 1928 and functioned effectively until 1933, when the coming of the New Deal and NRA called for individual associations in each field, has already been related. If the chains have nothing else to thank the New Deal for they may at least be grateful for the trade associations which came into being as a result of it.

Four of the most influential have been the National Association of Food Chains, the Limited Price Variety Stores Association, whose name was changed in 1957 to Variety Stores Association, the National Association of Chain Drug Stores and the Institute of Distribution.

Almost continuously since 1933 business has had to operate under Governmental controls and regulations imposed to help us fight successively the depression, World War II, postwar inflation, the cold war in Europe and the hot war in Korea. Under these conditions the chains, in common with most other business enterprises, were compelled to lean heavily on their own trade associations for guidance, information, official contacts, representation on industry committees cooperating with the Government, and as a medium for the exchange of ideas on current problems and operating policies. How indeed any chain could have operated within the law, with all its complexities, during these difficult years without the benefit of such information and help as these associations were equipped to furnish would be hard to conceive.

The chains were particularly fortunate in their choice of executives to direct the activities of their associations. Although the members themselves naturally had to make the final decisions on most of the important questions which arose, they were aided materially in arriving at them by the experience, ability and energy of their association directors.

John A. Logan, president of the National Association of Food Chains, directed its activities from the time it was organized, March 7, 1934, until his retirement in 1960. It was under his leadership that the far-reaching farm-relief program, which has already been described, was initiated in 1936. Without attempting even to list the many other important achievements of this Association under Mr. Logan's direction during the past 25 years, suffice it to say that it is generally regarded as one of the most effective organizations in the entire field of trade associations.

Mr. Logan was succeeded by Clarence G. Adamy, as Executive Vice-President, the present incumbent.

The variety chains were equally fortunate when they secured Dr. Paul H. Nystrom to head up the activities of the Limited Price Variety Stores Association, which was organized in the summer of 1933. As one of the outstanding authorities on marketing in general and retailing in particular, serving as professor of marketing at Columbia University since 1926, Dr. Nystrom commanded universal respect in trade and Governmental circles as well as in the academic field. As the spokesman for the entire variety-store trade, independents as well as chains comprising the membership of his association, he was particularly effective in clarifying the special problems confronting his field. On the other hand, his broad experience and sound judgment proved invaluable to his members in helping them to formulate their own policies, both individual and collective. When Dr. Nystrom retired in 1954 he was succeeded by Philip W. Schindel, as Executive Director.

Fred Griffiths, president of the Pennsylvania Drug Stores, served as executive secretary of the National Association of Chain Drug Stores from the date of its organization in 1933 until his death in 1949. His long experience in the chain-drug field as a top executive gave him a practical approach to the problems which faced the drug chains as a group which few men outside of the field could have equalled. To this was added a personality which made him particularly effective as a trade-association executive. His own experience as a retail druggist having convinced him of the need for price-maintenance legislation, Mr. Griffiths was an ardent advocate of the Fair Trade laws which some of the States had already passed and others were considering when his association was organized. As most of the other drug-chain operators felt the same way about it as he did, Mr. Griffiths was able to offer the full cooperation of his organization to the National Association of Retail Druggists, which was the principal proponent of such legislation. With the chains thus joining forces with the independent druggists in the effort to end price-cutting on standard drug products, the main grievance the independents had entertained against the chains for so many years was eliminated.

Before many more years were to elapse, Mr. Griffiths had the gratification of seeing Fair Trade laws in effect in 45 States and enjoying Federal sanctions as well through the passage of the Miller-Tydings Act in 1937. From then on and until his death, Mr. Griffiths' main concern was to protect Fair Trade against the attacks of those who were opposed to it, including the Federal Trade Commission and the Department of Justice. When, in 1947, Fair Trade was being blamed in some quarters as one of the factors responsible for high prices, he lost no time in launching a survey to establish the facts. The resulting study[17] revealed that whereas the cost of living between 1939 and 1947 had increased some 60 per cent, the prices of more than 7,000 Fair-Traded drug and cosmetic items had increased only 3 per cent. The only conclusion to be drawn from that showing was that instead of being responsible for rising prices, Fair Trade had exercised a definite stabilizing effect, which was absent in the case of items which were not Fair-Traded.

Effective as this study was to establish the economic facts about Fair Trade, it carried no weight, of course, with the U.S. Supreme Court several years later when the scope of the vital

[17] *Chain Store Age,* Druggist Edition, October, 1947.

Miller-Tydings Act was successfully challenged on legal rather than economic grounds.[18] The subsequent fate of Fair Trade has been related in an earlier chapter. See page 115.

Upon the death of Mr. Griffiths, Carl Willingham, who had worked with him on Association matters for four years, was appointed secretary and treasurer. He died July 1, 1961 and was succeeded by James H. Merritt, formerly Secretary of the Proprietary Association.

In the shoe field, the National Association of Shoe Chain Stores, directed by Edward Atkins, has served its members well for many years.

The apparel chains and the mail-order chains have likewise maintained their own specialized associations.

The Institute of Distribution serves a different purpose of a more general nature. It was founded in 1935 by a group of important chains outside of the food field for the purpose of carrying on the educational work and public relation activities which the National Chain Store Association had begun prior to its dissolution in 1933. One of its most constructive activities was the development of the regional and State Chain Store Councils which have been described in an earlier chapter. Another important purpose it serves is to provide its member companies with statistical and other data relating to distribution and to keep them advised of the introduction and progress of legislative proposals affecting retailers in general and chain stores in particular. This work has been carried on effectively right from the start under the direction of Mrs. Gladys M. Kiernan.

What of the future? Have the chains gone about as far as they are destined to go in the fields in which they have made their greatest progress? Or is the evidence of their maturity revealed in the history of the last 32 years to be taken at less than its face value—as evidence only of a temporary slowdown in a movement which may be later resumed?

[18] Calvert Distiller's Corp. v. Schwegmann, 341 U.S. 384 (1951).

So far as the over-all retail picture is concerned, the chain-store ratio, as to both stores and sales, is likely, in the author's opinion, to increase in the years ahead. The gains, however, are likely to be both gradual and slight. They will come from the natural growth of the smaller chains and the entry of newcomers rather than from any substantial expansion on the part of the big companies.

This conclusion is based primarily on the basic merits of the chain-store system as they have been reviewed in these pages—on the fundamental fact that operating more than one store offers greater opportunity than operating only one. That principle will continue to encourage single-store operators in all fields to open a second store as long as ambition and vision are to be found among retail merchants, and the success of such ventures will encourage still further expansion. Small chains are unlikely to remain small if and when the opportunity arrives for further expansion.

So far as the bigger chains are concerned, they too may be expected to expand in order to keep pace with population growth and to meet the need in new shopping centers and expanding communities for the kind of stores the chains operate. But such normal expansion will not tend to change present chain-store ratios in the general sales picture in any appreciable degree.

Several factors argue against a resumption of chain-store expansion on anything like the frantic scale which marked their development between 1920 and 1930. In the first place, the kind of small stores which then prevailed favored rapid expansion because of the nominal capital investment involved. The trend towards bigger stores in all fields has materially changed that picture. Secondly, the caliber of the competition offered today by independents affiliated with voluntary chains and other cooperative groups has narrowed the wide-open opportunity the chains once enjoyed. Finally the law of diminishing returns, the rising costs of operation and the weight of oppressive taxes combine to discourage widespread expansion even if it were otherwise feasible.

This is not to say that the chains have reached saturation point. On the contrary, as long as new shopping centers continue to spring up all over the country, new chain store units will be needed to tenant them. Furthermore, as has already been pointed out, the burgeoning discount field lends itself ideally to chain store operation. Nevertheless, such additional units as the chains may need in those areas will be offset to some extent by the closing down of less profitable stores in traditional locations.

In the years which lie ahead, the main task of the chains will be not merely to maintain the favorable position they now hold but to measure up to the greater economic, social, national and even international responsibilities their status will impose on them.

For the fact is that what the author said of the food chains on the occasion of the celebration of the 25th anniversary of the founding of the National Association of Food Chains[19] applies with equal force to the chain store system in general. During the past 25 years that system has matured into one of the most vital elements of our economy—a distributive dynamo upon whose power depend in large measure the well-being and prosperity of the entire nation. But for the kind of job the chains are doing, we could not enjoy our enviable standards of living and the output of industry would inevitably be reduced as a result of the consumer's diminished buying power. For in keeping the cost of food, clothing and other basic necessities down to the lowest possible level, the chains enable the consumer to stretch her dollars—enable her to buy more of the things and services that would otherwise be beyond her reach.

The substantial growth of our population which the next

[19] "Twenty-Five Years of Progress," an address before the National Association of Food Chains, October 6, 1958.

two decades will bring, coupled with the increase in our productive capacity which technological advances assure will demand a corresponding increase in the capacity of our distributive facilities. The responsibility for providing it will fall largely upon the chains.

Because of the sheer magnitude of their operations and its impact on our economy, the chains will likewise incur additional social responsibilities and increased obligations in the area of cooperation with the government.

An interesting illustration of how the chains regard their responsibility to the government was provided in 1956 when, in cooperation with the State Department and through the initiative of the National Association of Food Chains, the food industry set up in Rome a fully-equipped and fully-stocked supermarket. It was operated under the direction of chain experts for the edification of the public in connection with an international conference on food distribution. The State Department's interest stemmed from its need to do something in the "cold war" to dramatize the American way of life. No more eloquent symbol of the way we live than this up-to-date supermarket could have been conceived. Commonplace as it has become to us, it was little less than sensational to several hundred thousand Italians and other visitors who had never before seen anything like it. It was so favorably received that the following year the food chains again cooperated with the government to set up a similar exhibit in a city where it might be even more useful ideologically— Zagreb, Yugoslavia. In 1959, a similar project was sponsored at a Trade Fair in Barcelona, Spain.

No doubt the chains will be called upon by the government for other extra-curricular cooperation in the years which lie ahead, and it will be forthcoming. But the prime responsibility of the chains will always be to improve the efficiency of our own distribution system. That they will be equal to whatever challenge the future will bring would seem to be evident from the vision and flexibility they have demonstrated through the years.

So long, therefore, as the public retains its present freedom to patronize the stores of its choice and the chains retain the right, and the ability, to provide the kind of stores the public likes best, the future of the chains woud seem to be secure.

APPENDIX

GROWTH OF LEADING CHAINS
IN SELECTED CATEGORIES

Sources: Company reports
Hugh M. Foster's 1937 Study, *Printers' Ink Monthly*
Chain Store Age
Miscellaneous

W. C. Shaw, Sr., of G. C. MURPHY Co.,
for average sales per store data
in variety store field.

GROWTH OF LEADING CHAINS
GROCERY CHAINS

ACME MARKETS, INC. (formerly AMERICAN STORES, INC.) PHILADELPHIA, PA.			COLONIAL STORES, INC. ATLANTA, GA.		
YEAR	STORES	SALES (MILLIONS)	YEAR	STORES	SALES (MILLIONS)
1918	1,149	$ 68.3	1940	585	$ 57.0
1919	1,175	76.4	1941	570	74.0
1920	1,243	103.1	1942	564	103.0
1921	1,274	86.1	1943	487	112.7
1922	1,375	85.9	1944	481	119.3
1923	1,474	94.6	1945	472	121.1
1924	1,629	98.2	1946	457	157.9
1925	1,792	108.9	1947	432	199.5
1926	1,982	116.9	1948	418	214.9
1927	2,133	120.7	1949	430	215.6
1928	2,548	137.3	1950	426	236.8
1929	2,644	143.3	1951	409	269.6
1930	2,728	142.8	1952	407	288.9
1931	2,806	135.2	1953	411	314.7
1932	2,977	115.5	1954	401	333.3
1933	2,882	109.4	1955	432	380.0
1934	2,859	114.4	1956	449	423.0
1935	2,826	115.9	1957	461	442.2
1936	2,816	113.4	1958	473	437.1
1937	2,620	114.6	1959	459	450.7
1938	2,416	109.9	1960	447	445.4
1939	2,272	114.8	1961	447	441.5
1940	2,157	124.8	1962	439	449.9
1941	2,130	157.7			
1942	2,099	209.1			
1943	2,066	212.1			
1944	2,020	227.6			
1945	1,964	233.5			
1946	2,012	314.6			
1947	1,921	388.6			
1948	1,833	417.5			
1949*	1,776				
1950	1,637	416.6			
1951	1,505	469.8			
1952	1,408	521.3			
1953	1,289	542.0			
1954	1,132	603.7			
1955	1,076	624.6			
1956	953	654.7			
1957	903	779.9			
1958	844	837.3			
1959	823	874.8			
1960	810	889.4			
1961	840	1,011.5**			
1962	845	1,034.9			

* Fiscal year changed from year-end to 3/31 of year given.

** Includes Alpha Beta stores and sales.

GROCERY CHAINS (Continued)

FIRST NATIONAL STORES, INC.
SOMERVILLE, MASS.

FOOD FAIR, INC.
PHILADELPHIA, PA.

YEAR*	STORES	SALES (MILLIONS)	YEAR	STORES	SALES (MILLIONS)
1927	1,681	$ 59.0	1935	9	$ 5.7
1928	1,717	64.4	1936	14	8.7
1929	2,002	75.9	1937	22	13.8
1930	2,549	107.6	1938	34	18.3
1931	2,548	108.2	1939	67	24.5
1932	2,546	107.6	1940	73	29.2
1933	2,705	100.9	1941	75	34.1
1934	2,653	105.8	1942	77	41.7
1935	2,623	111.3	1943	73	42.2
1936	2,556	119.6	1944	89	44.8
1937	2,473	120.7	1945	89	60.6
1938	2,350	124.3	1946	89	101.2
1939	2,244	124.2	1947	95	121.8
1940	2,137	131.0	1948	105	142.0
1941	1,923	142.7	1950*	113	164.6
1942	1,748	174.4	1951	123	205.6
1943	1,585	187.8	1952	151	259.6
1944	1,463	164.9	1953	162	292.7
1945	1,340	170.2	1954	196	348.2
1946	1,236	182.1	1955	216	410.1
1947	1,201	156.5	1956	238	475.2
1948	1,150	315.9	1957	273	545.1
1949	1,083	354.4	1958	332	654.8
1950	1,033	344.2	1959	368	733.9
1951	979	371.9	1960	404	771.2
1952	922	406.8	1961	450**	840.2
1953	847	424.5	1962	500	923.2
1954	761	442.2			
1955	702	470.6			
1956	661	491.7			
1957	607	507.4			
1958	575	521.5			
1959	543	531.5			
1960	534	525.3			
1961	516	536.5			
1962	632**	711.3			

* Calendar years from 1935 to 1948 inclusive; fiscal years thereafter ending April 30 of year given.
** Includes 55 J. M. Fields stores.

* Fiscal years ending March of year indicated.
** Reflects acquisition in October, 1961 of all stores of the New York division of Safeway Stores, Inc.

GROCERY CHAINS (Continued)

Grand Union Company
East Paterson, N. J.

Year	Stores	Sales (millions)
1928	—	$ 31.9
1929	612	36.9
1930	611	37.0
1931	—	35.6
1932	—	30.4
1933	—	28.3
1934	568	28.6
1935	563	28.0
1936	566	29.5
1937	551	31.1
1938	499	31.4
1939	487	37.2
1940	476	35.1
1941	417	39.6
1942	358	43.9
1943	347	43.9
1944	329	50.1
1945	319	55.4
1946	318	83.4
1947	308	99.8
1948	293	116.1
1949	287	135.0
1950	289	161.0
1951	322	179.4
1952	296	184.1
1953	316	201.8
1954	320	219.5
1955	347	283.0
1956	354	374.2
1957	381	427.9
1958	472	503.7
1959	451	603.5
1960	472	604.3
1961	475	640.6

Great Atlantic & Pacific Tea Co.
New York, N. Y.

Year*	Stores	Sales (millions)
1859	1	—
1865	25	—
1880	100	—
1900	200	—
1906	291	—
1910	372	—
1911	400	—
1912	480	—
1913	585	—
1914	991	—
1915	1,817	—

Great Atlantic & Pacific Tea Co.
New York, N. Y.
(Continued)

Year*	Stores	Sales (millions)
1916	2,866	—
1917	3,782	—
1918	3,799	—
1919	4,224	$ 195
1920	4,621	235
1921	5,217	202
1922	7,350	247
1923	9,303	303
1924	11,421	352
1925	14,034	440
1926	14,811	574
1927	15,671	761
1928	15,177	973
1929	15,418	1,054
1930	15,737	1,066
1931	15,670	1,008
1932	15,427	864
1933	15,131	820
1934	15,035	842
1935	14,926	872
1936	14,746	907
1937	13,314	882
1938	10,900	879
1939	9,200	990
1940	7,230	1,116
1941	6,170	1,379
1942	6,000	1,471
1943	5,900	1,311
1944	5,800	1,402
1945	5,600	1,435
1946	5,200	1,909
1947	5,075	2,546
1948	4,900	2,837
1949	4,700	2,905
1950	4,500	3,180
1951	4,400	3,392
1952	4,300	3,756
1953	4,250	3,989
1954	4,200	4,140
1955	4,150	4,305
1956*	4,200	4,482
1957	4,200	4,769
1958	4,252	5,095
1959	4,276	5,049
1960	4,351	5,247
1961	4,409	5,240

* Fiscal years ending February 28 following year given, until 1955; thereafter on last Saturday in February following year given.

GROCERY CHAINS (Continued)

JEWEL TEA CO., INC.
MELROSE PARK, ILL.

THE KROGER CO.
CINCINNATI, OHIO

YEAR	STORES*	SALES (MILLIONS)	YEAR	STORES	SALES (MILLIONS
1921	0	$ 11.2	1882	1	—
1922	0	10.2	1885	2	—
1923	0	12.6	1891	7	—
1924	0	13.6	1902	40	$ 1.8
1925	0	14.2	1920	799	50.1
1926	0	14.6	1921	947	44.9
1927	0	14.5	1922	1,224	53.8
1928	0	15.9	1923	1,641	74.3
1929	0	16.8	1924	1,973	90.1
1930	0	15.5	1925	2,559	116.2
1931	0	13.7	1926	3,100	146.0
1932	85	14.7	1927	3,564	161.3
1933	84	14.4	1928	4,307	207.4
1934	87	17.2	1929	5,575	286.6
1935	87	18.8	1930	5,165	267.1
1936	100	20.7	1931	4,884	244.4
1937	109	23.3	1932	4,737	213.2
1938	109	23.7	1933	4,400	205.7
1939	116	24.6	1934	4,352	221.2
1940	132	29.1	1935	4,250	229.9
1941	148	40.9	1936	4,212	242.3
1942	154	52.4	1937	4,108	248.4
1943	152	51.4	1938	3,992	231.3
1944	152	56.0	1939	3,958	243.4
1945	150	62.4	1940	3,727	260.4
1946	150	86.9	1941	3,477	302.8
1947	149	128.5	1942	3,174	388.8
1948	154	150.6	1943	2,999	422.4
1949	153	166.1	1944	2,896	448.4
1950	154	185.7	1945	2,730	457.3
1951	157	205.9	1946	2,611	573.8
1952	160	222.6	1947	2,516	754.3
1953	164	238.7	1948	2,349	825.7
1954	173	270.6	1949	2,190	807.7
1955	179	300.4	1950	2,054	861.2
1956	184	334.8	1951	1,978	997.1
1957	227**	414.5	1952	1,891	1,051.8
1958	253	443.8	1953	1,810	1,058.6
1959	274	460.6	1954	1,678	1,108.7
1960	315***	509.1	1955	1,587	1,219.5
1961	323	552.2	1956	1,476	1,492.6
			1957	1,421	1,674.1
			1958	1,428	1,776.1
			1959	1,393	1,911.9
			1960	1,372	1,870.3
			1961	1,354	1,842.3
			1962	1,369	1,946.3

* Home service sales from 1921 to 1932; home service plus store sales thereafter. Retail sales are exclusive of sales tax collections.
** Includes 39 Eisner Grocery Stores acquired March 12, 1957.
*** Includes 30 Osco Drug Stores.

GROCERY CHAINS (Continued)

NATIONAL TEA CO. CHICAGO, ILL.			SAFEWAY STORES* OAKLAND, CALIF.		
YEAR	STORES	SALES (MILLIONS)	YEAR	STORES	SALES (MILLIONS)
1899	1	—	1914	4	$ 0.3
1921	261	$ 16.3	1922	118	5.8
1922	295	20.6	1923	193	8.6
1923	514	31.3	1924	263	11.9
1924	598	39.1	1925	330	13.4
1925	761	47.5	1926	673	50.5
1926	840	53.7	1927	840	69.6
1927	1,237	58.8	1928	1,191	103.3
1928	1,600	85.9	1929	2,340	213.5
1929	1,627	90.2	1930	2,675	219.3
1930	1,600	85.2	1931	3,264	246.8
1931	1,512	76.7	1932	3,411	229.2
1932	1,389	65.7	1933	3,306	220.2
1933	1,299	64.9	1934		242.9
1934	1,245	62.8	1935	3,330	294.7
1935	1,224	63.1	1936	3,370	346.2
1936	1,221	62.5	1937	3,327	381.9
1937	1,213	62.1	1938	3,227	368.3
1938	1,103	55.6	1939	2,967	385.9
1939	1,073	56.7	1940	2,671	399.3
1940	1,062	61.9	1941	2,660	475.1
1941	1,015	72.2	1942	2,697	611.1
1942	950	89.9	1943	2,493	588.8
1943	874	91.8	1944	2,463	656.6
1944	827	99.9	1945	2,452	664.8
1945	749	106.9	1946	2,428	847.5
1946	693	157.6	1947	2,401	1,117.1
1947	702	217.9	1948	2,308	1,276.8
1948	659	270.2	1949	2,202	1,197.8
1949	655	274.3	1950	2,084	1,209.9
1950	634	315.2	1951	2,104	1,454.6
1951	624	361.3	1952	2,104	1,639.1
1952	765	405.2	1953	2,054	1,751.8
1953	688	462.3	1954	2,008	1,813.5
1954	711	520.3	1955	1,998	1,932.2
1955	744	575.6	1956	1,980	1,989.3
1956	761	617.6	1957	1,958	2,117.7
1957	883	681.1	1958	2,117	2,225.4
1958	932	794.2	1959	2,164	2,383.0
1959	910	829.5	1960	2,207	2,469.9
1960	897	855.8	1961	2,063**	2,548.0
1961	897	888.9	1962	2,069	2,509.6

* Includes Canadian Stores.
** Reflects sale of N. Y. stores to First National.

GROCERY CHAINS (Continued)

WINN-DIXIE STORES, INC.
JACKSONVILLE, FLA.

YEAR ENDING	STORES*	SALES (MILLIONS)	YEAR ENDING	STORES*	SALES (MILLIONS)
June 28, 1952	335	$246.4	June 28, 1958	473	$588.6
27, 1953	335	278.4	27, 1959	495	666.4
26, 1954	347	312.7	25, 1960	519	721.5
25, 1955	370	358.6	24, 1961	536	767.0
30, 1956	412	421.3	30, 1962	561	772.2
29, 1957	462	513.5			

* Predecessor chains which were combined in the course of this chain's development included Table Supply Stores, Winn & Lovett, Steiden Stores, Dixie-Home, Margaret Ann and Kwikchek.

VARIETY STORE CHAINS

W. T. GRANT CO.
NEW YORK, N. Y.

YEAR	STORES	ANNUAL SALES		YEAR	STORES	ANNUAL SALES	
		TOTAL (Millions)	PER STORE (Thousands)			TOTAL (Millions)	PER STORE (Thousands)
1907	1	$ 0.1	$ 99.5	1935	171	$ 91.9	$195.3
1908	2	0.2	84.6	1936	477	98.3	206.2
1909	4	0.4	99.7	1937	480	99.1	206.5
1910	6	0.8	125.5	1938	489	97.5	199.4
1911	9	1.1	120.4	1939	492	103.8	210.9
1912	12	1.4	113.5	1940	492	111.8	227.2
1913	16	2.0	125.1	1941	495	130.6	263.7
1914	20	2.6	128.3	1942	493	154.2	312.8
1915	23	3.1	133.1	1943	493	163.9	332.6
1916	25	3.7	146.4	1944	490	175.5	358.1
1917	30	4.5	150.4	1945	488	180.3	369.5
1918	32	6.0	188.4	1946	484	212.3	438.6
1919	33	7.9	240.7	1947	483	228.6	473.3
1920	38	10.2	268.2	1948	482	233.9	485.2
1921	45	12.7	282.9	1949	480	233.2	485.8
1922	50	15.4	307.7	1950	477	250.6	525.3
1923	60	20.6	343.8	1951	482	268.3	556.6
1924	70	25.3	361.7	1952	491	283.4	576.7
1925	77	30.4	394.9	1953	503	299.8	597.2
1926	109	36.1	330.9	1954	520	317.2	610.0
1927	157	43.7	278.6	1955	574	351.8	612.9
1928	221	55.7	251.9	1956	632	380.9	602.6
1929	279	65.9	236.2	1957	691	406.3	588.0
1930	350	71.4	204.0	1958	739	432.2	584.8
1931	404	75.7	187.3	1959	801	479.9	599.1
1932	446	73.1	163.9	1960	864	512.7	593.4
1933	457	78.2	171.1	1961	952	574.5	603.4
1934	465	85.1	182.9	1962	1,051	682.2	649.1

VARIETY STORE CHAINS (Continued)

H. L. Green Co.
(Merged with McCrory Stores Corp. 1960)
New York, N. Y.

YEAR	STORES	ANNUAL SALES		YEAR	STORES	ANNUAL SALES	
		TOTAL (Millions)	PER STORE (Thousands)			TOTAL (Millions)	PER STORE (Thousands)
1933	182	$ 28.9	$159.2	1947	212	$ 94.2	$444.3
1934	178	33.6	188.9	1948	217	101.2	466.4
1935	184	35.5	192.8	1949	222	99.1	446.4
1936	190	40.5	213.4	1950	225	101.9	453.0
1937	193	41.9	217.6	1951	228	106.5	467.1
1938	195	40.4	207.2	1952	222	106.9	481.5
1939	196	52.2	266.2	1953	224	108.7	485.3
1940	217	56.5	260.3	1954	221	108.5	491.0
1941	219	64.2	292.9	1955	227	111.7	492.7
1942	218	73.9	339.1	1956	225	112.5	500.0
1943	217	77.4	356.6	1957	224	110.6	514.0
1944	216	79.7	370.0	1958*	354	133.4	377.0
1945	213	79.1	371.3	1959	372	133.3	358.3
1946	209	90.4	432.7				

S. S. Kresge Co.
Detroit, Mich.

YEAR	STORES	ANNUAL SALES		YEAR	STORES	ANNUAL SALES	
		TOTAL (Millions)	PER STORE (Thousands)			TOTAL (Millions)	PER STORE (Thousands)
1909	42	$ 5.1	$121.8	1936	734	$149.5	$203.6
1910	51	6.5	127.4	1937	741	155.2	209.5
1911	64	7.9	123.8	1938	745	149.3	200.4
1912	85	10.3	121.5	1939	745	153.9	206.6
1913	101	13.3	131.3	1940	743	158.7	213.6
1914	118	16.1	136.4	1941	736	176.2	239.4
1915	139	20.9	150.6	1942	731	198.7	258.1
1916	160	26.4	164.9	1943	716	206.0	287.8
1917	164	30.1	183.5	1944	711	216.5	304.4
1918	170	36.3	213.6	1945	705	223.2	316.6
1919	174	42.7	245.2	1946	696	251.4	361.2
1920	184	51.2	278.5	1947	696	270.1	388.1
1921	200	55.9	279.3	1948	700	289.1	413.0
1922	211	65.2	308.9	1949	702	288.7	411.6
1923	234	81.8	349.8	1950	694	294.8	424.7
1924	257	90.1	350.6	1951	690	310.9	450.6
1925	306	105.9	346.3	1952	695	326.4	469.6
1926	367	119.3	324.8	1953	692	337.3	487.4
1927	435	133.8	307.5	1954	690	337.9	489.7
1928	506	147.5	291.2	1955	673	354.7	527.0
1929	597	156.3	261.9	1956	676	366.4	542.0
1930	678	150.5	221.8	1957	692	377.2	545.0
1931	711	145.8	205.0	1958	706	384.4	544.4
1932	719	124.5	173.0	1959	725	404.9	558.4
1933	720	125.9	174.6	1960	759	418.2	551.0
1934	731	137.7	187.9	1961	777	432.8	557.0
1935	745	138.3	185.6	1962	821	450.7	547.7

* Includes Olen Co.

VARIETY STORE CHAINS (Continued)

S. H. KRESS & Co.
NEW YORK, N. Y.

YEAR	STORES	ANNUAL SALES TOTAL (Millions)	ANNUAL SALES PER STORE (Thousands)	YEAR	STORES	ANNUAL SALES TOTAL (Millions)	ANNUAL SALES PER STORE (Thousands)
1896	1	$ .03	$ 31.1	1930	212	$ 69.3	$326.8
1897	2	.07	36.2	1931	221	69.0	312.4
1898	5	.16	32.0	1932	230	62.8	272.9
1899	6	.23	37.8	1933	230	65.0	282.7
1900	11	.49	44.5	1934	232	75.7	326.1
1901	13	.68	52.4	1935	234	78.5	335.4
1902	16	.87	54.1	1936	235	86.8	369.2
1903	19	1.1	59.9	1937	234	87.9	275.5
1904	25	1.6	63.7	1938	240	82.2	342.4
1905	38	2.2	57.4	1939	240	84.9	353.6
1906	51	3.1	60.9	1940	242	88.3	364.9
1907	56	3.8	67.2	1941	242	101.4	418.9
1908	62	4.6	74.4	1942	244	116.9	479.3
1909	75	6.6	88.2	1943	244	124.0	508.3
1910	84	8.4	99.4	1944	243	127.9	526.6
1911	91	8.8	96.9	1945	244	126.0	516.4
1912	100	10.0	100.0	1946	242	150.9	623.7
1913	114	10.8	94.5	1947	243	155.4	639.5
1914	118	11.9	100.1	1948	250	165.4	661.6
1915	123	12.4	101.0	1949	256	163.9	640.3
1916	130	15.1	115.8	1950	259	161.7	624.2
1917	144	17.6	122.5	1951	259	172.4	665.6
1918	144	21.2	146.9	1952	261	176.2	675.3
1919	145	25.2	174.1	1953	262	172.9	660.0
1920	145	28.9	199.8	1954	264	169.4	641.6
1921	142	28.9	203.6	1955	262	167.9	640.8
1922	145	30.1	211.4	1956	260	167.6	644.8
1923	152	34.0	223.7	1957	261	158.6	607.6
1924	161	40.3	250.1	1958	262	159.4	608.2
1925	166	45.9	276.9	1959	266	154.4	580.4
1926	169	51.9	306.9	1960	275	144.6	525.8
1927	183	58.1	317.3	1961	271	145.1	535.4
1928	193	65.1	336.7	1962	272	149.9	551.1
1929	203	68.5	337.3				

VARIETY CHAIN STORES (Continued)

McCRORY STORES CORPORATION
NEW YORK, N. Y.

YEAR	STORES	ANNUAL SALES		YEAR	STORES	ANNUAL SALES	
		TOTAL (Millions)	PER STORE (Thousands)			TOTAL (Millions)	PER STORE (Thousands)
1901	20	$ .49	$ 24.9	1931	244	$ 43.3	$177.4
1902	26	.67	25.7	1932	242	39.6	163.4
1903	28	.78	28.0	1933	222	35.4	159.4
1904	31	.82	26.4	1934	207	38.2	184.7
1905	35	1.0	28.9	1935	201	37.4	186.2
1906	41	1.2	29.3	1936	195	40.2	206.3
1907	46	1.7	37.1	1937	200	41.0	205.0
1908	46	1.8	40.2	1938	200	40.1	200.3
1909	47	2.4	50.9	1939	200	43.2	215.9
1910	60	3.2	53.2	1940	199	46.2	232.2
1911	69	3.9	56.5	1941	202	53.0	262.4
1912	93	4.9	53.5	1942	202	62.6	309.9
1913	110	5.6	50.5	1943	201	67.4	335.1
1914	116	5.2	45.0	1944	203	71.3	351.4
1915	117	5.9	50.7	1945	199	71.3	358.3
1916	132	6.8	51.4	1946	199	84.5	424.7
1917	143	7.8	54.8	1947	199	91.2	456.1
1918	147	9.6	65.4	1948	202	97.6	483.1
1919	148	11.5	77.6	1949	201	95.8	476.4
1920	156	14.2	91.0	1950	205	98.6	481.0
1921	159	14.4	90.6	1951	206	104.2	505.8
1922	161	17.1	106.4	1952	211	107.0	507.2
1923	167	21.4	127.9	1953	211	104.8	497.6
1924	175	25.2	144.1	1954	210	103.9	494.8
1925	182	29.6	162.6	1955	214	109.7	512.6
1926	199	33.4	168.8	1956	213	113.1	531.1
1927	220	39.3	178.8	1957	215	111.8	520.0
1928	228	41.1	180.3	1958	216	109.8	500.8
1929	241	44.7	185.5	1959*	446	171.6	384.7
1930	242	43.2	178.6				

* Includes McLellan. Subsequent acquisition by McCrory of chains outside of the variety store field made reported figures no longer comparable. See page 38 *ante*.

VARIETY STORE CHAINS (Continued)

McLellan Stores Co., New York, N. Y.

YEAR	STORES	ANNUAL SALES TOTAL (Millions)	PER STORE (Thousands)	YEAR	STORES	ANNUAL SALES TOTAL (Millions)	PER STORE (Thousands)
1921	72	$ 2.2	$30.3	1940	232	$24.0	$103.6
1922	75	3.5	46.4	1941	233	28.0	120.3
1923	77	4.7	61.0	1942	231	32.8	141.9
1924	80	5.6	69.4	1943	230	37.7	163.8
1925	94	6.7	71.6	1944	226	41.1	181.7
1926	112	9.5	84.7	1945	225	43.5	193.3
1927	128	11.9	93.3	1946	224	49.1	219.2
1928	150	13.9	92.9	1947	224	50.9	227.2
1929	259	23.8	91.8	1948	227	55.5	244.5
1930	277	24.0	86.8	1949	230	54.5	237.7
1931	278	21.9	78.9	1950	231	56.6	245.1
1932	277	19.9	71.8	1951	231	61.1	264.5
1933	238	18.3	76.9	1952	231	62.5	270.5
1934	234	19.6	83.9	1953	232	60.7	261.6
1935	230	19.9	86.5	1954	234	60.7	259.4
1936	235	21.9	93.6	1955	232	61.4	264.7
1937	236	22.6	95.8	1956	232	61.9	266.6
1938	236	22.3	94.4	1957	235	60.7	258.3
1939	231	23.1	99.9	1958*	235	60.5	257.4

* Absorbed by McCrory Stores Corporation in 1959.

G. C. Murphy Co., McKeesport, Pa.

YEAR	STORES	ANNUAL SALES TOTAL (Millions)	PER STORE (Thousands)	YEAR	STORES	ANNUAL SALES TOTAL (Millions)	PER STORE (Thousands)
1910	10	$ .26	$ 26.3	1938	201	$ 42.2	$209.9
1911	12	.26	20.9	1939	202	47.3	234.1
1912	18	.37	20.6	1940	204	53.4	261.6
1913	23	.47	20.6	1941	207	63.5	306.8
1914	27	.50	18.6	1942	207	76.9	371.9
1915	30	.60	20.1	1943	207	82.1	396.5
1916	32	.77	24.1	1944	207	88.9	429.6
1917	38	1.0	27.2	1945	208	95.9	461.1
1918	42	1.4	32.2	1946	209	110.3	527.9
1919	46	1.4	31.2	1947	209	119.3	571.0
1920	51	2.1	40.2	1948	210	137.6	655.1
1921	60	2.2	37.2	1949	218	141.3	648.2
1922	61	2.7	44.3	1950	219	150.5	687.2
1923	75	3.9	52.7	1951	223	165.2	740.9
1924	85	5.2	60.7	1951	294	168.9	574.5*
1925	88	6.5	73.8	1952	295	184.1	620.6
1926	92	8.6	93.1	1953	297	187.2	630.2
1927	113	10.2	90.6	1954	298	182.2	611.3
1928	133	12.1	91.1	1955	303	196.4	648.3
1929	153	15.7	102.8	1956	309	204.8	662.9
1930	166	17.5	105.4	1957	316	208.2	658.9
1931	172	19.2	111.9	1958	323	208.9	646.8
1932	176	18.5	105.3	1959	418**	238.8	571.4
1933	180	21.9	121.6	1960	437	245.6	561.9
1934	186	28.0	150.5	1961	480	256.4	534.2
1935	189	31.6	167.2	1962	511	272.4	533.1
1936	195	37.9	194.8				
1937	200	42.5	212.6				

* Including 71 Morris Stores.
** Includes Morgan & Lindsay.

VARIETY STORE CHAINS (Continued)

NEISNER BROTHERS, INC., ROCHESTER, N. Y.

YEAR	STORES	ANNUAL SALES TOTAL (Millions)	PER STORE (Thousands)	YEAR	STORES	ANNUAL SALES TOTAL (Millions)	PER STORE (Thousands)
1920	4	$ .9	$238.9	1941	116	$26.5	$228.2
1921	6	1.2	203.9	1942	117	33.1	283.3
1922	7	1.3	184.6	1943	117	37.3	319.1
1923	9	1.7	188.4	1944	115	38.2	332.3
1924	11	1.9	173.4	1945	112	38.9	347.3
1925	13	2.7	207.4	1946	112	45.7	408.0
1926	17	4.5	264.5	1947	114	50.9	447.3
1927	22	6.5	294.4	1948	117	57.6	492.6
1928	35	10.3	294.3	1949	121	57.8	477.6
1929	58	15.1	260.2	1950	123	58.3	473.7
1930	75	16.5	220.1	1951	125	61.8	494.7
1931	78	15.9	204.6	1952	127	63.8	502.6
1932	79	14.4	182.6	1953	129	66.7	517.0
1933	79	14.4	181.7	1954	132	64.9	491.6
1934	80	16.6	207.1	1955	139	68.8	495.2
1935	95	18.6	198.1	1956	142	69.2	487.3
1936	99	20.9	211.4	1957	149	69.6	467.1
1937	108	22.4	207.6	1958	152	67.1	441.4
1938	109	20.1	184.8	1959	162	69.7	430.2
1939	112	22.6	200.8	1960	170	73.5	432.3
1940	114	22.5	198.6	1961	173	76.3	441.0

J. J. NEWBERRY CO., NEW YORK, N. Y.

YEAR	STORES	ANNUAL SALES TOTAL (Millions)	PER STORE (Thousands)	YEAR	STORES	ANNUAL SALES TOTAL (Millions)	PER STORE (Thousands)
1912	1	$ .03	$32.3	1938	476	$ 49.0	$103.0
1913	2	.04	21.1	1939	479	52.3	109.1
1914	3	.09	30.9	1940	486	55.9	114.9
1915	5	.12	23.2	1941	488	64.2	131.6
1916	5	.15	30.3	1942	492	77.3	157.1
1917	6	.15	24.9	1943	491	91.0	185.4
1918	7	.28	39.5	1944	491	95.9	195.2
1919	17	.50	29.6	1945	488	100.9	206.7
1920	17	.75	44.2	1946	487	113.2	232.4
1921	26	1.2	44.5	1947	485	117.9	243.1
1922	33	1.8	53.0	1948	484	134.8	278.5
1923	51	3.6	69.9	1949	482	136.8	283.8
1924	68	5.1	75.2	1950	483	145.7	301.6
1925	86	6.9	80.2	1951	480	161.3	336.0
1926	112	9.9	89.2	1952	477	166.3	348.6
1927	151	15.1	99.8	1953	476	171.2	359.6
1928	210	20.6	98.1	1954	476	179.8	377.7
1929	279	27.8	99.6	1955	476	190.7	400.6
1930	335	30.2	90.1	1956	476	203.4	427.3
1931	379	31.1	82.2	1957	476	213.0	447.4
1932	406	33.1	81.6	1958	469	221.9	451.8
1933	417	35.1	84.3	1959	462	238.0	515.1
1934	431	41.1	95.3	1960	559	265.8	475.5
1935	450	43.4	96.4	1961	564	291.2	516.3
1936	461	48.4	104.9	1962	570	312.5	548.2
1937	469	50.3	107.3				

CHAIN STORES IN AMERICA

VARIETY STORE CHAINS (Continued)

F. W. Woolworth Co., New York, N. Y.

YEAR	STORES	ANNUAL SALES TOTAI (Moillins)	PER STORE (Thousands)	YEAR	STORES	ANNUAL SALES TOTAL (Millions)	PER STORE (Thousands)
1912	631	$ 60.6	$ 95.9	1938	2,015	$ 304.3	$ 151.0
1913	684	66.2	96.8	1939	2,021	318.8	157.8
1914	737	69.6	94.5	1940	2,027	335.5	165.5
1915	805	75.9	94.4	1941	2,023	377.1	185.4
1916	920	87.1	94.7	1942	2,015	423.2	210.0
1917	1,000	98.1	98.1	1943	2,008	439.0	218.6
1918	1,039	107.2	103.2	1944	2,004	459.8	229.5
1919	1,081	119.5	110.5	1945	1,971	477.1	242.1
1920	1,111	140.9	126.8	1946	1,958	552.4	282.1
1921	1,137	147.7	129.9	1947	1,945	593.4	305.0
1922	1,176	167.3	142.3	1948	1,944	623.9	320.9
1923	1,260	193.4	153.5	1949	1,938	615.6	317.6
1924	1,356	215.5	158.9	1950	1,936	632.1	326.5
1925	1,423	239.0	167.9	1951	1,943	684.2	352.1
1926	1,480	253.6	171.4	1952	1,960	712.6	363.6
1927	1,581	272.8	172.5	1953	1,981	713.9	360.3
1928	1,725	287.3	166.6	1954	2,021	721.3	356.9
1929	1,825	303.0	166.0	1955	2,064	767.8	371.9
1930	1,881	289.3	153.8	1956	2,101	806.2	383.7
1931	1,903	282.7	148.5	1957	2,121	823.9	388.4
1932	1,932	249.9	129.3	1958	2,152	864.6	401.7
1933	1,941	250.5	129.1	1959	2,221	916.8	412.8
1934	1,960	270.7	138.3	1960	2,430*	1,035.3	425.9
1935	1,980	268.8	135.7	1961	2,502	1,061.4	424.2
1936	1,998	290.4	145.3	1962	2,521	1,110.1	440.3
1937	2,010	304.8	151.6				

* Includes stores and sales of German, Mexican and other subsidiaries.

DRUG CHAINS

Cunningham Drug Stores, Inc., Detroit, Mich.

YEAR ENDING SEPT. 30	STORES	SALES (MILLIONS)	YEAR ENDING SEPT. 30	STORES	SALES (MILLIONS)
1935	76	$ 6.8	1949	110	$25.0
1936	80	8.0	1950	165*	34.0
1937	84	9.2	1951	167	38.2
1938	90	8.8	1952	173	40.1
1939	95	9.5	1953	175	42.4
1940	97	10.4	1954	180	40.9
1941	98	12.3	1955	179	42.6
1942	98	15.1	1956	188**	45.5
1943	98	18.9	1957	191	47.4
1944	100	20.4	1958	221	48.8
1945	99	20.9	1959	213	54.2
1946	99	23.2	1960	211	54.7
1947	103	24.6	1961	206	52.5
1948	106	24.7	1962	214	53.2

* Includes Marshall and Schettler.　　** Includes Miller Drug Stores, Inc.

DRUG CHAINS (Continued)

GRAY DRUG STORES, INC.
CLEVELAND, OHIO

YEAR*	STORES	SALES (MILLIONS)	YEAR	STORES*	SALES (MILLIONS)
1929	17	$1.5	1946	91	$14.7
1930	21	2.1	1947	91	17.5
1931	24	2.6	1948	78	16.2
1932	26	2.5	1949	79	15.6
1933	26	2.5	1950	77	15.2
1934	29	3.2	1951	74	16.8
1935	29	1.8	1952	80	19.3
1936	33	4.4	1953	78	21.1
1937	37	5.4	1954	80	22.6
1938	38	5.4	1955	78	23.4
1939	38	5.1	1956	81	25.5
1940	40	5.5	1957	86	29.3
1941	39	6.9	1958	102	32.2
1942	44	7.9	1959	107	35.9
1943	43	9.1	1960	111	37.6
1944	43	9.5	1961	117	39.6
1945	78	10.0	1962	134**	44.9

* Calendar years 1929 to 1934 inclusive; 1935, six months to June 30; thereafter fiscal year ending June 30 of year given.
** Includes 25 leased depts.

KATZ DRUG CO.
KANSAS CITY, MO.

YEAR	STORES	SALES (MILLIONS)	YEAR	STORES	SALES (MILLIONS)
1929	3	$ 5.5	1946	23	$24.3
1930	4	6.6	1947	24	26.4
1931	8	7.4	1948	27	26.9
1932	8	6.8	1949	28	29.9
1933	8	7.2	1950	29	31.9
1934	9	8.3	1951	30	35.1
1935	10	8.9	1952	31	34.2
1936	12	8.8	1953	31	34.3
1937	13	9.7	1954	33	35.8
1938	13	8.6	1955	33	39.5
1939	13	8.3	1956	35	40.9
1940	15	8.1	1957	39	44.8
1941	18	9.6	1958	39	46.9
1942	20	13.7	1959	39	50.8
1943	20	17.1	1960	40	52.6
1944	20	17.2	1961	39	53.6
1945	20	20.1			

DRUG CHAINS (Continued)

PEOPLES DRUG STORES, INC.
WASHINGTON, D. C.

YEAR	STORES	SALES (MILLIONS)	YEAR	STORES	SALES (MILLIONS)
1920	8	$ 2.4	1942	137	$32.6
1921	11	3.1	1943	131	34.8
1922	13	3.7	1944	131	34.7
1923	16	4.0	1945	131	36.1
1924	18	4.8	1946	134	44.2
1925	18	7.3	1947	136	46.0
1926	46	8.4	1948	140	46.9
1927	73	10.2	1949	141	46.8
1928	82	11.3	1950	143	47.2
1929	112	15.5	1951	146	50.7
1930	118	16.8	1952	152	54.0
1931	124	17.4	1953	150	54.5
1932	117	16.2	1954	156	54.9
1933	113	15.5	1955	158	57.6
1934	117	16.9	1956	162	61.9
1935	122	19.2	1957	170	67.1
1936	129	21.1	1958	173	74.9
1937	133	22.4	1959	188	85.7
1938	135	21.7	1960	196	93.2
1939	136	22.8	1961	205	98.7
1940	136	23.9	1962	223	108.5
1941	136	27.7			

REXALL DRUG COMPANY
LOS ANGELES, CALIF.

YEAR	STORES*	CONSOLIDATED SALES** (MILLIONS)	YEAR	STORES*	CONSOLIDATED SALES** (MILLIONS)
1941	584	$102.5	1952	289	$178.3
1942	573	122.0	1953	270	189.2
1943	568	138.9	1954	202	176.1
1944	591	147.8	1955	165	153.5
1945	558	158.2	1956	158	155.6
1946	594	178.9	1957	160	167.6
1947	541	182.7	1958	180	182.4
1948	464	173.9	1959	174	227.0
1949	387	156.4	1960	159	242.6
1950	339	153.6	1961	174	260.9
1951	309	164.3			

* Includes only stores operated by wholly owned subsidiaries, of which Liggett and Owl are the principal ones.

** Sales of Rexall Drug Company and its consolidated subsidiaries, of which the Retail Division is only one.

DRUG CHAINS (Continued)

SUN RAY DRUG CO. (now CONSOLIDATED SUN RAY, INC.)
PHILADELPHIA, PA.

YEAR*	STORES	SALES (MILLIONS)	YEAR*	STORES	SALES (MILLIONS)
1930	2	$ .6	1945	43	$11.1
1931	4	.9	1946	120**	16.6
1932	8	1.2	1947	130	19.9
1933	13	1.9	1948	141	22.0
1934	19	3.2	1949	140	24.1
1935	23	4.0	1950	138	23.9
1936*			1951	134	24.8
1937	29	5.9	1952	133	26.4
1938	37	6.2	1953	134	28.5
1939	38	6.5	1954	138	29.9
1940	47	7.4	1955	132	29.6
1941	48	7.9	1956	135	29.8
1942	45	8.6	1957	139	32.4
1943	44	9.8	1958	143	36.4
1944	44	10.7	1959***	160	41.0

* Calendar years from 1930 to 1935 inclusive; fiscal years thereafter ending January 31 of year given.

** Includes stores and sales of Nevins Drug Co. and also agency stores for this and all subsequent years.

*** After consolidation with Consolidated Retail Stores in 1959, including apparel stores, data became no longer comparable.

THRIFTY DRUG STORES CO., INC.
LOS ANGELES, CALIF.

YEAR*	STORES	SALES (MILLIONS)	YEAR*	STORES	SALES (MILLIONS)
1947	72	$39.4	1955	114	$66.7
1948	78	43.6	1956	123	74.9
1949	82	45.3	1957	129	86.8
1950	85	45.9	1958	136	97.7
1951	94	51.1	1959	145	115.6
1952	96	54.0	1960	160	134.3
1953	103	60.6	1961	178	152.0
1954	108	63.1	1962	196	170.1

* Fiscal year ending August 31 of year given.

DRUG CHAINS (Continued)

UNITED WHELAN CORPORATION*
(formerly United Cigar-Whelan Stores Corporation)
BROOKLYN, N. Y.

YEAR	DRUG STORES	CIGAR STORES	AGENCY STORES	SALES (MILLIONS)	YEAR	DRUG STORES	CIGAR STORES	AGENCY STORES	SALES (MILLIONS)
1935	187	579	830	$54.2	1949	208	113	987	$75.4
1936	185	563	848	55.3	1950	202	69	1,007	74.3
1937	186	541	804	54.9	1951	197	58	898	74.2
1938	181	499	837	50.3	1952	186	48	820	67.6
1939	191	407	925	50.1	1953	175	37	697	63.9
1940	186	328	995	50.0	1954	167	15	627	58.7
1941	179	284	1,033	50.0	1955	152	8	610	56.5
1942	178	275	926	57.2	1956	146	—	583	54.8
1943	177	264	879	64.2	1957	136	—	534	52.5
1944	164	248	876	65.4	1958	131	—	494	49.6
1945	166	237	846	67.0	1959	120	—	446	45.2
1946	194	227	909	79.3	1960	113	—	432	50.8
1947	200	194	973	78.3	1961**	107	—	409	47.9
1948	202	145	1,031	77.4					

* This corporation commenced business July 17, 1937. Figures for 1935, 1936 and part of 1937, therefore, represent business of the Trustee of the Estate of United Cigar Stores Company of America and its subsidiaries. Consolidated figures for years prior to 1935 are not available.

** Includes Charles Stores sales.

WALGREEN COMPANY
CHICAGO, ILL.

YEAR*	STORES	SALES** (MILLIONS)	YEAR*	STORES	SALES** (MILLIONS)
1920	23	$ 2.2	1942	480	$ 95.3
1921	29	2.6	1943	460	112.2
1922	33	2.5	1944	442	120.0
1923	41	3.6	1945	427	118.8
1924	56	5.6	1946	412	140.7
1925	87	9.3	1947	410	154.5
1926	107	13.5	1948	413	163.3
1927	170	20.9	1949	414	163.4
1928	230	31.4	1950	410	163.4
1929	397	46.6	1951	406	171.5
1930*	440	39.1*	1952	400	177.9
1931	468	54.0	1953	390	181.5
1932	471	47.6	1954	388	184.3
1933	474	46.0	1955	388	192.7
1934	487	53.7	1956	386	212.3
1935	501	58.1	1957	407	235.1
1936	496	61.8	1958	406	260.0
1937	504	67.9	1959	422	285.1
1938	508	67.7	1960	451	312.4
1939	494	70.8	1961	467	331.7
1940	489	74.3	1962	476	353.1
1941	487	82.5			

* Calendar years 1920 to 1930 inclusive, except that 1930 covers only 9 months. Fiscal years thereafter ending September 30 of year given.

** Sales to agency stores are included in company sales.

MAIL ORDER CHAINS

MONTGOMERY WARD & COMPANY, CHICAGO, ILL.

YEAR	STORES	SALES* (MILLIONS)	YEAR	STORES	SALES* (MILLIONS)
1926	10	$ 184	1944	632	$ 621
1927	36	187	1945	630	655
1928	248	214	1946	628	974
1929	532	267	1947	622	1,159
1930	554	249	1948	621	1,212
1931	548	200	1949	621	1,084
1932**	492	176	1950	614	1,170
1933***	488	188	1951	606	1,106
1934	489	250	1952	599	1,085
1935	508	293	1953	590	999
1936	548	361	1954	568	887
1937	575	414	1955	566	970
1938	599	414	1956	562	1,046
1939	618	475	1957	554	1,074
1940	648	516	1958****	548	1,092
1941	646	633	1959	547	1,222
1942	641	635	1960	529	1,249
1943	637	596	1961	517	1,326

* Includes sales of mail-order houses.
** 13 months ending Jan. 31, 1933.
*** Fiscal years hereafter, ending Jan. 31 of year following year given.
**** Fiscal years hereafter end nearest Wednesday to January 31 following year given.

SEARS, ROEBUCK & CO., CHICAGO, ILL.

YEAR ENDING	STORES	NET SALES* (MILLIONS)	NET SALES** (MILLIONS)
Dec. 31, 1925	8	$ 200.	$ 11.
" 31, 1926	9	234.	22.
" 31, 1927	27	249.	39.
" 31, 1928	192	329.	103.
" 31, 1929	324	415.	168.
" 31, 1930	351	355.	190.
" 31, 1931	390	320.	195.
Jan. 28, 1933	384	275.	159.
" 28, 1934	403	273.	160.
" 29, 1935	417	318.	192.
" 29, 1936	429	392.	229.
" 29, 1937	450	495.	303.
" 31, 1938	485	537.	342.
" 31, 1939	496	502.	322.

* Total, including mail order.
** Store sales only; since 1942 store sales have not been available separately, but they have been consistently running at the rate of 75% of total sales.

MAIL ORDER CHAINS (Continued)

Sears, Roebuck & Co. (Continued)
Chicago, Ill.

YEAR ENDING	STORES	NET SALES* (MILLIONS)	NET SALES** (MILLIONS)
Jan. 31, 1940	529	$ 617.	$409.
" 31, 1941	596	704.	480.
" 31, 1942	618	915.	615.
" 31, 1943	598	868.	
" 31, 1944	595	853.	
" 31, 1945	605	989.	
" 31, 1946	603	1,045.	
" 31, 1947	609	1,613.	
" 31, 1948	623	1,982.	
" 31, 1949	628	2,296.	
" 31, 1950	647	2,169.	
" 31, 1951	654	2,556.	
" 31, 1952	674	2,657.	
" 31, 1953	684	2,932.	
" 31, 1954	694	2,982.	
" 31, 1955	699	2,965.	
" 31, 1956	707	3,307.	
" 31, 1957	717	3,556.	
" 31, 1958	724	3,601.	
" 31, 1959	728	3,721.	
" 31, 1960	734	4,036.	
" 31, 1961	740	4,134.	
" 31, 1962	740	4,267.	

* Total, including mail order.
** Store sales only; since 1942 store sales have not been available separately, but they have been consistently running at the rate of 75% of total sales.

SHOE CHAINS

EDISON BROTHERS STORES, INC., ST. LOUIS, MO.

YEAR*	STORES	SALES (MILLIONS)	YEAR*	STORES	SALES (MILLIONS)
1923	1	$ .3	1943	166	$39.8
1924	3	.5	1944	169	44.6
1925	6	.9	1945	170	53.2
1926	8	1.4	1946	180	65.7
1927	11	2.2	1947	188	70.9
1928	17	3.2	1948	202	75.0
1929	34	3.8	1949	213	74.2
1930	42	4.9	1950	220	73.8
1931	50	6.4	1951	228	78.0
1932	63	8.0	1952	237	80.7
1933	75	10.2	1953	245	81.6
1934	85	14.1	1954	251	80.2
1935	92	16.3	1955	267	87.2
1936	102	19.7	1956	297	91.1
1937	121	23.8	1957	322	99.3
1938	123	24.2	1958	334	109.1
1939	131	24.9	1959	357	124.1
1940	142	26.5	1960	404	133.2
1941	162	33.6	1961	440	137.2
1942	168	45.9	1962	479	147.5

* Calendar years in all cases except 1929 when fiscal year was changed to January 31 of following year and gave 1929 13 months; 1930 to 1932 inclusive, when fiscal year ended January 31 following year given; and 1933 in which a return to the calendar year gave that year only 11 months.

G. R. KINNEY CO., NEW YORK, N. Y.

YEAR	STORES	SALES (MILLIONS)	YEAR	STORES	SALES (MILLIONS)
1894	1		1940	343	$15.6
1909	24	$ .6	1941	346	20.1
1914	40	2.9	1942	339	27.1
1920	75	15.1	1943	338	24.4
1921	102	12.2	1944	330	25.9
1922	120	12.3	1945	317	28.2
1923	152	14.1	1946	306	32.6
1924	207	16.3	1947	310	33.1
1925	250	17.4	1948	308	34.8
1926	274	18.4	1949	305	35.2
1927	295	18.1	1950	311	36.7
1928	317	19.5	1951	318	43.1
1929	365	20.9	1952	324	43.8
1930	405	17.9	1953	327	44.4
1931	423	14.0	1954	344	46.9
1932	388	11.9	1955	352	51.7
1933	354	12.2	1956	360	52.2
1934	333	13.2	1957	411	59.2
1935	333	13.2	1958*	422	66.8
1936	327	14.8	1959	488	81.7
1937	321	15.7	1960	519	87.3
1938	333	14.5	1961	560	90.3
1939	344	15.5	1962	575	94.2

Sources: *The First Sixty Years*, by Edw. Holloway, New York; Company reports and Hugh M. Foster, *Printers' Ink Monthly*, 1937.

* Kinney sales not separately reported by Brown Shoe after merger, which, however, was voided by U. S. Supreme Court in 1962.

SHOE CHAINS (Continued)

MELVILLE SHOE CORPORATION, NEW YORK, N. Y.

YEAR	STORES	SALES* (MILLIONS)	YEAR	STORES	SALES* (MILLIONS)
1892	1		1941	659	$46.7
1920	20	$ 3.7	1942	579	51.6
1921	19	4.5	1943	556	39.2
1922	19	4.7	1944	549	37.1
1923	31	6.4	1945	536	41.2
1924	83	9.0	1946	519	60.2
1925	148	10.9	1947	519	71.9
1926	247	14.1	1948	547	75.6
1927	321	17.8	1949	560	71.9
1928	410	22.6	1950	560	70.9
1929	459	25.5	1951	577	71.1
1930	480	28.7	1952	739	77.4
1931	476	26.3	1953	794	99.6
1932	499	20.6	1954	834	100.8
1933	535	21.1	1955	886	106.7
1934	588	27.2	1956	947	115.9
1935	609	30.4	1957	1,018	122.1
1936	651	35.3	1958	1,053	129.1
1937	690	38.1	1959	1,110	145.3
1938	677	36.0	1960	1,156	157.7
1939	663	38.3	1961	1,212	161.9
1940	666	40.3	1962	1,244	171.3

* Retail sales only.

SHOE CORPORATION OF AMERICA*, COLUMBUS, OHIO

YEAR	STORES	SALES (MILLIONS)	YEAR	STORES	SALES (MILLIONS)
1920	6	$ .3	1946	315	$ 28.6
1930	173	9.9	1947	306	33.2
1931	179	10.2	1948	326	37.6
1932	187	8.9	1949	332	39.7
1933	202	9.4	1950	440	49.1
1934	233	10.9	1951	467	62.5
1935	239	11.7	1952	485	66.0
1936	255	13.0	1953	511	70.1
1937	278	13.5	1954	528	73.2
1938	276	12.6	1955	591	89.5
1939	284	13.3	1956	625	101.8
1940	285	14.2	1957	656	106.5
1941	294	16.3	1958	676	107.1
1942	288	20.1	1959	711	118.2
1943	284	19.3	1960	702	126.7
1944	284	21.4	1961	716	130.1
1945	301	24.6			

* Originally The Schiff Co. Present name adopted Nov. 3, 1947.

DEPARTMENT STORE AND APPAREL CHAINS

ALLIED STORES CORPORATION
NEW YORK, N. Y.

YEAR*	STORES	SALES (MILLIONS)	YEAR*	STORES	SALES (MILLIONS)
1934	31	$ 82.1	1948	79	$419.2
1935	31	89.9	1949	73	407.8
1936	33	103.3	1950	73	439.9
1937	54	107.6	1951	71	476.7
1938	56	103.2	1952	72	501.8
1939	58	112.1	1953	73	515.8
1940	60	121.3	1954	75	544.0
1941	61	151.8	1955	79	581.9
1942	63	170.8	1956	84	615.8
1943	63	203.7	1957	87	632.8
1944	70	241.9	1958	86	643.8
1945	70	281.6	1959	85	679.5
1946	71	361.7	1960	87	680.5
1947	75	392.2	1961	95	713.5

* Fiscal years ending January 31 following year given.

FEDERATED DEPARTMENT STORES
CINCINNATI, OHIO

YEAR*	STORES	SALES (MILLIONS)	YEAR*	STORES	SALES (MILLIONS)
1930	12	$113.0	1946	14	$265.4
1931	12	105.3	1947	17	304.7
1932	12	85.0	1948	21	346.5
1933	12	82.6	1949	21	358.6
1934	12	89.1	1950	24	389.1
1935	12	91.6	1951	24	408.8
1936	12	103.2	1952	28	447.9
1937	12	107.7	1953	34	478.8
1938	12	105.9	1954	34	500.6
1939	12	110.1	1955	33	537.7
1940	13	114.7	1956	37	601.5
1941	14	131.4	1957	42	635.6
1942	14	142.5	1958	42	653.2
1943	14	163.4	1959	45	759.9
1944	13	182.3	1960	56	785.4
1945	14	200.9	1961	56	856.4

* Years ending January 31 or nearest Saturday thereto following year given.

DEPARTMENT STORES, etc. (Continued)

LERNER STORES CORPORATION
NEW YORK, N. Y.

YEAR*	STORES	SALES (MILLIONS)	YEAR*	STORES	SALES (MILLIONS)
1933	160	$ 22.1	1949	197	$126.9
1935	158	30.4	1950	207	120.6
1936	159	32.2	1951	209	125.8
1937	159	37.2	1952	209	140.9
1938	160	39.6	1953	214	154.4
1939	164	37.9	1954	215	147.8
1940	166	40.5	1955	224	151.2
1941	171	42.5	1956	230	161.1
1942	179	50.5	1957	246	170.6
1943	180	64.8	1958	263	179.5
1944	180	75.6	1959	271	179.3
1945	181	87.3	1960	284	188.9
1946	179	91.9	1961	304	197.9
1947	185	97.0	1962**		
1948	191	107.3			

* Calendar year in 1933; thereafter fiscal years ending January 31 of year given.
** Merged with McCrory Stores Corporation.

THE MAY DEPARTMENT STORES CO.
ST. LOUIS, MO.

YEAR*	STORES	SALES (MILLIONS)	YEAR*	STORES	SALES (MILLIONS)
1949	21	$407.3	1956	31	$494.4
1950	22	392.9	1957	31	521.4
1951	23	416.7	1958	35	533.6
1952	25	424.9	1959	46	645.1
1953	26	447.5	1960**	55	683.9
1954	26	454.1	1961	56	684.8
1955	26	444.4	1962	56	708.5

* Year ending January 31 of year given.
** Includes sales and stores of Hecht Co., acquired Feb. 2, 1959.

DEPARTMENT STORES, etc. (Continued)

J. C. PENNEY CO.
NEW YORK, N. Y.

YEAR*	STORES	SALES (MILLIONS)	YEAR*	STORES	SALES (MILLIONS)
1902	1	$ .03	1932	1,473	$ 155.3
1903	1	.06	1933	1,466	178.8
1904	2	.09	1934	1,474	212.1
1905	2	.09	1935	1,481	225.9
1906	2	.13	1936	1,496	258.3
1907	2	.17	1937	1,523	275.4
1908	4	.22	1938	1,539	257.9
1909	6	.31	1939	1,554	282.1
1910	14	.66	1940	1,586	304.6
1911	22	1.2	1941	1,605	377.6
1912	34	2.1	1942	1,611	490.3
1913	48	2.6	1943	1,610	489.9
1914	71	3.6	1944	1,608	535.4
1915	86	4.8	1945	1,602	549.1
1916	127	8.4	1946	1,601	767.6
1917	177	14.9	1947	1,601	775.9
1918	197	31.3	1948	1,601	885.2
1919	197	28.8	1949	1,609	880.2
1920	312	42.8	1950	1,612	949.7
1921	313	46.6	1951	1,621	1,035.2
1922	371	49.0	1952	1,632	1,079.3
1923	475	62.2	1953	1,634	1,109.6
1924	569	74.3	1954	1,644	1,107.2
1925	674	91.1	1955	1,666	1,220.1
1926	747	115.7	1956	1,687	1,291.9
1927	892	151.9	1957	1,694	1,312.3
1928	1,023	176.7	1958**	1,687	1,409.9
1929	1,395	209.7	1959	1,683	1,437.5
1930	1,042	192.9	1960	1,695	1,468.9
1931	1,459	173.7	1961	1,686	1,553.5

* Calendar year until 1957. Thereafter fiscal years ending Jan. 31 following year given.
** 13 months.

INDEX

INDEX

419

This book may be kept

FOURTEEN DAYS

A fine will be charged for each day the book is kept overtime.

May 15 ˙68			
Aug 1 6 8			
DEC 3 '68			
GAYLORD 142			PRINTED IN U.S.A.